Crisis in the Eurozone

Also by Mark Baimbridge

FROM ROME TO MAASTRICHT: A Reappraisal of Britain's Membership of the European Community

THERE IS AN ALTERNATIVE: Britain and Its Relationship with the EU

THE IMPACT OF THE EURO: Debating Britain's Future

ECONOMIC AND MONETARY UNION IN EUROPE: Theory, Evidence and Practice

FISCAL FEDERALISM AND EUROPEAN ECONOMIC INTEGRATION

CURRENT ECONOMIC ISSUES IN EU INTEGRATION

BRITAIN AND THE EUROPEAN UNION: Alternative Futures

IMPLICATIONS OF THE EURO: A Critical Perspective from the Left

THE 1975 REFERENDUM ON EUROPE: Current Analysis and Lessons for the Future

THE 1975 REFERENDUM ON EUROPE: Reflections of the Participants

BRITAIN, THE EURO, AND BEYOND

BRITAIN IN A GLOBAL WORLD: Options for a New Beginning

MOORED TO THE CONTINENT? Future Options for Britain and the EU

THE POLITICAL ECONOMY OF THE EUROPEAN SOCIAL MODEL

Also by Philip B. Whyman

THERE IS AN ALTERNATIVE: Britain and Its Relationship with the EU

THE IMPACT OF THE EURO: Debating Britain's Future

ECONOMIC AND MONETARY UNION IN EUROPE: Theory, Evidence and Practice

FISCAL FEDERALISM AND EUROPEAN ECONOMIC INTEGRATION

SWEDEN AND THE 'THIRD WAY': A Macroeconomic Evaluation

AN ANALYSIS OF THE ECONOMIC DEMOCRACY REFORMS IN SWEDEN

BRITAIN AND THE EUROPEAN UNION: Alternative Futures

IMPLICATIONS OF THE EURO: A Critical Perspective from the Left

THIRD WAY ECONOMICS: An Evaluation

THE 1975 REFERENDUM ON EUROPE: Current Analysis and Lessons for the Future

BRITAIN, THE EURO AND BEYOND

BRITAIN IN A GLOBAL WORLD: Options for a New Beginning

MOORED TO THE CONTINENT? Future Options for Britain and the EU

THE POLITICAL ECONOMY OF THE EUROPEAN SOCIAL MODEL

Crisis in the Eurozone

Causes, Dilemmas and Solutions

Mark Baimbridge
University of Bradford, UK

Philip B. Whyman
University of Central Lancashire, UK

palgrave
macmillan

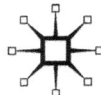

First published 2015 by
PALGRAVE MACMILLAN

Palgrave Macmillan in the UK is an imprint of Macmillan Publishers Limited, registered in England, company number 785998, of Houndmills, Basingstoke, Hampshire RG21 6XS.

Palgrave Macmillan in the US is a division of St Martin's Press LLC, 175 Fifth Avenue, New York, NY 10010.

Palgrave Macmillan is the global academic imprint of the above companies and has companies and representatives throughout the world.

Palgrave® and Macmillan® are registered trademarks in the United States, the United Kingdom, Europe and other countries

ISBN: 978–1–137–32902–8

This book is printed on paper suitable for recycling and made from fully managed and sustained forest sources. Logging, pulping and manufacturing processes are expected to conform to the environmental regulations of the country of origin.

A catalogue record for this book is available from the British Library.

Library of Congress Cataloging-in-Publication Data

Baimbridge, Mark.
    Crisis in the eurozone : causes, dilemmas and solutions / Mark Baimbridge, University of Bradford, UK, Philip B. Whyman, University of Central Lancashire, UK.
        pages cm
    ISBN 978–1–137–32902–8 (hardback)
    1. Financial crises – European Union countries. 2. Eurozone. 3. Monetary policy – European Union countries. 4. European Union countries–Economic conditions – 21st century. I. Whyman, Philip. II. Title.
HB3782.B347 2015

330.94—dc23   2014028337

Transferred to Digital Printing in 2014

Contents

List of Illustrations

Figures

Tables

Acknowledgements

There are many people to thank for their input in making this book possible. Most obviously, we must thank our commissioning editor at Palgrave Macmillan, Taiba Batool, for her support for this project and Ania Wronski (editorial assistant) for her very enduring patience. Second, we are grateful to several students; in particular, Zhang He, Jessica Carswell and Saba Javed, who have provided inspiration for aspects of the book. Third, we would like to thank our long-time colleague Brian Burkitt, together with those at the universities of Bradford and Central Lancashire, for their comradeship and general support for our research on European economic integration. Finally, we owe a deep sense of gratitude to our families for their forbearance during the preparation of this book. It is to them that this book is dedicated: M.B.: Mary, Beibei and Douglas; P.W.: Barbara, Boyd and Claire.

Any remaining errors and omissions we gladly attribute to each other.

Haworth and Heaton Norris
June 2014

European Integration Timeline

1948   The Organisation for European Economic Cooperation (OEEC) is
       set up in Paris in April 1948, coordinating the distribution of the
       Marshall Plan financial aid, which will amount to $12.5 billion
       from 1948 to 1951. The OEEC consists of one representative from
       each of the 17 Western European countries that join the organisa-
       tion. In May 1948, in The Hague, the Congress of Europe (a meeting
       of delegates from 16 European countries) agree to form the Council
       of Europe with the aim of establishing closer economic and social
       ties.

1951   The European Coal and Steel Community (ECSC) is established
       by the signing of the Treaty of Paris in April 1951. Along with
       France and West Germany, Italy, Belgium, Luxembourg and The
       Netherlands have also chosen to join the organisation. Members
       of the ECSC pledge to remove all import duties and quota restric-
       tions on the trade of coal, iron ore, and steel between the member
       states.

1952   The European Defence Community (EDC) Treaty is signed by
       France, West Germany, Italy, Belgium, Holland and Luxembourg in
       May 1952. It includes the provision for the formation of a parallel
       European Political Community (EPC). However, both initiatives
       are destined to founder since the French National Assembly never
       ratifies the EDC Treaty, finally rejecting it in August 1954.

1955   The process of further European integration is given fresh impetus
       by a conference of ECSC foreign ministers at Messina, Italy, in June
       1955. The meeting agrees to develop the community by encour-
       aging free trade between member states through the removal of
       tariffs and quotas. Agreement is also reached to form an Atomic
       Energy Community to encourage cooperation in the nuclear
       energy industry.

1958   The two Treaties of Rome are signed, establishing the European
       Economic Community (EEC) and the European Atomic Energy
       Community (Euratom). As well as stipulating the eventual removal
       of customs duties on trade between member countries (over a
       period of 12 years) the EEC Treaty sets out to allow the free move-
       ment of workers, capital and services across borders and to harmo-
       nise policies on agriculture and transport.

1960   At the Stockholm Convention in January 1960, Austria, Britain,
       Denmark, Norway, Portugal, Sweden and Switzerland form the

European Free Trade Association (EFTA). The objective of EFTA is to promote free trade but without the formal structures of the EEC.

1961 UK applies to join the EEC.

1963 British application for EEC membership fails.

1967 UK submits second application to join EEC.

1968 Customs union completed and Common Agricultural Policy enacted.

1972 In October, following the recommendations of the Werner Report, the EEC launches its first attempt at harmonising exchange rates. The mechanism adopted is the so called 'snake in the tunnel', whereby participating governments are required to confine the fluctuations of their currencies within a range of +/–1% against each other. The value of the group of currencies (the snake) is also to be maintained within a range of +/–2.25% against the U.S. dollar (the tunnel). Countries requiring assistance to keep their currencies within the required band may receive help only in the form of loans.

1973 Denmark, Ireland and the UK join the EEC.

1975 UK referendum supports staying in EEC.

1978 At a summit in Bremen in July, the French and West German governments announce their intention to create the European Monetary System (EMS). At the centre of the EMS is the European Currency Unit (ECU). The value of the ECU is to be derived from a weighted basket of all participating currencies with the greatest weighting against the West German mark.

1981 Greece joins the EC.

1986 Portugal and Spain join the EC.

1990 UK joins EMS.

1992 At a summit of the European Council in Maastricht, Holland, the Treaty on European Union (TEU), also known as the Maastricht Treaty, is signed. Originally intended to include a declaration of an intention to move towards federal union, at Britain's insistence this aspect is played down. Subsequent to the signing of the Maastricht Treaty, the European Community is referred to as the European Union (EU).
UK leaves EMS.

1993 The Single European Market takes effect. Trade tariffs are scrapped, but duty-free shopping remains until 1999.

1994 Stage 2 of EMU is initiated on January 1st with the establishment of the European Monetary Institute (EMI) to oversee the co-ordination of the monetary policies of the individual national central banks. The EMI will also work towards the introduction of stage 3 by organising the creation of the European Central Bank.

1995   Austria, Finland and Sweden join the EU, bringing membership to 15.

The Schengen Agreement comes into force and scraps border controls. UK and Ireland stay out of the agreement.

1997   Heads of government draft a new agreement in Amsterdam which updates the Maastricht Treaty and prepares the EU for its eastward expansion. Qualified majority voting is introduced into new areas, reducing individual countries' powers to veto new measures.

1998   At the beginning of May, at a summit of EU officials and heads of state in Brussels, the announcement is made as to which countries will participate in the launch of the euro the following January. In June the European Central Bank (ECB) is established in Frankfurt, Germany. The ECB together with the national central banks of the 15 EU member states form the European System of Central Banks (ESCB), which will be responsible for setting monetary policy for the euro countries and managing those countries' foreign reserves.

The EU opens accession negotiations with Hungary, Poland, Estonia, the Czech Republic, Slovenia and Cyprus.

1999   Romania, Slovakia, Latvia, Lithuania, Bulgaria and Malta are invited to begin accession negotiations.

Eleven countries adopt the euro as their official currency (although national currency notes and coins remain in circulation), but Sweden, Denmark and the UK stay out.

2000   The Nice summit agrees to limit the size of the Commission and increase the president's powers. Qualified majority voting is introduced in new areas, but members keep their vetoes on social security and tax. A timetable for taking forward accession negotiations is endorsed.

2001   The Laeken European Council establishes the Convention on the Future of Europe.

2002   Euro notes and coins are introduced in 12 EU countries.

The European Commission announces that ten countries are on course to meet the criteria for accession to the EU in 2004.

2003   The UK has been a member of the EU for 30 years.

2004   EU enlargement to 25 member states with addition of Slovakia, Latvia, Lithuania, Malta, Hungary, Poland, Estonia, the Czech Republic, Slovenia and Cyprus.

2005   EU Constitution ratification ended by referendum defeats in France and the Netherlands.

The UK holds EU presidency, but fails to make progress on new 2007–2013 budget.

Accession negotiations are opened with Turkey and Croatia.

2006   Slovenia's entry into the euro on 1 January 2007 is confirmed.

Accession negotiations with Turkey are suspended.

2007   EU enlargement to 27 member states with addition of Bulgaria and Romania.

2008   Slovenia becomes the first of the recent enlargement member to hold the presidency of the Council of the EU.

Treaty of Lisbon ratification ended by referendum defeat in Ireland.

2009   Final year of the Barroso Commission.

Seventh series of elections to the European Parliament.

Second referendum on the Treaty of Lisbon in Ireland.

2010   Spain is the first country to hold the Presidency of the Council of the EU under the Lisbon Treaty and the new `trio presidency system' with Belgium and Hungary.

Heads of state and government agree to support the Greek government in its efforts to meet the Stability Programme targets for 2010.

European Council adopts a ten-year strategy for smart, sustainable and inclusive growth: Europe 2020.

The EU agrees to support the Irish economy to help safeguard the stability of the euro.

2011   Estonia adopts the euro, becoming the seventeenth member of the euro area.

The first 'European semester' of economic policy coordination between EU countries to help prevent economic crises like the one in 2008–2010.

A comprehensive package of measures to strengthen the European economy is finalised with the Euro Plus Pact to reinforce economic policy coordination in the EMU.

Three new European financial supervisory authorities begin operating: the European Banking Authority, the European Insurance and Occupational Pensions Authority and the European Securities and Markets Authority.

European Council agrees that the accession negotiations with Croatia should be concluded by the end of June 2011, paving the way for the country to become the twenty-eighth EU member in 2013.

The EU seeks to resolve the eurozone crisis centered on Greece through establishing the European Financial Stability Facility (EFSF) to become the European Stability Mechanism (ESM) from 2013.

2012   Denmark takes over the six-month rotating presidency of the Council.

Croatia vote 'yes' by 66 to 33% in its accession referendum and so will become the twenty-eighth EU member on 1 July 2013.

The European Council proposes a new treaty on stability, coordination and governance in the economic and monetary union, which is agreed by all EU countries with the exception of the Czech Republic and the UK.

A treaty to create a European Stability Mechanism (ESM) is signed.

The European Council grants candidate status to Serbia.

The European Citizens' Initiative becomes a reality, enabling citizens to propose EU legislation on specific issues for the first time.

As part of the 'European Semester', the Commission adopts recommendations for each member state, offering guidance on 2012–2013 national budgets and economic policies.

Cyprus takes over the six-month rotating presidency of the Council.

The European Stability Mechanism (ESM) enters into force.

The European Union is awarded the Nobel Peace Prize 2012.

2013   Ireland takes over the six-month rotating presidency of the Council.

The Treaty on Stability, Coordination and Governance in the Economic and Monetary Union enters into force.

Croatia joins the EU, bringing the total number of member countries to 28.

Lithuania takes over the six-month rotating presidency of the Council.

2014   Greece takes over the six-month rotating presidency of the Council.

Latvia adopts the euro as its currency, becoming the eighteenth member of the euro area.

The European Parliament adopts a set of rulebooks on how to deal with banks in serious difficulties, as the final element of the EU's Banking Union.

Chronology of Eurozone Crisis

1970   EC Commission resolution to establish Economic and Monetary Union (EMU). Werner Committee Report on EMU issued.

1973   Collapse of 'snake in the tunnel' policy.

1977   European Monetary System (EMS) launched.

1979   EMS comes into operation.

1991   European Council meeting in Maastricht agrees the Treaty on European Union.

1992   Crisis in the ERM leading to the UK and Italy suspending their memberships.

1998   European Council decides that 11 EU member states will participate when the euro is launched in 1999 (France, Germany, Italy, Belgium, Luxembourg, the Netherlands, Ireland, Spain, Portugal, Finland and Austria).

1999   Exchange rate parities of the participating member states and their conversion rates into euros are irrevocably fixed. The euro becomes a currency in its own right. Member states' monetary policy, exchange-rate policy carried out, and new public-sector debt instruments issued, in euros. The ESCB, national and EU public authorities to oversee and assist with currency changeover.

2001   Greece is added to list of eurozone member states.

2002   Euro banknotes and coins to circulate alongside national currency notes and coins.

2007   January: Slovenia joins the euro.

2008   January: Malta and Cyprus join the euro. EU leaders agree on a €200bn stimulus plan to help boost European growth following the global financial crisis.

2009   January: Slovakia joins the euro. Estonia, Denmark, Latvia and Lithuania join the Exchange Rate Mechanism (ERM) to bring their currencies and monetary policy into line with the euro in preparation for joining. The EU orders France, Spain, the Irish Republic and Greece to reduce their budget deficits.

April: Standard and Poor's downgrades Greece's debt ratings below investment-grade to junk-bond status; downgrades Portuguese debt two notches and issues negative outlook; downgrades Spanish bonds.

October: Amid much anger in Greece towards the previous government over corruption and spending, George Papandreou's Socialists win a general election.

December: Greece admits that its debts have reached €300bn, the highest in modern history, such that it is burdened with debt amounting to 113% of GDP.

2010   January: An EU report condemns 'severe irregularities' in Greek accounting procedures. Greece's budget deficit in 2009 is revised upwards to 12.7%, from 3.7%, and more than four times the maximum allowed by EU rules. The ECB dismisses speculation that Greece will have to leave the EU. Greece unveils a series of austerity measures aimed at curbing the deficit from 12.7% in 2009 to 2.8% in 2012.

March: The eurozone and IMF agree a safety net of €22bn to help Greece, raised to €30bn in April. Papandreou continues to insist that no bailout is needed. ECB extends softer rules on collateral to avoid a situation where one ratings agency decides if a eurozone country's bonds are eligible for use as ECB collateral.

April: The EU announces that the Greek deficit is even worse than thought at 13.6% of GDP, not 12.7%.

May: The ECB announces that it will accept Greek government bonds as collateral no matter what their rating is. The eurozone members and the IMF agree a €110bn bailout package to rescue Greece. Ireland's debt starts to come under scrutiny.

June: The EU releases the results of 'stress tests' conducted on 91 European financial institutions, with seven failing to maintain the minimum amount of ready capital required by examiners.

September: EU finance ministers and IMF approve second of the bailout instalments for Greece of €6.5bn and €2.57bn respectively. Ireland's central bank announces that the cost of bailing out Anglo Irish Bank could reach as much as €34.3bn, pushing its budget deficit to 32% of GDP.

November: Ireland starts talks and then accepts an €85bn package to help alleviate its debt burden, contrary to previous denials that it would need external help. Ireland then passes an austerity budget.

2011   January: Estonia joins the euro. Fitch becomes the third ratings agency to cut Greek debt to 'junk' status after S&P and Moody's.
February: Eurozone finance ministers set up a permanent bailout fund, the European Stability Mechanism (ESM), of €500bn.
May: The eurozone and IMF approve a €78bn bailout for Portugal.
June: Eurozone ministers say Greece must impose new austerity measures before it gets the next tranche of its loan, without which the country will probably default on its debts. Standard & Poor's downgrades Greece's credit rating, making it the country with the world's lowest-rated sovereign debt.

July: A second bailout for Greece is agreed. The eurozone agrees a comprehensive €109bn package designed to resolve the Greek crisis and prevent contagion among other European economies. The Greek parliament votes in favour of a fresh round of austerity measures; the EU approves the latest tranche of the Greek loan of €12bn.

August: Interest rates on ten-year Italian government bonds top 6% as confidence in the coalition led by Prime Minister Silvio Berlusconi is undermined by personal scandals and his on-going disagreements with Finance Minister Giulio Tremonti. Italy's €1.9tr public debt falls under increasing scrutiny from investors and, at 120% of GDP, Italy's rate of indebtedness is second only to Greece. The ECB says it will buy Italian and Spanish government bonds to try to bring down their borrowing costs, as concern grows that the debt crisis may spread to the larger economies of Italy and Spain.

September: A meeting of finance ministers and central bankers in Washington leads to more calls for urgent action, but a lack of concrete proposals sparks further falls in share markets. Greece holds 'productive and substantive' talks with its international supporters, the European Central Bank, European Commission and IMF. Spain passes a constitutional amendment to add in a 'golden rule,' keeping future budget deficits to a strict limit. Italy's legislature approves a €54bn austerity package with the intention of wiping out Italy's budget deficit by 2013, but Italy has its debt rating cut by S&P.

October: The Bank of England injects a further £75bn into the UK economy through quantitative easing, while the ECB unveils emergency loan measures to help banks. European leaders reach a 'three-pronged' agreement described as vital to solve the region's huge debt crisis. Some private banks holding Greek debt have accepted a loss of 50%. Banks must also raise more capital to protect themselves against losses resulting from any future government defaults. Slovakia's coalition government collapses when Prime Minister Iveta Radičová ties her country's approval of the expansion of the EFSF (requiring unanimous consent of all eurozone members) to a confidence motion. Eurozone finance ministers approve the next €8 bn tranche of Greek bailout loans, potentially saving the country from default.

November: Summit of G20 leaders discusses the eurozone crisis, and European leaders publicly declare that Greece's departure from the single currency is a possibility. Prime Minister Papandreou announces a Greek referendum on the new eurozone debt deal, but then withdraws promised referendum amid heavy pressure from Germany and France. Papandreou responds by abandoning the planned referendum. Spain becomes the third eurozone country in three weeks to see a change in government. Spanish voters sweep the ruling Spanish Socialist Workers' Party (PSOE) from power, handing the Popular Party (PP) an overall majority in parliament. Zapatero remains caretaker prime minister while PP leader Mariano Rajoy begins the task of forming a new government. Berlusconi's budget passes, and he resigns to be replaced by Mario Monti, a politically independent economist who previously served on the European Commission. S&P downgrades Belgium's long-term sovereign credit ratings.

December: All eurozone members and six countries that aspire to join agree on a new intergovernmental treaty (a fiscal stability union) to cap government spending and borrowing, with penalties for those countries that violate the limits. All other non-eurozone countries, except the UK, are also prepared to join in. The ECB starts the biggest infusion of credit into the European banking system by loaning €489bn to 523 banks at a rate of just 1% over a three-year period. In Greece a new interim national union government led by Lucas Papademos (former ECB vice-president) submits its plans for the 2012 budget, promising to cut its deficit from 9% of GDP 2011 to 5.4% in 2012; however, both Fitch and Moody's cuts Greece's rating, with a negative outlook.

2012   January: The 'fiscal pact' initially proposed in December 2001, containing for new rules that make it harder to break budget deficits, is signed by 25 EU members, with the UK and the Czech Republic opting-out. Talks stall between Greece and its private creditors over a debt write-off deal. The deal is necessary if Greece is to receive the bailout funds it needs to repay billions of euros of debt in March. Standard & Poor's downgrades France and eight other eurozone countries, together with the EFSF blaming the failure of eurozone leaders to deal with the debt crisis.

February: The ECB holds a second auction, providing 800 Eurozone banks with further €529.5bn in loans. Following negotiations with private lenders and the EU/IMF/ECB troika as Greece tries to get a debt write-off and make even more spending cuts to get its second bailout, its coalition government finally agrees to pass the demands made of it by international lenders. But the eurozone effectively casts doubt on the figures, requiring a further €325m in budget cuts.

March: 25 EU countries sign the new pact on fiscal discipline. While it will be binding only for those countries that use the euro, other signatories can choose to abide by its guidelines. However, unlike previous EU treaties, unanimous support from member countries is not required, and the agreement enters into force upon ratification by 12 of the 17 eurozone countries. Eurozone finance ministers announce an expansion of the EFSF and ESM to a combined €800bn in funding. This increase is made at the urging of the G20 and the IMF, who had expressed concern that the existing rescue funds were not sufficient to manage the bailout of a country such as Spain or Italy. The government of Prime Minister Mariano Rajoy unveils a budget that cuts some €27bn in spending, intended to bring Spain back into line with the new EU fiscal pact. The eurozone governments and IMF finally back a second Greek bailout of €130bn. With a majority of private bondholders agreeing to swap their existing Greek government bonds for ones with a longer term, a lower interest rate and less than half the previous face value, the Greek government exercises 'collective action clauses' to force the remaining bondholders to accept the deal. The action allows Greece to erase some €100bn in government debt. Unlike the 'selective default' of July 2011 the activation of the collective action clauses marks the event as a true loan default. The International Swaps and Derivatives Association declares that a 'credit event' has occurred, a decision that triggers the payout of credit-default swap insurance.

April: Spanish shares hit by worries over the country's economy, and the Spanish government's ten-year cost of borrowing rose back towards 6%, signalling fear over the country's creditworthiness. Italian borrowing costs increase in a sign of fresh concerns among investors about the country's ability to reduce its high levels of debt. In an auction of three-year bonds, Italy pays an interest rate of 3.89%, up from 2.76% in a sale of similar bonds the previous month.

May: The European Commission adopts a package of recommendations for budgetary measures and economic reforms and recommends that the euro area make steps towards a 'full economic and monetary union', including a banking union, integrated supervision and a common deposit insurance scheme. Spain's fourth largest bank, Bankia, is effectively nationalised as the government announces a €23.5bn bailout. A majority of Greeks vote in a general election for parties that reject the country's bailout agreement. Market analysts begin to discuss a 'Grexit', so capital flight becomes a growing concern as depositors fear a possible return to the drachma. Greece agrees to repay in full a €435m bond after previously declaring that it would default on any investors that did not participate in its €206bn debt swap. It is reported that depositors withdrew €700m from banks, sparking fears of a bank run.

June: EU leaders' meeting is dominated by Rajoy and Monti, who secure more-favourable lending terms, and eurozone leaders agree that countries obtaining loans from the ESM will not be subject to troika oversight. Additionally, steps are taken to establish a eurozone banking union, with supervisory powers vested in the ECB. The European Council adopts a 'growth compact' and tasks the president of the European Council, the president of the Commission, the president of the Eurogroup and the president of the ECB (the 'Four Presidents') with developing a specific, time-bound roadmap for the achievement of a genuine eurozone. In Greece, new elections held after attempts to form a coalition government fail. The pro-austerity party, New Democracy, wins most votes, allaying fears about Greece leaving the eurozone. In an effort to shore up its undercapitalised banking sector, Cyprus becomes the fifth eurozone country to apply for a bailout (€4bn). After emergency talks Economy Minister Luis de Guindos of Spain says that the country will shortly make a formal request for up to €100bn in loans from eurozone funds to try to help shore up its banks. Although Prime Minister Rajoy characterises the transaction as a 'soft loan' rather than a bailout, EU officials emphasise that the troika will oversee both the loan and any conditions that might be attached to it.

July: The ECB drops a key interest rate to 0.75%, which lowers the cost of borrowing for banks in the eurozone. Representatives of the troika arrive to investigate Cyprus's financial problems and submit bailout terms. The Cypriot government expresses disagreement over the terms. EU regulators agree to €18bn in aid for four Greek banks (Alpha Bank AE, EFG Eurobank Ergasias SA, Piraeus Bank SA, and National Bank of Greece SA). Prime Minister Rajoy of Spain announces an austerity budget that includes some €65bn in additional spending cuts and tax increases. Eurozone finance ministers agree to a plan for Spain's €100bn bank bailout plan. It is expected that the first €30bn will be delivered by the end of July.

August: Catalonia becomes the third Spanish region to ask the nation's central government for a €5bn bailout. The region faces €5.6bn of further bond maturities in 2012.

September: The ECB announces it would launch an unlimited but sterilised bond-buying program that would offset bond purchases by taking money out of circulation to avoid increasing the money supply. The new program known as Outright Monetary Transactions will replace the Securities Markets Program. Spaniards withdrew a record €75bn from Spanish banks in July, equivalent to 7% of GDP. The IMF approves a new €920m tranche for Ireland, the latest in financial aid that started in 2010.

October: The EU discusses the completion of EMU on the basis of an interim report presented by Herman Van Rompuy and agrees to have the legal framework for the single supervisory mechanism in place by January 2013. This agreement clears the way for the ESM to directly recapitalise banks, rather than having to act through national governments. It is hoped that this will break the vicious cycle of interconnected sovereigns and their systemically important banks. The Greek government submits its 2013 budget draft. The plan outlines further austerity measures of around €8bn, designed to placate the nation's lenders.

November: EU leaders fail to reach a deal on a common budget for its 27 members. A delay is expected until early 2013. EU Commission president, Barroso, says that he supports the 17-member eurozone nations integrating their economies faster than the wider, 27-member EU to facilitate a unified budget and the ability to issue eurozone-wide bonds. However, the Eurogroup approves a two-year extension to Greece's fiscal-adjustment period. The IMF and eurozone reach a debt-reduction agreement for Greece amounting to €40bn. The reduction is expected to help Greece re-emerge from its crippled state by 2020. Greece announces that it will borrow €10–14bn to finance the repurchase of debt demanded under the new terms of its bailout agreement.

December: EU finance ministers announce that they have reached an agreement to form a banking union. A single banking regulator, the ECB, is thought to be a key to resolving the crisis. Authority is granted to force troubled banks to close their doors and for bank capital ratios to be raised. Credit ratings are lowered for the EFSF and ESM by Moody's.

2013 March: The Eurogroup and troika agree a €10bn bailout with Cyprus (the fifth country to receive money from the EU-IMF); in return for Cyprus agreeing to close its second largest bank, the Cyprus Popular Bank (also known as Laiki Bank), levying all uninsured deposits there, and possibly around 40% of uninsured deposits in the Bank of Cyprus, many held by wealthy citizens of other countries who were using Cyprus as a tax haven. As part of the deal, a one-off bank deposit levy of 6.7% for deposits up to €100,000 and 9.9% for higher deposits, was announced on all domestic bank accounts. No insured deposit of €100,000 or less would be affected. Savers were to be compensated with shares in their banks and measures were put in place to prevent withdrawal or transfer of moneys representing the prescribed levy. However, when the final agreement was settled the idea of imposing any sort of deposit levy was dropped, as it was now possible instead to reach a mutual agreement with the Cypriot authorities accepting a direct closure of the most troubled Laiki Bank (with remaining good assets and deposits below €100,000 being saved and transferred to the Bank of Cyprus, while shareholder capital would be written off, and the uninsured deposits above €100,000, along with other creditor claims, would be lost to the degree being decided by how much the receivership subsequently can recover from liquidation of the remaining bad assets. As an extra safety measure, uninsured deposits above €100,000 in the Bank of Cyprus will also remain frozen until a recapitalisation has been implemented (with a possible imposed haircut if this is later deemed needed to reach the requirement for a 9% tier-1 capital ratio). Italy's general election failed to deliver a clear majority in the Senate. The centre-left coalition led by Pier Luigi Bersani won a narrow majority in the Lower House, but the Five-Star Movement, led by anti-euro comedian Beppe Grillo, emerged as the largest single party in the lower house and the second-largest party in the Senate. Outgoing PM Mario Monti was the biggest loser, with his party getting less than 10% of votes in both houses.

April: After several inconclusive ballots in which neither Prodi nor Marini (nor anyone else) found a majority, Giorgio Napolitano accepts to stand for re-election as Italian president in the hope that this will lead to a resolution of the Italian political crisis. Subsequently, Bersani resigns as leader of the Democratic Party (PD) and is replaced by Matteo Renzi. Enrico Letta, deputy leader of the PD, is invited by the president to form a government, after enough support is found for his leadership.

June: During state visit to Japan, President François Hollande of France declares that the eurozone crisis is over.

July: The IMF warns that it may be forced to write off some Greek debt after identifying an $11bn 'black hole' in the finances.

August: The Eurozone is brought out of 18-month recession by Germany and France, but Economic Commissioner Olli Rehn warns that the crisis is far from over as the eurozone reports 0.3% second-quarter growth.

December: Ireland leaves the EU/IMF bailout programme with government debt at 130.4% of GDP in 2013. Portugal also passes a bailout review of its economy.

2014   January: As foreign investor confidence in the country has been restored, Spain formally exits the EU/IMF bailout mechanism.

April: Greece returns to international capital markets, issuing bonds worth €3bn.

Glossary of Terms

Asymmetric and symmetric external shocks   External shocks refer to the impact upon the domestic economy generated by activities beyond the control of UK authorities, for example a sudden rise in oil prices or change in global demand for raw materials. If an external shock has a similar effect upon a given group of countries, it is said to be a *symmetric* shock since the policy response will be largely the same for all countries. *Asymmetric* shocks, alternatively, refer to those changes in the external environment that have significantly different effects upon different countries, requiring very different policy responses by each country in order to respond effectively.

Cyclical and structural convergence   Economic convergence refers to potential eurozone participants becoming economically similar prior to membership. Cyclical convergence occurs when the business cycles of boom and recession become increasingly similar amongst participating economies, so that a recession in the UK would occur approximately at the same time as a comparable slow-down in Germany, rather than one or two years in advance as at present. Similarly, structural convergence refers to changes in industrial and financial structure of the participating economies, which have the effect of ensuring similar reactions to external forces over the long term.

Deflation/Reflation   Deflation may be defined as a reduction in economic activity in the economy, which is associated with a sustained reduction in inflation, output and employment. Reflation refers to an increase in economic activity which stimulates output, employment and inflation in varying degrees.

Devaluation/revaluation/over-valuation   Devaluation refers to a reduction in the value of a given exchange rate relative to other rates, whilst revaluation concerns the increase in the exchange rate. For example, if the exchange rate on a given day is £1 equals $1.67, if the value of sterling increases so that £1 could now buy $2 worth of goods, the value of the pound would be said to have appreciated, whereas if the value falls to perhaps $1.50, sterling would be said to have fallen in value or devalued. Over-valuation refers to the circumstance wherein the value of sterling is so high that British exporters find it difficult to compete and this possibly leads to a trade deficit where more is imported than exported. Too high an over-valuation could lead to economic recession, as export companies reduce output and lay off workers. This then may spread to the remainder of the economy.

Economic and Monetary Union (EMU)   As a matter of definition, monetary union occurs when exchange rates are *permanently and irrevocably* fixed and may therefore precede the introduction of a single currency. However, the two terms are generally used interchangeably. Economic union involves a further transfer of macroeconomic policy to the federal level – particularly monetary policy, but typically also 'coordination' of fiscal policy within prescribed limits.

European Central Bank (ECB)   The ECB supersedes national central banks in those EU nations participating in the eurozone. Based in Frankfurt, the ECB will be in sole charge of exchange-rate and monetary policy for all the eurozone countries, setting one common interest rate, which will apply irrespective of the particular needs of individual countries at any period of time. Its sole policy goal is to achieve price stability without a similar responsibility to assist employment creation or economic growth. Policy conflict between ECB and the wider economic responsibilities of individual governments is difficult to resolve since the ECB is beyond the control of both member states and the EU Commission.

European Economic Area (EEA)   The EEA came into being on 1 January 1994, following an agreement between the European Free Trade Association (EFTA) and the EU. It was designed to allow EFTA countries to participate in the European SIM without having to join the EU. In an obligatory referendum, Switzerland's citizens chose not to participate in the EEA. Instead, the Swiss are linked to the EU by bilateral agreements, with a different content than that of the EEA agreement. Thus, the current members/contracting parties are three of the four EFTA states (Iceland, Liechtenstein and Norway) and the EU25. The EEA is based on four 'freedoms': the free movement of goods, persons, services and capital between the EEA countries. The non EU members of the EEA have agreed to enact legislation similar to that passed in the EU in the areas of social policy, consumer protection, environment, company law and statistics.

European Free Trade Association (EFTA)   The EFTA was established on 3 May 1960 as an alternative for European states that were not allowed, or did not wish, to join the EU. The treaty was signed on 4 January 1960 in Stockholm by seven states (United Kingdom, Denmark, Norway, Sweden, Austria, Switzerland and Portugal). Finland became an associate member in 1961 (becoming a full member in 1986), whilst Iceland joined in 1970. The United Kingdom, Denmark and Ireland joined the EU in 1973, and hence ceased to be EFTA members, whilst Portugal left EFTA for the EU in 1986. Liechtenstein joined in 1991 (previously its interests in EFTA had been represented by Switzerland). Finally, Austria, Sweden and Finland joined the EU in 1995 and hence ceased to be EFTA members. Currently, only Iceland, Norway, Switzerland and Liechtenstein remain members of EFTA. The EFTA states have jointly concluded free-trade agreements with a number of countries worldwide. EFTA has the following institutions: the

Secretariat, the EFTA Council, the EFTA Surveillance Authority, and the EFTA Court.

European Monetary Institute (EMI) The forerunner of the European Central Bank (ECB).

European System of Central Banks (ESCB) The central banks of all member states participating in the eurozone, which will act as subsidiaries of the ECB, implementing its policies.

European Union (EU) Formally the European Community (EC) and Common Market, the change of name occurred after ratification of the Maastricht Treaty, signifying a changed relationship between the 12 (now 25) participating nation states (called 'member states' in EU terminology), from a loose trading community towards a federal state encompassing one currency, a central bank and discussion of parallel moves towards political union.

Euro-X Committee A committee of those member states participating in the eurozone where discussions may include market-sensitive preferences for interest and exchange rates.

Excessive Deficit Procedure (EDP) The EDP is a feature of the Maastricht Treaty, whereby a budget deficit is deemed excessive if it exceeds 3% of GDP and if government debt exceeds 60% of GDP.

Fiscal federalism Fiscal federalism involves a redistribution of resources from more-successful to weaker regions of a federal state or, in the case of the single currency, between regions or member states participating in the eurozone. In practice, fiscal federalism acts in a similar manner to regional transfers in a nation state, whereby it seeks to stabilise the entire eurozone by reducing inflationary pressure in booming areas and kick-starting recoveries in depressed areas through a transfer of tax revenue from the former into public expenditure (or a tax cut) in the latter. Fiscal federalism may, therefore, assist macroeconomic management, particularly due to the existence of regional spill-overs or externalities, thereby preventing individual regions from 'going it alone'. It may also aid social cohesion by acting as an interregional public insurance scheme, preventing 'unlucky' areas bearing a disproportionate financial burden.

Fiscal policy Fiscal policy refers to the interaction between government expenditure and taxation. Under the eurozone, fiscal policy will remain under the control of national economic authorities, although constrained by the TEU convergence criteria and Stability and Growth Pact rules.

G7/G8 An informal grouping of seven of the largest industrialised economies (United States, Canada, Germany, France, United Kingdom, Australia and Japan). On occasion Russia has been invited to participate in recent summits, giving rise to the G8.

Gold Standard A currency arrangement whereby the central bank is obliged to give a fixed amount of gold in exchange for its currency. If a number of countries all fix their currencies relative to gold, they must, by definition, fix their exchange rates amongst themselves. The gold standard that existed between the majority of the industrialised economies during the 30 years-or-so before the First World War, imposed certain rules upon participating economies, the most important of which being a distaste for 'debasing the currency' by devaluing. Moreover, a participating nation experiencing a balance-of-payments deficit would have to take corrective deflationary action, thus preferring external over internal balance. The increased international volatility caused by war conditions terminated the system and its replication in 1925 was disastrous for the United Kingdom as it occurred upon pre-First World War parities, which no longer represented the true economic balance between nations.

Gross Domestic Product (GDP)/Gross National Product (GNP) These are two methods of measuring the value of the total flow of goods and services produced by an economy over a specified period of time – usually a year. The difference between the two is that GNP equals GDP *plus* net income earned by domestic residents from overseas investments.

International Monetary Fund (IMF) Established in 1944, by 2004 the IMF counted 184 members. It is intended to encourage international co-operation in monetary matters and the removal of foreign-exchange restrictions. Members are required to contribute a quota calculated upon the basis of GDP, and its fund can then be utilised to help members over temporary balance of payments difficulties, although usually in parallel with adopting corrective economic policies, such as domestic deflation and devaluation, intended to stimulate exports and reduce imports.

Treaty on European Union Convergence Criteria Established by the Treaty on European Union to ensure economic convergence amongst potential participants prior to their entry to the eurozone, there are five criteria which each country must achieve before they are permitted to participate in the single currency. They are: (a) each country's rate of inflation must be no more than 1.5% above the average of the lowest three inflation rates in the EMS; (b) its long-term interest rates must be within 2% of the same three countries chosen for the previous condition; (c) it must have been a member of the narrow band of fluctuation of the ERM for at least two years without a realignment; (d) its budget deficit must not be regarded as 'excessive' by the European Council, with 'excessive' defined to be where deficits are greater than 3% of GDP for reasons other than those of a 'temporary' or 'exceptional' nature; (e) its national debt must not be 'excessive', defined as where it is above 60% of GDP and is not declining at a 'satisfactory' pace.

Monetary policy Monetary policy is typically concerned with the level of interest rates, the availability of credit, banking regulations and the control of the money supply by the central bank. Under the eurozone, monetary policy will be transferred from national authorities to the ECB.

Nominal and real-wage rigidity   Nominal wages refer to money wages, whereas real wages refer to the purchasing power of those wages. Thus, a 3% rise in nominal wages during a period of 2% inflation produces a 1% rise in real wages. Wage rigidity refers to a situation in which wages are observed not to be perfectly flexible in response to a change in economic circumstances: for example, if wages should fail to fall sufficiently to price people back into work during a recession.

Non-accelerating inflation rate of unemployment (NAIRU)   NAIRU is the rate of unemployment, whether it be 1% or 8%, where inflation remains stable. The importance of this measure is that, if unemployment falls below its NAIRU rate, inflation will accelerate, whilst if above the NAIRU, inflation will fall.

Optimum Currency Area (OCA) Theory   This theory is utilised by economists to identify those factors which indicate the *optimum* size of a currency arrangement. Consequently, the theory proposes that objective tests can be employed to decide whether it is in the common interests of, for example, Ireland and Italy, or France and Germany, as to whether they should join together in the eurozone, or whether it is to their mutual advantage to retain separate currencies and monetary systems. Similarly, the theory could be used to identify whether *regions*, rather than countries, should form a currency union. In practice, however, whilst nation states remain the principal form of government for the majority of the world's population, OCA theory will be concerned in deciding where monetary integration should and should not be formed between groups of countries.

Single European Act (SEA)   The 1986 Single European Act introduced the single internal market, but also extended qualified majority voting within the Council of Ministers and further committed the EU to 'the objective of the progressive realisation of European and Monetary Union'.

Single Internal Market (SIM)   Resulting from the 1986 Single European Act, the single market refers to the removal of trade, capital and physical barriers across Europe, supposedly achieved by 1 January 1993, which allows free competition across the entire EU market.

Stability and Growth Pact (SGP)   Proposed by Germany to avoid excessive fiscal profligacy by individual member states within the eurozone, it limits budget deficits to 3% of GDP (as per TEU convergence criteria prior to membership). If this limit is ignored, and the country is not in recession (defined as GDP falling by 0.75%), fines of between 0.2 and 0.5% of GDP will be levied by the EU financial authorities. The Stability and Growth Pact additionally suggests that budget deficits be limited to 1% of GDP in the long term, thus increasing fiscal tightening.

1
The Eurozone as a Flawed Currency Area

Introduction

Advocates of membership in the eurozone argued that a European single currency could unleash economic potential that would increase economic growth and investment, achieve low and stable inflation and build a strong European economy through: encouraging greater trade; reducing transaction costs; and increasing price transparency. In terms of new institutions, the European Central Bank (ECB), through ensuring price stability, would result in lower inflation and interest rates, thereby again boosting investment and economic growth. Additionally, the euro would establish itself as a major world currency, conferring economic advantages and political prestige based upon the European Union's combined economic strength. Finally, arguments that eurozone membership reduces national sovereignty were rejected on the grounds that, due to the globalisation of financial markets and to voluntary limitations imposed by international treaties, sovereignty is not absolute any more (Baimbridge et al., 2000).However, many critics have argued that the costs of entry into the eurozone were, in fact, potentially far greater where the loss of monetary and exchange-rate policies weakens national economic management, which is further constrained by the restraints upon fiscal policy. Further, the lack of prior cyclical and structural convergence created strains such that unsynchronised business cycles and/or structural differences magnify the effects of asymmetric external shocks. This is potentially further exacerbated by the absence of any substantial fiscal redistribution mechanism to offset less competitive areas suffering declining incomes and persistent unemployment. Additionally, a unified monetary policy would be unable to meet the needs of all economies through concentrating upon the 'average' member state. In terms of rules and institutions, the 'generous' interpretation of the Treaty on European Union (TEU) convergence criteria implied that the majority of participants must continue to deflate their economies in order to meet the rigid financial criteria established by the Stability and Growth Pact (SGP). Finally, the ECB is fundamentally undemocratic because it is deliberately insulated from all political influence (Baimbridge et al., 2000).

There is sufficient evidence to suggest that the combination of tight fiscal policy, mandated by the SGP and the conservatism of the ECB has already resulted in the eurozone economy suffering a decade or more of slow growth. Since the inception of the euro many commentators have argued that, despite its resilience against immediate collapse due to the volume of political, and from 2010 financial, capital invested in it by the EU establishment, the euro remains a fundamentally flawed creation (Minford, 2002; Baimbridge and Whyman, 2008). Therefore, the eurozone constitutes a 'leap in the dark' with potentially destructive implications if its participants are insufficiently convergent, cyclically and structurally (Eichengreen, 1990, 1992, 1993).The reasons are varied: The eurozone fails to fulfil, or even approach, the optimum convergence criteria agreed by economists to be the minimum requirement for the efficient operation of a monetary union; crucially, the Eurozone lacks an adjustment mechanism to meet inevitably changing economic circumstances, both internal and external, other than price and income deflation; its governing institutions, the ECB and the European Commission, are not subject to democratic accountability, let alone democratic control; the eurozone was adopted for essentially non-economic motives as the next stage of an integrationist European project, but without the necessary political coordination underpinning it.

In addition to these longstanding potential problems inherent with the creation of the eurozone, its design – in terms of risks emanating from spill-over and free-rider effects that result from a lack of fiscal discipline – has been relentlessly exposed following the 2008 credit-crunch-induced recession. Whilst fiscal policy should theoretically be used as a countercyclical tool, governments can also use fiscal policy for purely political reasons; however, if this is the case, fiscal policy may become challenging within a monetary union such as the eurozone through the occurrence of spill-over or free-rider effects (von Hagen and Wyplosz, 2008). The former effect may occur if eurozone members run large budget deficits over a prolonged period of time, which leads to their fiscal stance being on an unsustainable path and which, given its financing through the financial markets, results in ever-higher interest rates on sovereign debt. Additionally, with such a growing recourse to the financial market, the availability of financing may decrease and, therefore, drive interest rates up further. Thus, one member's debt issue spills over to others as financing sovereign debt becomes more expensive for all countries (Arezki et al., 2011).The potential hazard of free-rider effects materialises when a country cannot meet the repayment of its outstanding debt and, with default on the horizon, undertakes either a surprise devaluation or inflation to reduce its debt's real value. However, for eurozone members without sovereign monetary policy, these methods are no longer available, thereby increasing the possibility of outright default

(McKinnon, 1996). Moreover, with the integration of financial markets, one country's bonds may be widely held by other members. Thus, outright debt default harms not only domestic bond holders, but other government and private investors holding such bonds. Consequently, the pressure to bailout troubled fellow members may increase and, without restrictions on fiscal behaviour, a member country may allow its debt to increase continuously if its government believes that other governments will bail it out. Under a currency union, member countries lose not only their monetary independence but also a central bank to back their sovereign debts; thus, when it comes to possible default, eurozone governments become uniquely vulnerable to self-fulfilling panic. Additionally, the connection between the operation of the euro and the recent worldwide economic recession provides an illustration that national self-governance offers the potential for superior economic performance.

To review the economic performance across the economies of the EU with particular reference to recent events, Tables 1.1 and 1.2 present an overview of mean GDP growth and unemployment rates for several key time periods: from the completion of the Single Internal Market to the fixing of exchange rates for eurozone countries (1993–1998), to the operation of the eurozone prior to the 'Great Recession' (1999–2007) and to the recession itself (2008–2011). For comparative purposes the information is shown for a number of economic regions in addition to the eurozone itself. It is noticeable how relatively poorly the eurozone has performed, with the slowest GDP growth and the highest unemployment rate across all periods. Such stylised facts lend support to the hypotheses that the eurozone is far from optimal, through having failed to provide the 'safety in numbers' that can contribute to weathering shocks.

Further problematic symptoms that the financial crisis has highlighted within the eurozone are the balance of payments (BoP) difficulties that some members have experienced, together with the divergence of external balances between members (see Figure 1.1). In relation to the rest of the world (RoW), the countries in the North (e.g., Germany, the Netherlands and Austria) have persistently experienced current account surpluses, whilst those in the South/Periphery (e.g., Greece, Ireland, Portugal and Spain) have experienced persistent current account deficits, despite an approximately

Table 1.1 Mean GDP growth rates (%)

	1993–1998	1999–2007	2008–2011
Eurozone	1.85	2.26	−0.11
European Union	2.17	2.54	−0.08
USA	3.70	2.85	0.21
OECD	2.62	2.56	0.19
World	2.89	3.26	1.55

balanced overall position (Holinski et al., 2012). Although originally perceived to be irrelevant, with the focus being on the global balance of the eurozone, these divergences are now partially identified as sources of the eurozone crisis (Sawyer, 2012). It is therefore pertinent to review the policy options for individual eurozone members to correct such BoP disequilibria and evaluate their desirability.

Initially, following the advent of Keynesian demand management, policy prescriptions were advocated to resolve external imbalances and aid adjustment mechanisms (Crockett, 1982); however, several policies are unavailable to individual eurozone members. For example, notwithstanding their criticisms, the short-term, expenditure switching policies/elasticities approach that advocates changes in relative price levels between countries, through either appreciations/revaluations or depreciations/devaluations (Södersten and Reed, 1994; Pilbeam, 2006). However, despite the unavailability of such policies, Jaumotte and Sodsriwiboon (2010) argue that eurozone countries could mimic this approach in the short term through 'internal devaluation' to restore competitiveness by decreasing labour costs and, hence, relative price levels. Policy options include decreased social security payments, reducing indexation of wage increases, or through minimising minimum wage growth. For example, if Greece and Portugal moderated minimum wage increases to those experienced by northern eurozone members, this would improve current account balances by 2–2.5% points (Jaumotte and Sodsriwiboon, 2010). Indeed, such measures are essentially those imposed upon bailout economies that have proved politically and socially problematic; however, it should be noted that if all southern eurozone members adopted such policies there would be little gained in relative competitiveness (Duwicquet et al., 2012).

Furthermore, the use of direct controls (e.g., tariffs, quotas and embargoes) are also excluded policy options, whereby trade policies are negotiated on behalf of all EU members, thus individual nations are unable to apply direct controls against the RoW (Lea, 2010). Additionally, longer-term policy options that emphasise BoP imbalances as entirely monetary phenomena are also unfeasible (Williamson and Milner, 1991); since eurozone members cannot control their narrow money supply, together with the prohibition of capital controls, then they possess no control over credit creation (Arestis and Sawyer, 2012). Therefore, eurozone members must either control their

Table 1.2   Mean unemployment rate (%)

	1993–1998	1999–2007	2008–2011
Eurozone	11.26	8.77	9.25
European Union	10.65	8.71	8.74
USA	5.57	4.94	8.40
OECD	7.32	6.45	7.59
World	5.30	5.83	5.86

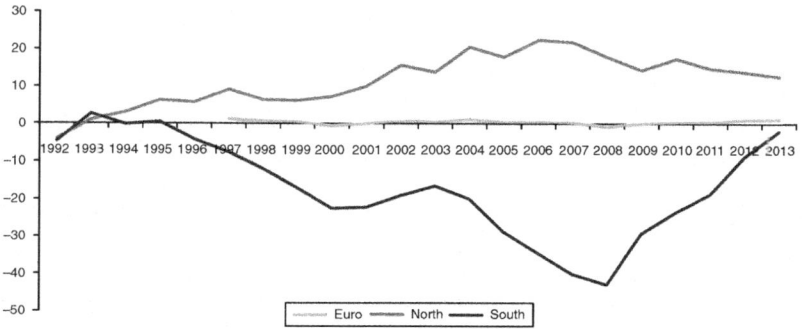

Figure 1.1   Current account balance (%of GDP) for eurozone members 1992–2013
Source: IMF (2012).

growth rates to prevent inflation, or face losing international competitiveness (McCombie and Thirlwall, 1994). Consequently, only a limited number of policy options are available to individual eurozone members. In the short term, the traditional approach emphasises the use of changes in the level of domestic spending, or absorption (Pilbeam, 2006). For example, in current account surplus countries such as Germany the policy prescription would be expansionary fiscal policy to stimulate the economy and increase imports to resolve the imbalance (Jirankova and Hnat, 2012). However such policies may conflict with internal balance; for example, Germany has typically operated at full employment output, such that any expansionary fiscal policy to increase absorption would create inflation (Arestis and Sawyer, 2012). Furthermore, since fiscal policy is limited due to the Stability and Growth Pact, the burden of adjustment is asymmetrically imposed on deficit countries (Ahearne et al., 2007). Similarly, in BoP deficit countries, contractionary fiscal policy is required; however, domestically these countries are experiencing low growth and high levels of unemployment (Chen et al., 2012); thus, such policies create a trade-off between internal and external balances, whereby there is a sacrifice of domestic goals (Thirlwall and Gibson, 1992). Hence, obtaining simultaneous internal and external equilibrium using only one policy is problematic; Tinbergen (1952) seminally proposed that the number of targets requires at least an equal number of instruments, whilst Mundell (1968) advocated that policies should be assigned based on their relative effectiveness. Arguably, fiscal policy has a greater effect on the domestic economy, whilst monetary policy (through interest rate differentials) attracts capital flows and is therefore more effectively assigned to the BoP (Pilbeam, 2006). However, for eurozone countries monetary policy is controlled at the ECB supranational level, such that national governments are (residually) left with fiscal policy to attain simultaneous equilibrium (Holinski et al., 2012); therefore, the adjustment mechanism is more difficult and uncertain (Duwicquet et al., 2012).

The eurozone's fundamental structural weakness

These aforementioned weaknesses in the design of the eurozone are permanent, but they become more damaging in times of crisis. In the wake of the worldwide financial recession, the eurozone suffered a series of debt crises in individual member states. To date, the eurozone's response has been piecemeal: ad hoc loans have been provided, whilst minor revisions to the Lisbon Treaty were agreed to enable the creation of a bail-out fund, the European Financial Stability Facility (EFSF) to become the European Stability Mechanism (ESM) from 2013. Such 'solutions', however, deal with the symptoms rather than the fundamental causes of the euro's structural weaknesses. This weakness ensures that recurrent problems will emerge that vitiate proposed remedies once they affect a large member country. Although the immediate origin of present discontents is usually located in the September 2008 collapse of the American investment bank, Lehman Brothers, its European antecedents lie in the bubble of speculative finance that occurred in the initial decade of the 21st century. This was intensified by the requirement to impose uniform interest rates in order to create an artificial monetary union amongst nations that did not always meet even their own restricted (financial not 'real') convergence criteria. Specifically, when the euro was introduced, the prevailing interest rate on 2 January 1999 stood at 3.25% for the three month Euribar (Euro Interbank Offered Rate), and, to achieve this target, nominal rates in France, Italy, Spain and Germany had fallen significantly in the previous nine years (O'Connor, 2009). Unsurprisingly, massive foreign investment ensued and stock markets boomed, whilst house prices and household debt levels soared. Inevitably, in such a low interest rate environment, investment banks and pension funds sought greater rates of return from alternative asset classes. Consequently 'structured products' developed, becoming the norm for investment in higher-yielding loan assets.

The strength of the euro until 2010 was determined by the German economy's competitive power, which brought about deflation in several other eurozone members, since having the same interest rate for all countries created a 'boom–bust' cycle in a number of them. Hence, the growth rate across the zone languished, whilst unemployment as well as government budget and trade deficits multiplied. Additionally, in 2007 the German coalition increased value-added tax by 3%, which financed concessions to industry so that Germany could compete at a higher exchange rate, but in the process intensified the problems of its eurozone 'partners'. Furthermore, the actions of the ECB – as the institution responsible for the one-size-fits-all monetary policy in the eurozone – also contributed to the series of events contributing to the crisis. Initially, in 2002–2003 the ECB adopted a low interest rate policy, which stimulated financial speculation. However, after 2005 the ECB changed its strategy so that rates climbed until the autumn 2008 crash. Indeed, it bowed to German pressure in June 2007 and as late as July 2008, raising interest rates to curb 'external inflation', despite an already-tight monetary environment. By definition, the ECB operates monetary policy for the eurozone as a whole, typically focusing upon the 'average' member state, so that the policy is often too tight for some nations, whilst too loose for others. Moreover, it is more difficult for the ECB to utilise monetary policy to regulate asset prices, whether stocks or housing, in individual nation states, where bubbles may occur. Thus, whilst few would claim ECB action to be the sole cause, it would be naïve to dismiss it as irrelevant rather than as a contributory influence. Although it might be argued that it is unfair to criticise the eurozone for struggling to deal with the negative consequences of the financial crisis, since it is by no means alone in this respect. Indeed, the Anglo-Saxon model was complicit in the loose regulation and speculative financial innovation that helped to precipitate the crisis in the first place. Nevertheless, although the 'old' European model could have avoided the worst of these failings through stronger financial-sector regulation and a more managed economy, it did not, and the current eurozone framework was at least a contributory factor.

Although this series of events exacerbated the inherent problems regarding the functioning of the eurozone, such difficulties could have been tempered if it had incorporated a coherent adjustment mechanism to meet inevitably changing economic circumstances. In a dynamic market economy characterised by technological and organisational progress, change is continuous: what Schumpeter (1942) famously termed the 'gale of creative destruction'. Furthermore, since the Industrial Revolution all capitalist economies have experienced a cycle of periodic booms followed by periodic depressions. Consequently, it is crucial to the health of every economy that it possess a robust adjustment mechanism to enable it to accommodate efficiently to the inevitable transformations that will occur in its internal and external environment. However, the eurozone lacks this crucial element in its structure whilst simultaneously harbouring potentially damaging spill-over and free-rider problems. Thus, in the recent recession the eurozone's members no longer possess independent monetary policies, so they cannot set interest rates or exchange rates to stabilise their economies. The current sovereign-debt problems faced by several participating nations demonstrate the simultaneous dangers of losing control of their borrowing costs and of the value of their currency to an external agency. Consequently, deflation – with all its economic, political and social costs – has become the eurozone's sole adjustment mechanism, to the detriment of its citizens.

Conventional wisdom is that these contemporary crises are the product of deficient policymaking in the suffering countries, often expressed in moral terms as 'indiscipline' (Mills, 2011). In particular, budgetary policy has been too expansive and economies too competitively inflexible. The consequences of such errors are public expenditure cuts, increases in taxation and/or declining real wages. Additionally, conventional wisdom declares that once fiscal consolidation has occurred and labour market flexibility introduced, the countries concerned can return to non-inflationary growth, as Germany did after 2003. However, such conventional wisdom is misplaced, subjecting the eurozone to inefficient and ultimately unsustainable tensions. So long as the ECB tolerates weak demand in the eurozone as a whole and so long as the EU's founder members (especially Germany) run trade surpluses, it will prove impossible for less-competitive nations to avoid insolvency. Their problems cannot be resolved by fiscal austerity alone, but only by a large rise in the external demand for their output. However, in a eurozone without monetary or exchange-rate offsets, any reduction in public expenditure generates at least an equivalent reduction in output. For example, an attempt to cut a fiscal deficit by 10% of GDP through reductions in spending would involve an actual reduction of 15% in GDP once declining tax revenues have been taken into account (Holland, 1995). A diminution in purchasing power of this magnitude would create a spiral of debt deflation in which the cost of meeting unpaid debts leads to low growth, falling prices, loss of jobs and declining living standards (Minsky, 2008). This 'perfect storm' increases the risk of default and, therefore, is likely to cause long-term interest rates to rise, the very thing that the adjustment policy was designed to avoid. Such a scenario carries dire consequences for future productive potential, leading to political dislocation and social distress (Baimbridge et al., 1994).

Almunia et al. (2010) compared the operation of the interwar gold standard with that of the euro, arguing that both systems are undermined as much by persistent surplus countries as by persistent deficit countries. Indeed, the more so because those in surplus are under no compulsion to change and are unwilling to contemplate this scenario. However, Germany now needs to reconsider its position, because the only way for other eurozone countries to lower fiscal deficits without their economies collapsing is through a huge net export expansion based upon both improved productivity and, crucially, buoyant external demand. Currently, neither is forthcoming, so that it is difficult to regain competitiveness when the euro is strong, partly because Germany is so competitive and partly also because eurozone inflation is low. Furthermore, the financial markets are correct in questioning the willingness of governments, and societies as a whole, to suffer the enormous deflationary burden imposed by euro membership. Indeed, the most direct method for eurozone nations to avoid the consequent deflationary effects of the eurozone is by dismantling or, at the very least, reconstructing its entire mode of operation.

Compatibility of the eurozone with economic progressivism

In addition to discussing the general background to the eurozone– the resulting economic policymaking framework and potential solutions/ outcomes from the recent crisis – a key central theme of this book is our belief that that the notion of the EU, via the eurozone, providing the potential for realising a progressive social and economic policy is problematic (Whyman et al., 2012). Considerable faith has been placed in the creation of a 'Social Europe' through the European Social Model (ESM), yet this model remains patchy in both coverage and generosity because at least four variants exist (Whyman, 2001). Moreover, the neo-liberal framework associated with the eurozone requires the formulation of monetary policy by the independent ECB to be separate from nationally determined fiscal policy (itself constrained by the SGP), thereby leading to a lack of policy coordination, a situation that is prejudicial to the construction of a progressive economic framework. In particular, the neo-liberal drift within the EU was precipitated by the TEU, which institutionalised monetarism through the constitution of the ECB and the provisions of the SGP (Baimbridge et al., 2007). Consequently, progressive forces must either redouble their efforts in a struggle within the EU to realise a fundamental reform of its institutions and policy framework, or else consider other, more globally orientated, alternatives. The latter choice could embrace: a competitive exchange rate; higher investment; a social contract to restrain inflationary pressures via planned redistribution; the reintroduction of exchange controls through a transactions tax on dealings unrelated to trade; and the pursuit of an active industrial policy to increase the long-run competitiveness of British industry. However, to facilitate such strategies the nature of the EU is called into question, leading to debate regarding whether championing internal reform of the organisation, its institutions and policy framework, or pursuing a more arm's-length, independent approach might produce more egalitarian results. The former has been explored extensively in the literature (Clift, 2004; Marquand, 1999; Arestis et al., 2001; Arestis and Sawyer, 2006), whilst the latter remains largely unexplored territory. Consequently, this book also analyses a number of these options and evaluates their potential benefits and costs from a social-science-wide political economy framework.

One of the most notable arguments proffered to explain social democratic support for European integration relates to the oft-repeated claim that the globalisation of the world economy has created a new environment within which progressive forces need to adapt traditional programmes to remain relevant and arrest a perceived decline in the efficiency of their preferred policy instruments (Daniels, 2003; Whyman, 2002). A vision of globalisation has been popularised wherein stateless corporations operate within a 'borderless world', relocating production facilities with relative ease on the basis of calculations that optimise profits and productivity (Ohmae, 1990; Reich, 1992). Moreover, disconnected capital has experienced an exponential increase in importance, whereby it dwarfs the value of world trade (Eatwell, 2000; Watson, 2002). Accordingly, theorists have claimed that the very concept of a national economy is becoming meaningless, whilst globalisation has been implicated in a 'decline' or 'crisis' of a 'hollowed out' nation state (Ohmae, 1990, 1995; Strange, 1996, 2000).

From this perspective, the implications for democratic socialist strategy are catastrophic, since there remains no room for manoeuvre for discretionary Keynesian policy, with governments compelled to revise policy to conform to the dictates of international financial markets (Gray, 1998; Veseth, 1998; Perraton et al., 2000). Indeed, Chancellor of the Exchequer Gordon Brown argues that, in an economy characterised by " ... deregulated, liberalized financial markets ... the Keynesian fine tuning of the past which worked in relatively sheltered, closed national economies and which tried to exploit a supposed long-term trade-off between inflation and unemployment, will simply not work" (Brown, 1998). Thus, 'luxuries' such as full employment, redistribution and the development of a universalistic welfare state may be no longer be affordable due to greater economic constraints (Hay, 1999).

The view amongst progressive forces that European integration could provide a positive response to globalisation is, however, problematic. For some, regionalisation can represent a 'macro-nationalist', 'neo-protectionist' reaction against the dominance of global market forces (Scholte, 2000). Thus the EU offers the possibility of resisting the worst ravages of the operation of market forces through the adoption of a form of Euro-Keynesianism (Strange, 2002). Thereby, pursuit of full employment, development of an advanced common system of social protection and an inclusive form of industrial relations are facilitated (Marquand, 1999; Baker et al., 2002). However, the political conditions have remained lacking for this approach to be implemented at European level (Fouskas, 1998; Callaghan, 2000). For others, however, the EU is viewed not as 'Fortress Europe', intended to protect a distinctive form of European capitalism from the full impact of market forces, but rather as a region where the power of the state should be used to adapt institutions and individual behaviour in ways that maximise their strength within the market (Giddens, 2001). Thus, regional integration can be viewed as a consequence of globalisation and may represent an intermediate step upon the road towards full globalisation (Tober, 1993). Hence, the appropriate response should be to adapt to these changes rather than seek to minimise their impact through deregulation, labour market flexibilisation and the marketisation of the public sector. Such a perception of globalisation constitutes a gross exaggeration. Specifically, nation states retain considerable autonomy in national economic policy and, hence, choices available to progressive forces are nowhere near as limited as is often suggested, as witnessed by Britain's economic performance after exiting the Exchange Rate Mechanism (ERM) in 1992 (Garrett, 1995; Hirst and Thompson, 1996). Nevertheless, as is so often the case in political debate, it is a fatalistic reaction to the *perception* of the impact arising from globalisation, rather than to its *reality*, that has shaped progressive forces' response to changes in the external economic environment (Hay, 1998; Rosamond, 1999; Hay and Rosamond, 2002; Whyman, 2003, 2006).

A second significant attraction concerns the existence of what is often described as the ESM (Strange, 1997). Essentially, this refers to an idealised form of the post-war German social market, which combined a successful, competitive market economy with generous welfare provision and labour protection. Its central features include the encouragement of social institutions to mediate between state and market, whilst 'social partnership' is intended to facilitate 'voice' rather than 'exit', thereby facilitating productive investment (in physical and human capital), innovation and co-operation in adaptation to change (Glasman, 1997; Coates, 1999). A comprehensive system of welfare provision, combining quality public services with social transfers providing a high replacement ratio, a partial socialisation of risk and decommodification of employees, should enable all citizens to participate fully within society. Hence, it is perhaps not surprising that this Delorsian vision should prove attractive to progressive forces after two decades of financial crises in the public sector and deregulation in the labour market. Nevertheless, it is the vision that proves attractive and not the realisation of democratic socialist aspirations. For example, whilst the current form of social dimension being constructed across the EU has had an impact in less-regulated EU member states (such as the UK), this form remains a minimalist version of a fully fledged system of social protection of the kind idealised in discussion of the ESM (Whyman, 2001, 2007). Indeed, Streeck (1992:218–219) considers that the 'retarded advancement of European-level political rights' and the 'almost complete absence of a European system of industrial citizenship' indicates the minimal impact of the ESM. Underpinning these arguments is an assumption that a distinct, indefinable ESM exists. However, EU welfare states differ significantly from each other, so that they can be classified into separate 'clusters' based on the concept of decommodification (Esping-Anderson, 1990). On this basis, four different kinds of welfare state have been identified within the EU before its 2005 enlargement: the social democratic (occurring in Scandinavia – 'the northern model'), the conservative-corporatist (located in France, Germany and the Benelux countries – 'the central model'), the Mediterranean (found in Greece, Italy, Portugal and Spain – 'the southern model') and the uniquely hybrid UK system ('the offshore island model'). However, the ESM model, to which the social democratic advocates aspire, is the conservative-corporatist variant, implemented by five of the six original signatories to the Treaty of Rome. These countries are now a minority within the EU, but their founder status gives them influence far greater than their numbers would suggest (Burkitt, 2006).

A further reason for questioning enthusiasm for EU integration is that was predicated upon the creation of a 'social Europe' concerns the existence of pressure within the EU for a series of reforms intended to create a model more attuned to the neo-liberal precepts of the EU's economic framework (Bulmer, 2000; Whyman, 2001). It is within this context that Tony Blair argued that 'we need to curb the European social model, not play around with it', suggesting that New Labour's approach can construct 'the foundation of a reformed European social model of which Britain can not only be part, but take a lead in helping to create', based upon the promotion of an enterprise agenda and improving competitiveness through increased flexibility and employability in labour markets, alongside a renewed commitment to equality of opportunity (Blair, 1998a&b; Clift, 2001; Favretto, 2003). Moreover, this neo-liberal approach is reflected in the approach of the EU Commission, which increasingly views social policy as a means of promoting adaptability and flexibility across the EU economy (Vaughan-Whitehead, 2003). Thus, the future direction of the EU remains a subject for political struggle, whilst the attraction of a regional means of pursuing traditional democratic socialist objectives must be assessed by whether the regional possesses a superior probability to advance an egalitarian programme when compared to available national and global alternatives (Whyman et al., 2012).

Finally, a further key aspect of the EU that has been embraced by large sections of progressive forces is the eurozone which is one of the most far-reaching recent economic reforms, and the focus of this book. Advocates claim the eurozone enhances competition through price transparency and completing the Single Internal Market (SIM), thereby reducing prices for consumers and ensuring a superior allocation of resources as corporate restructuring facilitates global competitiveness. An economic infrastructure has been established to focus upon the promise of low inflation, resulting in superior economic performance. However, critics of the eurozone point to the combination of substantial initial transfer costs and the danger of being trapped within a permanently fixed exchange rate system, magnified by the deflationary impact of the monetarist-inspired creation of the ECB whose sole objective is control of inflation through a 'one-size-fits-all' interest rate policy (Gill, 1998; Van Apeldoorn, 2002). The SGP ensures that this deflationary approach will be maintained once countries have achieved membership in the eurozone. Permanently maintaining fiscal deficits below 3% of GDP requires a more intensive 'reform' of welfare provision than has already occurred. It is no coincidence that speculation concerning the unaffordable nature of current levels of public and final-salary company pensions coincides with the restrictions placed upon government expenditure by the TEU convergence criteria and SGP. Furthermore, maintenance of a budget balance within the SGP limits will require further public-sector cuts, as large surpluses are necessary in periods of relatively rapid economic growth to ensure that state finances do not breach the 3% of GDP limit during periods of recession associated with the business cycle (Baimbridge et al., 1999a). Hence, Keynesian measures are further constrained, restricting the potential of counter-cyclical economic strategy. This constraint is quite intentional and is based upon monetarist assertions that Keynesian economics no longer work. However, many democratic socialists argue that the loss of national economic autonomy, combined with the multiple restrictions that eurozone participation places upon the pursuit of macroeconomic policy, reduces the scope for achieving their traditional objectives (Whyman et al., 2012).

Furthermore, in relation to the eurozone, there remains the fundamental problem of central bank independence, such that the democratic socialist case rests largely upon Keynesian rather than on monetarist/neo-classical assumptions, so that the market economy is perceived as experiencing significant market failure, cumulative causation and thus unequal exchange. Consequently, government intervention has the potential, if properly directed and accurately timed, for improving economic performance. Such a perspective rejects the neo-classical concept of time inconsistency, which implies that all government intervention worsens those circumstances it is intended to improve, together with the monetarist belief in a long-term equilibrium rate of unemployment determined solely by labour-market factors. Moreover, this democratic socialist perspective rejects the viewpoint that globalisation and the international free flow of capital have rendered national economic policy instruments impotent; if this viewpoint were true, undertaking economic policy within, the eurozone framework would be ineffective, because government autonomy has already been eroded by the external economic environment. Whilst the eurozone, in the shape of the TEU convergence criteria and SGP, directly impacts upon national policy-making, the ECB is the sole body credited with determining the appropriate monetary and exchange-rate policy for the entire eurozone (Baimbridge, 2006). Consequently, the ECB's ability to fulfil its stated objectives will be crucial to the eventual success or failure of the eurozone since its architects sought to insulate it completely from political pressures, thereby permitting no clear accountability to either national or EU institutions. The crucial operational features of the ECB are that its sole policy objective is the pursuit of price stability. This is founded upon both theoretical (Barro and Gordon, 1983; Alesina and Grilli, 1991) and empirical (Bade and Parkin, 1988; Alesina, 1988 and 1989; Cukierman, 1992) studies, which imply that the transfer of monetary policy from governments to an independent central bank is likely to result in lower inflation. However, the paucity of analysis regarding the ECB's ability to achieve low inflation, full employment and a satisfactory rate of economic growth, should be of great concern for all interested in contesting the neo-liberal path of European integration.

Overview of book themes

Over the past two decades the EU has increasingly embraced further financial market integration, culminating in the eurozone, as a bulwark to globalisation; however, the view that the EU provides the potential for realising progressive/social democratic social and economic policy is problematic. Thus, progressive forces have to either redouble their efforts to realise a fundamental reform of EU institutions and policy framework, or consider alternatives that inevitably question the fundamental nature of the EU. Consequently, this is a recurrent theme throughout this book, whereby we initially outline the direction of travel in mainstream macroeconomic thinking, such that its levels of abstraction are in danger of becoming detached from reality. Hence, in Chapter 2 we discuss a number of the key developments in macroeconomics following the breakdown of the post-Second World War consensus based upon Keynesian aggregate demand management. In particular, we evaluate the rise of New Classical economists who sought to provide more appropriate answers based on a return to classical notions. In response to its loss of the dominant position, New Keynesian economics emerged to defend Keynes's legacy through explanation of nominal and real rigidities, albeit combined with elements of New Classical ideas. Chapter 3 discusses how these different approaches have evolved into the so-called New Consensus Macroeconomics (NCM), which forms the current mainstream macroeconomic model comprising a blend of New Classical and New Keynesian theories through adopting the rational behaviour hypothesis and supply-side-determined long-term equilibrium of output. In addition to the general backdrop of macroeconomics it is essential to consider the impact of monetary union between countries under the rubric of Optimum Currency Area (OCA) theory. This theory concludes that a single currency boosts participants' living standards when they possess similar economic structures and international trading patterns, but proves detrimental where these structures and patterns diverge. In Chapter 4, these ideas of convergence are extended to include an examination of the euro-zone business cycle synchronicity.

A particular feature of these new ideas has been the inclusion of rules and institutions that are perceived to result in time-consistent policymaking through essentially precluding politicians from undertaking non-optimal behaviour for either opportunistic, partisan or non-rational expectations reasons. Chapters 6 and 7 discuss how such ideas have increasingly gained acceptance over the past two decades so that they have migrated from economic theory to become the actual policymaking structures of many contemporary economies. Indeed, they form the bedrock of the eurozone, where the TEU convergence criteria and SGP form the rules, whilst the European Central Bank is the key institution tasked with delivering low and stable price inflation: discussed in Chapter 8. However, although these notions have become the staple diet of a generation of mainstream economists, they comprehensively failed to insulate the eurozone from its sovereign debt crisis, triggered by the global financial crisis/Great Recession. Consequently, we present an alternative, post-Keynesian perspective to both neo-liberal macroeconomic thought and the operation of the economy. Specifically, we argue that the methods of economic management and democratic accountability have been fundamentally altered as the TEU convergence criteria/SGP reduce national fiscal flexibility whilst the eurozone strengthens financial market integration and thereby reduces seigniorage revenues: currently, a particularly acute issue for the Mediterranean member states.

Additionally, since at the present time there is no large federal fiscal system in place, then fiscal policy is confined to backward-looking automatic stabilisers such that the only channel for a forward-looking policy is through interest rates. Hence, the eurozone fiscal framework increases the burden on monetary policy to react to shocks even before they have fed fully through into output and inflation. Moreover, for some eurozone economies this policy straitjacket is further tightened through recourse to bailouts, whilst non-eurozone member states retain considerable policy autonomy, albeit theoretically subject to the monitoring of deficit and debt levels. Not only has this increased the complexity of domestic economic policymaking, but it also potentially weakens macroeconomic policy coordination across the EU as a whole. Thus, the Great Recession has demonstrated that the persistence of asymmetric external shocks requires an alternative stabilising mechanism to be developed to prevent the eurozone being undermined by diverse economic and social forces to the extent that it could collapse; however, as discussed in Chapter 5, almost all other similar international monetary arrangements that have not been based upon a firm national identity have failed.

Chapters 9 through 11 discuss how an alternative stabilising mechanism might be achieved within the context of the eurozone where there are several potential routes of varying effectiveness and likelihood that appear available for varying degrees of economic efficiency. For example, as has been witnessed, the initial response to the eurozone crisis was that of moral suasion; namely, castigating debtor countries for their profligacy. Such a shaming process may exert a limited effect, but is likely to be of only short duration given its illogicality in terms of Germany's urging budget cuts on the Mediterranean nations, but without acknowledging how its own surpluses has been built partly upon their willingness to buy German commodities with borrowed money. Thus, if the euro is to prove permanent, it requires a firmly based equilibrating mechanism. One development in this direction has been the provision of ad hoc financial relief, usually subject to guarantees of a changed economic policy backed by market and political pressures: This was the reaction to the eurozone crises during 2010 and the early months of 2011. As bailouts encompassed Greece, Ireland and Portugal, with market sentiment indicating the possibility of future loans to Belgium, Italy and Spain, a permanent source of funding is required. Consequently, eurozone members agreed to establish the EFSF to be replaced by the ESM after 2013, so that by 2017 the latter will possess a fully paid-up capital base of €80billion, which provides a lending ceiling of €500billion that is more than adequate to cover the cost of existing bailouts. However, the weakness in this approach lies in the fact that the gap between the €80billion base and the €500billion ceiling is composed of guarantees from eurozone member states, and calling upon these guarantees could prove problematic. It is at least conceivable that some countries may be financially unable to meet their obligations (e.g., Italy), whilst others may be politically unwilling (e.g., Germany).

Therefore, the formation of the ESM may prove insufficient to the task. Moreover, the rescheduling of debts and/or partial default may be the end result of this process, with resultant concern over the size of the 'haircut' suffered by the holders of the debt should this take place. Thus, the creation of the ESM and the associated deflationary measures forced upon deficit nations merely postpones the eventual clash between the irresistible force of euro-zone-wide crisis resolution and the immovable object of national democratic decision-making. Although the eurozone package of a second €109billion bailout for Greece, agreed on 21 July 2011, implies that the Greek debt-to-GDP ratio would not peak at 172% as previously forecast but at 148%, neither of these numbers is even close to a sustainable debt level. Moreover, an integral part of the Greek plan to repay its debts is a €30billion provision for privatisation receipts by 2014, which is unlikely to materialise; hence, this and other gaps suggests that the cost of refinancing will be significantly higher as indicated by later renegotiations that initiated even further austerity policies.

As discussed in Chapter 10, fiscal federalism offers an alternative means of stabilising the eurozone in the absence of differentiated (national) monetary policy. In one conception, it would substitute for natural arrangements within a political union– without which, former German chancellor, Helmut Kohl, famously asserted the euro was just a 'castle in the air'. Indeed, Bordo and Jonung's (2000) analysis of the history of currency unions between unitary states supports Kohl's conclusion. However, as Mills argued (2010), the difference between unitary states and multi-nation associations is that the former are more internally cohesive, making it possible for their governments to at least substantially resolve economic differences within them. Without such redistributive funds, the cost bases of constituent economies become so unaligned that currency-value adjustments are essential. For example, Mills (2010) demonstrated that, compared to 2005, labour costs in Spain were 15% higher than in Germany and in Italy were 18% higher, thus illustrating the magnitude of divergence between eurozone members. However, whilst advocacy of fiscal federation to prevent the fracturing of the eurozone may possess theoretical coherence, it ignores constraints imposed by current political reality. German doubts about extending the EFSF's proposed capacity would be multiplied in the face of fiscal federal problems. Indeed, current UK prime minister, David Cameron, is attempting to move in the opposite direction by building a coalition of members to limit the EU budget to no more than 1% of its GDP between 2014 and 2020. Additionally, to consolidate the euro, further harmonisation of economic and social policies may be necessary, but political acceptability of this harmonisation will be hard-fought and it will be only grudgingly accepted by many participants. Therefore, its development is likely to prove problematic and, if it occurs, will be a lengthy process incapable of alleviating present dilemmas. It also intensifies long-held fears about the diminution of national sovereignty as a result of closer integration (Redwood, 1997); such an attack upon the independence of nation states camouflages the fact that the single currency project was inadequately conceived, ignoring many of the tenents of OCA theory in favour of a preference for a political 'fix'.

Consequently, fiscal federalism without democratic support would potentially create new problems. Taxpayers in the eurozone's core already resent underwriting what they perceive to be profligate, uncompetitive partners, whilst voters in the periphery equally resent economic austerity being imposed upon them. Far from bringing nations together, a common currency and the consequent one-size-fits-all monetary policy are driving member states further apart. However, EU leaders who are fearful that their integrationist project is failing tend implicitly to favour greater fiscal union. Yet even if they can persuade their electorate of the need for large, permanent cross-border transfers, experience suggests that the euro's problems will remain unresolved. For example, two decades after reunification, no part of eastern Germany is as wealthy as the poorest part of western Germany, whilst a century of transfers from northern Italy to the Mezzogiorno has not generated regional equality. Hence, if subsidies within one nation exert only a limited impact, they are unlikely to be any more effective when applied to societies with different languages and profoundly different ways of life. In contrast, the tested formula for economic recovery always includes, albeit not exclusively, devaluation.

In addition to the newfound interest in fiscal federalism, Eurobonds have become a fashionable 'solution' to the crisis as debt issues pledging 'joint and several' liability by all nations using the euro. However, the ruling of the German Constitutional Court on 7 September 2011 makes Eurobonds' adoption improbable. Whilst it upheld the EFSF, it stated that the German government cannot accept permanent mechanisms that carry the following criteria: if they involve a permanent German liability to other countries; if these liabilities are large or incalculable; or if the actions of foreign governments trigger the payment of guarantees. This verdict implies that Eurobonds are unconstitutional in Germany, since: they are a permanent mechanism; require a permanent loss of control; could be of a size that would need to be substantial to resolve the eurozone crisis efficiently. Therefore, a Eurobond matches the conditions set by the Constitutional Court for an arrangement that violates the German constitution. Moreover, the procedure necessary to achieve Eurobonds –through negotiating a new European treaty and subsequently ratifying it across 27 countries, in the midst of a fast-moving crisis– renders their creation extremely unlikely. Consequently, any future eurozone fiscal policy will either be too small and too temporary to be effective, or will prove impossible to implement.

Chapter 11 discusses how the creation of a clearing union, suggested by Keynes (1942) on an international basis during the Second World War, could not only remove the sovereign-debt problems of particular countries, but more significantly in the long term could restore international confidence in the single currency. Presently, fund managers in the United States and Asia suspect the euro's future is limited, so they are divesting. Keynes's response to such problems rested on analysis of the operation of the gold standard–a system that failed because adjustment to imbalances, as in the present eurozone, was compulsory for the debtor but voluntary for the creditor. His solution was that all international transactions, giving rise to balance of payments surpluses and deficits, were to be settled through clearing accounts held by member central banks at an international clearing bank (ICB), which has more recently been advocated by Davidson (2002, 2009), from a Post-Keynesian perspective. The central idea of this proposal was 'the establishment of a currency union based on international money accepted by all members for the purpose of setting international balances' (Keynes, 1942). At first sight, the eurozone appears to meet this definition within its geographical area of application. However, it lacks the underlying equilibrating mechanism (recommended by Keynes) to eliminate both deficits and surpluses. Moreover, his measures for debtor adjustment, unlike those of the eurozone, 'do not include a deflationary policy...having the effect of causing unemployment' (Keynes, 1942). Moreover, the Keynes proposal also possesses the major advantages of redistributing resources within the zone, without the political encumbrance of a fiscal union apparatus, whilst addressing the problem of private, as well as public, debt.

The difficulties of securing the acceptability of long-term resource redistribution within the eurozone remain immense. Despite the eurozone's overwhelming economic and social advantages over the contemporary deflationary alternative, in terms of lost output, employment and associated social costs, surplus countries are unlikely to accept a loss of funds easily, other than as a 'one-off' response. Germany's political and legal manoeuvres to limit its liability demonstrate the magnitude of the task ahead for those who want to preserve the future viability of the euro. Consequently, advocates of a single European currency face a fundamental dilemma, as the present operation of the eurozone lacks the equilibrating mechanism essential for its long-run sustainability. However, the responses of moral suasion and the provision of ad hoc financial relief are plainly inadequate, whilst fiscal federalism and the creation of a clearing union lack political acceptability. Thus, so long as this state of affairs persists, consideration must eventually be given to a fifth response, albeit one unacceptable to conventional wisdom: the collapse of the euro, at least in its current form and with its current membership. Hence, as discussed in Chapter 12, the placement of all adjustment costs upon specific (i.e., deficit) members has never worked in the long term, of which periodic crises and the ultimate collapse of the silver and gold standards are evident proof (Eichengreen, 1996). Moreover, whilst unilateral ending of eurozone membership for outlier states (who, in any case, never met the convergence criteria on a sustainable basis) would solve the worst problems in the short run, the fundamental design flaws would remain and impose future costs upon another member state finding itself an outlier at some future point. Thus, the inability or unwillingness of surplus nations to share part of the necessary adjustment that is a common feature of currency arrangements between sovereign nations is the flaw which tends to undermine the long-term sustainability of those arrangements.

Finally, in Chapter 13 we argue that the demise of the currently constituted eurozone would impose fewer costs than would the status quo or alternative scenarios. Moreover, these costs could be minimised if accomplished through an orderly process, which would involve internal euro devaluation in each of the debtor economies, accompanied by capital and exchange controls on all external transactions until new non-euro currencies have been established. The main problem facing such a policy, however, arises from the substantial cross-border lending that has occurred within the EU over the last decade (encouraged by its authorities) which will leave many banks carrying large losses. Therefore, the key requirement becomes stopping banks from defaulting on their deposits, which would involve their widespread public ownership and support, including extending public ownership where necessary, whilst the ECB concentrates its borrowing power on securing bank liabilities. Although elaborate and costly efforts to save the euro are conventionally justified by the notion that the alternative is too alarming to contemplate, evaluation of the benefits and costs of eurozone's dissolution is inevitably problematic as there are many different permutations surrounding any eurozone collapse, with a panoply of choices for departing and remaining states to make afterwards. Two crucial issues are involved. The first is the time scale over which the impact is assessed, as the short-term withdrawal effects become dwarfed over a longer period by the impact of the lost production, employment and consequent social dislocation imposed by resort to the eurozone's sole equilibrating mechanism, deflation. The second issue concerns the manner in which the eurozone is dissolved; an enforced, disorderly breakdown under the pressure of events would entail greater costs than a planned dissolution. Therefore, it is in the interest of both members and non-members that the eurozone's leaders retract their mantra that a collapse of the single currency is 'unthinkable' and, instead, devise mechanisms to minimise the costs of such an occurrence where short-term losses would be small compared to long-term gains from greater flexibility and, hence, economic efficiency, together with enhanced accountability in political decision-making.

Conclusion

The deflationary strategy now being imposed upon the least competitive eurozone countries carries frightening implications. The Club Med governments can slash their budget deficits only at the cost of huge falls in current economic activity and a substantial loss of future productive capacity. However, without the possibility of devaluation, they cannot hope for substantial export gains or even capital inflows. The weaker members of the eurozone are being forcibly encouraged by the EU to pursue measures guaranteed to prolong and deepen their recessions, instead of pursuing the broadly Keynesian policies that revived growth (until subsequently reversed) not only in America and Britain, but also in France and Germany. To make matters worse, on 22 June 2009, the German parliament voted to amend the country's constitution to impose upon its federal government a 'debt brake' in the form of a balanced-budget requirement. Thus, Germany intends to rely for the next phase of its recovery on export-led growth, which can only eliminate even more Club Med businesses unable to compete against German goods.

The EU leadership's priority is to prevent the single currency's collapse, but such a stance creates immense danger, since the EU possesses only a limited volume of both borrowing capacity and political will (Mills, 2011). If these become exhausted in providing loans to preserve an unsustainable future for the eurozone, there may be insufficient financial firepower to prevent bank defaults if a number of countries decide to leave the single currency and devalue. This risk has been intensified by EU encouragement of cross-border loans within its jurisdiction, thus leaving European banks more exposed than they would otherwise have been. While the experience of the eurozone has proved a disaster in economic integration, financial integration has proceeded rapidly. Consequently, the more loans are denominated in German-backed euros, the greater the probability that these liabilities are inflated by devaluation. However, the longer the EU extends additional loans to preserve the status quo, the greater will become the divergences between member economies. Therefore, the sums of money owed abroad by banks in vulnerable economies can only become larger, and the worse the eventual crash will be, as the whole eurozone spirals down in debt deflation. This is truly a Greek tragedy, with devastating economic consequences for the people of Europe and, indirectly, for the rest of the world. The crisis has demonstrated the defective design of the eurozone, but it has also revealed, and exacerbated, a fundamental lack of trust, let alone a source of shared identity, among the peoples locked together in what has become a marriage of inconvenience.

Part I
The Economics of Monetary Integration

2
The Development of Microfoundations of Macroeconomics

Introduction

In this part of the book we briefly highlight the development of macroeconomics, since this is a key tool and a foundation used for analysing/forecasting aspects of economic performance, such as output, inflation and unemployment. Therefore, macroeconomics is crucial to policymakers in terms of designing/implementing an appropriate economic policy that can respond to the needs of the economy at the aggregate level. The purpose of this book is to evaluate, from the macroeconomic perspective, the sustainability of the eurozone. Hence, an overview of relevant macroeconomic models is a necessary initial step that helps us gain a basic understanding of the theoretical foundation that determines the eurozone's economic operations.

These chapters review the state of modern macroeconomics by highlighting key theories and their developments. The initial Keynesian view explained economic fluctuations as the consequence of demand deficiency and thereby established modern macroeconomics wherein fiscal policy needs to be conducted to stimulate economic recovery through direct spending and improvements on confidence and expectations among private economic agents as the results of expansionary fiscal policy. However, since the late 1960s and early 1970s Keynesian theory has been no longer able to fully explain and resolve contemporary economic problems. Hence, monetarists and then New Classical economists rose to provide – based on a return to classical notions – more appropriate answers to the ongoing economic issues. In response to its loss of the dominant position, New Keynesian emerged to defend Keynes's legacy through explanation of nominal and real rigidities, albeit combined with elements of New Classical ideas. Subsequently, these different approaches have evolved into the so-called New Consensus Macroeconomics (NCM) that forms the current mainstream macroeconomic model comprising a blend of New Classical and New Keynesian theories through adopting the rational behaviour hypothesis and supply-side-determined long-term equilibrium of output (Fontana, 2009). Additionally, NCM also recognises that price/wage rigidities in the short-term are the cause of the business cycle and of the deviation of unemployment/output from its natural rate; therefore, it rejects the postulation of continuous market-clearing; thus, it is also being called the New Neoclassical Synthesis (Goodfriend and King, 1997; Fontana, 2009). As the result of rational behaviour and supply-side-determined long-term equilibrium, vertical Phillips Curves are continually used to indicate the limitations of discretionary economic stabilising policy and to indicate that monetary policy has to be rule-based and mainly used to achieve price stability.

Although this might sound detached with regard to the daily lives of eurozone citizens, these developments in macroeconomic theory possess profound consequences for the eurozone crisis, since in our view it reaches back to the wrong type of unreality-based microfoundations to macroeconomics, starting in the 1970s – microfoundations that have subsequently evolved to reach this point. For example, fiscal policy has been downgraded to become considered as an ineffective policy tool for real economic activities, and one which is harmful to 'price stability' monetary policy. The independent position of the ECB and its policy goal and implementation of monetary policy are, by and large, consistent with the NCM model. The fiscal policy framework designed by the EU, which aims to discipline the fiscal behaviour of eurozone members, also reflects the adoption of the NCM model as the theoretical foundation of the eurozone's economic operations. For the financial markets, where governments interact with lenders in accessing funds to finance their budget deficits and national debt, the underlying assumption put forward by the NCM is that the market should perform rationally and efficiently. The implication is that the behaviour of fiscal activities of eurozone members could be monitored and enforced through a dual mechanism of rules and financial markets. Hence, if both fiscal-discipline mechanisms operated normally, as they should, then fiscal behaviour within the eurozone could be well-managed and maintained.

In this and the next two chapters we outline the background economic theory underpinning the eurozone and argue that these were foundations built on sand such that the eurozone is a fundamentally unsustainable economic system in terms of the development of modern macroeconomic theory and in terms of that theory specifically designed to evaluate the appropriateness of creating and joining in a single currency, together with evaluating business-cycle synchronisation to examine whether general economic conditions have sufficiently converged to allow for the implementation of an appropriate union-wide monetary policy. Hence, Part II carries on these themes through focusing upon the ensuing applied policymaking in terms of the operation of international monetary systems, the diminution of national fiscal policy within the eurozone and the effectiveness of monetary policy on controlling inflation and its impact on other macroeconomic indicators through the auspices of the ECB.

The development of microfoundations of macroeconomics

The debate concerning the desirability of macroeconomics being based upon a firm microeconomic framework began essentially from the time of the Keynesian revolution. Prior to the 1930s, the classical approach derived its macroeconomic model from microeconomic theory, such that all real variables are determined by the labour market, whilst the price level is determined by changes in the money supply. Assuming perfectly competitive markets, the expectations of all agents (firms and consumers) are fulfilled and so there is neither involuntary unemployment nor unsold goods. However, the onset of the Great Depression in the 1930s shattered universal acceptance of this theoretical model and facilitated the triumph of the Keynesians critique, together with the adoption of discretionary demand-management economic policy. The triumph of the Keynesian revolution was not, however, complete. Indeed, whilst the Keynesians had clearly won the policy battle during the post-war period, their theoretical hegemony was far less secure. The traditionally 'conservative' economics profession was loath to disregard its Walrasian inheritance and sought to reconcile the classical and Keynesian strands of economics by means of a new comprehensive framework. This endeavour was possible because of Keynes's general acceptance of many precepts of classical theory. Once this fault had been rectified, Keynes believed that classical theory would come into its own again; thus, he accepted the assumptions of perfect competition in the product market and thought that the price mechanism would solve the distributional and productive problems associated with the economic problem of scarcity. However, the time lags associated with the 'invisible hand' market-adjustment mechanism were far too slow and were very costly in terms of unemployment and lost output, so Keynes argued that sluggish market forces should be enhanced, and sometimes replaced, by government intervention (Snowdon and Vane, 2005).

The distinction was thereby created between the economics of resource allocation, production and distribution (microeconomics) and issues concerning the level and long-term trend of aggregate output, employment and the rate of inflation (macroeconomics) – which, in the process, fractured economic theory into two largely separate and mutually independent spheres. Microeconomics retained the classical theory rejected by the Keynesians' macroeconomics which, alternatively, preferred to base its policy proposals upon empirical analysis of observed data rather than on theoretical predictions concerning how individuals react to external stimuli. Computer-aided macroeconomic models therefore became increasingly complex and sought to explain variations in macroeconomic variables through multiple regression models rather than through theoretical concentration upon the response pattern of individual economic agents. The distinction between macroeconomics and microeconomics began to be broken down during the 1960s, and particularly in the 1970s, because of the interaction of two principal factors. First: Keynes had written the 'General Theory' in response to 1930s mass unemployment, which meant the theory had relatively less concern about problems of inflation that (partly because of the success of Keynesian demand-management policies) had progressively become the main economic problem. Acceptance of classical microeconomic assumptions of perfect competition meant that inflationary pressure could not be located in the product market and, so, Keynesians adopted the empirical Phillips Curve relationship to explain wage inflation. Many economists were unconvinced about the applicability of using empirical relations as predictive theoretical tools, and they appeared to be proved correct when the Phillips relationship seemed to lose its significance almost as soon as it had been adopted. Second: Confidence in the Keynesian model eroded during the 1970s as the OPEC cost–price shock created an economic climate in which industrial economies experienced simultaneously rising unemployment and inflation combined with slow growth. The demand-orientated Keynesian approach was forced to reconsider the importance of the supply-side and relatively swiftly devised new models; however, the temporary confusion caused by the apparent inability to solve the new economic problems generated widespread dissatisfaction with Keynesian economics and resulted in a sudden surge of interest in alternative approaches (Greenwald and Stiglitz, 1987).

One feature all alternative economic schools of thought had in common (monetarism generating the least enthusiasm) was increased interest in the microfoundations for macroeconomic models. Theorists concerned with reinvigorating the classical approach argued that Keynesianism failed because it did not fully understand the behavioural patterns of rational economic agents in response to a range of changing incentives. When combined with classical assumptions of perfect competition and continuous market clearing, this new classical approach dismissed the existence of involuntary unemployment and argued that inflation was caused by lax government monetary policy.

New classical macroeconomics

The New Classical School (NCS) responded to Keynesian assumptions of non-rational and non-optimising behaviour of economic agents as a fundamental flaw with the whole approach. Accordingly, the NCS approach explicitly sought to devise a macroeconomic model from the ground up, based upon the analysis of rational, self-interested economic agents operating in an economy denoted by competitive markets. The resulting macroeconomics would therefore be based upon rigorous, classically determined microfoundations. Although principally devised in reaction to Keynesianism, the NCS was also dissatisfied with the monetarist tendency to analyse the behaviour of economic aggregates, such as inflation and unemployment, in terms of empirical relationships rather than first developing microeconomic theories that could then be tested using econometric techniques. This was a reversal of the traditional scientific technique, which states that a theory is first developed that can subsequently be tested empirically and rests upon the assumptions of rational expectations, continuous market clearing and the aggregate supply hypothesis (Sachs, 1999).

In contrast to the Friedman–monetarist assumption of *adaptive expectations* that allowed for economic agents making mistaken decisions that caused outcomes temporarily unequal to the natural rate equilibrium position, the NCS required the alternative assumption of *rational expectations* in order to restore the inevitability of classical outcomes in the short- as well as long-term. However, it is important to note that there are both strong and weak versions of the rational expectations hypothesis (Muth, 1961). The weak version argues that, when forming expectations or predictions about the future value of a variable, economic agents will make the most efficient usage of all publicly available information about those factors they believe will determine the behaviour of that variable. In contrast, the strong version of the rational expectations hypothesis may be summarised as: Those informed predictions of future events are essentially the same as the predictions of the relevant economic theory. Thus, economic agents' subjective expectations of the future behaviour of economic variables will coincide with the 'objective' predictions formed by economic models. This requires the following assumptions to be shared by all economic agents: that universal knowledge of the structural equations characterising the economy, universal belief that all markets are cleared and universal understanding that all other agents also share the initial assumptions so they are common knowledge (Snowdon and Vane, 2005).

These assumptions mean that there exists a unique level of employment that clears the labour market and, as a result, there is a unique natural rate of unemployment. This level of employment translates into a unique output level, via the short-run production function, and hence both employment and output are derived from the labour market in accordance with transitional classical theory. Moreover, for aggregate demand to equal this unique output level, the real money supply must remain fixed. Any variation in the nominal money supply and prices must immediately rise in order that the real money supply is kept at this constant level. Finally, because output and employment are fixed by their natural rates, any increase in government expenditure causes the crowding-out of an equal amount of private expenditure, implying the absence of an effective role for fiscal policy. Finally, it is important to note that rational expectations should not be equated with the existence of perfect foresight. Rational economic agents are assumed to take into account the predictions made by what they collectively believe to be the 'true' macroeconomic model of the economy. However, incomplete information and the existence of 'surprises' may result in forecasting errors; nevertheless, the rational expectations hypothesis does argue that, on average, expectations will be correct and predictions equal objective reality. Moreover, rational economic agents will form their expectations without a systematic bias that persists over time such that agents learn from mistakes and thereby eliminate any initial systematic errors. Consequently, whilst not absolutely without error in every individual case, in aggregate the rational formation of expectations produces the correct results (Redman, 1992).

The rational-expectations hypothesis is criticised on two main grounds. Firstly, the acquisition and calculation of information is costly in terms of time and money. The weak version of the hypothesis counters this claim by stating that information will only be gathered until the marginal benefit of so doing equals the marginal cost. However, since this implies that not all information will be used in the formation of expectations, predictions are therefore not perfectly efficient (Frydman and Phelps, 1983; Evans and Honkapohja, 1999). Secondly, the rational expectations hypothesis is criticised because it assumes that agents understand and act upon the 'true' macroeconomic model of the economy. This critique is slightly misleading, however, since the strong version of the theory does not actually require economic agents to understand an objective model of the economy, but rather to act as if they did. However, the secondary assumption that expectations are, in aggregate, unbiased and on average equal to objective reality, means that this defence is partly based upon semantics (Lovell, 1986). The fundamental point is that the rational expectations hypothesis assumes that economic agents have a considerable amount of complex information, which they process in a sophisticated manner. If this is not the case, and individuals are largely ignorant of how the economy works or of the effect of government actions, then active macroeconomic policy retains the potential to have a significant effect upon real variables (Shackle, 1972).

The assumption of continuous market clearing is the most contentious and crucial assumption underpinning the NCS model. Based upon the Walrasian tradition, the economy is perceived as being in continual short- and long-run equilibrium due to the interaction of rational economic agents and perfect price flexibility. Adjustment from one equilibrium position to another occurs instantly, thereby preventing the existence of a period of disequilibrium adjustment, whilst prices, output and employment are temporarily away from their natural equilibrium position (Dixon, 1997). This assumption is in contrast to the previous debates concerning the speed of economic adjustment, where Keynesians traditionally argued that markets might be slow to clear because of sticky wages and prices, thereby implying that the economy might remain in a state of disequilibrium for long periods of time. In contrast, monetarists argued that price adjustment occurred relatively quickly so that long-run equilibrium would return to the natural equilibrium rate of output and employment, although the possibility of short-run disequilibrium was conceded. Consequently, the NCS approach represents a significant hardening of the position held by orthodox monetarists. The principal criticism of the NCS model is its assumption of continuous market clearing. It is this assumption which, like its Walrasian predecessor, enables the absence of involuntary unemployment and therefore dismisses the need for, or even the effectiveness of, fiscal and monetary policy in either short- or long-run. However, the argument that all observed unemployment is voluntary, since economic actors prefer leisure to work at the equilibrium wage rate, is hard to sustain during periods of mass unemployment such as the 1930s Great Depression and more recently during the last decade throughout Europe (Lucas, 1978; Tobin, 1993, 1996).

Starting with the labour market, the NCS suggests that, as rational optimising economic agents, workers are faced with the decision of how to allocate their time between work and leisure. Assuming they have a clear understanding what the normal or expected average real wage will be, if the current real wage exceeds this level, the workers will have an incentive to substitute work for leisure in the current period in the expectation that the real wage will eventually fall back to its normal level and they can then, at that point, consume more leisure. Similarly, if the real wage is temporarily lower than the expected normal real-wage level, workers have the incentive to take more leisure (work less) on the basis that the real wage will eventually rise to its normal level and they can then substitute more work for leisure. This behaviour is described as intertemporal substitution since the supply of labour responds to changes in the real wage, which changes are perceived to be of temporary duration. Thus, at any one period of time, observed unemployment is wholly voluntary and reflects the optimising behaviour of rational economic agents (Lucas and Rapping, 1969). It is assumed that, whilst firms in the goods market know their own prices and costs, the general price level for all other markets is only available after a time lag. Thus, when an individual firm experiences a rise in the current price of its goods, it must decide whether this change reflects a shift in demand towards its product or a nominal increase in demand across all markets associated with an increase in the general level of prices. Clearly, the rational response to the first situation would be for the firm to expand output to take advantage of the higher demand and market price for its products, whereas the rational response to the second scenario would be to leave output and employment as they were because there has been no shift in relative prices, only a rise in nominal prices caused by inflation. This poses a 'signal extraction' problem for the firm, since it must distinguish between nominal and real price changes (Lucas, 1972, 1973).

As a result of the expectation-forming process facing both firms and labour there is a 'surprise' supply function: $Y - Y_N = (I - I^e)$ where output deviates from its natural level only if actual inflation deviates from its expected level. This is, in effect, a restatement of the Friedman expectations–augmented Phillips Curve relationship, since a temporary movement in output away from the natural equilibrium level is only possible if changes in price or inflation 'surprise' economic actors and cause expectations to be temporarily fooled. However, this process enables the NCS to explain the observable business cycle by pointing to unanticipated, random shocks that cause temporary errors in price and inflation expectations, thereby encouraging temporary output and employment deviations from the natural equilibrium level. However, introducing the rational expectations hypothesis into this theory means that any fluctuations around the natural equilibrium point will be random in nature and, on average, will have a mean deviation of zero (Lucas, 1972, 1973).

The policy implications of the NCS model are unequivocal: Since the economy continually operates at the natural equilibrium level (apart from random disturbances), both in the short- and long-term, there is therefore no role for government policy. Moreover, any systematic attempt to reduce unemployment below the natural rate will be completely unsuccessful in the short-run, as well as in the long-run. Economic agents are aware that a unique equilibrium position exists and therefore will respond to any government demand expansion by simply revising prices and wages immediately upwards, thereby leaving real prices and wages unchanged at a higher nominal price level. Specifically, an initial equilibrium position is disturbed by a government-induced increase in the money supply, which implies that all economic agents would realise that the initial equilibrium position occurred at the long-run natural equilibrium level of output, and thus any increase caused by the government stimulus would only be temporary. Therefore, all rational economic agents form their expectations on the basis that the effect of the increase in money supply will (eventually) be fully reflected in a higher price level, with no increase in long-run output. As a direct result of rational expectations, output and employment will remain unchanged even in the short run; hence, the NCS prediction is that government policy has no effect upon output and employment, only upon the price level. However, the NCS reliance upon continual market clearing also raises a problem in explaining the existence of the business cycle. The response that this is caused by random shocks that create unpredictable monetary disturbances fits poorly with the evidence of serially correlated fluctuations in national output and employment. Moreover, the existence of incomplete information in otherwise perfect markets populated by economic actors governed by rational expectations, does not seem sufficient to generate the size of observed variation in output (Sargent and Wallace, 1975, 1976).

The desire to strengthen macroeconomic models through the use of microfoundations has been an increasing feature of economics throughout recent decades. Largely as a result of disenchantment with the predictive power of traditional Keynesianism, with its reliance upon empirical analysis rather than being derived more directly from microeconomic theory, the increase in interest in this element of macroeconomics has stimulated interest both amongst those who sought to reconstruct Keynesianism and those who wished to bury it. However, it is important to note that additional models constructed by alternative economic schools have all expended considerable effort in devising microfoundations for their macroeconomic models to justify and explain their particular policy conclusions.

New Keynesian Economics

Throughout the three decades after Keynes first published the General Theory, unprecedented rates of economic growth, continual full employment and low (but slowly rising) rates of inflation sustained the neo-classical-Keynesian synthesis that had supplanted the classical approach as hegemonic throughout the majority of the economics profession. However, the stagflation experienced in the 1970s fractured this consensus and – despite Keynesian models being rapidly modified to incorporate supply-side cost-push inflationary effects – provided the opportunity for monetarist and NCS alternatives to gain increasing credibility and acceptance within academia, financial markets and government. Certain converts were undoubtedly attracted by the 'political' consequences of these approaches, as they were clearly more consistent with the preferences of the political Right for 'small government' and for restricting government intervention. However, academic criticism focused on the uncritical acceptance, by the orthodox neo-classical-Keynesian synthesis, of the existence of a sluggish or imperfect adjustment of prices and wages – an acceptance made in the absence of a microeconomic theoretical framework that could satisfactorily explain this behaviour. Moreover, the economic failures of the 1980s along with low growth and the return of some form of trade-off between inflation and unemployment, increased dissatisfaction with monetarist and NCS theories, with the persistence of unemployment in Europe causing increased interest in Keynesian policy prescriptions. Hence, New Keynesianism emerged out of criticism of the neo-classical-Keynesian synthesis for having an insufficient microeconomic theoretical basis, and reinforced by disillusionment with the resulting NCS attempts to construct macroeconomic theories from a tight neo-classical microfoundation that struggled to fit the observed stylised facts. Perhaps, naturally, due to their initial starting point, New Keynesians accepted a large part of the NCS world view, most significantly including: acceptance of the broad predictions of monetarism (at least in the long run) that fluctuations in the money supply are the primary source of fluctuations in aggregate demand; adoption of the Phelps–Friedman expectations-augmented Phillips Curve; and sympathy with rational expectations theory, although this is not universally the case. However, New Keynesianism refutes the NCS assumption of universal and continuous market clearing (Gordon, 1990, 1993).

Accordingly, in the absence of this key NCS assumption, unemployment may persist, with employment constrained by a lack of effective aggregate demand. Thus, New Keynesians agree with orthodox Keynesians that expansionary government policies will have an effect upon real output and employment. They both point to the sluggishness exhibited by prices and wages as suggesting that demand and supply shocks will have real effects upon the economy, effects that can be substantial and of lengthy duration. It is important to emphasise, at this point, that New Keynesian theories are concerned with an incomplete adjustment of nominal wages and prices rather than simply a temporal delay in the operations of a Walrasian market-clearing mechanism. Time lags due to uncertainty or information costs, or to price imperfections caused by poor incentives or re-negotiation costs, certainly undermine the assumption of perfect market adjustment (Mankiw and Romer, 1991). However, in the absence of more substantial dislocation, these imperfections will not prevent economic adjustment to a form of Walrasian equilibrium, albeit perhaps after a short time lag. Consequently, New Keynesians claim that a business-cycle theory derived from markets failing to clear continuously is more realistic than the NCS alternatives, whilst their explanation of the persistence of mass unemployment as at least partially demand-constrained, is more in tune with observable stylised facts than are arguments claiming it is due to mistaken expectations derived from imperfect information or that unemployment is entirely voluntary. However, New Keynesianism differs from its older form in that, whilst the orthodox neo-classical-Keynesian synthesis assumed wage and price stickiness (often fixed short-term nominal wages), the more recent version desires to construct an acceptable microeconomic explanation for this effect (Dixon and Rankin, 1994).

Furthermore, New Keynesianism may be distinguished from other schools of economic thought by reference to its assumed product and labour-market behaviour that embraces a theoretical model that incorporates imperfect competition, incomplete market clearing, asymmetric information, heterogeneous labour and where rational economic agents adopt norms of 'fairness' and reward 'loyalty'. Coordination failures and externalities impinge upon the working of the market mechanism. However, the very complexity of this approach – whilst arguably more closely approximating the 'real world' than classical microeconomic assumptions – nevertheless increases the difficulty in unifying all New Keynesian research into one model (Colander, 1988). Hence, two noticeable strands of New Keynesianism may be identified. The first argues that nominal price rigidities explain why market economies differ from the Walrasian theory: In the absence of these rigidities, flexible prices would ensure speedy adjustment to shocks much in the manner the neo-classical models predict. Rigidities, therefore, enable monetary policy to have a real effect upon output and employment, not simply on the price level where small frictions can cause nominal disturbances to have large effects upon aggregate economic activity. Moreover, it accepts the varied reasons presented in the New Keynesian literature for real-wage rigidity causing stickiness of nominal wages and reducing firms' incentives to vary prices in response to demand shifts, such as relative nominal wages and early contract theory. The second approach agrees that wage and price rigidity exists, but claims that output and employment would remain highly volatile even if perfect wage and price flexibility existed, with shocks being amplified and persisting because of market failure principally due to incomplete contracts and imperfect indexation. Thus, monetary policy will have a real effect upon the economy even if wages and prices were perfectly flexible! Indeed, increased flexibility of wages and prices may actually exacerbate the magnitude of economic fluctuations. This approach promotes the concept of risk-averse firms and financial institutions, which increases uncertainty and the cost of capital during a recession, thereby inhibiting output and employment. Sticky real wages are explained by reference to efficiency wages, implicit contracts, insider–outsider models and the like (Gordon, 1990).

However, theories describing real-wage rigidities may explain the persistence of unemployment but, on their own, do not undermine the classical model, since if the money supply changes in an economy characterised by real-wage rigidity, nominal prices and wages could change, leaving relative prices and real outcomes unchanged, despite the existence of non-Walrasian elements in the labour market. Moreover, despite wage stickiness, if profits can vary sufficiently to secure flexible prices, the classical model can still be preserved. Consequently, New Keynesian theories of price rigidities have accounted for a considerable amount of theoretical energy, including menu costs, judging quality by price, capital market imperfection, market-search costs and monopolistic customer markets (Pindyck and Rubinfeld, 1998).

In relation to their policy implications, all variants of New Keynesianism accept the potential for active government demand-management policies to minimise the costs inherent in lost output and involuntary unemployment, caused by nominal wage and price rigidities. However, because demand and supply fluctuations are unpredictable in nature, New Keynesians do not support the macroeconomic 'fine-tuning' (Taylor, 2000). Instead, they prefer a more general discretionary government policy intended to offset or prevent large macroeconomic disturbances, known as 'coarse tuning'. Policy prescriptions advocated to reduce real-wage rigidity, and thereby decrease persistent unemployment, may include reducing insiders' bargaining strength through industrial relations legislation aimed at weakening trade unions and reducing the possibility of strikes and other disruptive activity and the weakening social-security legislation to reduce the costs for the firm of recruitment and redundancy. Alternatively, outsiders could be made more employable through reducing unemployment and social-security benefits in order to encourage both a more rapid job search and a lower reserve wage as well as: labour mobility policies, such as the provision of inexpensive rented accommodation or grants to facilitate relocation to areas with a tighter labour market; retraining programmes to improve outsiders' human capital and, hence, productivity and piece-work; and bonuses or profit-sharing schemes designed to increase wage flexibility (Lindbeck, 1992). New Keynesianism is a relatively new theoretical development and, as it lies at one cutting edge of theoretical research, perhaps asks more questions than it answers. Nevertheless, its attempts to draw all disparate theoretical threads into one model remain premature. Whilst theories of real-wage rigidities are the most advanced and complete of all the approaches examined, the results cannot be described as uniquely Keynesian, since many neo-classical and monetarist (as opposed to the NCS) theorists accept the existence of market imperfections that marginally impede the efficient market mechanism. Explanation of nominal wage and price rigidities, and the alternative ideas concerning risk-averse firms and financial institutions, are in this respect more radical theories, since they aim to prove the failure of the classical adjustment mechanism. However, even here, the general acceptance of long-term price and wage flexibility means that, for most adherents, Keynesian solutions only apply in the short- and medium-term.

Politics, time inconsistency, credibility and reputation

Following the incorporation of the rational expectations hypothesis into macroeconomic models, the theoretical literature on economic policy has been dominated by the game-theoretic approach with policymakers seen to be engaged in a complicated dynamic game with private-sector economic agents (who are also voters). Accordingly, governments that are free from rules (i.e., pre-commitment) can use discretionary policies, but they will be unable to persuade rational agents that they will keep to low-inflation policies. Hence, agents know that if they lower their inflation expectations the government will have an incentive to cheat and, by creating an inflation surprise, increase employment temporarily (Kydland and Prescott, 1977). However, because rational agents are aware of the policymakers' incentives, the time-consistent policy involves an inflationary bias. Thus, if a government has discretion, low-inflation declarations are time-inconsistent and not credible. Therefore a credible policy announcement can be defined as one which is time-consistent. Solutions to the time-inconsistency problem include contractual arrangements, delegation of decisions and institutional and legal constraints (i.e., a need to bind government/politicians into rules/pre-commitment) (Drazen, 2000a & b): for example, in recent years the idea of monetary policy being delegated to independent central banks while fiscal policy is constrained by rules such as those for eurozone countries on budget deficits (maximum of 3% of GDP) and national debt (maximum of 60% of GDP). However, in industrial democracies subject to regular democratic elections, politicians have an incentive to deviate from optimal policies and create an inflation surprise. In a game-theoretic context the reputation of a player (i.e., politician) will depend on the way they have played and reacted to events in the past such that rational agents (i.e., voters) will only believe politicians who make ex ante policy announcements that are also optimal to implement ex post. Consequently, as Table 2.1 illustrates, it is not just the eurozone economies that have embraced budgetary rules, but such rules have now become prevalent across OECD countries. However, voters possess imperfect information about the real motives of politicians as compared to their pre-election promises; therefore voters will need to analyse carefully the various signals politicians give out. In this scenario it may be difficult for voters to distinguish 'hard-nosed' (inflation averse) from 'wet' (inflation-prone) politicians, since the latter will always have an incentive to masquerade as 'hard-nosed' (Backus and Driffill, 1985).

Additionally, the prediction of the median voter theorem that in a two-party system there will be policy convergence is time-inconsistent since there is no mechanism for holding an elected government to its promises. After the election the influence of partisan considerations will predominate as the elected politicians re-optimise and follow a programme that best fits their ideological stances. Thus the time-consistent equilibrium involves no policy convergence and the two parties follow their most preferred policy, which inevitably creates too much volatility in policy-making which, in turn, causes politically induced business cycles (Alesina, 1987). It follows from the above analysis that only those pre-election announcements and promises that are consistent with a party's ideology should be taken seriously by voters. Once elected, politicians will tend to follow a more partisan strategy. This may prove to be a particular problem for parties of the left that declare themselves to be 'tough on inflation'. In the context of the United Kingdom, these issues were very pertinent in there in the run-up to the 1997 election, when the 'New' Labour Party, led by Tony Blair, declared that it intended to be 'tough on inflation', and that it also aimed to achieve much lower unemployment. Thus, the statement on inflation was clearly time-inconsistent. However, to give credibility to its anti-inflation rhetoric, on winning the 1997 election, New Labour immediately granted operational independence to the Bank of England, thereby delegating decisions on monetary policy, and also developed a 'golden rule' regarding borrowing over the economic cycle (Snowdon, 1997). Similarly, in the context of the eurozone this policy is reflected in the behaviour of the ECB to gain credibility by having to develop an overly hawkish posture on inflation, together with both the instigation of budget deficit and national debt criteria that were rapidly strengthened through the SGP (Hibbs, 1977a, b; Alesina, 1987).

Conclusion

The desire to strengthen macroeconomic models through the use of micro-foundations has increasingly been a feature of economics, largely as a result of disenchantment with the predictive power of traditional Keynesianism,

Table 2.1 Fiscal and prudent rules in industrialised economies

		Characteristics of Rules			
				Rule to Deal with	
Country	Date and Name	Budget Target	Expenditure Target	Windfall Revenues	Golden Rule
Australia	Charter of Budget Honesty (1998)	Yes	No	No	No
Austria	Stability and Growth Pact (1997) Stability Pact (2000)	Yes	No	No	No
Belgium	Stability and Growth Pact (1997) National Budget Rule (2000)	Yes	No	Yes	No
Canada	Debt Repayment Plan (1998)	Yes	No	Yes	No
Czech Republic	Stability and Growth Pact (2004) Law on Budgetary Rules (2004)	Yes	Yes	No	No
Denmark	Medium Term Fiscal Strategy (1998)	Yes	Yes	No	No
Finland	Stability and Growth Pact (1997) Spending Limits (1991, rev. 1995, 1999)	Yes	Yes	No	No
France	Stability and Growth Pact (1997) Central Government Expenditure Ceiling (1998)	Yes	Yes	Since 2006	No
Germany	Stability and Growth Pact (1997) Domestic Stability Pact (2002)	Yes	Yes	No	Yes
Greece	Stability and Growth Pact (1997)	Yes	No	No	No
Hungary	Stability and Growth Pact (2004)	Yes	No	No	No
Ireland	Stability and Growth Pact (1997)	Yes	No	No	No
Italy	Stability and Growth Pact (1997) Nominal Ceiling on Expenditure Growth (2002)	Yes	Yes	No	No
Japan	Cabinet Decision on the Medium Term Fiscal Perspective (2002)	Yes	Yes	No	No

Luxembourg	Stability and Growth Pact (1997)	Yes	No	No	No
	Coalition Agreement on Expenditure Ceiling (1999, 2004)			No	No
Mexico	Budget and Fiscal Responsibility Law (2006)	Yes	No	Yes	No
Netherlands	Stability and Growth Pact (1997)	Yes	Yes	Yes	No
	Coalition Agreement on Multiyear Expenditure Targets (1994, rev. 2003)				
Norway	Fiscal Stability Guidelines (2001)	Yes	Yes	No	No
Poland	Stability and Growth Pact (2004)	Yes	No	No	No
	Act on Public Finance (1999)				
Portugal	Stability and Growth Pact (1997)	Yes	No	No	No
Slovak Republic	Stability and Growth Pact (2004)	Yes	No	No	No
Spain	Stability and Growth Pact (1997)	Yes	No	No	No
	Fiscal Stability Law (2001, rev. 2006)				
Sweden	Fiscal Budget Act (1996, rev. 1999)	Yes	Yes	No	No
Switzerland	Debt Containment Rule (2001, in force since 2003)	Yes	Yes	Yes	No
UK	Code for Fiscal Stability (1999)	Yes	No	No	Yes

with its reliance upon empirical analysis rather than its predictions being derived more directly from microeconomic theory. The increase in interest in this element of macroeconomics has stimulated interest both amongst those who have sought to reconstruct Keynesianism and those who wished to bury it. The most important initial responses from either side of the argument have been described in this chapter, whilst the more recent models constructed by alternative economic schools will be considered in Chapter 3; but in general these have all expended considerable effort in devising microfoundations for their macroeconomic models in order to justify and explain their particular policy conclusions.

In relation to the NCS model, particular criticism is levelled at its assumption of continuous market clearing which, like its Walrasian predecessor, enables the absence of involuntary unemployment and therefore dismisses the need for, or even the effectiveness of, fiscal and monetary policy in either the short run or long run. However, the argument that all observed unemployment is voluntary – since economic actors prefer leisure over work at the equilibrium wage rate – is hard to sustain during periods of mass unemployment, such as the 1930s Great Depression and, more recently, during the last decade throughout Europe. Furthermore, the NCS reliance upon continual market clearing also raises a problem in explaining the existence of the business cycle. The response that this is caused by random shocks that cause unpredictable monetary disturbances fits poorly with the evidence of serially correlated fluctuations in national output and employment. Moreover, the existence of incomplete information in otherwise perfect markets populated by economic actors governed by rational expectations, does not seem sufficient to generate the size of observed variation in output (Dixon, 1997).

Finally, the rational expectations hypothesis is criticised on two main grounds. Firstly, the acquisition and calculation of information is costly in terms of time and money. The weak version of the hypothesis counters this claim by stating that information will only be gathered until the marginal benefit of so doing equals the marginal cost. However, since this implies that not all information will be used in the formation of expectations, predictions are therefore not perfectly efficient (Snowdon and Vane, 2005). Secondly, the rational expectations hypothesis is criticised because it assumes that agents understand and act upon the 'true' macroeconomic model of the economy, which is hard to comprehend since professional economists often find it difficult to agree! This critique is slightly misleading, however, since the strong version of the theory does not actually require economic agents *to understand* an objective model of the economy, but rather *to act as if* they did. However, the secondary assumption that expectations are, in aggregate, unbiased and on average equal to objective reality, means that this defence is partly based upon semantics. The fundamental point is that the rational expectations hypothesis assumes that economic agents have a considerable amount of complex information that they process in a sophisticated manner. If this is not the case, and individuals are largely ignorant about how the economy works or about the effect of government actions, then active macroeconomic policy retains the potential to have a significant effect upon real variables (Frydman and Phelps, 1983).

The second major approach reviewed in this chapter is the New Keynesian model, which has been criticised by both 'old' Keynesians as well as NCS theorists; in particular, the principal objections are that individual research projects concerning wage and price rigidities have inspired multiple theories which, whilst consistent and interesting, have yet to be fully encapsulated within a single macroeconomic model. Second, that the model has a bias towards theoretical developments (again the result of the yet-immature nature of the New Keynesian approach) means that its predictions are insufficiently subjected to empirical testing. Third, the acceptance by most New Keynesians of the rational expectations hypothesis is criticised by those who do not find the theory persuasive; whilst, fourth, continued use of traditional Keynesian explanatory tools, such as the IS–LM model, is criticised as precluding discussion of the role of expectations. Fifth, to the extent that New Keynesian models predict disequilibria, economic movements will become less predictable and thereby could reduce the ability to predict how the economy will react to government economic policies. Consequently, Keynesian aggregate-demand management remedies will have uncertain outcomes and should therefore be avoided (Lindbeck, 1998).

Finally, 'old' Keynesians argue that the New Keynesian concentration upon nominal wage and price rigidity, and their arguments that this rigidity is the central theoretical insight common to all forms of Keynesian macroeconomics, is incorrect. In fact, it is argued that the only thing Keynesian macroeconomics requires is that markets are not continually or instantly cleared by movements in prices. If this is so, then output and employment may be constrained by aggregate demand, and Keynesian policy prescriptions are effective. However, in a world where firms that operate in an economy beset by non-uniformity and imperfect information establish prices and wages amid uncertainty, it is logical to expect price and wage inertia (or stickiness) to be the result. Similarly, the idea that one rigidity may amplify the effect of other market imperfections would also seem to be consistent with this scenario. Thus, the New Keynesian approach provides one promising route by which to explain the observable business cycle. However, New Keynesianism has reinforced the Keynesian tradition by adopting many aspects of NCS theory, but still indicates that aggregate demand management may be necessary to address the reduced welfare associated with the output losses and involuntary unemployment caused by wage and price rigidities, or by the existence of risk-averse firms and financial institutions (Ball et al., 1988).

3
Contemporary Macroeconomic Thought and Its Discontents

Introduction

As discussed in Chapter 2, the New Classical School (NCS), developed in the context of stagflation in the 1970s, forms the bedrock of contemporary neo-liberal economics by shifting the focus from the demand-side to the supply-side of the economy, a position that was previously not well developed. Thus, prevailing models were criticised, first, for not fully incorporating rational optimising behaviour of individual agents, leading to a new paradigm based on comprehensive adoption of market-clearing microeconomic foundations. Second, the assumptions and outcomes are that all economic agents are rational optimisers who base their decisions only on real factors and on the postulation that markets clear more or less continuously: these being the key pillars that support outcomes of the model. Third, that prices are correctly anticipated because of rational expectations; hence, there are no systematic errors in making price forecasts. This aggregate supply hypothesis explains how temporary fluctuations away from full employment may be possible. These fluctuations are said to have these results: that output and employment are determined in the labour market; that there is a unique natural rate of unemployment; that anticipated changes in the growth of the money supply lead directly to inflation; that they have no real effects; and that there is total crowding-out of fiscal policy.

However, in reality there are observed fluctuations in unemployment and other real variables, such as output – variables the NCS addressed through associating changes with confusion by agents between changes in general price level and changes in relative prices. Within the labour market, workers choose to allocate time between work and leisure – so-called 'intertemporal substitution', whereby the labour supply is said to respond to perceived temporary changes in real wages, such that unemployment is seen to be wholly voluntary. In the goods market, the assumption is that firms know the price of their own goods, but in reality the general price level is only known with a time lag. The combination of these is therefore the 'surprise' supply function, whereby if inflation differs from the expected level then output similarly differs from the natural level. Thus the NCS explanation of the business cycle is through postulating that unanticipated random shocks lead to temporary errors in price/inflation expectations. Consequently, there are a number of criticisms of NCS: first, for example, in relation to the notion of continuous market clearing that effectively rules out involuntary unemployment, with workers merely preferring leisure over employment. Second, the implication that business cycles are random although evidence suggests that such economic fluctuations are serially correlated, together with the question whether information problems sufficiently large enough to generate the size of observed output variations associated with recessions and booms. Third, that in relation to rational expectations, information is frequently costly to gather and process, such that economic agents do not act 'as if' they understand macroeconomic models (Woodford, 1999).

New Consensus Macroeconomics

Subsequently, the microfoundations approach of the NCS and the split from the traditional Keynesian perspective meant that finding a broad consensus in macroeconomics became increasingly elusive; however, common ground has now appeared around the term 'New Keynesian' economics. Here neoclassical aspects of the model are standard methodological features: for example, optimising behaviour of micro agents in terms of rational expectations, but also price and wage rigidities. Moreover, the 'Keynesian' refers to the idea that such models allow for prolonged departures from optimal levels resulting from instability in aggregate expenditure (Goodfriend and King, 1997; Woodford, 2002; Romer, 2000; Taylor, 2000a & b; Walsh, 2002). An established version of this world of New Consensus Macroeconomics (NCM) is the IS-PC-MR model that offers an analytical framework to examine contemporary macroeconomics, where these are derived from the optimising behaviour of the monetary authority (e.g., central bank), price setters and households in imperfect product and labour markets, together with some nominal rigidities (Carlin and Soskice, 2005, 2009). In particular, the central bank chooses its preferred combination of output and inflation along the Phillips Curve that it faces in that particular time period, and it then uses the IS function to calculate what interest rate (r) it must set so that aggregate demand moves to the desired level, that is, to stabilise the economy around an inflation target. Hence, the IS-PC-MR model is useful for explaining the optimising behaviour of the central bank and its reactions to disturbances (Carlin and Soskice, 2005, 2009).

In terms of summarising the IS-PC-MR model: the IS function represents combinations of interest rates and output that give equilibrium in the real side of the economy, whilst equilibrium requires planned real expenditure on goods and services to be equal to real output, where planned expenditure is comprised of consumption, investment and government. The microfoundations are provided by the labour market in terms of the Phillips Curve, where equilibrium unemployment implies that inflation is constant (i.e., NAIRU holds) such that when unemployment is below equilibrium, then inflation is accelerating, and when unemployment is above equilibrium, then inflation is decelerating. Although there is the possibility of a short-run trade-off of lower unemployment and higher inflation, this is regarded as fundamentally unsustainable in the long run given wage setters' concern about real wages resulting in action to prevent real wage erosion by higher nominal wage claims. Thus, in the long run there is no trade-off between unemployment and inflation leading to the familiar vertical Phillips Curve. The key institution and policymaking actor within this framework is the central bank that manages monetary policy through interest-rate adjustment, not via money-supply growth targets, where the aim is to keep the economy close to its inflation target at the equilibrium level of output. The central bank's role is important due to the disturbances/shocks that shift inflation away from its target or output away from the equilibrium level, or both, such that central banks seek to minimise these suboptimal fluctuations (Carlin and Soskice, 2005, 2009).

In terms of disinflation and central bank preferences, then, although any point on the initial Phillips Curve is feasible, the issue becomes which point along this curve the central bank would choose when implementing a deflationary policy, operating upon the assumption that the central bank aims to return the economy to the equilibrium rate on unemployment, with inflation at its designated target level. At one extreme the central bank could choose to bring inflation down to the target in the next period, but at cost of high unemployment and low output; however, once achieved the central bank can cut interest rates to stabilise output (Clarida et al., 1999). An alternative approach is for the central bank to choose a position for the economy whereby the fall in inflation and rise in unemployment would be less severe. This illustrates the inflation aversion of the central bank whereby it will have preferences between a deviation of inflation from its target, or of unemployment from its equilibrium rate. Hence, the notion of sacrifice ratios becomes a crucial aspect of both contemporary macroeconomic thought and associated policymaking by central banks, where the response from more inflation-averse central banks to an inflationary shock is to dampen output by raising interest rates more than do the less inflation-averse central banks. This involves a faster rise in unemployment to get a faster fall in inflation such that unemployment can return more quickly to equilibrium. This form of 'shock therapy' contrasts with the more gradualist approach of less inflation-averse central banks that results in unemployment rising more slowly and disinflation taking longer. From this contrast in central bank reaction styles, the issue is: Which is preferable? That is, whether there is a difference in the cumulative level of unemployment under 'shock therapy' or gradualism

(Goodfriend and King, 1997). In essence, if the Phillips Curves are linear and parallel, then the cumulative amount of unemployment to achieve the inflation target is equal in both scenarios. Hence, the sacrifice ratio in terms of the cumulative unemployment to achieve a given reduction in inflation is independent of the degree of central bank inflation aversion. However, this model does not consider: the presence in the economy of institutional features that may prevent it quickly returning to equilibrium following a disturbance/shock; nor that the monetary rule will become ineffective if nominal interest rates approach zero (i.e., a liquidity trap) – for example as occurred in many economies during the financial crisis as central banks lowered interest rates to historically low levels, thereby necessitating the requirement for other policy instruments such as quantitative easing (Gali, 2008).

Economics of contemporary fiscal policy

Following from this development of the overall NCM framework, we can now explore the key tools of fiscal and monetary policy in terms of how they have been developed at a theoretical level and redefined in terms of their actual implementation. First, fiscal policy has traditionally been seen as possessing several macroeconomic roles within an economy: providing automatic stabilisers to insulate the economy from shocks (stabilisers that are designed in relation to microeconomic goals); the use of discretionary policy to stabilise output and to plan financing of expenditure in terms of maintaining a sustainable burden of public debt; and overall, the differences in the macroeconomic effects of changes in government expenditure are the result of how these changes are financed and its sustainability, which have led to the development of fiscal-policy rules. Consequently, there is a need to interpret budget deficit in relation to whether output is above/below or at equilibrium, leading to the issue of a cyclically adjusted budget deficit and the situation given existing taxes and expenditure if the economy is at equilibrium output. In simple terms, the relationship between different concepts of the fiscal balance are such that the (primary) budget deficit ≡ cyclical adjusted budget deficit + impact of automatic stabilisers, alternatively the (primary) budget deficit ≡ discretionary fiscal impulse + impact of automatic stabilisers. From these relationships we can note that if the economy is in recession, then automatic stabilisers raise government expenditure and depress tax revenue, thereby pushing up the deficit. The impact on the budget deficit of the automatic stabilisers is zero when at equilibrium output, such that a zero cyclically adjusted budget deficit has zero discretionary fiscal impulse; however, a cyclically adjusted budget deficit leads to an expansionary fiscal stance, whilst a cyclically adjusted budget surplus results in a contractionary fiscal stance. Thus, if the cyclically adjusted budget deficit or surplus is zero, then the actual deficit reflects automatic stabilisers and will disappear once economy returns to equilibrium (Buiter, 2001).

However, the situation becomes more contentious when considering discretionary fiscal policy which, as we have previously discussed, is essentially ruled out under the NCS approach. Here, government expenditure is assumed to be exogenous, but we need to consider how this is financed and the consequences of changes in the government deficit for the asset stocks (money and bonds) in the economy. First, we assume that the private sector view government bonds as comprising part of their wealth in terms of the comparison between different methods of financing increases in government expenditure through taxation, bonds or the creation of high-powered money. Alternatively, under the guise of the NCS-inspired NCM, we consider that bonds are not regarded as wealth for the private sector as extolled by the Ricardian equivalence doctrine, such that far-sighted bond-holders realise that bonds issued to finance increased government expenditure will have to be repaid by higher taxation in the future (Seater, 1993). Consequently, tax- or bond-financed increases in government expenditure are indistinguishable. Hence, we can develop a government budget identity for each period, whereby the government must finance its expenditure and pay interest on its debt consisting of stock of bonds previously sold to the private sector. In the below identity the sources of funds are shown on the right and the uses of funds on left:

$$G + iB \equiv T + \Delta B + \Delta H$$

Where:

G = government expenditure in nominal terms
B = outstanding stock of bonds and value of national debt
T = tax revenue measure in net transfers
ΔB = value of new bonds issued
ΔH = new high-powered money printed by government

The fiscal policy transmission mechanism that follows from this exposition is such that an expenditure multiplier magnifies the impact of the fiscal impulse leading to income rising and the demand for money following suit; consequently, interest rates rise, thereby crowding out some interest-sensitive spending by the private sector. Furthermore, in relation to tax finance and the balanced-budget multiplier, this does not depend on the assumption that taxes are exogenous, but rather the key issue is that government spending results in extra output/income, whereas increases in taxation redistributes spending power from taxpayers to those who provide goods and services. This is important for policy purposes since, if a government is unable or unwilling to use debt or money financing, then it can still raise economic activity. Concerning the third option of bond finance, a rise in government expenditure will not induce sufficient extra tax revenue to eradicate the deficit, thereby requiring the government to sell bonds to cover this gap. However, the implications depend on whether bonds are considered by private-sector agents to represent net wealth (Seater, 1993). If bonds are seen as wealth, then changes in the stock of wealth influences consumption and money demand, which government has to consider when undertaking fiscal and monetary policy. For example, bond-financed government expansionary policy raises the proportion of bonds to money in the economy, assuming a fixed money supply, increasing the demand for money, and so restoring portfolio balance.

However, the Ricardian equivalence debate suggests that a bond-financed increase in government spending will have the same effect on output as a tax financed increase if bonds are not considered as net wealth. As a result, changes in wealth disappear as the government's debt rises, and the expansionary impact of the spending programme reverts to that of a balanced budget. Subsequently, the consensus is that changes in fiscal policy are only partly offset by changes in private-sector savings, whilst the sources of 'non-equivalence' in the real world indicate that the Ricardian equivalence is not a good representation of macroeconomic behaviour. An alternative source of funds for undertaking fiscal policy is money-financed expansion, where increases in government expenditure occur through an increase in the monetary base. Here, the government sells bonds to the central bank and spends the newly printed money on its expenditure initiative; however, this potentially creates severe medium-run consequences from such monetary financing, because monetary policy cannot fulfil both functions of providing the nominal anchor for the economy whilst being used to finance government expenditure (Auerbach and Feenberg, 2000).

Following from the government budget identity, the next issue concerns budget deficits and national debt, in terms of what determines the path of government's debt over time and, if debt is rising, will it continue rising indefinitely? To explore this issue we move beyond the single-period budget identity to exclude the possibility that governments can borrow from the central bank, that is, generate new high-powered money so that the government budget identity becomes: $G + iB \equiv T + \Delta B$. Further, we can distinguish between total expenditure and revenue, so that the actual government deficit $\equiv G + iB - T$ and the primary deficit, which excludes the interest payments on the debt. Hence, the actual deficit is equal to the change in the stock of government debt: $\Delta B \equiv (G - T) + iB$, where the change in debt $\equiv$ primary deficit + interest on outstanding debt, whilst the change in debt $\equiv$ actual deficit. Defining the government debt relative to national income in terms of a debt ratio where: $b = B/Py$. The next step is to rewrite the budget identity equation by dividing through by Py and thereby giving an expression for the change in the debt to GDP ratio (where γy = growth rate of output): $\Delta b = d + (i - \pi - \gamma y)b$ so that $\Delta b = d + (r - \gamma y)b$ where this equation provides the key to understanding the four determinants of the growth of the debt to GDP ratio and provides the framework for examining fiscal rules such as those within the eurozone whereby the costs of high and rising government debt differs according to whether the interest rate (r) is higher or lower than the growth rate (γy), leading to the evolution of debt ratio, where if γy > r then the economy is converging to a stable debt ratio and there is no problem with solvency. However, if γy < r then the economy is diverging to an unstable debt ratio and there will be a problem with solvency, to the extent that a substantial primary surplus may be required to prevent the debt ratio rising further, and so an even-larger primary surplus is required to reduce the debt burden.

The steps to achieving an increasing primary surplus are essentially reductions in expenditure and/or increases in taxes. The latter potentially lead to supply-side problems and a higher level of equilibrium unemployment, whilst the generation of high debt raises concerns about default so that higher interest rates on borrowing result in a potential feedback from debt ratio to interest rates. Consequently, the notion of fiscal consolidation has come to the policymaking forefront, which is consistent with a lower long-run primary surplus since the primary surplus required to offset the interest burden of the debt is lower. Hence, the implementation of fiscal policy is undertaken to achieve a sustainable debt ratio so that the trade-off government faces in order to reduce debt ratio is either one of gradualism or shock therapy (Alesina et al., 1998). Thus, although fiscal consolidation relates to a choice of policy options, the post-2008 recession path taken across most economies, and in particular within the stricken eurozone countries, has been the shock-therapy route through the tightening of fiscal policy and attempts to raise the primary surplus until the desired debt ratio has reached an optimal point at which the fiscal stance can be relaxed. This contrasts with the alternative of gradualism – although gradualism's aim is similarly to raise the primary surplus, but after a period of debt reduction the primary surplus is again adjusted and the process is repeated over an extended time horizon. Although there is an implicit assumption that fiscal consolidation will be contractionary through increasing the primary surplus and thereby reducing output and employment in the short run, the key attendant debate is about whether fiscal consolidation has expansionary effects sufficiently strong to offset contractionary effects. This has been agued by its advocates through the channel where an unsustainable fiscal position increases risk premium leading to interest rates becoming higher than they should be; in contrast, credible fiscal consolidation reduces the risk premium, thereby boosting investment and consumption. The key to this process is the initial cutting of government consumption expenditure (i.e., austerity), which signals commitment to fiscal reform and, in turn, triggers the belief that taxes will be lower, lowers both interest rates and the risk premium, and results in the boosting of investment and consumption. This still remains the official policy of not only national governments, such as the United Kingdom's, but also of the EU Commission and the other members of the EU/IMF/ECB Troika in terms of how to address the euro-zone crisis.

An alternative strategy is the monetising of debt through seignorage and hyperinflation, where if the government has high debt levels, but still seeks to continue and/or expand expenditure policies, then carrying out this policy becomes difficult due to the risk of defaulting and raising taxes. Thus, the only option is monetary financing of government expenditure. As previously discussed, the growth of the debt to GDP ratio will be reduced to the extent that the deficit is being financed by new money creation; thus in essence higher inflation reduces the growth of the debt ratio and acts as a so-called 'inflation tax'. A further contemporary development is the adoption of a prudent fiscal policy rule restricting the government to being solvent based on long-run or 'permanent' values of relevant variables, where deviations from such permanent values occur due to factors such as cyclical fluctuations and/or structural changes to government expenditure. In essence a budget constraint equates to the change in the debt to GDP ratio, whilst a prudent fiscal policy rule begins with the condition of the debt ratio not increasing and so sets the share of tax revenues in GDP at a constant level equal to the 'permanent' or long-run requirement. This implies that if government expenditure is temporarily above its permanent level, then borrowing should finance it, and that if the real interest rate is confidently known to be temporarily above its permanent value, or if growth is depressed relative to its long-run value, then the rule indicates that the deficit can be allowed to widen. However, any expected rise in permanent government expenditure should be funded by a rise in taxation.

Economics of contemporary monetary policy

As previously discussed, within NCM, the pivotal institution is the central bank, which controls monetary policy, with the bank's behaviour modelled through a 'reaction function' that responds to shocks in pursuit of its inflation target – a function that provides a medium-run, 'nominal anchor' and guidance for adjusting interest rates (Carlstrom and Fuerst, 2003). Therefore, the structure of monetary policy is based on this optimal monetary policy rule in combination with private-sector constraints. Following the monetarist revolution, economists then focus on the idea that low and stable inflation is an accepted/appropriate goal for policy-makers to the extent that they establish a nominal anchor that keeps infla-tion low and stable, but they also need to consider why higher output is potentially undesirable. First, we should note that, with the advent of the new consensus view, there has been a shift in the monetary-policy para-digm, from the money-supply paradigm to the interest-rate-reaction func-tion paradigm. Although both share a number of common features, the contemporary interest-rate-reaction function paradigm is based on the idea that policy changes are determinants of price level and inflation where the short-term nominal interest rate is the key policy instrument, which is guided through an interest rule in terms of a mechanism to adjust equilibrium with constant inflation following a shock. Hence, this paradigm shift centres on the choice of monetary policy instrument and the choice of an active or a passive policy, based on empirical evidence suggesting that operating monetary policy passively was not optimal and that, for an economy with shocks and adjustment lags, active monetary policy was superior to passive. Contemporary thought encapsulates an active monetary policy reaction function using the interest rate as an instrument of an activist policy framework, with central banks following a 'rule-based' approach to monetary policy whilst remaining very active through frequent interest-rate adjustments (Allsopp and Vines, 2000).

Key to this new paradigm is the notion of the central bank's utility function, whereby it possesses a trade-off in preference between inflation and unemployment, assuming that the central bank has two concerns: first to minimise fluctuations around the target inflation rate, which assumes a symmetrical target and attaches greater importance to returning inflation back to its target the further it is away from target; second, to minimise the gap between actual and equilibrium output which again assumes a symmetrical attitude to such deviations. In relation to the actual operation of these monetary policy rules, there is first the assumption that the central bank can control output via monetary policy to manage aggregate demand, but via output it can only control inflation indirectly. If a shock occurs and inflation rises above target, the central bank then faces a trade-off, the extremities of which are either a fully accommodating policy of preserving output at equilibrium level, or a non-accommodating policy of attaining the inflation target in the next period. However, in reality, the central bank will choose a policy response between these extremes (Cecchetti, 2000). The key to the predicament of the eurozone following its creation was that the ECB was given a symmetrical inflation target whilst simultaneously seeking to prove its anti-inflationary credentials and thereby being more included in pursuing a non-accommodating monetary policy. However, once the 2008 credit-crunch-induced recession began to tighten its grip across the eurozone; the ECB remained wedded to this general approach and found itself unable to respond in a flexible manner before significant damage had been inflicted upon the eurozone economy. The second factor influencing the monetary rule is the responsiveness of inflation to output (i.e., the slope of the Phillips Curve), with the starting point assuming an equal short-run trade-off between output and inflation. However, if Phillips Curves are steeper (shallower), then any given reduction in output has a greater (less) effect in reducing inflation, so that the monetary rule schedule of the central bank is less (more) elastic compared to its generic slope. A steeper (shallower) Phillips Curve makes it easier (more difficult) for the central bank, since a smaller (larger) rise in unemployment and fall (rise) in output is required to achieve any desired fall in inflation (Carlin and Soskice, 2005, 2009).

We can now devise the more general form of the central bank's monetary rule and add the timing structure so that the larger the responsiveness of wages to employment, or the more inflation-averse is the central bank, then the slope of the monetary rule would be less elastic. Consequently, the steeper the Phillips Curve, any reduction in aggregate demand leads to a larger reduction in inflation, whilst in the case of a more inflation-averse central bank, no matter what the labour market position, then a more inflation-averse central bank will wish to reduce inflation by more than a more accommodating central bank. Finally, in addition to this new macroeconomic framework, we can add the ideas of credibility, time inconsistency and rules versus discretion where economists have forwarded several potential solutions, or at least mitigation, to the time-inconsistency problem. First, is replacing discretion by a rule to demonstrate commitment, such as the well-known Taylor Rule; second, is the delegation of monetary policy by government to an independent central bank with an output target closer to the equilibrium level of output and increased inflation aversion. Thus, the reputation of the government/central bank as being tough on inflation is therefore reflected upon wage and price setters, who observe these policy decisions; however, the central bank needs to be inflation-averse over several time periods (Taylor, 1993). Again, this mirrors the behaviour of the ECB, which exacerbated the depth and longevity of the eurozone crisis through feeling the need to generate this reputation by maintaining interest rates above the required level. However, advocates would point to the anticipated benefits resulting from rules and expectations versus from discretion and learning. These include no inflation bias in the adoption of rules rather than discretion for the operation of policy such that gains arise as economic agents anticipate the central bank's reaction to shocks; otherwise, the central bank fails to 'learn' about the economy (King, 1997).

Critical assessment of New Consensus Macroeconomics

As previously mentioned, the development of the contemporary New Consensus Macroeconomics (NCM) framework is not without criticism, and it comes largely from a Post-Keynesian perspective (Lavoie, 2004, 2006; Rochon, 2004; Setterfield, 2004; Smithin, 2004; Palley, 2006; Monvoisin and Rochon, 2006). The Post-Keynesian school was initially treated as a variant within the general Keynesian approach, being slow to emerge as a separate entity; however, it may be contrasted with New Keynesian ideas, partly because of its more comprehensive rejection of the classical model as unhelpful and the theoretical abstractions of which impair, rather than enhance, understanding about economic processes. Whilst New Keynesianism largely accepts rational expectations, the monetarist concentration upon the importance of the money supply and the existence of an equilibrium (natural or NAIRU) rate of unemployment, Post-Keynesians reject all these propositions. Similarities between the two schools do exist to the extent that New Keynesians have largely adopted the imperfect competition approach originated by Post-Keynesians; however, whilst New Keynesians mainly concentrate upon temporary wage and price rigidities, Post-Keynesians prefer to locate fundamental economic instabilities as being the result of the effect of expectations within an uncertain world (Sawyer, 1988). Hence, the Post-Keynesian approach diverges from New Keynesianism in terms of the microeconomic framework upon which it constructs its macroeconomic model that is intended to conform closely to observable reality. Industrial structure is assumed to exhibit characteristics of imperfect competition, oligopoly or monopoly, whilst the labour market is characterised by heterogeneous labour organising collectively in trade unions in order to maximise bargaining power. Markets with relatively flexible prices are generally distinguished from relatively fix-price markets for manufacturing, where changes in demand and supply generally cause variations in output rather than price (Davidson, 1991, 1994). One of the most important microeconomic theories is that nominal prices are largely based upon a markup over costs. This markup varies between different products, and within industrial sectors, as a result of different degrees of monopoly power, normal rates of capacity utilisation and planned levels of investment. However, the markup tends to remain largely stable over time. Prices charged by individual firms are determined by a markup added to average total costs, whilst aggregate costs and markup together determine the general price level (Arestis and Chick, 1992). These Post-Keynesian microfoundations have three principal implications. Firstly, that product prices and money wages are determined by the relative bargaining strengths enjoyed by oligopolistic firms and trade unions, and under a variety of market conditions, which leads to the conclusion that inflation may be the result of this conflict over the distribution of income, with trade union strength greatest during conditions of full employment. Secondly, since prices are determined by a markup on top of nominal wage costs, this means that an adjustment of nominal wages in the labour market cannot achieve a reduction in real wages and thereby create the conditions required by the classical model to achieve a reduction in unemployment. Thirdly, since money prices remain essentially constant until a change in underlying costs (particularly wage costs) causes them to shift, Post-Keynesians conclude that fluctuations in economic activity will initially impact upon output, not prices, which in turn influences the demand for credit (needed to finance inventories and investment) and hence the quantity of money supplied (Rochon, 1999; Fontana, 2003).

In general terms, many Post-Keynesians are critical of the IS function that underlies the analysis, together with the efficiency of monetary policy in the short run and monetary neutrality in the long run, whilst all Post-Keynesians reject the concept of a vertical long run Phillips Curve. In relation to the former, rejection of the simple interest rate/investment relationship implied in the IS model occurs, since this is more complex than the simple function assumes. Post-Keynesians do not believe that there is a one-for-one relationship between the short-term interest rate set by the central bank and the long-term interest rates or the lending rates that affect the components of aggregate demand; indeed, empirical evidence suggests that the interest elasticity of investment is non-linear and asymmetric, where an increase in interest rates is likely to reduce investment in times of economic boom the reverse is not true and is unlikely to stimulate investment in times of recession (Arestis and Sawyer, 2008).

Furthermore, Post-Keynesian criticisms of the efficiency of monetary policy and monetary neutrality derive from the belief that monetary policy takes a considerable amount of time to have any effect, especially on the inflation rate, unless interest rates are changed by the drastic amounts theory (Rochon, 1999; Fontana, 2003). Hence, monetary policy is known to be a particularly blunt instrument, with long and variable lags, so that it acts upon inflationary forces by weakening aggregate demand and labour conditions. Post-Keynesians also reject the so-called neutrality of money in both the short run and the long run, at the same time denying that logic requires that in the long run the actual rate of capacity utilisation ought to converge towards an exogenously given normal rate of capacity utilisation. Thus they reject the notion of a supply-determined natural growth rate; a critique applies equally to the classical model and to the endogenous growth models. Rather, they believe that if the concept of a natural growth rate is to be of any assistance, it is determined by the path taken by the actual growth rate (Arestis, 2009). Additionally, Post-Keynesians reject the vertical long-run Phillips Curve with many of them even sceptical about short-run trade-offs between GDP/capacity and inflation, since there is a large range of capacity utilization rates that are consistent with an absence of demand-led pressures (for reasons tied to the absence of decreasing returns over a large range of production levels). Thus, it is believed that, with coordinated wage bargaining, a constant inflation rate becomes compatible with a range of employment levels and the NAIRU, as the short-run limit to employment is no longer unique (Arestis, 2009).

However, aside from these broad points of difference, the key Post-Keynesian criticism is that the NCM model is characterised by an interest-rate rule whereby the money markets and financial institutions are typically not mentioned, let alone modelled (Fontana, 2009). Thus, in the NCM model there is no mention of banks, but as witnessed in the credit-crunch-financial-crisis banks and their decisions play a considerably significant role in the transmission mechanism of monetary policy. Decisions by banks as to whether or not to grant credit plays a major role in the expansion of the economy, in the sense that failure of banks to supply credit would imply that expansion of expenditure cannot occur. Consequently, many economic agents are liquidity constrained and do not have sufficient assets to sell or the ability to borrow, therefore expenditures are limited to their current income and few assets. Through the perfect capital market assumption, this implies the absence of credit rationing, meaning that some individuals are credit-constrained to the extent that the only effect of monetary policy would be a 'price effect' as the rate of interest is changed. However, this implies that parts of the transmission mechanism of monetary policy that involve credit rationing and changes in the non-price terms on which credit is supplied are excluded by assumption (Woodford, 2001). Consequently, Post-Keynesians' criticisms of monetary policy are that policy designed to eliminate bubbles would lead to the problematic result of 'financial repression', whereby the experience with financial liberalization is that it caused a number of deep financial crises and problems unparalleled in world financial history, to the extent that when bubbles emerged, monetary authorities argued that monetary policy should not interfere with the free functioning of financial markets (Arestis and Sawyer, 2004). However, proactive monetary policy requires authorities to outperform market participants, whereas central banks prefer to deal with the consequences of the burst of a bubble by mini-mising the damages to the real economy. Thus, monetary policy should be tightened (loosened) as the ratio of net wealth-to-disposable income, over a period of time, is above (below) a predetermined threshold. This would allow asset-price booms, but it would prevent them from becoming bubbles that would ultimately burst with huge adverse consequences for the economy as a whole. Such an approach would also help regulate financial engineering, since the central bank would monitor the implications of financial innova-tions as they impact net wealth, even if the bank is ignorant of them.

Additionally, Post-Keynesians argue that another serious omission by the NCM is the role of what Keynes described as *animal spirits*, namely the possibility that individuals act irrationally and for noneconomic reasons; failure to recognise their importance in monetary policy can lead to wrong conclusions, such that monetary policy can become ineffective. Monetary policy may also influence aggregate supply through changes in the rate of interest whereby fixed and working capital may need financial resources, since current inputs should be paid before output can be sold, and these resources carry financial costs (Smithin, 2004; Arestis, 2009). Therefore, the interest rate paid on working capital affects production costs and in turn the supply side of aggregate output. Furthermore, Post-Keynesian criticisms relate to the key concept of the equilibrium real rate of interest, which plays a crucial role in the NCM model, to the extent that the discrepancy between the actual and the equilibrium rates of interest has been termed the real interest-rate gap and can be used to evaluate the stance of monetary policy. This is thereby a useful theoretical concept in the analysis of the relation-ship between the independence of monetary policy and economic fluctua-tions, where the equilibrium real rate of interest secures output at the supply equilibrium level (i.e., zero output gap) consistent with constant inflation or when the real rate of interest is reached – then there is no problem of deficient (or indeed excessive) aggregate demand. This equilibrium rate is often seen to correspond to what is called the Wicksellian 'natural rate' of interest. Although it is not self-evident from the NCM, this 'natural rate' of interest equates savings and investment and does so at a zero output gap; it is implicitly assumed to be consistent with the full employment of labour inasmuch as flexible real wages would permit the labour market to clear with full-employment, compatible with the zero output gap (Rochon and Setterfield, 2007).

It is also the case that the use of the equilibrium real rate of interest in NCM models with the emphasis on price stability provides an important benchmark for monetary policy analysis in the context of models with a single rate of interest, with no banks and no monetary aggregates. Under these assumptions the reaction of the interest-rate policy instrument to movements in the equilibrium real rate of interest can ensure price stability. Thus, when the rate of interest on bank loans differs from the policy rate of interest, the equilibrium real rate of interest may not be a useful indicator for monetary policy since the crucial distinguishing assumption in this context is whether markets are frictionless, such that in markets characterised by friction a further implication is that monetary policy exerts real effects even in the long run. Hence, whilst the NCM model portrays an economy in which the interest rate can be adjusted to secure equilibrium in terms of a zero output gap and a balance between aggregate demand and aggregate supply, where the rate at which this materialises is the real equilibrium rate of interest that provides an 'anchor' or benchmark for monetary policy; however, a shift in the state of confidence and expectations leads to a shift in the investment schedule and so to a shift in the real equilibrium rate of interest (Moore, 1988; Palley, 2006). In view of the difficulties that relate to the real rate of interest, two questions emerge. First, whether or not the natural rate can be a surrogate for a detailed analysis of the real and monetary forces relevant to the identification of risks to price stability; and, second, whether a great deal of discretion should be applied in the conduct of monetary policy, although the degree of discretion required might not be compatible with the inflation-targeting theoretical principles.

Most Post-Keynesian economists reject key elements of the NCM, in particular disagreeing with the underlying IS curve as well as the vertical long-run Phillips Curve. Moreover, it has been shown that accepting all the basic equations of the NCM amended with the suggested Post-Keynesian modifications with respect to the Phillips Curve equation, will fundamentally change the model's conclusions, thereby creating important roles for fiscal (Smithin, 2007; Wray, 2007) and monetary policy interest (Moore, 1988; Palley, 2006; Fontana, 2009) in influencing the level of output, capacity utilisation and employment.

Conclusion

Since the late 1980s there has been a major revival of political economy, utilizing the tools of modern economic analysis where a common theme running throughout this new political macroeconomics is the need to integrate the political process into mainstream economics – in particular, through the idea of political business cycles that can be traced back to the work of Schumpeter and Kalecki. However, for a period, interest in politico-economic models lost momentum as theoretical shortcomings and inconclusive empirical results led to a temporary demise of this line of research. However, this area was revived as new classical theorists traced the policy implications of rational expectations market-clearing models, where the emphasis on policy ineffectiveness and rationality was initially interpreted as being inconsistent with politically motivated policy manipulations. Consequently, new rational politico-economic models have been developed that incorporate features such as asymmetric/imperfect information, non-contingent nominal wage contracts and uncertainty over election results. Accordingly, the policymaking process consists of a complex game played out by various competing groups whose interests do not necessarily coincide.

A particular aspect of this development in macroeconomics, discussed in this chapter, is that economists have sought to enhance understanding of aggregate instability by adding a political dimension to their models in terms of the issue of credibility of policy announcements, known as time-inconsistency, and the subsequent need to bind politicians to rules/ pre-commitment, and through the creation of politically neutral institutions such as independent central banks. As we will see in Chapters 6 and 7, these ideas of rules and institutions have been central to the design of the eurozone based upon the generally recognised solutions, or at least mitigation, to time-inconsistency problems. The rationales presented are, first, replace discretion by rules to demonstrate commitment such as those rules contained within the TEU convergence criteria and SGP; second, delegate monetary policy from government to an independent central bank with an output target closer to the equilibrium level of output and more inflation aversion; third, the reputation of government or central bank leads to it being tough on inflation so that wage and price setters observe decisions taken; however, to be credible the central bank needs to be inflation-averse over several time periods. Hence, overall there is seen to be a fundamental dichotomy in terms of rules and expectations versus discretion and learning. In relation to inflation bias, the issue of rules versus discretion means gains rise as economic agents anticipate the central bank's reaction to shocks, compared to an emphasis on rules whereby the central bank fails to 'learn' about the economy.

4
Theoretical Considerations of a Single Currency

Introduction

The advert of the single currency was a momentous event that, as the euro-zone crisis has illustrated, entailed profound consequences for people across the Continent and beyond. The euro has become the currency in which individual citizens are paid and denotes the price of all goods, services and labour across the whole eurozone. Most academic social science literature either accepts that closer EU integration is desirable or, more usually given the political will of EU leaders, that it is inevitable. Therefore, economists, political scientists and sociologists frequently devote their research to the dynamics of the eurozone, the political institutions fostering 'ever-closer union' and the social implications of these momentous changes. However, whilst such detailed analyses generate important policy proposals, they tend by their weight to obscure the crucial strategic issue: Is the eurozone benefi-cial or not for the EU as a whole? The purpose of this chapter is to analyse this issue. More specifically, it seeks to evaluate the criteria that have been advanced by different authorities to assess whether or not membership in the single currency would prove beneficial.

Under the rubric of optimum currency-area theory, economists have long studied the potential impact of monetary union between countries. This theory concludes that a single currency boosts participants' living standards when they possess similar economic structures and international trading patterns, but proves detrimental where these diverge (De Grauwe, 1994; Corden, 2003). This extensive literature points to a number of distinct, yet interrelated characteristics that are likely to determine the probable consequences of monetary union: degree of factor mobility (Mundell, 1961; Ingram, 1962); degree of commodities' market integration (Mundell, 1961); openness and size of the economy (McKinnon, 1963); degree of commodity diversification (Kenen, 1969); level of fiscal integration and interregion transfers (Kenen, 1969); degree of policy integration (Ingram, 1969; Haberler, 1970; Tower and Willett, 1970); similarity of inflation rates

(Haberler, 1970; Fleming, 1971; Magnifico, 1973); price and wage flexibility (Friedman, 1953b); real exchange-rate variability (Vaubel, 1976, 1978). However, numerous studies (Bruno and Sachs, 1985; Eichengreen, 1990, 1993a, b, 1997; MacDougall, 1992, 2003; Bini-Smaghi and Vori, 1992; Blanchard and Katz, 1992) have indicated that the eurozone failed to sufficiently meet these optimum currency area (OCA) theory criteria.

Subsequently, modern OCA theory focuses upon an endogeneity hypothesis that economic structures can be dramatically changed due to participation in a monetary union, thereby providing a pro-eurozone argument whereby the improvements of intra-eurozone trade will lead to a convergence among business cycles (Artis and Zhang, 1995; Baxter and Koupartitas, 2005). Consequently, fluctuations of prices also tend to be similar among members; therefore, a flexible exchange-rate policy is not required (Frankel and Rose, 1997). However, in contrast to this endogeneity perspective, the counter-endogeneity view is represented by a specialisation hypothesis (Krugman, 1993; Bayoumi and Eichengreen, 1993, 1996), postulating that trade integration will enhance the specialisation of each country's production, thereby reducing OCA cohesion. Furthermore, monetary integration may not able to enforce the correlation of business cycles (Baxter and Stockman, 1989; Bordo and Helbling, 2003; Bergman, 2004), since asymmetric shocks force adjustments to occur in the real economy rather than via the exchange rate.

The danger of locking a country's currency within an international regime ill-suited to meeting domestic and external economic goals is illustrated by the mass unemployment under the gold standard of the 1920s. Consequently, to avoid making a potentially costly mistake, especially since single-currency membership is intended to be permanent and irrevocable, with no exit clause negotiated in the Treaty on European Union (TEU), there is an obvious need for taking a series of measures to determine whether an individual economy is prepared for the demands of membership (EC Commission, 1992). These indicators must incontrovertibly demonstrate the existence of prior and sustainable 'real' convergence between participating economies before the formation of a single currency between these countries is in their economic interests. However, despite the critical importance of such indicators in establishing whether or not membership of the eurozone is 'good' or 'bad' for a particular country, the construction of these indicators has been paid relatively scant attention.

Indeed, the convergence criteria contained within the TEU are more concerned with examining transitory cyclical movements in financial indicators than in concentrating upon structural convergence in the real economy (EC Commission, 1992). Thus, the only questions asked are those concerning levels of price inflation, interest rates, exchange-rate stability, public debt and annual budget deficits. The TEU focused upon 'nominal' convergence, measured by reference values (e.g., 60% debt; 3% deficit) that largely reflect historical levels of debt and deficit in the 'core' EU countries. Their relevance to future conditions is unclear. In contrast, the TEU contained no similar tests to compare the wealth of the various countries, their unemployment, productivity and growth rates, nor the sectoral composition of economic activity. Perhaps this is not entirely surprising as the eurozone project was designed by a committee dominated by central bankers, whose particular concern was to devise rules restraining potentially profligate national governments from destabilising the monetary system. However, whilst these matters are important, it is problematic that the eurozone is designed to proceed from such a narrow, theoretically questionable, foundation. Such concerns are magnified by the fact that the eurozone possesses no historical precedents. No monetary union has ever existed independently of political union, and no independent country had ever unilaterally abandoned its own currency (Goodhart, 1995). The eurozone is therefore a 'leap in the dark' that has potentially destructive implications if its participants are not sufficiently converged prior to its establishment (Eichengreen, 1992, 1993).

Optimality of international monetary systems

In order to fully understand what is involved by a monetary union, we must first establish why the exchange rate is an important macroeconomic policy instrument. Essentially the exchange rate acts as the price of one country's currency when translated into the currency of another for the purposes of international trade and financial movements. Consequently, these rates can exert a decisive impact upon inflation, balance of payments, employment and, ultimately, economic growth. However, history demonstrates that an exchange-rate regime that is too rigid over a long period of time will inevitably collapse because it prevents individual economies adjusting to the divergent impact, caused by external shocks and changes in the pattern of demand, upon production and employment structures (Foreman-Peck, 1995). In other words the question is: Where over this spectrum lies the 'ideal' exchange-rate mechanism? Unfortunately, there is no simple or conclusive answer to this problem, with each set of arguments possessing its own merits. Moreover, in the dynamic modern world, the 'ideal' exchange-rate regime can change over time, depending upon the domestic economic circumstances of the country involved and the global economic environment in which it finds itself. Most policymakers would agree that, in general, the 'ideal' situation is for the exchange rate to possess short-term stability but long-term flexibility. This offers the best possible environment for business, investment and trade – which prefer stability – whilst not locking the country into an exchange-rate position that may prove harmful in the long run, as regional, national and global economic circumstances change over time. Hence, a key aspect of international monetary arrangements is the choice of an exchange-rate regime (Ghosh et al., 2002; Sarno and Taylor, 2002). Although a number of attempts have been undertaken to secure the greater predictability that a fixed exchange-rate regime can provide, badly constructed systems have been associated with economic recessions, bankruptcies and mass unemployment.

The importance of this point is reinforced by the fact that the eurozone is intended to be an irrevocable act, such that even greater emphasis is placed upon the estimated balance of costs and benefits by which a country decides whether or not to participate in this unique currency arrangement (Wyplosz, 2003). If the advocates of membership are correct, joining the single currency would unleash economic potential that would increase economic growth and investment throughout the eurozone, achieve low and stable inflation, and build a strong European economy to be the envy of the rest of the world. Some of the main economic and political benefits claimed would include that greater nominal exchange-rate stability will occur, which reduces the risk associated with fluctuating exchange rates and is, therefore, assumed to encourage greater trade and investment that, in turn, should result in higher growth and employment in the longer run. Furthermore, a reduction in transaction costs should occur, since firms exporting or importing goods and services to another participating country will no longer have to exchange currency to complete the sale, thereby saving on commission charges. Whilst less onerous for large companies than tourists changing small amounts of foreign currency, the removal of this minor but significant charge upon international trade should encourage exports and thereby stimulate economic growth. Even a small annual boost to economic activity may become significant if its effects are cumulative over time. Additionally, price transparency should increase, because goods, services and labour are priced in the same currency, facilitating traders to make cheaper purchases and increase competition across the eurozone, thereby exerting a downward pressure upon prices to the benefit of European consumers. It is further argued that this price transparency is a precondition to the final completion of the single market.

As the key institution at the heart of the eurozone, the ECB is charged with ensuring price stability above all alternative economic goals and, therefore, many proponents argue that inflation is likely to be lower for those countries with the single currency, particularly in the longer run, and accordingly interest rates should be lower, thereby boosting investment and economic growth. Moreover, the creation of the euro would establish a major world currency capable of rivalling the U.S. dollar and Japanese yen, which could confer certain economic advantages as well as providing political prestige based upon the EU's combined economic strength and greater world political influence. This might, or might not, involve closer political integration between EU member states, which would rival the United States in terms of population and wealth. However, arguments that the euro reduces national sovereignty are rejected on the grounds that sovereignty is not an absolute right any more, due to the globalisation of financial markets and voluntary limitations imposed by international treaties such as membership in

NATO, the Geneva Convention, the United Nations and the World Trade Organisation. Sovereignty is not relinquished, because nations are still able to influence decision-making through the European Council; thus, sovereignty is shared, or pooled, within the EU, with decision-making subject to the collective viewpoint of participating member states.

However, many critics of the single currency argue that the costs of entry are in fact potentially far larger, such that the principal arguments advanced by those critical of the eurozone include: the loss of control over monetary policy and of influence over the exchange-rate weakens national economic management, which is further constrained by the restraints upon fiscal policy resulting from the TEU convergence criteria and SGP rules on government borrowing. This combination reduces the potential capacity of a country to respond to internal or external shocks, exacerbating the danger of national destabilisation. Furthermore, the lack of prior cyclical and structural convergence amongst all participating member states would create strains. Consequently, unsynchronised business cycles and/or structural differences magnify the effects of asymmetric external shocks, whilst a unified monetary policy will be unable to meet satisfactorily the needs of all economies, concentrating upon the 'average' member state as it is likely to do. Thus, incorrectly set interest rates may damage individual economies, increasing their initial misfortunes rather than moderating them. Moreover, the 'generous' interpretation of the TEU convergence criteria in order to ensure as many countries as possible participated in the eurozone implies that the majority of participants must continue to deflate their economies by raising taxes or cutting government spending in order to meet the rigid financial criteria established by the TEU convergence criteria and SGP. The combination of these measures will result in higher unemployment and slower growth within the eurozone. Indeed, the absence of any substantial fiscal redistribution mechanism, which could stabilise the eurozone by transferring resources from favoured to weaker regions, means that less competitive areas may suffer declining incomes and persistent mass unemployment, thereby increasing inequality and social tension across the single currency area. Consequently, many of the economic objectives claimed by single currency advocates could be achieved through effective national economic management, such as price stability, high economic growth and full employment. Moreover, since the ECB will include Mediterranean countries as well as Germany, it is unlikely that it will initially possess the anti-inflation credibility that the Bundesbank enjoyed, meaning that the euro might be a weak currency.

Additionally, opponents of the eurozone dismiss the threat of loss of markets through protectionist measures enacted by single currency members against the United Kingdom, since these would flout the various EU treaties (Rome, SIM, TEU) and WTO rules. Similarly, critics of European integration generally reject the view that sovereignty can be pooled, instead suggesting that sovereignty refers to a national authority using every means at its disposal to achieve its objectives, within the constraints imposed by international markets and treaty obligations. Thus, sovereignty can be exercised either by a national government or by the EU, but not by both; the eurozone would result in the loss of economic sovereignty to the ECB, with national authorities losing autonomy. Moreover, there is the issue that the ECB is undemocratic because it is deliberately insulated from all political influence; the authors of the TEU believed that such insulation would enhance its ability to secure price stability. Thus, electors would no longer be able to influence monetary and exchange-rate policies, whilst fiscal policy is also tightly constrained through the SGP. These policies deeply affect individual citizens' lives, from setting the cost of their mortgage to the possibility of losing their job. One final criticism is that, rather than the eurozone creating a European super-state, it is in fact designed to 'roll back' the state and reduce its ability to regulate the actions of the owners of private capital and the international financial markets in the interests of their citizens. Increased constraints placed upon government economic autonomy reduce the choices available through the democratic process, whilst limiting the ability of one country to pursue a significantly unorthodox economic strategy intended to meet nation-specific goals.

The eurozone and optimum currency-area theory

The debate surrounding the prospects for a single EU currency has begun to focus upon the prior necessity for structural economic convergence, which is wider than simply meeting the TEU convergence criteria or the Treasury tests. These criteria may be largely necessary for a successful and sustainable eurozone, but they are not sufficient to fulfil this objective. Therefore a need exists to develop a more comprehensive set of criteria to complement the convergence criteria. To do so, it is necessary to examine that section of economic theory that discusses the optimality of monetary unions and exchange-rate arrangements, namely the theory of Optimum Currency Areas (OCA) (De Grauwe, 1994; Corden, 2003). Extensive literature points to a number of distinct, yet interrelated, characteristics that are likely to determine the probable consequences of monetary union.

Countries between which there is a high degree of factor mobility are viewed as better candidates for monetary integration, since this integration provides a substitute for exchange-rate flexibility in promoting external adjustment (Mundell, 1961; Ingram, 1962). However, in practice it is unlikely that the EU – with different cultures, languages and traditions across member states – displays sufficient inter-regional labour mobility to act as a mechanism for payments adjustment. Available evidence suggests that labour mobility within European nation states is one-third the level found in a mature 'eurozone' such as the United States, despite the existence of greater regional inequality and unemployment in Europe. This implies that European labour mobility is less responsive to employment and income incentives (OECD, 1986). Moreover, the figures in this evidence relate to labour mobility *within* individual countries, whereas mobility *between* countries is likely to be much lower due to language barriers, cultural differences and residual non-recognition of qualifications (Ermisch, 1991; Masson and Taylor, 1993). Furthermore, due to the time lags involved in the movement of physical capital, capital mobility is unlikely to generate sufficient short-term stabilisation whilst factor movements, due to the transaction costs involved, are an inefficient means of reacting to transitory regional shocks (von Hagen, 1993; Romer, 1994).

The level of commodities' market integration is concerned with structural convergence and, specifically, with the requirement that countries should possess similar production structures. Economies exhibiting such symmetry are deemed to be more welfare-efficient candidates for currency area participation than those whose production structures are markedly different (Mundell, 1961). The reason for this belief is that external shocks will tend to impact upon given industries in certain ways and, therefore, a group of economies with similar industrial structures should experience similar effects, making it easier for a common monetary and exchange-rate policy to mitigate any negative results of the shock. Furthermore, the openness and size of the economy are observed facts that economies in which international trade accounts for a high proportion of national income tend to prefer fixed exchange rates, because exchange-rate changes in such economies are unlikely to be accompanied by significant effects on real competitiveness. In this sense, the greater the potential for damage to the economy from a fluctuating currency, the more business leaders and employees desire exchange-rate stability. If a fluctuating exchange rate affects only an insignificant proportion of the economy, the pressure for such arrangements is lower. Moreover, in open economies frequent exchange-rate adjustments diminish the liquidity property of money, since the overall price index varies more than in relatively closed economies (McKinnon, 1963). However, whilst relatively open economies might prefer exchange-rate stability, they also require the ability to correct any fundamental misalignment of their currency. Such over- or under-valuation could occur gradually, over time, as the competitiveness and productivity of the economy changes relative to others with whom the country has a fixed exchange rate, or more rapidly as a result of an internal (e.g., wage–price explosion) or external shock (e.g., oil price rise). Irrespective of the cause, failure to adjust exchange rates to their long-term equilibrium value (itself changing over time) prove damaging to the economy in question, unless alternative adjustment mechanisms are sufficient to achieve the same outcome. Most small- or medium-sized industrialised nations fulfil this condition.

Highly diversified economies are better candidates for currency areas than less-diversified economies, since their diversification provides some insulation against a variety of shocks, thereby forestalling the need for frequent changes in the exchange rate (Kenen, 1969). Countries reliant upon a small number of prominent industries react significantly differently to other monetary union participants in the face of changes within those particular markets. This would increase the difficulty of operating a common monetary policy that could stabilise all participants. In general terms, virtually all industrialised member states fulfil this particular criterion, at least prior to the establishment of a single currency. However, the combination of a single market and the eurozone is likely to generate a degree of specialisation that potentially undermines such insulation. Multinational corporations, in particular, are anticipated to respond to the opening of markets and greater transparency of prices by expanding throughout Europe. Indeed, the creation of large European corporations, intensifying specialisation in fewer, larger concerns better equipped to compete globally, was one principal impetus behind the push towards greater European integration (EC Commission, 1990).

The higher the level of fiscal harmonisation, the greater is the ability to smooth divergent shocks through transfers from low- to high-unemployment regions. This feature is important for the emerging eurozone because, in the absence of national exchange-rate variation, wage–price flexibility and/or labour mobility are unlikely to prove sufficiently powerful to adjust economies in the face of asymmetric external shocks. Consequently, budgetary policy can be an important tool to cushion individual countries from shocks. Such fiscal flexibility may involve the discretionary strategies associated with 'fine tuning', but can also arise from the operation of automatic stabilisers (Kenen, 1969). This can also occur at the national as well as the federal level. Therefore, despite the constraints placed upon national fiscal policy by the operation of the convergence criteria and the Stability and Growth Pact, it is probable that federal policy will expand over time. The current size of the EU budget, at only 1.24% of total EU GDP, appears to preclude the development of any significant inter-regional fiscal transfer system for the foreseeable future (MacDougall, 1992, 2003). Moreover, the cost of such a system may defer meaningful consideration of this potential mechanism to stabilise the eurozone (Burkitt et al., 1997; Whyman, 1997a, b). However, in the absence of alternative stabilising mechanisms, fiscal integration may be the only practical means of sustaining the eurozone in the medium and long term, given the likely persistence of asymmetric external shocks.

The fact that monetary union requires the establishment of a common monetary and exchange-rate policy, applied across the entire union, means that external shocks that impact upon individual economies in a significantly different manner than for the majority require different policy instruments in order to restore stability (Ingram, 1969; Haberler, 1970; Tower and Willett, 1970). Fiscal policy variations between member countries can potentially offset nationally based disequilibria, but the constraints imposed by the convergence criteria effectively limit what can be achieved on a national basis. In any case, the argument for greater macroeconomic-policy coordination is independent of whether a monetary union exists: namely, that a more efficient outcome results if all countries affected by a given shock respond in an optimum manner. For example, if France suffers a negative shock that reduces its competitiveness and increases unemployment, whilst Germany experiences the opposite effect (an increase in competitiveness and an over-tight labour market), mutual benefit flows from a coordinated policy response by both countries. In this case, Germany would raise taxes or reduce government spending in order to prevent inflationary pressure, whilst France would reflate its economy. If fiscal federalism existed, part of the resources needed for such reflation could be transferred from Germany to France, thereby enhancing the stabilisation of the union between them. However, although the need for an 'economic' as well as monetary union is recognised by the TEU, its only practical applications thus far have been the continuation of European Monetary System (EMS) membership until monetary union and the SGP.

The similarity of inflation rates focuses upon the significance of divergent trends in national inflation rates as a source of balance-of-payments problems. Diverse price changes impacting upon national competitiveness arise from a variety of potential causes, including: differences in national propensities for trade-union wage militancy, acute shortages of highly trained employees or differences in investment rates and, therefore, industrial-capacity growth (Haberler, 1970; Fleming, 1971; Magnifico, 1973). The architects of the eurozone were aware of the danger and included this target as one of the five convergence criteria. Moreover, Exchange Rate Mechanism (ERM) membership resulted in most EU member states adapting their economic strategies in order to achieve similar inflation rates, particularly during the 1980s, when the mechanism was reinterpreted as a means of achieving monetary union through the absence of further realignments. This strategy was partially successful, with average EU inflation rates declining from 10.7% during the 1970s to 6.5% in the following decade and declining further during the 1990s, with the variance between most EU member states also declining dramatically during this period.

When prices and wages are flexible between regions, adjustment to destabilising shocks is less likely to be associated with unemployment in one region and inflation in another. The need for exchange-rate changes is diminished, because wage–price flexibility takes the place of exchange-rate variations in maintaining a competitive balance between countries (Friedman, 1953). However, available evidence indicates that substantial wage–price rigidity persists across Europe, so that market flexibility is unlikely to restore former competitiveness, neither easily nor quickly. As a result, wage–price flexibility cannot prevent the generation of areas blighted by high and persistent unemployment, a fact confirmed by the large literature concerning nominal and real-wage rigidity in Europe (Bruno and Sachs, 1985; Eichengreen, 1990, 1993 and 1997; Bini-Smaghi and Vori, 1992; Blanchard and Katz, 1992). If wage–price rigidity prevents an immediate and full restoration of former competitiveness, output will fall and unemployment will rise, until wage reductions, or at least slower wage growth, enhance competitiveness. However, the country in question may suffer from the dual problems of persistent high unemployment and a decline in incomes for its citizens relative to the monetary union as a whole.

The need for real exchange-rate variability is regarded as important since it measures the shifts in a nation's competitiveness. Thus, when a country participates in a monetary union, and its nominal exchange rate is fixed at a given value relative to those of other members, the real exchange rate denotes whether that country (now a region of the monetary union) remains competitive over time. A negative shift in competitiveness will typically cause a deterioration in the balance of payments. However, in the absence of any changes permitted in the nominal exchange rate, a lack of competitiveness could result in areas of high, persistent unemployment. The only available method of reducing the real exchange rate, and thereby restoring competitiveness, is to reduce relative prices. This could be achieved over time if investment in capital and education produced a new competitive edge. However, a more immediate method would be to reduce relative wages, leading to lower income growth than in the rest of the monetary union. The smallness of countries' real exchange-rate movements is a crucial characteristic for determining currency-area optimality, because real exchange-rate changes are clearly measurable and automatically give the appropriate weights to the economic forces of which they are the result (Vaubel, 1976, 1978).

In contrast to the preceding discussion, the endogeneity hypothesis of OCA theory emphasises the positive relationship between monetary integration and economic convergence. This somewhat 'optimistic view' argues that further economic and monetary integration can lead to less divergence among members of a currency union (Frankel and Rose, 1997). In other words, the business cycles' synchronisation will improve among member states after the creation of the union; therefore, the cost of not having their own national-level monetary policy, which could be used for adjusting internal imbalance, is minimised. This theory can be interpreted as: Once a country enters a common-currency area, (even if it did not satisfy the criteria ex ante), eventually, through economic integration such as improvements in intra-union trading relationships, the country can satisfy the criteria ex post. This argument implies that even if monetary union is established with non-optimal members, it will still shift towards an optimal currency area through continued economic interaction, and over time the single monetary policy is more likely to be appropriate union-wide.

In particular, with the creation of the currency union and removal of trading barriers (such as custom and border controls, exchange-rate uncertainty and transaction costs), then the correlation among movements of key business-cycle variables (e.g., GDP, consumption, exports and imports) will increase if intra-union trade prevails or common demand shocks prevail

(Frankel and Rose, 1997; Frankel, 1999; De Grauwe and Mongelli, 2005). This implies that the international trade-pattern and international business-cycle correlation are endogenous and based on a forward-looking model, where the principle foundation of the endogeneity hypothesis is built upon the Lucas critique (Lucas, 1976), which states that a prediction based on historical data, especially highly aggregated data, would be invalid if the relationship between relevant variables can be altered by the conducting of economic policies. If the policy change alters the relationship between the variables, then the future relationship between the variables may not be fully represented by the historical relationship.

Empirical studies suggest that the endogeneity hypothesis is pronounced for the EU where increasing bilateral trade integration shifted countries towards a universal business cycle (Artis and Zhang, 1995; Baxter and Koupartitas, 2005). Although a more succinct view that confirms the endogeneity hypothesis is that, it is not the increase of trade that affects convergence, but it is the increase in structural similarities of foreign trade that does so (Fidrmuc, 2004). With reference to monetary union, studies have shown that adoption of the single currency can lead to a significant improvement in the volume of trade among members, thereby providing the fundamental ground for the endogeneity hypothesis (Rose, 2000; Persson, 2001; Mélitz, 2001; Glick and Rose, 2002).

However, in contrast to these pro-endogeneity OCA theory studies, the counter-endogeneity view is represented by the specialisation hypothesis (Bayoumi and Eichengreen, 1992, 1996; Krugman, 1993), arguing that trade integration will enhance the specialisation of each country's production since countries will tend to export more of those goods where they possess a comparative advantage. This, in turn, will reduce the income correlation such that even if the country did not fully satisfy OCA criteria before they joined the monetary union, then trade integration may not generate a move towards satisfaction ex post. For example, Krugman (1993) applies data from North America that indicates the increase in trade integration leads to increases in divergence rather than to rising in income correlation and economic convergence. Furthermore, another counter-argument that works in similar fashion suggests that monetary integration may not generate the correlation of business cycles, focusing on the costs of loss of exchange-rate policy. For instance, under a fixed exchange-rate regime, the central bank is required to maintain its peg on the objective currency, or within a currency union it will lose its monetary sovereignty. Consequently, for asymmetric shocks the exchange rate as a shock-absorbing mechanism is no longer available, thus adjustments take place in the real economy rather than via the exchange rate (Baxter and Stockman, 1989; Bordo and Helbling, 2003; Bergman, 2004).

In summary, although the eurozone does not fully meet the criteria in terms of traditional OCA theory, the modern view/endogeneity hypotheses of OCA theory has provided a theoretical argument for creating a monetary union even amongst seemingly non-optimal members. This theory suggests that even if a currency union fails to satisfy OCA criteria ex ante, then trade integration among member states can improve the situation ex post. This implies that improvements in synchronisation of business cycles through intra-trade in the eurozone can eventually solve the 'one-size-fits-all' monetary policy issue. Therefore, this may reflect some possibilities for improved convergence of members' economies; however, there also remains the possibility that the eurozone remains as a currency union with low levels of co-movement of the overall economic activities across the membership. Hence, it is important to the policymaker to review the issue of synchronisation of business cycles in the eurozone – especially, to understand whether there are grounds for the implementing a successfully single monetary policy.

Synchronicity of the eurozone business cycle

In addition to considering the above dimensions of OCA, the key focus for many economists is measuring business-cycle synchronisation, where researchers have employed two broad categories of techniques: the correlation method and the shock-accounting approach. The former evaluates the degree of business-cycle convergence by testing whether key output variables (e.g., GDP or industrial production) for the pair of objective countries are moving together in the same direction. The most commonly adopted approaches of correlation method are: the dynamic correlation measure (Croux et al., 2001), the concordance index (Harding and Pagan, 2002) and the phase-adjusted correlations method (Koopman and Azevedo, 2003). In relation to empirical analysis utilising these methods, Fatás (1997) concluded that during the period 1966–2002 the correlation of business cycles of the EU12 were higher during the post-EMS period than pre-EMS; similarly, Artis and Zhang (1999) found that the European business cycle had become more alike after the creation of the ERM. However, their result was contradicted by Inklaar and de Haan (2001) to the extent that the business cycles of European economies are better correlated with Germany alone, whilst correlation is higher during 1971–1979 than the later period of 1979–1987, therefore indicating no evidence to suggest that business cycles became more synchronised after the establishment of the ERM in 1979.

In relation to eurozone members, Agresti and Mojon (2001) and Belo (2001), using GDP as the measure of cycles, report a high and increasing correlation of business cycles over time; however, Massmann and Mitchell (2004), using monthly industrial production data, again found business-cycle convergence has been mixed over the last four decades, albeit with positive mean correlation on average. Studies covering shorter sample sizes – for example from 1980s to the early 2000s – have found evidence to show that the business-cycle synchronisation was improved during the run-up to the eurozone in the 1990s (Altavilla, 2004; Darvas and Szapary, 2004). In addition to the estimation of correlation there is the issue of the volatility and persistence of the cycle. For example, Darvas and Szpary (2004) suggested that the core eurozone members (i.e., France, Germany, Italy, the Netherlands, Austria and Belgium) possess a higher degree of business-cycle convergence than do other members, where those with the lowest level of correlation were Ireland, Finland and Portugal. Finally, in the more recent literature, Camacho et al. (2008) evaluate the synchronisation of European countries over the period 1960–2004, finding evidence against the argument that no common business cycle exists in either the EU or the eurozone.

However, the correlation methods for both parametric and non-parametric approaches fail to consider the 'drive' element of business cycles; therefore, although correlation methods are able to answer the question as to whether the cycles become similar, these methods are incapable of investigating the factors that may contribute to the convergence of business cycles. Hence, alternative approaches – such as the shock-accounting method based on the Vector Autoregressive (VAR) model and the Dynamic Factor Model (DFM) – are used to answer this issue. For example, Beine et al. (2003) applied a time-series VAR model with 23 years of monthly industrial production data, but failed to find the existence of common cyclical movements amongst leading eurozone countries (Austria, Belgium, France, Germany and the Netherlands); whilst Artis et al. (2004) also reach a similar conclusion by using GDP as the indicator of synchronisation, concluding that the European business cycle is rather an elusive phenomenon.

In contrast, Monfort et al. (2003) adopt the DFM with a selection of quarterly GDP data for G7 countries over the period 1970–2002, with France, Germany and Italy forming a coherent area distinct from the others. Similarly, Lumsdaine and Prasad (2003), using a large monthly industrial production dataset from 1963–1994 finds that for eurozone countries the correlation with the European component is much stronger than the correlation with the world component. In contrast, Kose et al. (2003), using variable of output and its key components (i.e., consumption and investment) with a time period similar to that of Lumsdaine and Prasad (2003), found that the common European factors have only a minor impact on the fluctuations of European aggregates, implying that there is no evidence of a European cycle. From a different perspective, Sidschlag and Tondl (2011) analyse the impact of trade integration and specialisation on business-cycle synchronisation and find that deeper trade integration within the eurozone has had a pronounced direct positive effect on the synchronisation of regional output growth, even though industrial specialisation was a source of cyclical divergence. Additionally, Giannone et al. (2010) and Lehwald (2012) reached similar conclusions in emphasising that business-cycle convergence diverged between the core and periphery groups; more specifically, Lee (2012) found that output and inflation among eurozone members was moving towards synchronisation during the run-up period of its creation; however, there is little evidence to show the eurozone factor still prevailed after the implementation of the single currency. Overall, the evidence on business-cycle synchronization across the eurozone is mixed, with results seeming to be sensitive depending on the periods specified and the benchmark used; however, most of the current evidence suggests that periods of greater and lesser synchronization tend to alternate.

Conclusion

This chapter discusses the theoretical background to the concept of the eurozone, where the process of the eurozone is a step along a theoretical road in terms of exchange-rate regimes. Although its practical consequences in terms of both economic and political national sovereignty are substantial and, therefore, these practical implications require deep analysis, the adoption of any exchange-rate regime is not a decision for any country to take lightly. Hence, the first part of this chapter reviewed the cost–benefit calculation required by participating member states. We summarised the principal advantages and disadvantages of joining a single-currency system, which in essence is the ultimate form of fixed exchange rates. There are, however, several complications to what appears to be a simple trade-off optimisation problem. Firstly, the various costs and benefits need to be assessed within the context of both the potential partner country and in relation to the already-established monetary union or to the other prospective members. Each economy is unique in its blend of sectoral strengths and weaknesses and comparative advantage; therefore, the national interest will be distinctively different for each potential participant. Secondly, there is no set rule with which to weigh the relative merits of the arguments associated with membership of a monetary union. Again, the above consideration of relative strengths and weaknesses needs to be taken into account. Thus, the final arbitration of decision making will be a political process rather than an economic one.

The decision whether to join the eurozone must depend upon an analysis of membership's probable benefits and costs. Economic theory suggests that a monetary union will prove generally beneficial, and be sustainable over time, if the participants are sufficiently converged *before* they enter. Thus, it is necessary to establish an unambiguous, comprehensive and theoretically sound set of convergence criteria that can indicate whether such convergence has occurred prior to participation. However, the decision on whether countries should participate carries further consequences, whereby the advantages of low inflation and high employment could be obtained by pursuing coherent domestic economic policies, whilst European co-operation may be undermined more effectively by increasing national divergences within a eurozone governed by inflexible rules rather than by countries opting out.

For example, even a cursory examination of available evidence suggests that the Central and Eastern Europe countries are not obvious candidates for monetary union without their first undertaking major structural changes – which are likely to take decades to complete. Such a situation could lead to the opposite outcome to that envisaged by the proponents; however, if participation is considered to be in the national interest, economic theory demonstrates that membership should await the achievement of prior convergence; optimum currency-area theory provides the tests to establish the validity of convergence. Unless these tests can be attained, monetary union could prove damaging to the existing and future eurozone countries, as a combination of external shocks to the system and a destabilising common monetary policy exacerbate existing differences between economies. Even the more 'the euro-zone-friendly' endogeneity approach to OCA again fails to provide a definitive set of criteria, whilst the empirical literature indicates that business-cycle convergence is fleeting at best and highly sensitive to the parameters of the study. Whilst such imprecision generates a multitude of possibilities for further research, this is of little comfort for any economies that find themselves within a system (such as the eurozone) without adequate release or policy mechanisms to counterbalance asymmetric shocks – as the eurozone crisis has unfortunately already demonstrated.

Part II

Contemporary Economic Policymaking

5
Rules and Institutions in International Monetary Systems

Introduction

In its present form, the eurozone is without precedent in the history of the civilised world. There has never been an economic and monetary union of a group of countries without a simultaneous movement towards political union, although a number of attempts have been undertaken to secure the greater predictability that a fixed exchange-rate regime can provide, the aim being to reduce exchange-rate risk and hence promote trade, investment and ultimately economic growth. The most successful fixed rate regimes, the classical gold standard and Bretton Woods, each helped to establish an international economic environment that facilitated decades of economic expansion, before a combination of political and economic factors forced their ultimate termination. However, a badly constructed fixed exchange-rate system – such as the 1920s return to the gold standard on pre-First World War parities or the United Kingdom's experience of ERM membership at too high a parity – has been associated with economic recession, bankruptcies, housing price collapses and mass unemployment. Consequently, whilst a properly constructed system can be a benefit to participating countries, a badly designed regime can cause its members untold damage. The importance of this point is reinforced by the fact that eurozone membership is intended to be an irrevocable act, with the TEU deliberately failing to specify a means by which a member state might exit the arrangement in the future. It is intended to be a one-way shift towards further economic integration. Consequently, even greater emphasis is placed upon the estimated balance of costs and benefits by which a country decides whether or not to participate in this unique currency arrangement.

In order to fully understand what is involved in joining the single currency, we must first establish why the exchange rate is an important macroeconomic policy instrument. The exchange rate acts as a price like any other; it is the price of one country's currency when translated into the currency of another for the purposes of international trade and financial movements. If the demand for sterling exceeds supply, the price rises (sterling appreciates in value). Alternatively, If the supply of sterling exceeds demand, the price falls (sterling depreciates) and is worth less in foreign currency. The appreciation of sterling benefits British citizens wishing to take a foreign holiday and those purchasing cheaper imports, but disadvantages those whose jobs depend upon British exports, the price of which is higher when valued in foreign currency. Consequently, changes in the value of one currency in terms of another can exert a decisive impact upon prices, balance of payments and employment.

Supporters of a single currency have, therefore, argued that by permanently fixing European currency exchange rates, uncertainty would be reduced, thereby stimulating trade between EU countries and, in the process, facilitating investment together with an expansion in output and employment. This apparently plausible argument is, however, based upon a number of questionable assumptions. For example, whilst it is undoubtedly true that a relatively stable environment encourages international trade and investment, the experience of the past quarter of a century has demonstrated that a dramatic increase in internationalisation can occur without the 'assistance' of a fixed exchange-rate regime. Indeed, history also demonstrates that an exchange-rate regime that is too rigid will, over a long period of time, inevitably collapse because it prevents individual economies adjusting to the divergent impact upon production and employment structures caused by external shocks and changes in the pattern of demand for specific product ranges.

Exchange-rate regimes

The main issue of debate concerning exchange-rate regimes regards the case for or against greater flexibility. In other words, the question is: Where, over this spectrum, lies the 'ideal' exchange-rate mechanism? Unfortunately, there is no simple or conclusive answer to this problem, with each set of arguments possessing its own merits. Moreover, in the dynamic modern world of ever-greater globalisation, the 'ideal' exchange-rate regime can change over time, depending upon the domestic economic circumstances of the country involved and the global economic environment in which it finds itself. Most policymakers would agree that, in general, the 'ideal' situation is for the exchange rate to possess short-term stability, but long-term flexibility. This offers the best possible environment for business, investment and trade – which prefer stability – whilst not locking the country into an exchange-rate position that may prove harmful in the long-run as national, regional and global economic circumstances change over time (Baimbridge and Whyman, 2008).

Hence, a key aspect of such international monetary arrangements is the choice of exchange-rate regime, which centres on the issue of flexibility

(Ghosh et al., 2002; Sarno and Taylor, 2002), where perhaps the most popular argument in favour of floating exchange rates can be summed up by the expression, 'The market knows best'. 'Best' here implies that a competitive foreign-exchange market would be a more efficient means of achieving balance-of-payments equilibrium and adjustments of the exchange rate over time. However, it may also reflect normative preferences that market mechanisms are more desirable than leaving decisions to government officials and/ or monetary authorities. A second argument notes that exchange rates always adjust to ensure continuous equilibrium between the demand and supply of the currency. Thus, based upon the current-account theory, an efficient market-clearing mechanism quickly eliminates temporary disequilibrium positions. Excess demand for a currency leads to its appreciation, thereby making imports cheaper and exports more expensive, and consequently reduces the excess demand for the currency as imports rise and exports fall. Similarly, excess supply of a currency leads to its fall in value, making exports cheaper and imports more expensive and, therefore, stimulating demand for the currency through higher exports and lower imports. No one expects the adjustment process to be quite as smooth as this. However, if arbitrage and speculation are stabilising, it provides an efficient and automatic solution to the balance-of-payments problems (Baimbridge and Whyman, 2008).

Furthermore, floating exchange rates enable countries to operate independent monetary policies. According to this viewpoint, floating is essential to restore monetary autonomy for each country – which would otherwise be constrained by an arbitrary exchange-rate target, thereby allowing it to determine its own employment and inflation rates. Under fixed systems, the need to maintain long-term competitiveness requires a country to achieve inflation rates essentially similar to other countries, thereby restricting the country from pursuing markedly different economic policies. Under fixed exchange-rate regimes, monetary policy is focused upon the maintenance of the exchange-rate parity and is therefore not available for other macroeconomic goals. This economic argument is also sometimes expanded to claim that this element of fixed exchange rates disempowers democracy since, for example, democratic decisions to pursue an economic strategy aimed at securing full employment would be derailed if inflation remained higher than elsewhere. A counter argument asserts that in a world of global financial capital flows and international money markets, monetary autonomy does not exist. This view holds that interest rates must move towards a world norm, which negates this criticism of fixed exchange rates to the extent that it is an accurate description of economic reality (Williamson and Milner, 1991). Additionally, interest rates may also partially insulate the domestic economy from foreign price shocks. If there is an increase in foreign prices under floating exchange rates – provided the exchange rate moves roughly in line with the fundamental balance of the economy, arguably expressed by the Purchasing Power Parity (PPP) relation – the domestic exchange rate would appreciate to prevent the importation of foreign inflation. Under a fixed exchange rate, the same scenario would leave the exchange rate over-competitive, thereby leading to increased demand for exports and stimulating domestic demand. Assuming the economy was already operating at full employment, this would cause inflation unless countered by compensatory fiscal or monetary measures. The more difficult scenario under fixed exchange rates is if the domestic exchange rate becomes uncompetitive. Instead of allowing a currency to depreciate, price and wage downward flexibility would be required to ensure a real depreciation (Williamson and Milner, 1991). This is a scenario that is difficult to achieve in the short term because of wage and price stickiness, and it would therefore be likely to require deflation and high unemployment. Under floating exchange rates some of this adjustment can be borne by changes in relative prices if the fall in the value of the currency allows expenditure switching to take place. This helps to cushion the country from deflationary pressures by making the rest of the world share some of the burden. Consequently, floating rates are deemed to be more conducive to economic stability because of their superior ability to adjust to external shocks and relative changes in domestic prices (Baimbridge and Whyman, 2008).

It is also argued that floating exchange rates release the balance-of-payments constraint on the growth of a country's economy in terms of simultaneously achieving both internal and external balance. The assumed advantage is that flexible exchange rates allow the government to 'forget' balance-of-payments problems, as they will automatically adjust themselves. In practice, flexible exchange rates have not eliminated the balance-of-payments constraint, as governments do not forget that deficits exist; it only makes external and internal economic management slightly easier. However, supporters of flexible exchange rates would argue that totally freely floating exchange rates have been given their chance. Finally, economies on foreign-exchange reserves could be achieved if the foreign-exchange market works efficiently under flexible exchange rates, because governments would not need to hold official reserves of foreign exchange (Williamson and Milner, 1991). Official 'accommodating transactions' are not required, as the exchange rate 'cures' the balance-of-payments deficit by falling in value in the foreign-exchange markets. Thus, the opportunity cost of holding foreign exchange reserves would be lower, thereby releasing considerable resources to finance alternative objectives, either stimulating consumption or investment in public and private sectors, or reducing domestic money supply and, therefore, inflationary pressure. This is especially important to less-developed countries, which may find that the necessity of holding extra reserves to cushion swings in the balance of payments to be high in terms of the development opportunities forgone by not being able to use these reserves to purchase scarce inputs from abroad. In reality, however, currency floating does not work perfectly; so governments still need to intervene to push the exchange rate in the required direction even if they are committed to floating. Nevertheless, even managed floating would probably require smaller foreign-exchange reserves than would a fixed exchange rate. Overall, these arguments were powerful enough in the 1970s and 1980s to tip the balance in favour of greater exchange-rate flexibility after a period (from before the First World War to after the Second World War) of almost continuous fixed rates. Nevertheless, there are some counter-arguments that are vociferously presented by those who believe that too much flexibility has been permitted and that a return to greater fixity would be appropriate (Williamson and Milner, 1991).

In contrast, the case against greater flexibility is supported by the suggestion that floating rates generate wider fluctuations in exchange rates, which increases uncertainty and leads to a contraction in the volume of international trade. Thus, fixed exchange rates should minimise uncertainty and, thereby, provide the optimum environment for international trade and productive investment. Small companies, in particular, will minimise their exposure to exchange-rate variations by either adding a premium to their prices to hedge against this risk (thereby reducing potential export sales) or concentrating upon domestic sales instead of expanding internationally. Creating a relatively stable trading environment will, therefore, stimulate international trade and investment. However, this argument is based upon the assumption that greater fluctuations in exchange value equate with greater uncertainty that will, in turn, depress trade flows. This is not, however, necessarily the case. Instability, in the broader sense of greater fluctuations in rates, is not the same thing as uncertainty, since regularly reversing fluctuations can be quite predictable. Moreover, fixed rates have also been frequently changed in practice and have often fluctuated quite strongly between certain limits. These changes could have been similarly off-putting for traders. Secondly, the transactors involved would have to be *risk averse* for the negative economic effects to occur, whereby traders are unwilling or unable to use forward markets to hedge the risks involved. Only if traders expect future exchange-rate movements to be unpredictable and are put off by the risks of fluctuations, will there then be adverse effects on the volume of trade.

A second argument against floating concerns its association with destabilising speculation. Speculation can be a stabilising influence upon exchange rates if speculators are able to calculate currency deviations from purchasing power parity rates and consequently speculate that they will return towards this long-term underlying rate. If, however, they guess wrongly or are unable to accurately assess the currency value most accurately expressing the underlying international competitive strength, then speculation will be destabilising and the currency will fluctuate more than it would have done otherwise. However, it must be stressed that speculation can be rife under fixed exchange rates if it is abundantly clear that the economy is suffering from 'fundamental disequilibrium' and that devaluation is imminent. Such was the situation before sterling's forced exit from the ERM, when speculators believed (rightly) that the pound was over-valued. These speculators were able to sell at the guaranteed fixed rate (since sterling had fallen to the lowest allowable value within its band) on the basis that, were they to be wrong, they could re-purchase the currency in the future at approximately the same rate, having to pay only the small commission charges that are charged for large volume transactions. Additionally, flexibility of the exchange rates is claimed to result in greater inflationary pressures on the domestic economy. If the value of the currency falls, this raises import prices and may result in 'cost-push' inflation, whilst an appreciation of the currency is unlikely to be passed on in the form of lower prices. Thus, there is an in-built 'ratchet' effect under flexible exchange rates. Furthermore, 'demand-pull' inflation is also possible if the economy is unable to respond rapidly (i.e., too inelastic supply) if a depreciation of the currency increases exporters' incomes.

Fixed rates may provide a greater degree of discipline upon government macroeconomic policies than a floating regime is able to exert. If a balance-of-payments deficit occurs under fixed exchange rates, a country must either be borrowing or running down reserves, thereby making the deficit immediately visible and leading to prompt corrective action. A flexible regime enables the authorities to delay corrective measures, since currency depreciation may mask the worst effect of this process; however, the country may suffer inflationary consequences as a result. A related issue is that fixed rates, by their nature, depend upon a degree of international co-operation and co-ordination between countries that is typically lacking under alternative floating regimes. At a minimum, fixed exchange-rate regimes require agreement to avoid damaging competitive devaluation's undermining the exchange-rate arrangement, such as occurred in the 1930s, and to negotiate rules preventing realignment apart from explicitly sanctioned scenarios, such as fundamental disequilibrium. At best, fixed exchange-rate regimes could facilitate macroeconomic co-ordination between participating nations, such as the G7 efforts in the late 1970s and the EU member states under the EMS regime. Co-ordinated reflation or deflation could minimise leakages and thereby enhance the success of the initiative. One final argument for fixed rates is that, if an economy is fairly rigid in the sense that resources are relatively immobile, then changes in the foreign-exchange market may not result in the necessary changes in trade flows for the balance of payments to be in a position of equilibrium. Devaluation (to stimulate export demand) requires producers to take advantage of their new competitive position by reducing prices abroad and increasing output. However, they may choose to maintain prices and reap higher profits, which blunts devaluation as a means of reducing unemployment. Alternatively, variation in exchange rates may be an attempt to use market prices to signal the need for one sector of the economy to expand relative to others. However, sticky prices and wages, particularly the latter, may frustrate this mechanism.

This is largely a reiteration of the structuralist school of thought, which has relatively little faith in market clearing. A counter argument asserts that exchange-rate adjustments can be effective, with those made by Britain in 1931, 1949 and 1992 having boosted exports, growth and production without triggering an inflationary spiral.

Alternative international monetary systems

The eurozone is the latest experiment in designing an international monetary system, although it has been on the drawing board of the architects for EU integration even prior to Treaties of Rome in 1957. International monetary systems are broadly defined as the set of conventions, rules, procedures and institutions that govern the conduct of financial relations between nations. The need for them derives from the inherent interdependence of open national economies, and different systems are designed to support specific forms of trade and economic development (Foreman-Peck, 1995). However, the design of international monetary systems has a considerable influence upon the ability of national economies to achieve their goals of maintaining internal and external balance. Moreover, it is interesting to note that since the industrial revolution there has been a movement away from fixed towards more flexible exchange-rate regimes for the industrialised world. This trend, however, now appears to be in reverse for the membership of the EU, where the European Exchange Rate Mechanism (ERM) of the European Monetary System (EMS) was a distinct shift back to less flexible exchange rates between the participating countries. Moreover, continuation along this path to the eurozone (with a single currency, the euro, being adopted for use) entailed the disappearance altogether of exchange rates between members.

The system of international monetary relations that had evolved by the late 19th century was a commodity money standard known as the classical gold standard (1870–1914). The historical origins of using gold as a medium of exchange derives from its use in ancient times and the more formal adoption of the gold standard in Britain in 1819, when Parliament resumed its practice of exchanging currency notes for gold on demand at a fixed rate. As the decade continued, Germany, Japan and other countries adopted the gold standard (rather than the alternative silver standard) as the basis for their currency exchange, with the United States joining in 1879. The essence of the gold standard was that each participating country was obliged to fix its currency in terms of gold. Consequently, national currencies were then fixed to each other. Since the exchange rate was fixed to gold, the money supply was restricted by the supply of gold. Prices could still rise and fall in relation to economic booms and slumps, but the tendency was for a return to a long-term stable level. As long as the gold stock grew at a steady rate, prices would follow a steady path; new discoveries of gold would cause discontinuous shifts in the price level. In order for the gold standard to operate in this way, a number of conditions had to be fulfilled: gold had to be acceptable as international money; governments had to be prepared to provide gold on demand in unlimited quantities at a fixed price and no restrictions could be placed on the import or export of gold.

It was especially important that governments obeyed the 'rules' and did not respond to a gold loss resulting from a BOP deficit by issuing more money, or otherwise 'sterilising' the contractionary effects of the gold loss on the domestic money supply. After about 1870 these conditions were sufficiently fulfilled for the major trading countries that an international monetary system based upon the gold standard could be said to be in operation. In particular, central banks were given the responsibility to preserve the parity of the nation's currency relative to gold. To fulfil this aim, central banks required an adequate stock of gold. Consequently, policy makers did not view external balance in terms of a current account target, but rather concerning whether the central bank was either gaining or losing gold to foreigners at too fast a rate. Since international trade flows were based upon the gold standard, shipments of gold from a deficit nation to a surplus nation were required to finance the trade gap. For the deficit nation, this outflow of gold reserves would lower the gold supply and, through the quantity theory of money, reduce the aggregate price level. This would make the deficit country's exports more competitive and imports more expensive, thereby improving the balance-of-payments situation. Simultaneously, the surplus country would receive an inflow of gold, thereby increasing money supply and inflation and subsequently weakening competitiveness, thus reducing the balance-of-payments surplus. It is important to note that the classical gold standard mechanism assumed that both countries adjusted to restore balance-of-payments equilibrium. Nevertheless, it was deficit countries that had the most immediate incentives to act, since their loss of gold meant that they might be unable to meet their obligation to redeem currency notes on demand.

In practice, the gold standard was relatively efficient, providing relatively stable exchange rates that helped to stimulate expanding international trade and factor mobility. However, the reality was that the gold standard worked rather differently than the pure model had suggested. For example, the assumption that adjustment to temporary balance-of-payments disequilibria would take the form of price adjustments appeared to be less pronounced than income adjustments, where a deficit typically caused a contraction in income and employment rather than a fall in prices and wages. Thus, the balance of payments was improved by a derived fall in import spending rather than an improvement in competitiveness. Secondly, relatively little gold actually flowed between countries because monetary authorities preferred to raise interest rates to attract foreign capital in order to improve a balance-of-payments deficit, rather than allowing the outflow of gold to contract the money supply. Thus, the adjustment occurred on the capital account rather than through the reduction in domestic prices. In practice, gold was not so much the principal medium of exchange as it was a reserve asset against which domestic banks issued a much larger quantity of money in the form of cash and bank deposits. Indeed, the decisive reason why the classical gold standard worked so well was probably because the late 19th century was a period of relatively free trade and economic expansion, such that most countries managed to expand without experiencing significant balance-of-payments problems. As such, the gold standard worked well largely because of the favourable prevailing economic environment.

The modified gold standard (1925–1931) was introduced in post-First World War Europe because of the apparent success of the classical gold standard. The new system should accurately be described as a *partial* gold exchange standard since smaller countries could hold the currencies of several large countries as reserves. These large countries would remain fixed to gold; hence the smaller countries would be linked to gold through this indirect association. One attraction for returning to a version of the gold standard was the hyperinflation prevailing in many European states in the early 1920s, with Germany the worst example. In the aftermath of a devastating world war, and with hyperinflation undermining what little confidence remained in the future, the desire to restore former economic stability, by reconstructing the gold standard, was understandable. Accordingly, the United States returned to the gold standard in 1919, followed by Britain and most other industrialised nations by 1925. However, the ultimately disastrous decision to return on the basis of pre-war exchange-rate parities undermined any chance of success. This decision was taken because of a fundamental misunderstanding of how the gold standard worked in the 19th century.

For the post-war policy makers, the gold standard had represented a period of relatively stable exchange rates during which countries had confidence in gold as the unit of account. Moreover, the classical interpretation of the adjustment mechanism had promoted minimal government intervention and seemed to offer a 'fair' way to settle payments imbalances by making deficit countries take the necessary domestic action to cure their own payments imbalances. Unfortunately, however, the war had fundamentally altered the balance of economic power in the world, which was reflected in the growing strength of the United States and the relative decline of Britain and France. Thus, pre-war exchange-rate parities were seriously out of line with economic realities, with sterling about 10% overvalued in 1925 and the French franc seriously undervalued. Since, under the logic of the gold standard a deficit country was obliged to deflate its prices and wages to restore external balance, Britain was forced into a severe contraction from 1925 onwards in order to re-establish competitiveness in a situation in which export prices were something in the region of 10% overpriced and imports 10% underpriced. In addition, the degree of common commitment to the gold standard rules, which had worked fairly well in the previous century, had diminished after the war. Moreover, adjustment costs were underestimated by participating nations that, when the full burden was experienced, preferred to use alternative methods to restore balance-of-payments equilibrium. Governments were now more concerned with maintaining internal balance, and the United States, in particular, was not averse to sterilising any inflow of gold as a means of containing domestic inflation. The determination of the United States to avoid inflationary pressures by deflating its economy made the adjustment process more painful for deficit nations since they needed to deflate their economies faster than the United States to restore trade balance. This led to a degree of competitive deflation, with disastrous consequences for internal balance. Downward rigidity of prices and wages compounded this still further by making deflation less effective, requiring higher rates of unemployment than previously in order to restore external balance and maintain fixed exchange-rate parities. Thus, a combination of wartime inflation, which had changed the exchange-rate parities required by economic fundamentals, and a deterioration in commitment to the adjustment mechanism imposed by the gold standard, led to the collapse of the modified gold standard.

As early as 1941, the Allies (especially the United Kingdom and United States) decided to cooperate on changes in the international monetary system with the clear intention of establishing a set of rules and institutions that would replace the chaotic system that had operated during the 1930s. Their objective was to agree the articles to three new institutions: the International Bank for Reconstruction and Development (IBRD) to ensure the availability of long-term investment finance to speed recovery in post-war Europe; the International Monetary Fund (IMF) to act as a supervisory body of monetary arrangements; and the International Trade Organisation (ITO) to reduce the level of world protectionism that had grown in the pre-war international economy. However, the Bretton Woods system was not merely the restoration of a workable system along the lines of the gold standard, but one that restored currency convertibility (i.e., confidence) and removed the dislocation and protectionism of the 1930s. This system did so with more built-in flexibility than the gold standard provided. What was at stake was not just another set of exchange-rate arrangements, but a set of rules by which payments imbalances between countries could be equitably settled and, at the same time, could promote the growth of international trade. More specifically, the objectives were to return to a fixed exchange-rate system, but with a degree of flexibility (+/− 1%) greater than under the previous gold standards, to: facilitate short-term assistance for balance of payments, that is, countries undergoing temporary crisis on BOP; reduce protectionism; and encourage countries to achieve domestic goals (i.e., full employment) within the context of freer trade and factor mobility.

In terms of exchange rates, the actual outcome of the Bretton Woods conference was very different from what had been conceptualised (Gavin, 1996), whereby instead of the participants creating a system of equal currencies, the U.S. dollar emerged as being the 'numeraire' of the system as the U.S. Treasury pegged the price of the dollar to gold at $35 per ounce such that it was to act as a reserve asset (Hall et al., 2011). However, as far as other countries were concerned, the link with gold was broken because they were obliged to defend their currencies only by buying and selling dollars. In effect the dollar was fixed in terms of gold, but other currencies were tied to the dollar directly, or sometimes indirectly, through another reserve currency such as sterling. This meant that the system was akin to the gold exchange standard as countries were willing to hold much of their reserves in dollars because they were confident that the dollar would retain its value in terms of other currencies and would remain convertible into gold. Gold was, therefore, viewed as a reserve asset rather than as an international currency. As far as the exchange-rate system was concerned, each country declared its par rate in terms of gold, but the authorities operated an adjustable peg exchange-rate mechanism (Blokker and Muller, 1994). Although the point was to combine the advantages of a fixed exchange-rate system with more flexibility than was allowed under the gold standard, the Bretton Woods system progressively became more of a gold–dollar system, resembling features with the gold exchange standard, and thus allowing for the re-emergence of the problems experienced in the interwar period (Bordo, 1993).

However, if national currencies moved outside of their parity range, governments were obliged to change policy through, for example, buying their own currency, undertaking expenditure-changing policies, borrowing from the IMF or pursuing any combination of these. Furthermore, if a country was in a position of 'fundamental disequilibrium' then it could, with IMF agreement, alter the fixed exchange-rate parity outside the original limits (Dominguez, 1993). The process of adjustment thus envisaged was that temporary imbalances would be financed from reserves or borrowing from the IMF, while more persistent imbalances would be cured by applying monetary and fiscal policies. Only if the domestic adjustments were considered likely to be large and persistent was there to be a change in the exchange rate outside the 1% limits either side of par. Exchange controls, however, were almost universally used to counter destabilising capital movements (Hall et al., 2011). The IMF saw itself primarily as a source of short-term assistance to overcome BOP problems and as the arbiter of an orderly system of exchange-rate adjustments. Each member was given a quota based upon a formula incorporating such factors as the size of its national income or its importance in international trade. This quota then determined the amount the country contributed to the IMF Fund that, in turn, defined the size of its potential borrowings and fixed its voting rights within the IMF's decision-making body. Deficit countries were permitted to withdraw foreign exchange by giving up their own currency in return, which they subsequently had to buy back when in a position to do so. These were known as 'tranches' of credit. However, the more a country borrowed, the greater the conditions attached to the loan by the IMF.

The Bretton Woods system did not operate effectively until the early 1950s, but thereafter proved highly successful until the mid-1960s mainly due to a combination of factors such as free international trade, a rapid expansion in trade and capital mobility, and sustained economic growth, meaning that individual countries did not experience too many problems. However, the system had within it a number of built-in contradictions. First, it had a fundamental weakness, since the expansion of international trade could only be maintained by a parallel expansion of international liquidity. However, the principal source of this liquidity, namely persistent U.S. balance-of-payments deficits, could not continue indefinitely. U.S. deficits were necessary for continued economic expansion, since they represented the only way that the growth in international reserves could be sustained in the absence of any other reserve asset, including gold. Participating countries wishing to expand their reserves, in line with the increase in trade value, could use dollars paid to them by the United States to finance its balance-of-payments deficit. However, if the U.S. deficit became too large, whilst its gold assets remained constant, it was only a matter of time before this would lead to a crisis of confidence in the U.S. commitment to convert dollars into gold at the fixed price ($35 per ounce). The question was whether the United States could guarantee to maintain the gold price if its gold assets remained constant. Either the United States had to correct its deficit and create a liquidity shortage, or foreign central banks that held dollars would lose confidence and demand conversion of their dollar holdings into gold, thereby pre-empting the collapse of the Bretton Woods system. Over time, U.S. dollar liabilities to the rest of the world increased faster than the addition to U.S. gold reserves by mining (Blanchard and SaKong, 2011).

Second, when there is a discrepancy between the official rate of exchange between two assets and their private market rate of exchange, the asset that is undervalued at the official rate will disappear from circulation, whilst the asset that is overvalued will continue in circulation. In other words, 'bad money drives out good money', the so-called law named after Sir Thomas Gresham (1519–1579). In the case of Bretton Woods, the two assets were gold and the U.S. dollar, with gold valued at $35 per ounce. Since U.S. inflation rose by some 40% between 1959 and 1969, the price of gold should have risen by a similar amount but did not since the fixed exchange-rate system required that it remain unchanged. Thus, the official price of gold became undervalued relative to the private value, meaning that central banks could have demanded conversion of their dollar holdings and made a profit selling the gold on the private market. To prevent this occurrence, the U.S. government secured an agreement with foreign banks not to convert their dollar holdings into gold, meaning that as of 1967, de facto, the dollar was no longer convertible (Rolnick and Weber, 1986). Furthermore, the central role of the dollar within the Bretton Woods system meant that it provided the majority of international liquidity. To acquire reserves, held in the form of dollars, participating nations needed to run balance-of-payments surpluses whilst the United States ran deficits, so the former would receive dollars the latter used to finance its trade deficit. Thus, the United States was able to print dollars that it exchanged with other nations for goods, services and assets (Prestowitz, 2004). Dollar treasury bills, typically yielding low rates of interest, would then be held as reserves by other nations whilst their purchasing power was gradually eroded by U.S. inflation. Hence, the United States was de facto borrowing from the rest of the world at very low real rates of interest (Aisen and Jos Veiga, 2005). This, whilst not itself proving a principal reason for the collapse of the Bretton Woods system, proved an irritant which undermined any resolve to save it.

Although Bretton Woods provided for exchange-rate realignment in the case of the 'fundamental disequilibrium' of a participating nation's balance of payments, in reality countries were extremely reluctant to devalue, revalue or implement macroeconomic policies consistent with ensuring a sustainable external balance (Grubel, 1977; Bordo and Eichengreen, 1993). The United States could not devalue, since it provided the cornerstone of the system, implying it had to implement deflationary policies to restrict the size of its balance-of-payments deficit. Not surprisingly it was reluctant to do so, and the inflationary effect of the Vietnam War further exacerbated this problem. Other countries preferred to avoid devaluation to solve balance-of-payments deficits, since this was perceived as a sign of weakness. Deflation was similarly avoided because of commitments to full employment and political considerations. Thus, the stability of the system depended upon surplus countries revaluing their currencies or expanding their economies (hence, importing a degree of inflation); however, countries such as Germany, Japan and Switzerland were reluctant to reduce their surpluses or risk inflation. The IMF articles did include a 'scarce currency' clause that would have permitted debtor countries to invoke penal measures against persistent surplus countries to force them to bear part of the burden of adjustment, but this was never invoked. Consequently, with neither deficit nor surplus countries willing to adjust their economies, a fixed exchange-rate system became untenable. Finally, the rapid growth of mobile, short-term capital made an already fragile fixed-rate system vulnerable to speculative movements. Balance of payments imbalances fuelled speculation that currency realignments were imminent, thereby increasing the pressure upon the system when it desperately required corrective measures to be taken to preserve the essence of the international monetary system. Any payments imbalances that persuaded capital holders that devaluation was imminent led to capital flight into currencies that seemed likely to appreciate. With a fixed set of currencies, speculation becomes a one-way bet, as a country with a balance-of-payments deficit will only devalue (Eichengreen and Wyplosz, 1995).

Hence, it is clear that the reasons for the fall of previous international monetary systems largely stemmed from countries failing to comply with rules and from the weaknesses of institutions. For significant periods of time these were masked by the general level of economic prosperity of the industrial revolution and post-Second World War recovery; however, once these positive externalities began to diminish, then the inherent deficiencies of these international monetary systems came to the forefront resulting in their demise. In terms of the Bretton Woods system, as the key supervisory body/institution, the IMF was responsible for maintaining exchange-rate stability but failed to achieve this because it could not enforce the requirements needed for the Bretton Woods system to succeed (World Gold Council, 2014). It neither took measures against surplus countries that were refusing to reduce surpluses by revaluing or expanding in order to aid deficit-suffering counterparts – which it could have done under the 'scarce currency' clause – nor was there any impetus put on deficit countries to deflate economies to address the imbalance. Hence, with the passive position it chose to undertake, the IMF was largely impotent in ensuring stability of the fixed exchange-rate system, although its structure partially explains the inadequate surveillance provided (Duggan, 2013; Tamny, 2013). For example, the fund structure of the IMF consisted of quotas assigned to member states reflecting relative economic power with a subscription proportionate to the quota. A quarter of this subscription had to be paid in gold, or currency convertible to gold, essentially meaning the dollar, which was the only currency directly convertible to gold (Chorev and Babb, 2009). This meant that the United States would have significant influence over the operations of the institution, which undoubtedly contributed to the passiveness of the IMF in questioning U.S. actions that ultimately destabilised the Bretton Woods system.

Conclusion

This chapter presented the background to the eurozone in relation to its being the latest in a series of attempts to devise international monetary systems since the advent of the Industrial Revolution; however, as history has repeatedly demonstrated, the ability of such systems to endure in both favourable and inclement economic climates is problematic. Whilst their architects have sought to rid, or at least minimise, the fault lines of successive systems, to date none have proved to be robust in the long term. Indeed, this harks back to the notion of the ideal exchange-rate system that results in a hybrid between the extremes of pure floating and fixed options, with the benefits of both and the disadvantages of neither. However, just as this has proved elusive, policymakers have instead pushed forward their attempts to develop more sophisticated international monetary frameworks encompassing the key elements of rules and institutions. Hence, the process of the eurozone is merely a step along a theoretical road in terms of exchange-rate regimes. Although its practical consequences are substantial in terms of both economic and political national sovereignty and, therefore, these practical implications require deep analysis, to the extent that the adoption of any exchange-rate regime is not a decision for any country to take lightly. Hence, the first part of this chapter summarises the arguments concerning the polar extremes of fixed and floating systems and, in particular, reviewed the development of adopted exchange-rate regimes. The lessons to be learnt from this historical experience are that the 'holy grail' of an ideal exchange-rate system is an elusive aspiration for policymakers: the key to understanding exchange-rate regimes is to realise their inherently temporary nature relative to the level of economic development experienced by the country in question and its main trading partners, together with the overall global trend in international monetary systems. Hence, the need for countries to maintain a degree of 'philosophical' flexibility given that an alternative regime might prove optimal as economic circumstances.

In relation to the eurozone, a similar cost–benefit calculation is required by states considering membership. We summarise the principal advantages and disadvantages of joining a single-currency system, which is in essence the ultimate form of fixed exchange rates. There are several complications to what appears as a simple trade-off optimisation problem. Firstly, the various cost and benefits need to be assessed within the context of both the potential partner country and in relation to the already-established monetary union or the other prospective members. Each economy is unique in its blend of sectoral strengths and weaknesses and comparative advantage; therefore the national interest will be distinctively different for each potential participant. Secondly, there is no set rule by which to weigh the relative merits of the arguments associated with membership of a monetary union. Again the above consideration of relative strengths and weaknesses need to be taken into account.

6
Fiscal Policy within the Eurozone

Introduction

As outlined in Chapter 3, the relationship between the economy and the political system has always attracted the interest of economists, since it is obvious that politics will influence the choice of economic policies and, consequently, economic performance. Of particular interest to macroeconomists is the influence that the interaction of political and economic factors has on such issues as business cycles, inflation, unemployment and the conduct and implementation of stabilisation policies together with the origin of persistent budget deficits.

Since the 2007–2008 financial crisis, countries worldwide have experienced deteriorated fiscal positions, particularly in the eurozone; Greece, notably, has witnessed a debt-to-GDP ratio of 165.3%, and a 9.2% budget deficit in 2011, with other peripheral countries facing similar circumstances. Such high public deficits and subsequent accumulations of debt have caused sustainability and default fears; this has compelled the 'troika' of the EU/IMF/ECB to provide bailout packages (Spiegel, 2012; Nag, 2012). Consequently, debate has been spurred regarding the causes of these fiscal positions and why supposedly implemented fiscal rules failed to prevent such debts (Featherstone, 2011). The study of the determinants of debt and deficits is not a new phenomenon; studies initially focused on the macroeconomic determinants of deficits, underpinned by Barro's (1979) tax-smoothing theory, which emphasised a normative approach (Pinho, 2004). However, accumulation of public debt in industrialised economies throughout the 1970s and 1980s called for the identification of determinants. Thus, studies evolved to incorporate political factors, such as opportunistic and partisan effects, which emphasised a positive approach to public debt and deficits (Svaljek, 1997).

With the creation of the eurozone, importance was placed on the ability of rules to prevent fiscal deterioration, where admission to the monetary union for member states was subject to the TEU convergence criteria and, subsequently, the Stability and Growth Pact (SGP) was enforced (Buiter, 2006). However, despite theoretical improvements, evidence indicated that many eurozone members failed to comply with the maximum 60% debt ratio and 3% deficit rules (Wierts, 2008); notably, Germany was the first to violate the 3% deficit rule in 2001, with France following in 2002, although no disciplinary action was taken (Nasad, 2012). The onset of the financial crisis exacerbated these positions and highlighted the fiscal difficulties experienced, with particular focus on southern members' vulnerability (i.e., Greece, Italy, Portugal and Spain) (Di Mascio and Natalini, 2012). This subsequently resulted in the 2013 Fiscal Compact Treaty, which reiterates fiscal discipline and aims to strengthen rules in the eurozone (Rooney, 2012), the efficacy of which we discuss in Chapter 9.

Political influences of economic stabilisation policy

Although classical economists did not deny that fluctuations in aggregate economic activity could occur, they believed that the self-correcting forces of the price mechanism would prevail and restore the system to full employment within an acceptable time period. However, by the mid-1920s Keynes was already expressing his disillusionment with this classical laissez-faire philosophy, such that the orthodox Keynesian view evolved out of the catastrophic experience of the Great Depression and suggested that market economies are inherently unstable. Consequently, this instability can and should be corrected by discretionary monetary and fiscal policies. However, economists soon challenged this rather naive assumption by presenting models of the electoral cycle whereby politicians compete for votes and thereby influence economic policies contributing to aggregate instability. This runs counter to traditional Keynesian models, which treat the government as exogenous to the circular flow of income and in which politicians are assumed to act in the interests of society, leading to an asymmetry in the application of Keynesian policies. Moreover, because voters do not understand that the government faces an intertemporal budget constraint, they underestimate the future tax liabilities of debt-financed expenditure programmes – that is, voters suffer from 'fiscal illusion'. Thus, given these considerations, it would seem that macroeconomists ought to consider the possibility that elected politicians may engage in economic manipulation for political profit. From a more modern new political economy perspective, policymakers are seen to be heavily influenced by powerful societal and state-centred forces rather than their acting impartially on the advice of economists. Therefore, the theoretical insights and policy advice economists can offer are mediated through a political system that reflects a balance of conflicting interests that inevitably arise in a country consisting of heterogeneous individuals. Hence, in modelling politico-economic relationships, the new political macroeconomics views the government as standing at the centre of the interaction between political and economic forces. Once this endogenous view of government is adopted, the welfare-maximizing approach to economic policy formulation associated with the normative approach is no longer logically possible (Snowdon and Vane, 2005).

Given the above ideas, the traditional Keynesian circular-flow model needs to be modified to take account of self-interested government behaviour creating a politico-economic system that results from this modification. However, in choosing to whom they will delegate decision-making power, voters are faced with a principal-agent problem since the agent (government) may have different preferences, which it can conceal from the imperfectly informed voters. Hence, within the politico-economic circular-flow model politicians are seen to be driven by a balance of both ideological and re-election considerations. Voters evaluate politicians on the basis of how successful they have been in achieving desirable economic goals; in particular, the state of the economy in the immediate pre-election period is crucial. Hence, economic conditions influence election results, and the incentive to get elected directly influences the choice and use of macroeconomic policies. Consequently, in the theoretical literature on the political business cycle we can distinguish four main approaches that have evolved in two separate phases. During the first phase, in the mid- to late 1970s, Nordhaus (1975) reawakened interest in this area by developing an opportunistic model of the political business cycle. This was followed by Hibbs (1977), who emphasised ideological (i.e., partisan) rather than office-motivated considerations. However, the Nordhaus and Hibbs models (the 'old' political macroeconomics) were swept aside during the rational-expectations revolution as Rogoff and Sibert (1988) developed rational-opportunistic models and Alesina (1987) produced a rational-partisan theory (the 'new' political macroeconomics).

In the wake of the rational-expectations revolution in macroeconomics, the models of the mid-1970s that incorporated adaptive expectations hypothesis were coming under heavy criticism from new classical theorists, as it implies that economic agents can make systematic errors. Hence, by the mid-1980s the literature on the relationship between politics and the macroeconomy underwent a significant revival as economists responded to the rational-expectations critique by producing a new generation of rational politico-economic models where economic agents are forward-looking. This makes it more difficult for the policymaker to manipulate real economic activity. Consequently, there is no exploitable short-run Phillips Curve that policymakers can use. Once the rational-expectations hypothesis is introduced, however, voters can be expected to recognize the incentives politicians have to manipulate the economy for electoral advantage. Thus, some of the insights of Nordhaus can survive even in a model with rational expectations, providing there is asymmetric information between voters and policymakers, so that forward-looking voters are not fully informed about some characteristics of the political and economic environment; hence, incumbents have the opportunity of creating a temporary illusion of prosperity in order to gain favour with the electorate.

In the rational-opportunistic models, electoral cycles are created in policy variables such as government spending, taxes and monetary growth, where such cycles are made possible by temporary information asymmetries. Although rational voters aim to choose politicians they believe can deliver the highest utility, they lack information on the competence of different policymakers – information voters acquire by observing outcomes. Therefore, before elections the incumbents engage in a 'signalling process' that aims to persuade voters that the politicians in power are competent. Consequently, rather than generating a regular inflation–unemployment cycle, as in the Nordhaus model, rational political business cycle theories predict the manipulation of various policy instruments before and after the election. The temptation of incumbents to cut taxes and increase spending before an election in order to appear competent clearly generates departures from optimality. Hence, opportunistic behaviour survives in rational-opportunistic models, although such models give rise to a different set of empirical predictions compared to the original Nordhaus model. In particular, because of rational expectations, any cycles resulting from the manipulation of monetary and fiscal policies will be predicted to be less regular and of shorter duration. Additionally, the assumption of rationality implies that since the output and employment effects of demand-management policies are only transitory in new classical models, then the identification of partisan influences on macroeconomic outcomes will be harder to detect. Furthermore, a significant problem for the partisan approach is the notion that low inflation is to the benefit of the poor more than to the rich – that is, that left-of-centre parties/voters would prefer lower unemployment at the cost of higher inflation.

Hence, following the rational-expectations revolution, theorists questioned the ability of policymakers to influence real economic activity by using aggregate-demand-management policies. However, the partisan theory of political business cycles can survive in models incorporating rational expectations providing that voters are uncertain about election outcomes, and noncontingent labour contracts are signed for discrete periods and are not subject to renegotiation after the election result is declared. Moreover, central to the rational-partisan theory is the idea that the political systems of many industrial democracies are polarised. In particular, the rational-partisan model emphasises the ideological preferences of politicians who aim to please their supporters by implementing policies that are likely to lead to a redistribution of income in their favour. Hence, the rational-partisan theory shows how parties follow different macroeconomic strategies because of their impact on the redistribution of income, whilst it is assumed that voters are well aware of these ideological differences between the parties. However, in this framework macroeconomic policies create short-run aggregate disturbances because rational voters are uncertain about election results. Overall, the more recent rational versions of politico-economic models of cycles have been much more successful empirically than the earlier models. In particular, partisan effects appear to be quite strong, while opportunistic effects appear to be small in magnitude and affect only certain policy instruments, particularly fiscal variables. However, there are a number of important weaknesses in the rational-partisan theory. Firstly, if the cyclical effects are due to the signing of wage contracts before an election, then one obvious solution is to delay the signing of contracts until the election result is known. This solution is, of course, not as applicable where the timing of elections is fixed endogenously. Secondly, in line with other models that assume nominal wage rigidity, the model implies a counter-cyclical real wage that is at odds with the stylised facts of the business cycle. Thirdly, there is a lack of microeconomic foundations in such models to explain the mechanism of nominal wage contracting. Fourthly, according to real business-cycle theorists, monetary policy cannot be used to produce real effects on output and employment, although the theorists agree that monetary growth determines the rate of inflation. Fifthly, in relation to hysteresis effects, if following an aggregate demand disturbance the natural rate properties of rational-partisan models do not hold, the political business cycle may be reversed. Sixthly, the empirical evidence suggests that monetary policy is not the source of political cycles in real variables. Finally, some theorists argue that partisan and opportunistic models are not incompatible and a more complete model should incorporate both influences.

This section has sought to introduce the idea of a relationship between the economy and the political system in terms of what is known as the 'new political macroeconomics'. In particular, this interrelationship has shifted from a view of politicians as largely exogenous to the economy, to one where they are regarded as endogenous. Consequently, it is now accepted that there is the possibility that politicians will set economic policy contrary to that required for stabilisation (as Keynes had originally envisaged), manipulating key macroeconomic variables to maximise their chances of re-election. While the importance given to political influences in causing aggregate instability in industrial democracies remains highly controversial, few commentators would challenge the view that politicians, faced with a regular election cycle, will tend to develop short-time horizons. The desire to be re-elected or regain office may lead politicians to pursue or promise an economic policy package which creates aggregate economic instability. If this line of argument is accepted, then it follows that what is needed is an institutional framework that creates an environment conducive to the more-frequent implementation of sustainable economic policies geared to longer-term objectives. The dilemma faced in industrial democracies is how, through institutional reform, to constrain the over-zealous short-term discretionary actions of politicians without threatening the basic principles of democratic government. Hence, the economic policymaking framework, particularly in relation to fiscal measures within the eurozone, is fundamentally based upon such ideas.

The political economy of debt and deficits

During the mid-1970s several OECD countries accumulated large public debts, a rise in the debt/GNP ratios during peacetime among a group of relatively homogeneous economies that was unprecedented and difficult to reconcile with the neoclassical approach to optimal fiscal policy represented by the 'tax smoothing' theory. In order to explain the variance of country experience and the timing of the emergence of these rising debt ratios, economists have argued that it is crucial to understand politico–institutional factors. To explain such wide differences, the two most significant factors are seen to be, firstly, the various rules and regulations that surround the budget process; and secondly, the structure of government in terms of whether the electoral system generates coalitions or single-party governments. The former were previously discussed, whilst for the latter the argument is that, in the face of large economic shocks, weak coalition governments are prone to delaying necessary fiscal adjustments. Consequently, in investigating the relationship between electoral rules, the form of government and fiscal outcomes, the main findings of economists are first that majoritarian elections lead to smaller government and smaller welfare programmes than elections based on proportional representation; and, second, presidential democracies lead to smaller government than do parliamentary democracies (Snowdon and Vane, 2005).

Additionally, the 'composition' of a fiscal adjustment matters for its success in terms of its sustainability and macroeconomic outcome, where two types of adjustment are identified, those fiscal adjustments relying on expenditure cuts, reductions in transfers and public sector wages and employment, together with those adjustments depending mainly on broad-based tax increases and cuts in public investment. Economists have found that the former induce more lasting consolidation of the budget and are more expansionary, while the latter are soon reversed by further deterioration of the budget and have contractionary consequences for the economy. Hence, any fiscal adjustment that avoids dealing with the problems of social security, welfare programs and inflated government bureaucracies is seen to be doomed to failure. Additionally, the former are also likely to have a more beneficial effect on competitiveness in terms of unit labour costs than policies that rely on distortionary increases in taxation. Similarly, the study of debt and deficit determinants has evolved greatly from its initial theoretical approaches towards more advanced models; firstly, the sustainability of fiscal positions is analysed to illustrate the necessary economic determinants. This is mirrored in the neoclassical tax-smoothing approach, although this was argued as insufficient; emphasis was later placed on political factors, as with the opportunistic and partisan models with their subsequent rational-expectations adaptions, together with political fragmentation within governments. Hence, it is due to these politico-institutional factors that fiscal rules have been advocated; these prevent accumulations in debt by setting numerical targets on fiscal components and/or through procedural reforms (Buti and Sapir, 1998). The case for fiscal rules in the eurozone is emphasised due to the potential negative spill-over effects on member states; if one develops excessive deficits and debt, the interest rate increases for the entire union, requiring other member states to undertake deflationary fiscal policies (Neck and Sturm, 2008). Indeed, even prior to the eurozone crisis, commentators hypothesised that the ECB may be pressured to relax monetary policy to alleviate these problems, or to 'bail out' a country through open-market purchases (De Grauwe, 2003).

Furthermore, as member states are unable to use monetary policy to influence national income, there may be an overreliance on fiscal policy for macroeconomic management, causing deteriorated fiscal positions (Baimbridge and Whyman, 2008). Also, the adoption of a common currency increases the size of the domestic capital market, reducing the need to borrow foreign currency and eliminating exchange-rate risks (Eijffinger and De Haan, 2000). Moreover, due to an inexplicit guarantee by the ECB, enabling excessive deficits, capital markets may not assign a higher default premium (De Grauwe, 2003). Hence, the seminal 1989 Delors Report recommended fiscal rules in the eurozone; these were implemented in the 1992 Treaty on European Union (TEU), which enforced convergence criteria for potential member states, namely a 3% deficit ceiling and a maximum 60% debt ratio (De Grauwe, 2003). After accession in 1999 (2001 for Greece) these rules were reinforced by the SGP, which additionally called for budgets in surplus or balance in the medium term, though this was revised in 2005 to account for cyclically adjusted budgets (Buiter, 2006); non-compliance results in sanctions of up to 0.5% of GDP, in the form of deposits or fines, except in exceptional circumstances, that is, unexpected events or severe economic downturns (formally a 2% fall in GDP) (Buiter, 2006). The SGP has undergone great criticism; opponents argue the numerical targets are arbitrary, balanced budgets contain no economic rationale, and there are concerns regarding accounting methods disguising fiscal positions (Jespersen, 2004). The main criticism of SGP is around its lack of flexibility: the rules limit crucial automatic stabilisers for macroeconomic stabilisation in recessions, thus worsening the downturn (De Grauwe, 2003). This is exacerbated in smaller and open eurozone countries that are argued to rely on active policy (Buti and Sapir, 1998). However, this assumes that rules are strictly enforced and adhered to, though evidence has shown this has not been the case (Wierts, 2008); thus, the success of fiscal rules is ambiguous.

Evidence for political business cycles

Having discussed the theoretical considerations of deficit and debt determinants, it is important to review the supporting evidence; hence, this section discusses both the main general empirical findings for economic, political and fiscal rules effects, together with those relating to the EU, where the most relevant recent studies have presented comprehensive models through incorporating a multitude of factors (see Mulas-Granados, 2003; Busemeyer, 2004; Tujula and Wolswijk, 2004; Castro, 2007; Bayar and Smeets, 2009; Wehner, 2011). Overall, the majority of the literature agrees that macroeconomic variables, such as those suggested by Barro (1979) and Lucas and Stokey (1983) in the tax-smoothing model, are necessary for modelling but do not sufficiently explain the determinants of fiscal deficits. Alesina and Perotti (1995a) argue that, whilst in some periods the empirical investigation by Barro holds, the theory is inconsistent in certain periods (notably the 1980s) and cannot explain differences in debt accumulation between countries; it is argued that the tax-smoothing model acts as a normative benchmark (a 'baseline') by which further political economy studies explain deviations from this model (Franzese, 2001).

The opportunistic political business cycle model has been empirically tested to determine whether election proximity causes budget deficit deteriorations; early empirical work found evidence for electoral cycles on transfers in the United States (e.g., Tufte, 1978; Alesina et al., 1992), and budget balances in OECD economies (Alesina et al., 1997; Franzese, 1999). However, these results are not unanimous, with Lowery (1985), Brender and Drazen (2005) and Shi and Svensson (2006) finding no evidence for electoral cycles, with the latter two studies arguing the effect is limited to developing countries – thus support for the electoral cycle theory is mixed. Similarly, the supports for ideological factors and partisan cycles are similarly inconclusive; in addition to the seminal work by Hibbs (1977) and Alesina (1989), further studies found party effects in OECD countries (e.g., Roubini and Sachs, 1989; Alt and Lowry, 1994; De Haan and Sturm, 1997; Volkerink and De Haan, 2001). However, later studies found insignificant or conflicting results (Persson and Svensson, 1989; Brauninger, 2005), whilst a meta-analysis by Imbeau et al. (2001) reviews 43 studies relating to ideological effects on policy, of which only 22% support the theory, 7% contradict the theory and 71% do not support the theory: indicating that partisan effects may be mostly theoretical.

A further body of research relates to the fragmentation view, whereby weak governments cause greater deficits; nevertheless, the evidence of this view is inconclusive and challenged. Roubini and Sachs (1989) initially devised a political index to capture the effect of single party, coalition and minority governments, and subsequently confirmed the hypothesis of greater deficits under more parties; this was corroborated by Alesina and

Perotti (1995b) and Kontopolous and Perotti (1999). However, many studies dispute this, especially the measure of the index (see Edin and Ohlsson, 1991; De Haan and Sturm, 1997); whilst Volkerink and De Haan (2001) indicate that dispersion within the coalition (e.g., number of spending ministers) is more significant. Finally, the effectiveness of fiscal rules has been studied, initially focusing on the U.S. economy, as budgetary rules are common in many states. Results show a general consensus that fiscal rules significantly improve fiscal outcomes (see Von Hagen, 1991; Alesina and Bayoumi, 1996; Bohn and Inman, 1996), although there are concerns for 'creative accounting' under ex ante rules (Poterba, 1996). Furthermore, studies of other countries, such as Swiss Municipalities (Feld and Kirchgassner, 1999), do not show evidence; thus the effect of rules may depend on their design, stringency and location.

In relation to the analysis with specific focus on EU and the eurozone countries, in the context of opportunism, Andrikopoulos et al. (2004) tested fiscal-target variables for 14 EU countries from 1970–1998, and concluded there was no evidence of electoral cycles. However, the lack of opportunistic effects in the EU may be specific to historical periods; further analysis by Buti and van den Noord (2003) and Mink and De Haan (2006) focus on 15 EU countries in more recent years (1999–2002 and 1999–2004 respectively). Both studies find evidence of electoral cycles of up to 0.5% of GDP and 0.96% of GDP respectively (using dummy variables and 'months until next election' variables), with the former showing support for pre-electoral effects. These studies thus conclude that despite the SGP, electoral cycles were still apparent in the early stages of the eurozone; however, conclusions are tentative due to the short time period. Wehner (2011) expands the analysis for the 15 eurozone countries from 1980–2007 and still finds a negative effect of 0.7% of GDP on budget balances in election years; therefore, an electoral budget cycle may still be prominent in eurozone economies. However, somewhat surprisingly, studies specifically on the ideological effects of debts/deficits in the eurozone are relatively uncommon; for example, Pamp (2008) researches partisan effects on fiscal retrenchment for 14 EU countries from 1990–2001. Using the percentage share of left, centre and right seats in government as dependents, there is no evidence for the theoretical approach that greater shares of left leads to worse deficits (less probability of retrenchment); this echoes similar analysis by Busemeyer (2004) and Castro (2007) and refutes some earlier studies – which could be attributable to more accurate variables.

In addition to the OECD models of fragmentation, the effects of party size on fiscal outcomes in the EU have been researched, although models do not study this effect solitarily; besides partisan effects, Pamp (2008) accounts for fragmentation through the number of parties in government, although finds insignificant results. Mulas-Granados (2003) also finds similar results for coalition size and number of spending ministers for 15 EU countries from 1970–2001, with the only significant effects present from 1970–1994; thus, the weak government hypothesis may have become obsolete in more recent years. Finally, it is consensually agreed that the eurozone accession and fiscal rules have significantly improved budgetary performance (see Ayuso-i-Casals et al., 2006; Guichard et al., 2007; Debrun et al., 2008). Marneffe et al. (2010) control for economic factors and specifically test fiscal rules for 16 eurozone members from 1995–2008; using a fiscal rules index (FRI) to represent the strength of fiscal rules in each country, the study found strong positive effects on fiscal balances. However, the FRI measure dates back to 1990, thus the strength of national rules before this period cannot be tested; furthermore, Hughes-Hallett and Lewis (2008) argue these effects are temporary and only applicable pre-eurozone.

There are, however, few studies that comprehensively test economic and politico-institutional determinants; Tujula and Wolswijk (2004) studied general government budget balances for 15 EU countries from 1970–2002 and found strong macroeconomic effects and election cycles – amounting to 0.3% deterioration in election years, although no support for fragmentation or ideology effects (using composition of ideology index, type of government and number of political parties). After using dummy variables to account for pre- and post-Maastricht, there is evidence that fiscal rules improved budgets by 0.8% of GDP from 1994–1997, although results afterward are insignificant; this suggests the eurozone-entry effects are temporary, though this may be prematurely concluded. More recently, Bayar and Smeets (2009) researched budget deficits in 15 EU countries from 1971–2006, using a PCSE approach. Again economic variables, such as unemployment and GDP growth, are strong and significant, with support found for both electoral cycles of up to 0.59% of GDP and the eurozone convergence of 0.5% of GDP (through using dummy variables). However, no support is found for fragmentation through using both the Roubini and Sachs (1989) index and subsequent dummies; lastly, contradictory and insignificant evidence of partisan effects is exhibited, using both a left dummy and a more accurate ideology scale index (although this is based on the authors' judgement).

A binary-dependent variable of 'excessive deficits' is employed by Castro (2007) in a fixed effects logit model for 15 EU countries, from 1970–2006. This study successfully found support for macroeconomic variables, electoral cycles and partisan effects (through both a dummy and the percentage share of Right seats in the cabinet). Furthermore, using dummy variables for pre- and post-eurozone, the author shows that fiscal rules improved budgetary positions, and this effect was not temporary in contrast to previous studies. However, fragmentation variables failed verification, with counterintuitive results from the Roubini and Sachs (1989) index, and no support for a single party dummy variable. Finally, Busemeyer (2004) uncommonly studies debt for 22 OECD countries from 1980–2002; there is strong and significant evidence for GDP growth and lagged unemployment and, contrary to previous studies, some weak partisan effects and strong fragmentation effects are shown (using ideological shares of seats, number of ministers and a majority government dummy). With its main focus on the eurozone accession, two dummy variables are constructed to account for pre- and post-eurozone convergence; both show significant effects, although the former is stronger, reiterating that fiscal rules' effects are temporary. Although relatively comprehensive, Busemeyer (2004) does not test for electoral cycles and, thus, opportunistic effects are overlooked; furthermore, although analysis starts in more recent years, the period is still significantly dated.

In summary, from the review of both theoretical and empirical evidence, political effects are inconclusive, such that although the results for macroeconomic variables and fiscal rules show more unanimity, it is still important to include all potential determinants, since results appear to be highly sensitive to the precise period, method or variables adopted.

Empirical evidence of adherence to eurozone fiscal rules

In terms of the trends and stylised facts regarding budget deficits and public debt, Figure 6.1 illustrates their volatility throughout the 1981–1992 period; despite no apparent trend for or between countries, some 10 out of 11 countries were in deficit. However, between 1992 and 1999 there is a clear improvement in all countries, with the largest increase being Ireland; this coincides with the TEU convergence criteria, which lends support to its effectiveness. However, post-membership in 1999 with SGP rules, budget balances deteriorate for all countries, indicating the SGP's ineffectiveness. Although 2003–2004 shows improvement in balances for some countries, the financial crisis generates subsequent deterioration.

Reiterating these findings, Figure 6.2 shows the average budget balance for all the eurozone members; budget balances were volatile pre-TEU convergence criteria, and subsequently improved from 1992–1999, such that on average all countries complied with the 3% limit at some point. However, post-membership in 1999, budget balances again deteriorated, paralleling the narrative above: although on average all countries did not exceed the 3% limit, this still indicates a relaxation in compliance. This corresponds with Hughes-Hallett and Lewis (2008: 421) who claim the eurozone countries experienced fiscal improvements that were 'more of a crash diet than a permanent improvement in fiscal discipline'.

Overall, these analyses indicate that many countries did not meet the criteria for convergence; indeed, Table 6.1 demonstrates that 7 out of the 11 countries violated the 60% debt-ratio, and that on average all countries exceeded the debt ceiling such that it is clear fiscal rules were not consistently adhered to, and were therefore arguably ineffective.

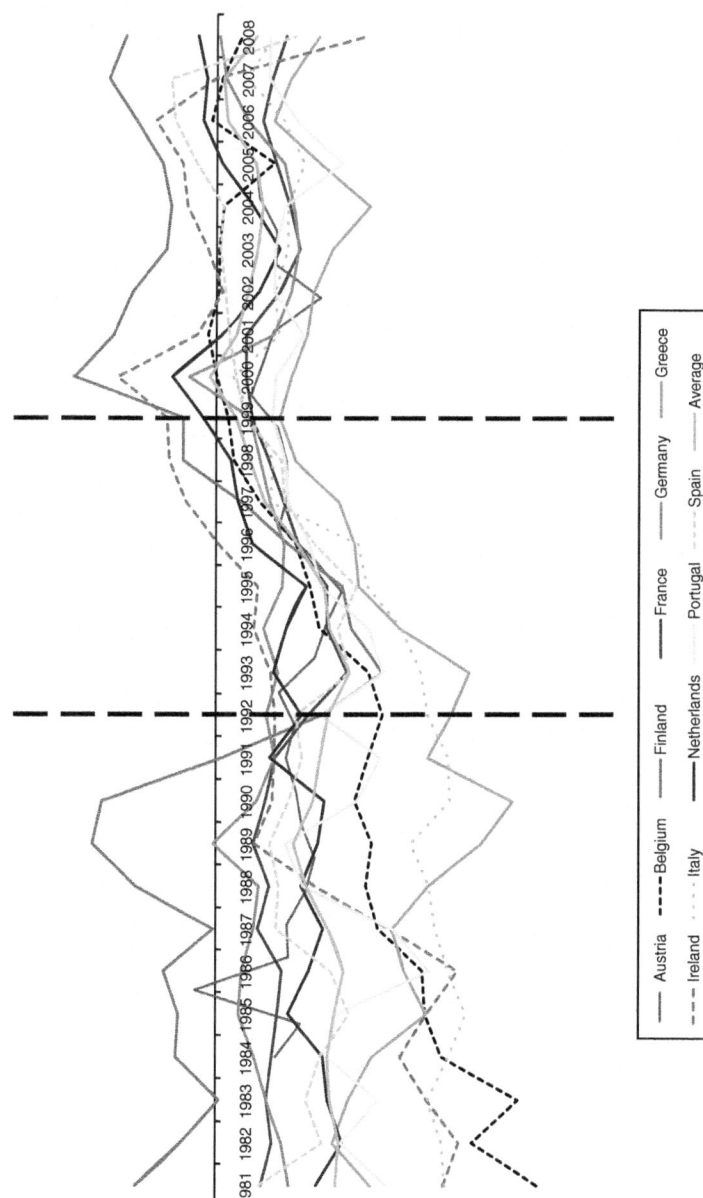

Figure 6.1 Budget balance to GDP (1981–2008)

Next, we consider the trend in each country's public debt-to-GDP ratio from 1981–2008; on average there is a steady trend upwards throughout the 1980's, which peaks in 1993 (see Figure 6.3). Subsequently, there is a steady decrease which coincides with the enforcement of the TEU convergence criteria (assuming a lagged impact) and eurozone membership, illustrated in 1992 and 1999 respectively. Although this does not necessarily illustrate causation, it is interesting to note its coincidence.

Secondly, throughout the period all countries have suffered deterioration in their public debt (except Ireland), although for some this is more notable than others; for example, Greece has experienced the largest increase in public debt, at almost 84% points (see Table 6.2). However, it is of interest to note that although countries such as Ireland, Italy, Greece, Spain and Portugal are perceived to have dangerously high debt, what might be described as the core eurozone member states also exhibit large increases in debt. Deteriorations commonly occurred between 1981–1992, whereas most countries experienced improvements between 1999–2008, when the SGP was enforced. Even still, there was considerable improvement in the 1992–1999 period that included the TEU convergence criteria; notably, Ireland has the most improvement of all countries with a fall of 43.05% points in this period. This would seem to indicate that fiscal rules were effective in decreasing debt ratios.

Consequently, to avoid making a potentially costly mistake, there is an obvious need for a series of measurements to determine whether an individual economy is prepared for the demands of eurozone membership (EC Commission, 1992). Hence, in terms of rules this is through the identification of those EU member states that have demonstrated their suitability for euro membership by their attainment of the five TEU convergence criteria

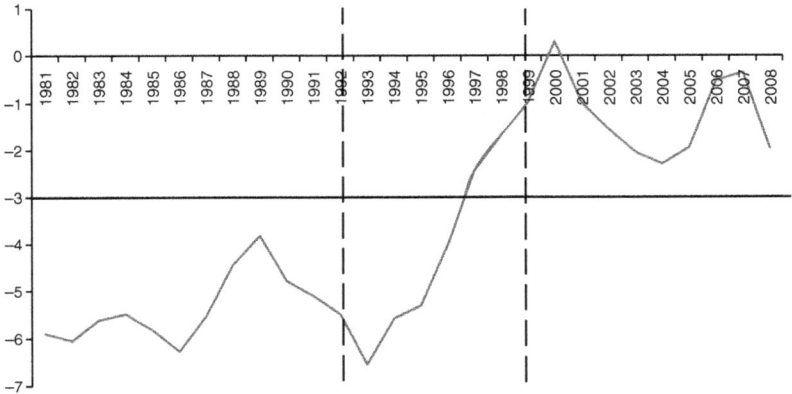

Figure 6.2   Country average for budget balance to GDP (1981–2008)

Table 6.1 Fiscal positions in year of entering the eurozone

Country	Budget Balance	Public Debt
Austria	−2.391%	67.21%
Belgium	−0.591%	113.78%
Finland	1.593%	45.70%
France	−1.776%	58.89%
Germany	−1.654%	60.90%
Greece*	−4.468%	103.72%
Ireland	2.394%	48.50%
Italy	−1.732%	113.71%
Netherlands	0.641%	61.1%
Portugal	−2.769%	49.55%
Spain	−1.423%	62.34%
Average	−0.985%	71.29%

*Greece's data are from 2001; all other countries' data are from 1999.

whereby each country's rate of inflation must be no more than 1.5% above the average of the lowest three inflation rates in the EMS; its long-term interest rates must be within 2% of the same three countries chosen for the previous condition; it must have been a member of the narrow band of fluctuation of the ERM for at least two years without a realignment; its budget deficit must not be regarded as 'excessive' by the European Council, 'excessive' being defined as deficits greater than 3% of GDP for reasons other than those of a 'temporary' or 'exceptional' nature; its national debt must not be 'excessive', defined as above 60% of GDP and not declining at a 'satisfactory'pace. The initial two criteria – each country's rate of inflation must be no more than 1.5% above the average of the lowest three inflation rates in the EMS, and its long-term interest rates must be within 2% of the same three countries chosen for the previous condition – have a clear rationale upon the achievement of prior cyclical convergence. The similarity of inflation rates denotes a low probability of a sudden loss of competitiveness inside a single currency that might lead to unemployment blackspots and a growing inequality. Moreover, comparable interest rates indicate a relatively straightforward transition to a common monetary policy that does not require dramatic changes in the formally pursued national strategies. However, whilst these two convergence criteria are theoretically sound, the latter three have generated both analytical and empirical controversy, whilst their relevance to current conditions in the Great Recession is equally unclear.

The notion of the 'normal' ERM fluctuation bands was, until 1992, interpreted as the relatively narrow margins of +/−2.25%; however, following the 1992–1993 exchange-rate crises, these were widened to +/−15% in order to reduce the speculative pressure. However, the redefinition significantly

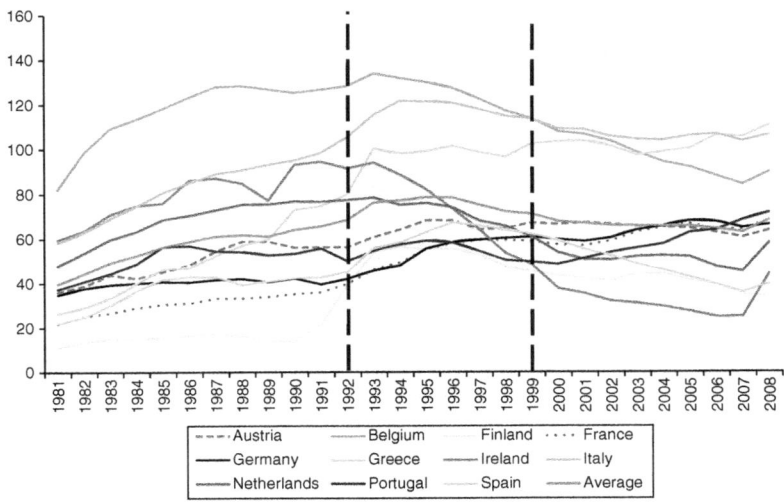

Figure 6.3   Percentage of public debt to GDP (1981–2008)

Table 6.2   Percentage-point change in public debt (1981–2008)

		Sub-period		
	1981–2008	1981–1992	1992–1999	1999–2008
Austria	27.67	20.29	10.84	−3.45
Belgium	7.44	46.17	−14.98	−23.99
Finland	22.64	27.91	6.31	−11.57
France	46.27	17.78	19.10	9.38
Germany	31.39	7.20	18.84	5.35
Greece*	83.98	53.40	23.57	7.01
Ireland	−15.46	31.75	−43.05	−4.16
Italy	47.84	47.03	8.21	−7.40
Netherlands	10.21	29.40	−16.30	−2.89
Portugal	34.17	12.61	−0.47	22.03
Spain	17.66	23.17	16.98	−22.49
Average	28.53	28.79	2.55	−2.82

*Greek sub-periods are 1992–2001, and 2001–2008, since Greece achieved membership in 2001.

reduced this indicator's utility, because the looser arrangement allowed for a currency to fluctuate by a potential of 30% and still be considered stable (Aglietta and Uctum, 1996). The inclusion of the final two targets – budget deficit must not be regarded as 'excessive', defined as deficits greater than 3% of GDP for reasons other than those of a 'temporary' or 'exceptional' nature; and national debt must not be 'excessive', defined as above 60% of GDP and

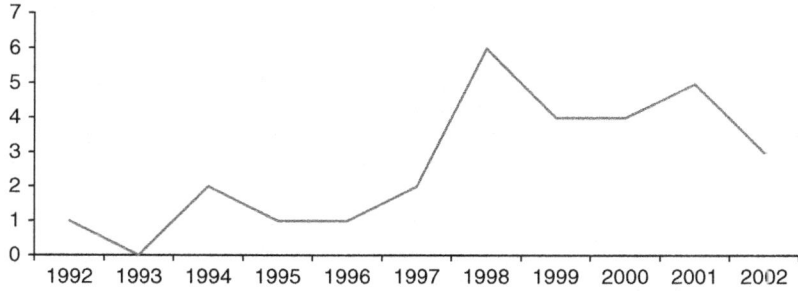

Figure 6.4 Attainment of convergence criteria by the EU15
Source: Adapted from Baimbridge (2005b).

not declining at a 'satisfactory' pace – as a means to establish compatibility raises further problems. The justifications for their use are that they would result in a stable debt ratio in a steady-state economy with 2% inflation and 3% real growth (Trades Union Congress, 1993); and advocacy of the 'golden rule' that current government expenditure and revenue should be equated, together with an estimate that EU public investment approximately averaged 3% over the period 1974–1991 (Buiter et al., 1993). However, this fails to provide a convincing case, since the fiscal reference values are compatible with any combination of inflation and growth, which sum to 5% per annum. The 60% national debt criterion is of doubtful use because it is primarily a consequence of the prior accretion of debt, reflecting past fiscal activities rather than current policy (Goodhart, 1992). Moreover, there is no evidence that attainment of these criteria would result in a steady-state economy (Arestis and Sawyer, 1996). In contrast, the TEU contained no similar tests to compare the wealth of the different countries, their unemployment, productivity and growth rates, nor the sectoral composition of economic activity.

Despite the problematic nature of the convergence criteria, the architects of the eurozone believed that their attainment would indicate the compatibility of potential participants, together with providing a guide to their subsequent maintenance (Baimbridge, 1997), where the prerequisite of prior convergence is significant over each stage of the economic cycle, and to prove robust against shocks (Eichengreen, 1992a, b; Bayoumi and Eichengreen, 1993). However, for the period between the TEU and advent of euro notes and coins, attainment of all five criteria was fulfilled on only 29 out of a possible 165 occasions, an achievement record of approximately 18%, even when member states still retained considerable control over their economies. Indeed, only seven member states have ever secured total compliance with the convergence indicators, whilst key eurozone countries such as Austria, Belgium, Italy and Greece have failed to ever achieve all five criteria. Furthermore, as Figure 6.4 illustrates, although the number of EU member states attaining all five convergence criteria peaked in 1998, it thereafter declined, thereby illustrating the difficulties in maintaining political willpower after the commencement of the eurozone and adherence in light of an economic slowdown.

Evidently, the reality of attainment by EU member states, both preceding and immediately following the creation of the eurozone, diverge significantly with the examination of the progress towards convergence and sustainability of the monetary union completed by the EU Commission (1998). The experience of those countries that narrowly complied with the convergence criteria suggested that they are not permanently converged, but have only achieved the necessary conditions in the most favourable economic circumstances. Such historical instability highlighted the potentially fragile nature of the eurozone as presently conceived. Hence, the implication that once severe shocks occur, such as the Global Financial Crisis, several participants would demonstrate a significant divergence from the established criteria.

Conclusion

In this chapter we have seen how economists have sought to enhance our understanding of aggregate instability by adding a political dimension to their models in terms of the linkage in developed countries of increased levels of national debt to budget rules and government structure. Indeed, since the late 1980s there has been a major revival of political economy utilizing the tools of modern economic analysis, whereby a common theme running throughout this 'new political macroeconomics' is the need to integrate the political process into mainstream economics. In particular, this interrelationship has shifted from a view of politicians as largely exogenous to the economy, to one where they are regarded as endogenous. Consequently, it is now accepted that there is the possibility that politicians will set economic policy contrary to that required for stabilisation as Keynes had originally envisaged. Instead, they are in a position to manipulate key macroeconomic variables, such as growth, employment and inflation, to maximise their chances of re-election. From this basis, economists have developed a number of models to examine the idea of a political business cycle expressed in terms of assumptions regarding politicians (opportunistic or partisan) and assumptions regarding voters/economic agents (non-rational or rational expectations). These ideas are examined and evaluated in terms of their empirical and theoretical support, which is largely found wanting.

However, while the importance given to political influences in causing aggregate instability in industrial democracies remains highly controversial, few commentators would challenge the view that politicians, faced with a regular election cycle, will tend to develop short-time horizons. The desire to be re-elected or regain office may lead politicians to pursue or promise an economic policy package that creates aggregate economic instability. If this line of argument is accepted, then it follows that what is needed is an institutional framework that creates an environment conducive to the more-frequent implementation of sustainable economic policies geared to longer-term objectives such as those within the eurozone. However, the dilemma faced in industrial democracies is how, through institutional reform and without threatening the basic principles of democratic government, to constrain the over-zealous short-term discretionary actions of politicians.

7
Monetary Policy within the Eurozone

Introduction

Following the prescription of contemporary economic theory to develop rules and institutions to enforce time-consistent policymaking, the European Central Bank (ECB) is a creation of the TEU, which designed it to be the most independent monetary authority in the world. The ECB's architects sought to insulate it completely from political pressures, both at the national government and at the eurozone level. The position of the ECB under the TEU permits no clear accountability to either national or federal European institutions. It stipulates that the ECB Council's deliberations remain confidential, whilst the only method of questioning the ECB's policies is through periodic reports to the European Parliament. Although commentators have concentrated upon criteria denoting initial convergence for eurozone membership, stringent rules restrict national fiscal policies, and the benefits deriving from the eurozone; however, far less attention has been paid to how the eurozone will operate in practice. In particular, the institutional design of the eurozone stipulates a central role for an ECB, established to be independent of government and charged with sustaining the stability of the currency zone in the face of asymmetric external shocks. The ECB is the sole body credited with determining the appropriate monetary and exchange-rate policy for the entire eurozone and as such its ability to fulfil its stated objectives is crucial to its success or failure, as has been demonstrated by the eurozone crisis. Consequently, the paucity of critical analysis of the ability of the ECB to stabilise the eurozone economy – complete with low inflation, full employment, a sustainable balance of payments and good level of economic growth – should be of great concern for all supporters of European integration.

This chapter seeks to compensate for the dearth of current analysis by examining the capability of the ECB to fulfil its designated role. Firstly, it evaluates the ECB design selected by the architects of the TEU and reviews the degree of independence attributed to the ECB in comparison to member states' national central banks (NCBs). It then summarises the leading conceptual issues and empirical literature in order to examine the merits of establishing the ECB to be independent from democratic influence. Subsequently, we review the hypothesised relationship between independence and macroeconomic indicators.

Evaluation of central bank independence

The belief that central banks should be independent from political influence has deep historical roots and featured in the discussions leading to the establishment of many 20th-century central banks (Toniolo, 1988). The historical desire to impose limits upon a government's ability to fund itself through seignorage is combined with the orthodox contemporary argument that politicians manipulate monetary policy to win elections, resulting in excessive concentration upon short-term macroeconomic fine tuning (Swinburne and Castello-Branco, 1991). Consequently it is argued that long-term economic efficiency requires the removal of monetary policy from the sphere of democratically accountable politics and its delegation to an independent central bank with an effectively designed constitution and internal reward system that impose price stability as the overriding policy objective. Few institutional reforms recommended by economists have gained such rapid and widespread acceptance as the demand to grant central banks independence from political control. Countries of the North and the South, the post-communist nations of Central and Eastern Europe as well as the established capitalist states have all been affected by the debate over the appropriate role and status of the central bank (Posen, 1993). Thus, the notion of central bank independence has taken on the character of a panacea, a quick institutional fix, producing desirable macroeconomic results in a wide variety of national contexts.

The conceptual case for central bank independence is primarily based on the view that arrangements raising the credibility of monetary policy will increase the bank's effectiveness in pursuit of price stability. Although this view has long been held, only in recent years has the concept of policy credibility been rigorously defined and analysed (Cukierman, 1986; Blackburn and Christensen, 1989). The establishment of an independent central bank with strong anti-inflationary preferences is seen as a way for the state to bind politicians' hands against the electoral temptation of inducing unanticipated increases in the price level. As commitment increases credibility, orthodox theory predicts that divergences between the central bank's policies and people's expectations will become smaller. Therefore, lower costs and fewer delays are incurred when adjusting to monetary policy shifts It is from this theoretical perspective of monetarism and rational expectations that the ECB was launched. However, this approach has been challenged. Firstly, if central bank independence increases credibility, it should be associated with greater rigidity in the setting of nominal prices and money wages, reflecting the fact that the bank's promise to keep inflation low is believed. However, studies of Organisation for Economic Co-operation and Development (OECD) countries by Posen (1993, 1998) indicate that neither effect occurs. Indeed, independence not only fails to reduce the cost of disinflation, but rather seems to increase it. Lowering inflation takes just as long and calls for a larger short-term sacrifice of output and jobs, on average, in countries with relatively independent central banks as compared to those democratically accountable monetary institutions.

Secondly, most of the contemporary support for central bank independence stems from a partial (and, frequently, historically naïve) view of the West German experience, whereby it is overlooked that any one item that helped to promote rapid post-war German growth, such as the independent Bundesbank, was part of a structural totality defining its role. Accordingly, it is unlikely to be effective if transferred by itself to other countries or onto the broader EU stage (Dowd, 1989, 1994). It may be more appropriate to reverse the fashionable view; the structural conditions that produced the strength of the German economy, allowing it to grow while maintaining a low inflation rate, also enabled it to afford the luxury of an independent central bank concentrating on monetary stability. For example, the wage-negotiations system in Germany has generally produced a less inflationary outcome than in many other countries over the post-war period, thus not requiring intervention from the Bundesbank. Therefore, it must be open to question whether the creation of a more independent central bank is significant in containing inflation, or whether the existence of an independent bank merely reflects a political economy in which price stability is a widely shared objective, where governments, as well as the central bank, regard low inflation as an overriding objective (Mitchell, 1993). Consequently, economists accept the possibility of 'reverse causality' as a significant constraint when interpreting the experience of countries with independent central banks.

Moreover, the theoretical case for independence is based on two analytical assumptions that have become generally accepted by economists. Firstly, the vertical long-term Phillips Curve, which implies that price stability can be achieved at no long-term cost of unemployment; and, secondly, the political business cycle. However, both rest on insecure foundations. The vertical Phillips Curve analysis rests upon the concept of a natural rate of unemployment, the frequently changing determinants of which economists remain largely ignorant (Davidson, 1998; Karanassou and Snower, 1998; Madsen, 1998; Nickell, 1998; Phelps and Zoega, 1998). Moreover, several studies indicate that relatively little evidence exists for the occurrence of any systematic political business cycle (Kalecki, 1943; Breton, 1974; Nordhaus, 1975; MacRae, 1977; Wagner, 1977; Frey, 1978; Alesina, 1989).

Fourthly, the empirical evidence concerning central bank independence and lower-than-average inflation – which again drew heavily upon the German Bundesbank, although counter-examples exist – compounds difficulties. For instance, the United States, with an independent central bank, has not enjoyed such a phenomenon. Moreover, German experience since reunification demonstrated that an independent central bank is unable to guarantee low inflation. However, the persuasive nature of monetarist ideas led to the widespread conviction that low inflation is an important condition for high and sustained growth. Thus its achievement should be the priority for government economic policy. The importance attached to low inflation as the prerequisite for high employment and rapid growth is central to the case for an independent central bank. However, the belief that low or zero inflation produces sustained growth is, once again, not supported by the available evidence. Indeed, many studies indicate that no significant relationship exists between low inflation and higher rates of growth, until double-digit rates of price increase occur, which do retard economic development (Thirlwall and Barton, 1971; Brown, 1985; Stanners, 1993). Thus, the consensus of research fails to provide the evidence to support the advantages of prioritising low inflation above all other objectives.

Moreover, economic policy objectives should be sufficiently comprehensive as to include the pursuit of multiple policy targets. However, if responsibility for price stability rests solely with an independent central bank, while others remain with government, economic management potentially becomes more difficult due to the separation of monetary and fiscal policy (Blake and Weale, 1998). Hence, an advantage of a non-independent central bank is that budgetary and monetary measures can complement each other, forging a coordinated strategy of economic management. A failure of policy coordination was demonstrated in the United States by the shortcomings of the Reagan–Volcker era and within the EU by Germany's problems in the aftermath of reunification. Such policy inconsistency highlights the ambiguous nature of 'independence', itself. Analysis of the role of a central bank confirms that, in a world of external shocks, the case for delegating monetary policy is weak, and that a coordinated approach is more likely to achieve the electorate's objectives (Rogoff, 1985a, b). Furthermore, if eliminating inflation is all-important, and elected politicians cannot be trusted to give it priority, the logical conclusion is that all economic instruments should be taken out of their hands. The assertion often made is that monetary policy is different because it is a technical operation with a single objective and with well-understood, reliable techniques. Such a belief is questionable, since monetary policy impacts upon employment and living standards just as vitally as does fiscal policy. Moreover, periods of high inflation have not occurred wholly, or even mainly, due to lax monetary expansion, whilst there is greater international evidence of fiscal, rather than monetary, policy being manipulated for electoral ends (Alesina, 1989).

When assessing the impact of central bank independence upon price stability, economists have mostly utilised imputed 'degrees of independence' to evaluate the heterogeneous character of central banks. A large body of literature focusing upon single or multi-country time-series studies has been accumulated, with an additional series of studies attempting to rank independence for a cross-section of countries. The majority of this research draws attention to the inherent difficulty of defining, let alone measuring, the concept of independence (Mangano, 1998). The initial method of imputing degrees of independence, based solely on legislative arrangements, found no relationship between inflation performance and central bank independence (Bodart, 1990). The index was refined by subsequent studies, which constructed a measure of central bank independence that reflected both 'political independence' and 'economic independence' (Alesina and Grilli, 1991; Grilli et al., 1991). Political independence relates to the ability of the monetary authorities to choose the goals of policy, whilst economic independence is defined by their capacity to choose the instruments with which to pursue policy objectives. The main conclusion from such analyses is that the average rate of inflation, and occasionally its variability, is significantly lower in countries that possess independent central banks. However, the value of such evidence is problematic (as the authors usually acknowledge), because measurement of 'degrees of independence' possesses serious weaknesses, which cast doubt upon the purported association between central bank independence and the attainment of price stability. The main failings of this approach are: Firstly, a limited spread of rankings inevitably restricts sensitivity across a wide number of inherently different countries, which raises difficulties concerning the index's analytical usefulness. Secondly, many of the studies cover overlapping time periods, opening up the possibility that they have found a result unique to that particular set of data. Therefore, it becomes crucial to test a hypothesis on data sets other than those that suggested the hypothesis (Friedman and Schwartz, 1991). Furthermore, the time periods covered by some studies increase concern over the reliability of their findings. For instance, the participation of countries within the EMS could be viewed as a potentially important determinant of inflation rates. Consequently, if all countries in a pegged exchange rate system are compelled to possess the same rate of inflation over the long run, whatever the various influences on that rate, the status of NCBs cannot be the main influence. Thirdly, disregard for non-economic factors that shape fiscal and monetary policy choices is a consistent feature of these studies, as illustrated by their assumption that electorates always prefer low inflation to the possible trade-off of higher economic growth and employment (Muscatelli, 1998).

However, even after analysing the role of political factors, other potential sources of differences in inflation rates are often neglected. For instance, even if EU countries were subject to the same exogenous shocks in the post-war period, structural differences between them (e.g., labour-relations systems, wage-indexation mechanisms, vulnerability to raw material price changes, varying preferences for inflation versus unemployment) may explain their different reactions. Indeed, the position of the government in the political spectrum, and various proxies of social consensus offer some explanation of inflation rates in different countries (Hansson, 1987). Likewise, the size of the public sector appears to be another significant factor (Alesina, 1988). Moreover, lower inflation in Germany and Switzerland could result from the presence, during periods of economic growth, of 'guest' workers who absorb part of the unemployment costs of disinflationary policies by having to return to their countries of origin when the work is no longer available (Burdekin and Willett, 1990).

Consequently, in an attempt to compare monetary regimes, many studies focus exclusively on institutional characteristics, disregarding behavioural indicators such as the average rate of growth of the money supply or the level and variability of interest rates. However, new research rarely at first possesses the reliable database it requires. Therefore, greater attention should be devoted to improving databases and to recording any national specificity that may exist or has occurred. Moreover, many studies suffer from the omission of indicators not identified as potential explanatory factors, so that influences other than central bank independence may be important, but as yet unidentified, determinants. Finally, a problematical aspect of this research is the statistical analysis of the link between central bank independence and inflation, with most studies relying upon the plotting of graphs. Indeed, Alesina and Summers (1993: 154) admit that 'our empirical procedure is extremely simple. We plot various measures of economic performance covering the entire 1955–1988 period against measures of central bank independence'. Furthermore, the manner in which the determined characteristics of central banks are aggregated to produce the overall index of central bank independence is a major area for concern. Consequently, the index is usually constructed through one of a number of alternative methods, none of which is universally valid. Indeed, despite the occasional econometric testing, the results provide little support for the notion that independent central banks consistently deliver low inflation, whilst the more common approach of the unscientific plotting of a line between inflation and only one other variable (when there are many determinants) constitutes scant evidence upon which to rest the case for central bank independence. Hence, in view of these potential difficulties associated with the frequently prevailing use of imputed degrees of independence, the chapter now re-examines this issue.

The design of the ECB

The structure and role of the ECB are detailed in the articles of the TEU. The ECB is headed by its Governing Council, comprising the governors of the NCBs together with members of the executive board of the ECB. The latter consists of professional bankers or monetary experts nominated by the member states for a single eight-year term of office (Article 109a). All members of the executive board and ECB in general, are expected to act independently of 'Community institutions or bodies, from any Government of a Member State or from any other body' (European Communities, 1991). However, the legal framework, institutional arrangements and emerging operating practices of the ECB are increasingly coming under closer scrutiny and criticism (Buiter, 1999; Howarth and Loedel, 2003). Elsewhere, however, the TEU provides for the Council and the European Commission to possess non-voting representation at meetings of the ECB's Executive Council, whilst the ECB must present an annual report to the EU's institutions and appear before the relevant committees of the European Parliament when requested (Article 109b).

The crucial operational features of the ECB are that its sole policy objective is the pursuit of price stability. It will also be responsible for defining and implementing the EU's monetary policy, together with supporting the attainment of general economic objectives. This design format is founded upon both theoretical (Kydland and Prescott, 1997; Barro and Gordon, 1983; Alesina, 1989; Alesina and Grilli, 1991) and empirical (Bade and Parkin, 1988; Alesina, 1988, 1989; Cukierman, 1992; Alesina and Summers, 1993) studies that suggest the transfer of monetary policy from governments to an independent central bank is likely to result in lower inflation. Additionally, the powers and tasks of the ECB are highly significant, with the bank exclusively responsible for authorising the issuance of bank notes (Article 105a). It is also able to make legally binding and directly applicable regulations on the minimum level of reserves to be held by NCBs, on the efficiency of clearing and payment systems and on the supervision of credit institutions. Moreover, where an undertaking fails to comply with an ECB regulation or decision, the bank will be able to impose a fine (Article 108a). Finally, the ECB is to be consulted by other EU institutions and national authorities and may issue opinions to them on matters within its competences (Article 105).

In particular, it is suggested that the capacity of the monetary authorities to choose the final objectives of policy is primarily determined by three aspects of a monetary regime. Firstly, the procedure for appointing the members of the central bank governing bodies; secondly, the relationship between these bodies and the government; and, thirdly, the formal responsibilities of the central bank. In principle, independence to determine ultimate macroeconomic goals may be defined without reference to their contents, but in practice the main virtue claimed for an independent central bank is that it can provide credibility. Hence, independence is frequently identified with autonomy from political interference to pursue the objective of low inflation, so that any institutional feature that enhances its capacity to pursue this goal is hypothesised to increase central bank independence. However, the architects of the TEU were faced with a wide range of alternative variations of central bank political and economic autonomy from government, out of which they created the institutional structure of the ECB. Contemporary examples of operationally independent central banks include the German Bundesbank, the Federal Reserve of the United States of

America, the Bank of England and the Reserve Bank of New Zealand. Each has a different degree of autonomy concerning different operational issues. The German Bundesbank is probably the most important of these alternatives, as it is perceived to have a track record of delivering consistently low inflation (Marsh, 1992). Faced with a number of alternative models (e.g., the U.S. Federal Reserve and the Reserve Bank of New Zealand), the designers of the TEU preferred to follow the Bundesbank blueprint when establishing the design of the ECB, given that Germany achieved low inflation over the period since 1961 and that those countries which pegged their currencies to the deutschmark, 'imported' a similar inflation performance. Hence, the ECB is anticipated to be as successful in safeguarding low inflation and price stability across the eurozone.

The apolitical status of the ECB can be examined in greater detail in relation to the concepts of economic and political independence. The latter refers to its decisions not being conditional on the approval of government, whilst the former pertains to its ability to operate monetary policy without government undertaking contrary actions. Tables 7.1 and 7.2 indicate the relative nature of political independence concerning the original signatories of the TEU when compared to the ECB, with an asterisk indicating possession of a specific feature.

Table 7.3 illustrates the comparative position in terms of the political, economic and combined indices of NCBs, following the adoption of the ECB criteria. The comparative figures are calculated by subtracting the value of the

Table 7.1 Political independence of central banks[1]

	Appointments (Governor + Board)			Relationship with government			Constitution		Index of political independence
	1	2	3	4	5	6	7	8	9
Belgium				*					1
Denmark		*				*	*		3
France		*		*					2
Germany		*		*	*	*	*	*	6
Greece			*					*	2
Ireland		*				*	*		3
Italy	*	*	*		*				4
Netherlands		*		*	*	*	*	*	6
Portugal					*				1
Spain				*	*		*		3
UK					*				1
Column total	1	6	2	5	6	4	5	3	
ECB		*		*	*	*	*	*	6

Sources: Adapted from Grilli et al. (1991) and EC Commission (1991).

Table 7.2 Economic independence of central banks[2]

	Monetary financing of budget deficit				Monetary instruments				Index of economic independence
	1	2	3	4	5	6	7	8	9
Belgium		*		*	*	*		*	5
Denmark		*			*	*		*	4
France				*	*	*		*	4
Germany	*	*	*	*	*	*	*		7
Greece				*		*			2
Ireland		*	*	*		*			4
Italy				*					1
Netherlands			*	*	*	*			4
Portugal				*		*			2
Spain			*	*			*		3
UK	*	*	*	*		*			5
Column total	2	5	5	10	5	9	2	3	
ECB	*	*	*	*	*	*	*		7

Sources: Adapted from Grilli et al. (1991) and EC Commission (1991).

Table 7.3 Comparison of central bank independence of EU member states and the ECB

	Present index of political independence	Comparison to political independence of ECB	Present index of economic independence	Comparison to economic independence of ECB	Comparison to combined independence of ECB
Belgium	1	−5	5	−2	−7
Denmark	3	−3	4	−3	−6
France	2	−4	4	−3	−7
Germany	6	0	7	0	0
Greece	2	−4	2	−5	−9
Ireland	3	−3	4	−3	−6
Italy	4	−2	1	−6	−8
Netherlands	6	0	4	−3	−3
Portugal	1	−5	2	−5	−10
Spain	3	−3	3	−4	−7
UK	1	−5	5	−2	−7
Mean	**3**	**−3**	**4**	**−3**	**−6**

Source: Derived from Tables 7.1 and 7.2.

ECB indices from those of the EU member states' central banks. This procedure clearly identifies the German Bundesbank as providing the blueprint for the ECB with no required revisions to its independence characteristics. The central bank of the Netherlands is the only other to fall below the overall mean comparison figure of six, whilst Denmark and Ireland coincide with the average. In contrast, those NCBs requiring the largest institutional reforms to meet the TEU requirements were, in ascending magnitude: Belgium, France, Spain, Britain, Italy, Greece and Portugal. It is interesting to note that this division of EU member states mirrors the established concept of 'core' and periphery groups regarding the formation of the single-currency area.

To empirically analyse central bank independence in relation to the ECB, we examine those EU member states (excluding Luxembourg, which at the time did not possess its own central bank), which were original signatories to the TEU (Baimbridge et al., 2002). Although this reduces the number of countries in comparison to several of the previous studies, it offers a logical basis for the subsequent analysis. For example, when examining the likely impact of the ECB little analytical precision is gained by including those countries which will never enter the eurozone (e.g., Australia, Canada, Japan, New Zealand and the United States). Moreover, few previous studies offer a rationale for the countries they include – for instance, whilst focusing upon industrialised economies, they all fail to incorporate every member of such a representative grouping as the OECD. A further aspect that differentiates this analysis is that it disaggregates central bank independence into its constituent features of political and economic independence. This approach involves dividing these principal features into 16 individual components, thereby enabling a detailed examination of the separate elements that comprise a central bank's independence alongside an evaluation of the aggregate level analysis pursued in previous research. Finally, in addition to the now-traditional comparison of central bank independence and inflation, GDP growth is introduced to evaluate the proposition that independence carries no detrimental consequences for output (Eijffinger et al., 1996).

The correlation results between the series of 16 measures of political and economic central bank independence (see Tables 7.1 and 7.2), together with both the rate of inflation and growth over the period 1961–1994 in terms of a positive hypothetical relationship between central bank independence and inflation, show that the only statistically significant factors include the 'board being appointed for a period exceeding 5 years' and the 'absence of prior government approval of monetary policy formulation'. Likewise, the fact the bank provides a 'direct credit facility at market interest rate' and is 'not participating in the primary market for public debt', are the sole significant economic characteristics. Hence, only 4 of a possible 16 features of central bank independence appear to contribute to lowering inflation. Such findings contrast with the blanket contention that an independent central bank is an effective anti-inflationary mechanism (Baimbridge et al., 2002). Although these findings partially support the conclusions of previous studies (Alesina, 1989; Grilli et al., 1991; Alesina and Summers, 1993), there are several important caveats. Firstly, the analysis of the individual features of political and economic independence indicates that only a limited number are statistically significant, raising difficulties concerning the necessity for all such characteristics to be present simultaneously within the ECB. Secondly, the overall index of political independence is insignificant, indicating that such criteria proved historically inconsequential to EU member states' inflation rates. Thirdly, although the indices of economic and combined independence are inversely related to inflation, only 66% of the variation of inflation is 'explained'. This appears to offer marginal evidence at best from which to launch such a fundamental institutional reform or to expect it to persist over the medium- to long-term, particularly if negative externalities are associated with greater independence.

The second part of this empirical analysis examines the relationship between central bank independence and output to evaluate the orthodox hypothesis that the former constitutes 'a free lunch' (Grilli et al., 1991: 375), because it carries no detrimental consequences for GDP growth. Hence, in terms of the correlation results for the individual features and the three overall indices of independence in relation to growth, then with respect to political independence, neither the individual factors nor the index are statistically significant. In contrast, three of the economic independence criteria are significant: 'direct credit facility not automatic', 'direct credit facility at market interest rate' and 'central bank does not participate in the primary market for public debt' (Baimbridge et al., 2002). Of particular interest, however, is the negative association between these features and GDP growth, which contradicts the previously established proposition that central bank independence has no 'costs in terms of macroeconomic performance' (Grilli et al., 1991: 375). The implication, therefore, is that independent central banks exert a negative impact on the rise in their citizens' standards of living and constitute an ominous background to the actual operation of the ECB.

Monetary policy and philosophy

The final aspect of this chapter briefly reviews the conduct of monetary policy by the ECB. Initially, the TEU left the role of the ECB uncertain, suggesting that it would mainly implement the policies determined by the NCBs by delegating the common monetary policy to the European System of Central Banks (ESCB) (von Hagen and Bruckner, 2002). In view of such institutional vagueness, key concerns have been: how ECB Council members could reach an agreement on a common monetary policy; to what extent that policy would be affected by national circumstances and preferences; and how it could be communicated effectively to a very heterogeneous European public (Cecchetti et al., 1999). Initially the European Monetary Institute (EMI) preparatory work narrowed the choice of a monetary policy strategy to monetary targeting versus inflation targeting (EMI, 1997). However, in October 1998, the Governing Council of the ECB announced that a key aspect of monetary policy strategy was a quantitative definition of price stability. Furthermore, in order to assess risks to price stability, the

ECB would make use of two pillars. Firstly, it attributes a prominent role to monetary indicators as signalled by the announcement of a quantitative reference value for the growth of a broad monetary aggregate and, secondly, it undertakes a comprehensive analysis of a wide range of other economic and financial variables as indicators of price developments (ECB, 1998, 1999, 2000, 2001; Issing et al., 2001).

In relation to the quantitative definition of price stability it does not give a precise definition. In order to specify this objective more precisely, in October 1998 the Governing Council announced the quantitative definition of price stability as 'a year-on-year increase in the Harmonised Index of Consumer Prices (HICP) for the euro area of below 2%', which was 'to be maintained over the medium term' (ECB, 1998). Such an announcement is supposed to enhance the transparency of the overall monetary policy framework and provide a clear and measurable benchmark against which to hold the ECB accountable. Furthermore, it gives guidance to expectations of future price developments, thereby helping to stabilise the economy. Consequently, the ECB (2003) argued that this definition of price stability has been conducive to a firm anchoring of inflation expectations in the euro area at levels compatible with the definition, thereby helping to contain the inflationary effects of the substantial price shocks that have occurred. While the announcement of a quantitative numerical value for the price stability objective of the ECB was welcomed, there has been criticism regarding specific features of the definition.

Firstly, regarding the choice of the price measure, it has been argued that the ECB should put more emphasis on measures of 'core' or 'underlying' inflation, or even specify the bank's objective in terms of a measure of core inflation (Gros et al., 2001; Alesina et al., 2001). Such measures could help to avoid the risk of monetary policymakers focusing excessively on temporary price fluctuations. Secondly, that the ECB's quantitative definition may be too ambitious, given a positive measurement bias in the HICP that could hamper the adjustment process at low levels of inflation, substantial divergences in inflation rates across countries that imply 'too low' a level of inflation, and possibly frequent deflationary situations and the presence of a zero boundary on nominal interest rates that could hamper the effectiveness of monetary policy in the face of large negative demand shocks and expose the euro area to the risks associated with deflation and deflationary spirals (Fitoussi and Creel, 2002; De Grauwe, 1994). Thirdly, the ECB's definition is imprecise and asymmetric as it specifies the upper boundary, but leaves the lower boundary undefined. This may result in the bank being less effective in anchoring inflation expectations and could possibly hinder the clarity of explanations of policy moves. Consequently, it has been suggested that the ECB should make its objective more precise by, for instance, officially announcing a lower boundary in the definition or by specifying the objective in terms of a point inflation rate (Svensson, 2002, 2003; IMF, 2002).

Finally, the choice of the specific quantitative objective requires a balance between the costs of inflation and rationales for small positive inflation rates. The costs primarily relate to: the misallocation of resources; the inflation tax on real balances; the effects of inflation on income distribution and inflation uncertainty; and associated risk premia, menu costs and those costs stemming from the interaction of inflation with the tax system. In contrast, the case for small positive inflation relates to: measurement bias in the price index; downward nominal rigidities; sustained inflation differentials; and the risk of protracted deflation or a deflationary spiral (Yates, 1998; Wynne and Rodriguez-Palenzuela, 2002; Coenen, 2003a, b; Klaeffing and Lopez-Perez, 2003). Unfortunately, such a review of the costs and benefits of moderate inflation does not allow the optimal rate of inflation to be precisely defined; it indicates the need for an inflation objective embodying a sufficient safety margin against deflation. In response to this criticism the ECB (2003) suggested that inflation objectives above 1% provide sufficient safety margins to ensure against these risks.

In relation to the first pillar, its key characteristic is the announcement of a reference value for the annual growth of M3. Hence, the ECB seeks to communicate the medium-term focus of monetary policy to the public, as it relieves the central bank from responding to short-run fluctuations in financial and other variables (ECB, 2003). Furthermore, by signalling continuity of the Bundesbank's strategy, the ESCB hoped to quickly establish credibility (von Hagen and Bruckner, 2002). However, the role of money and monetary analysis has generated controversy regarding the robustness of the chosen leading indicator's properties with respect to price developments, on the grounds that the correlation between money growth and inflation appears to have declined over time in parallel with restored conditions of price stability (Begg et al., 2002). In this context, the necessity for announcing a reference value for money growth has also been queried, together with the usefulness per se of a separate 'money' pillar (Svensson, 2003). In contrast, the second pillar consists of an assessment regarding future price developments (ECB, 1998). Initially, it represented the analysis of short-run price developments based on measures of real activity, wage cost, asset prices, fiscal policy indicators, together with indicators of business and consumer confidence (ECB, 1999). However, no framework was specified as to how these variables would be used to assess price developments, nor were their relative weights in such assessments. It is therefore an opaque aspect of the ESCB's strategy, being void of systematic analysis and fully discretionary (von Hagen and Bruckner, 2002). Furthermore, Gaspar et al. (2001) suggest that the analysis is now organised in the form of a macroeconomic projection, although the ECB does not provide confidence intervals for its projections (Gali, 2001).

According to the ECB (2003), the two pillars are used in parallel in monetary policy decision-making. However, there is no indication of what their relative weights are, resulting in an incomprehensible strategy, as Issing et al. (2001) partially acknowledge. Although there is nothing that would make the use and revelation of the relative weights of the two pillars impossible, the reason why the ECB has so far denied the public transparency of its strategy is more likely related to the internal decision-making processes (von Hagen and Bruckner, 2002). Finally, from its ostensively monetarist pre-history, the ECB argues that the majority of the eurozone's high unemployment originates from structural deficiencies on the supply-side of its member states' econo-mies. Consequently, the ECB denies responsibility for increasing aggregate demand to lower unemployment, since no scope exists to reduce unemploy-ment without accelerating inflation. However, if the sole objective of policy is to maintain a constant rate of inflation, wide variations in output and employment may be required. Insofar as a potential conflict exists between steady inflation and full employment, the latter should enjoy priority because the consequences of market failure in terms of high rates of employment are more serious than those associated with moderate levels of inflation.

Conclusion

The theoretical and empirical evidence surveyed in this chapter suggests that the creation of an independent central bank is a more finely balanced exercise than is frequently portrayed in particular given national economies that continue to experience varying economic cycles and possess divergent economic structures. Moreover, the interest-rate decisions taken by central banks are amongst the most sensitive actions deployed in a modern economy, influencing growth, living standards, the level of unemployment and the cost of credit and mortgages. However, the ECB neither publishes forecasts nor the minutes of its deliberations, and its members cannot be removed from office by the European Parliament, the Council of Ministers or even by the European Court. Hence, the ECB's problems arise from its lack of democratic accountability, transparency and democratic legitimacy, as well as from its arbitrary objectives, questionable economic philosophy and the potential for intermittent conflict with the national governments over whose destinies it possesses considerable influence. An alternative model of a democratically accountable and controlled ECB, operating in co-ordination with a combina-tion of nationally determined fiscal policies, or a newly established federal authority, would prove a more effective and desirable model.

Additionally, this chapter has sought to outline the 'new' shape of economic policymaking within the eurozone. Although this has evolved from the initial blueprint, the direction is diametrically opposite to what would be beneficial to the United Kingdom. For example, the introduction of SGP to reinforce the budgetary aspects of the convergence criteria poten-tially leads to an unprecedented loss of national autonomy in terms of fiscal policy. However, there is little comfort to be gained from the marked failure of the SGP (with numerous member states blithely flouting its provisions), since this illustrates the fallacy of the entire Maastricht process in seeking to curtail national well-being for the greater good of the EU. Similarly, in 2003 the ECB undertook a major reassessment of its monetary policy stance given the destabilising effect of the 'one-size-fits-all' interest rate policy: both upon domestic eurozone economies and in terms of the euro external position on global capital markets. However, once again the patchwork of remedial policies is far from those necessary to place monetary policy within the sphere of democratic accountability.

This leads us to the question of how economic policymaking could be improved within the eurozone? In the context of the monetary policy and the ECB, one radical, but effective, reform would be that control should be repatriated from the ECB to the nation states. Indeed, on 26 April 2004 the French finance minister complained that his job is to deliver economic growth, yet he was unable to do so because authority over the levers of growth had been given away to the ECB. Given the situation that was to follow the Great Recession when the ECB was sluggish in adjusting interest rates, then the conclusion that the centralisation of economic policy should be reversed is compelling.

Notes

1. Where: (1) governor not appointed by government; (2) governor appointed for >5 years; (3) all the board not appointed by government; (4) board appointed for >5 years; (5) no mandatory participation of government representative on the board; (6) no government approval of monetary policy formulation is required; (7) statutory requirements that central bank pursues monetary stability amongst its goals; (8) legal provisions that strengthen the central bank's position in conflicts with the government are present.
2. Where: (1) direct credit facility – not automatic; (2) direct credit facility – market interest rate; (3) direct credit facility – temporary; (4) direct credit facility – limited amount; (5) central bank does not participate in the primary market for public debt; (6) discount rate set by central bank; (7) banking supervision not entrusted to the central bank at all; (8) banking supervision not entrusted to the central bank alone.

8
Economic Policymaking within the Eurozone

Introduction

As previously outlined, a country within the eurozone faces a considerably different macroeconomic policy framework from that previously experienced by EU member states. Monetary policy is now set by the independent ECB, whilst national governments possess fiscal and supply-side policies. Hence, from an individual country's viewpoint, interest rates are now 'fixed' and will only move if the ECB decides that economic conditions are changing for the eurozone as a whole and not if an individual country, or group of countries, suffers an economic shock (McKinnon, 2003; von Hagen, 2003; Wyplosz, 2003). Thus, the eurozone participating countries now have two choices. Firstly, provided that it does not infringe the convergence criteria/SGP, a country can use fiscal policy to counteract whatever shock has occurred (Gali and Perotti, 2003). Secondly, that country can wait for its labour market to alter wages and then prices and, thus, its overall degree of international competitiveness.

Moreover, a particular problem for the eurozone countries is that at the present time there is no large federal fiscal system in place whereby a central government sets taxes and expenditure rules that apply in its constituent states or countries (see Chapter 10 for a discussion of this as a potential solution to the eurozone crisis). Hence, fiscal policy is confined to backward-looking automatic stabilisers, so that the only channel for a forward-looking policy is through interest rates. Hence, the fiscal framework in the eurozone increases the burden on monetary policy to react to shocks, even before they have fed fully through into output and inflation. Furthermore, many aspects of supply-side policies are inimical to the social model espoused by the majority of EU member states. Thus, in an attempt to extricate themselves from this self-inflicted deflationary position, the common reaction has been to blithely ignore the rules of the SGP and expand budget deficits (Germany, Greece and France) and debt-to-GDP ratios (Belgium, Germany, Greece, France, Italy, Austria and Portugal) beyond permitted limits (ECB,

2005). This, however, is not without potential costs in terms of stoking inflationary pressures and diminishing the external value of the euro, the consequence of which is that the ECB will be forced to maintain interest rates higher than is strictly necessary and, hence, initiating a vicious circle of exacerbating the high rates of unemployment that the breaking of SGP rules had sought to address.

The conduct of economic policy within the eurozone

The eurozone is based on a unique arrangement of public-finance relations whereby fiscal policy remains decentralised with regard to EU member states, but is subject to rules to combine discipline and flexibility (Buiter, 2003; Buti et al., 2003). This is provided by the SGP, which complements and tightens the fiscal provisions laid down in the TEU. Buti and van den Noord (2003: 4) argue that the SGP is 'unquestionably the most stringent supranational commitment technology ever adopted by sovereign governments on a voluntary basis in the attempt to establish and maintain sound public finances'. If fully applied, the SGP will have important implications for the behaviour of budgetary authorities in both the short-term (cyclical stabilisation, policy co-ordination) and long-term (sustainability of public finances). It seeks to achieve a balance between constraining national fiscal policy to protect the ECB whilst it has established credibility and permitted limited flexibility for counter-cyclical fiscal policy. This was deemed necessary since, although ECB policy might be expected to create stable macroeconomic conditions for the eurozone as a whole, it could not be expected to resolve regional cyclical imbalances. In particular, the SGP consists of several central elements (Buti et al., 1998; EU Commission, 2000). Firstly, a commitment to medium-term budgets that are 'close to balance or in surplus', which is interpreted by Canzoneri and Diba (2000) as an implied promise to balance structural (or cyclically adjusted) budgets. Secondly, submission of annual programs specifying medium-term budgetary objectives, thereby creating a track record when assessing compliance with the SGP, or convergence criteria in the case of member states who are not in the eurozone (EU Commission, 2000). Thirdly, countries that run excessive deficits will be subject to financial penalties and public approbation. Deficits are defined as 'excessive' if they exceed 3% of GDP, unless they occur under 'exceptional' circumstances, which are defined as an annual decline of more than 2% of GDP in real output, whilst a decline of 0.75% of GDP might be deemed 'exceptional' if there is additional supporting evidence. The sanctions associated with such deficits are that the member state has to make an interest-free deposit of 0.2% of GDP, plus 0.1% of the amount by which its deficit to GDP ratio exceeded 3%. The maximum deposit would be capped at 0.5% of GDP, which is forfeited after two years if the 'excessive deficit' persists. Canzoneri and Diba (2000) estimate that the foregone interest in the first year of sanctions would be in the range of €250–500 million for one of the larger member states.

However, the initial years of the eurozone have demonstrated little progress towards lower public deficits and debts by participating nations in terms of budgetary consolidation, let alone in structural terms. Furthermore, following the omission of the automatic effects of growth on the budget, countries relaxed their retrenchment efforts in the 1998–2002 period. In particular, the three largest countries of the euro area (Germany, France and Italy) as well as Portugal did not behave according to the SGP. Indeed, although the SGP appears rigid, it fails to address a typical failure of fiscal policy behaviour in Europe, namely the tendency to run expansionary pro-cyclical policies in good times (European Commission, 2000). Whilst an excess over the 3% of GDP deficit ceiling is sanctioned, there is no apparent reward for appropriate budgetary behaviour during cyclical upswings, leading Buti and van den Noord (2003) to argue that the political temptation to 'spend the money when it comes in' may prove irresistible. Hence, there is the suggestion that the SGP is 'all sticks and no carrots' (Bean, 1998) and may result in a pro-cyclical bias in the conduct of budgetary policy, since the only carrot is the opportunity for automatic stabilisers to operate during economic downturns. However, Buti and Martinot (2000) argue that if governments retain their historical budgetary culture they will tend to offset the working of the automatic stabilisers for sufficiently large, positive output gaps.

Furthermore, these questionable incentive structures may be further tested during electoral periods whereby, in contrast to the advent of the euro, when the incentive to maintain the announced fiscal consolidation path was evident, the situation may be different once in the eurozone, when adherence to the SGP's rules may be politically inefficient (Buti and Giudice, 2002). Resolving such political bias is likely to be problematic, with potential solutions ranging from the introduction of 'rainy-day' funds permitting countries to set aside revenue in good times (Buti et al., 2003) to the harmonisation of electoral cycles in the eurozone, which would reduce politically induced distortions and be welfare-enhancing (Sapir and Sekkat, 1999). Indeed, as witnessed from the eurozone crisis, the outcome has been the increasing of budgetary surveillance focussing on structural balances and using peer pressure and 'early warnings' to curb fiscal misbehaviour (Viren, 2001; Korkman, 2001; EU Commission, 2002). Additionally, to ensure member states adhere to the rules of the SGP, a further series of difficulties have arisen regarding the convergence criteria reference values for both the deficit and the debt-to-GDP ratios, whilst none were defined for structural deficits. Subsequently, the SGP added a commitment to structural balance, but the 'excessive deficits' procedure is its only explicit enforcement mechanism. Thus, actual deficits are the focus of the SGP, which appear to take primacy over both structural deficits and debt levels (Canzoneri and Diba, 2000). Consequently, it has been suggested that the SGP will become an impediment unless its focus is shifted from constraints on actual deficits and towards constraints on structural deficits or, better yet, constraints on debt levels (Canzoneri and Diba, 2000; Artis and Buti, 2001; Dalsgaard and de Serres, 2001; Rostangno et al., 2001; Missale, 2001). Furthermore, various studies regarding the flexibility built into the 'excessive deficits' procedure suggest that once governments have further reduced structural deficits the 'excessive deficits' procedure should not constrain normal counter-cyclical efforts (EU Commission, 2000), whilst countries that run excessive deficits have been subjected to financial penalties and public approbation (Baimbridge et al., 2012).

However, the initial years of the eurozone demonstrated little progress towards lower public deficits and debts by participating nations in terms of budgetary consolidation, let alone in structural terms, whilst in light of the Great Recession and subsequent Eurozone Crisis the current emphasis on the excessive deficits procedure seems misplaced (Balassone and Franco, 2001; Casella, 2001). Moreover, it remains unclear how strictly the EU will interpret the provisions in the SGP with it possessing a history of exerting discretion in such decisions. Furthermore, countries relaxed their retrenchment efforts in the period 1998–2002, such that the three largest countries of the eurozone (Germany, France and Italy) did not behave according to the SGP. Indeed, although the SGP appeared rigid, it failed to address a typical failure of fiscal policy behaviour, namely the tendency to run expansionary pro-cyclical policies (EU Commission, 2000). Whilst an excess over the 3% of GDP deficit ceiling is sanctioned, there is no apparent reward for appropriate budgetary behaviour during cyclical upswings, leading Buti and van den Noord (2003) to predict that the political temptation to 'spend the money when it comes in' may prove irresistible, which in some instances clearly occurred. Furthermore, at the present time there is no substantive federal fiscal system in place whereby a central government sets taxes and expenditure rules that apply in constituent states or countries (Whyman and Baimbridge, 2004).

The second dimension in the search for time-consistent policymaking was the creation of the ECB, designed to be the most independent monetary authority in the world in order to insulate it completely from political pressures. The historical desire to impose limits upon the government's ability to fund itself through seignorage is combined with the contemporary neoliberal argument that politicians manipulate monetary policy to win elections, resulting in an excessive concentration upon short-term macroeconomic fine tuning (Swinburne and Castello-Branco, 1991). Although this view has long been held, only relatively recently has the concept of policy credibility been defined and rigorously analysed (Cukierman, 1992). Consequently, it is argued that long-term economic efficiency requires the removal of monetary policy from the sphere of democratically accountable politics, and its delegation to an independent central bank that imposes price stability as the overriding policy objective. Consequently, few institutional reforms recommended by economists have gained such rapid, widespread acceptance as the demand to grant central banks independence from political control (Posen, 1993); however, as discussed in Chapter 7, this approach has been challenged.

Thus, the eurozone presents a novel policymaking framework that would prove challenging even under relatively benign circumstances. However, numerous empirical studies confirm that supply and demand shocks will prove asymmetric for eurozone participants, with 67% of supply shocks and 82% of demand shocks estimated to exert a divisive impact upon the EU economy (Weber, 1991; Bayoumi and Eichengreen, 1993). Advocates of monetary integration dismiss these findings by arguing that the development of the single market will reduce the frequency and impact of asymmetric shocks as individual economies become increasingly inter-dependent, and as large corporations straddle European borders (Goodhart, 1995). However, it is equally possible that industrial restructuring across Europe will concentrate certain industries in specific locations, thereby exacerbating existing differences (de Grauwe and Vanhaverbeke, 1993). Moreover, the literature concerning nominal and real wage rigidity undermines faith in price flexibility as an equilibrating mechanism to restore full employment in the aftermath of an asymmetric shock (Bini-Smaghi and Vori, 1992; Blanchard and Katz, 1992; Sala-i-Martin and Sachs, 1992; Goodhart and Smith, 1993; Pisani-Ferry et al., 1993; Kenen, 1995; Goodhart, 1995). With labour mobility far lower than experienced in mature monetary unions, such as the United States (Ermisch, 1991; Eichengreen, 1992; Masson and Taylor, 1993) and capital mobility unlikely to generate sufficient short-term stabilisation due to the time lags and transactions costs involved (von Hagen, 1993; Romer, 1994), fiscal policy is consequently left as the primary stabilising instrument (de Grauwe and Vanhaverbeke, 1993; Kenen, 1995). Thus, to generate labour mobility on the scale required to resolve regional imbalances in the absence of devaluation and wage/price flexibility may require substantially higher unemployment and regional inequality. This would be particularly destabilising for eurozone cohesion due to the political implications of large-scale emigration, together with the tensions created by unemployment and relative poverty within a Europe made more transparent through the introduction of a single currency. Although capital mobility can, in principal, substitute for labour mobility, its weakness in reducing long-term structural inequalities within existing nation states, together with the insights provided by studies in cumulative causation (Myrdal, 1957) and endogenous growth (Romer, 1994), results in being cautious against over-optimistic assumptions of a rapid elimination of unemployment caused by shocks. Moreover, due to the transactions costs involved, factor movements are an inefficient means of reacting to transitory regional shocks (von Hagen, 1993).

Hence, the eurozone remains vulnerable to any sizeable asymmetric external shock that highlights the inability of a single monetary authority to reconcile the different economic needs of individual participants by using only one policy instrument, the common interest rate, the level of which is set in the interests of the majority of nations. An alternative is for member states to run a budget surplus during favourable economic periods to avoid surpassing the 3% deficit limit during a downturn, but a surplus of this magnitude has little economic justification. Governments may, therefore, be faced with trying to cut public spending or to raise taxes in the middle of a slump, as has been recently witnessed, with the inevitable result being to deepen the recession, just as pro-cyclical fiscal policy worsened conditions during the 1930s depression (Ormerod 1999). Furthermore, as the eurozone crisis has shown, economic policy objectives should be sufficiently comprehensive as to include the pursuit of multiple policy targets. However, if responsibility for price stability rests solely with an independent central bank, while others remain with government, economic management potentially becomes more difficult due to the separation of monetary and fiscal policy. Hence, an advantage of a non-independent central bank is that budgetary and monetary measures can complement each other, forging a co-ordinated strategy of economic management that is more likely to achieve the electorate's objectives (Rogoff, 1985a, b). Furthermore, it is suggested that international policy coordination may undermine central bank credibility and cause an unanticipated increase in inflation by weakening the disciplining effects of excessive monetary growth upon the exchange rate (van der Ploeg, 1993). However, despite these criticisms, unless the discipline effect of the eurozone is powerful and immediate, the persistence of price and factor rigidities would appear to necessitate the use of fiscal policy as a stabilising instrument to reduce the incentive for any country to leave the eurozone and as an, albeit imperfect, substitute for exchange-rate flexibility.

The conclusion that fiscal policy may become the principal instrument to counteract asymmetric external shocks, and thereby prevent eurozone destabilisation, raises the issue of whether it should be deployed at the national or federal level. The adoption of the decentralisation theorem, whereby functions are performed by the lowest efficient layer of government, is in accord with the EU's professed belief in subsidiarity and would indicate an initial preference for national fiscal autonomy (Wheare, 1963; Oates, 1972; Bayoumi and Masson, 1995). However, the design and impact of monetary union upon member states significantly weakens this conclusion and restricts the pursuit of counter-cyclical fiscal policy at the national level (Holland, 1995; Burkitt et al., 1996, 1997; EU Commission, 1997).

Operation of economic policy within the eurozone

The IS–LM model was devised in 1937 by the British economist Sir John Hicks (one year after publication of Keynes's General Theory) to provide a determinate solution to the Keynesian system. It is a model that can be used to show new equilibria for income/output (Y) and the rate of interest (i) after any of the exogenous variables or parameters of the system change. In more recent years it has gone out of fashion, being regarded as too simplistic, given that its most basic form assumed that prices were fixed. Thus, it was unable to explain and illustrate the high inflation rates of the 1970s, together with the increasing attention applied to the supply-side of the economy (the second policy option outlined above). However, the IS–LM model has regained its relevancy because, firstly, there is a more stable inflation environment across the EU, which partially results from cheap labour in China and other emerging economies (*The Economist*, 2005); and, secondly, in relation to the eurozone policy debate, in that it combines the real (fiscal policy) and financial (monetary policy) sides of the economy in the IS and LM schedules respectively. In any event, the IS–LM approach provides a relatively straightforward means of evaluating the impact of the eurozone upon economic policy determination and, therefore is, for this reason at least, worthy of initial consideration. Figure 8.1 illustrates the basic IS–LM model representation that a eurozone country faces. The IS function retains its familiar downward-sloping nature; however, rather than thinking of it terms of its traditional description of illustrating equilibrium in product markets, we can view it in terms of fiscal policy (FP). This is the aspect of economic policy that national governments retain influence over, albeit within the stipulations of the SGP. In contrast, the LM function does not possess its usual upwards-sloping nature, since national economies are effectively 'price takers' in relation to the rate of interest, which is determined by the independent ECB (see Chapter 7). Hence, the LM or monetary policy (MP) is portrayed as being perfectly elastic (horizontal) and exogenously determined.

Through expansionary or contractionary fiscal policy, national governments can manipulate the economy (FP_1) to achieve a desired level of national income/output (FP_2); for example, in seeking to attain the full employment level of income/output (Y_{FE}). However, as Figure 8.1 indicates, the potential scenario facing the eurozone participants is that the SGP, if applied, could potentially impair the ability of governments to attain full employment through the sole use of fiscal policy (FP_3), with the economy achieving equilibrium at Y_2, thus resulting in a deflationary (unemployment) gap of $Y_2 - Y_{FE}$. Hence, without the ability to adjust interest rates via the national central bank to domestic economic conditions, the eurozone countries are left with only supply-side policies to attain full employment. Although most economists now accept the role of such policies, these are not an immediate remedy for the persistently high levels of unemployment that have been endemic across the continent of Europe for the past decade. Furthermore, many aspects of supply-side policies are inimical to the social model espoused by the majority of EU member states. Thus, in an attempt to extricate themselves from this self-inflicted deflationary position, the common reaction has been to blithely ignore the rules of the SGP

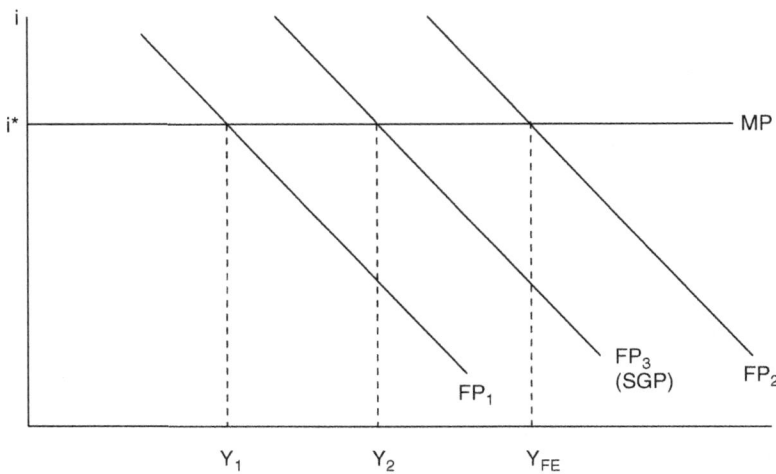

Figure 8.1   Economic policymaking within the eurozone

and expand budget deficits (Germany, Greece and France) and debt-to-GDP ratios (Belgium, Germany, Greece, France, Italy, Austria, Portugal) beyond permitted limits (ECB, 2005). This, however, is not without potential costs in terms of stoking inflationary pressures and diminishing the external value of the euro, the consequence of which is that the ECB will be forced to maintain interest rates higher than is strictly necessary and, hence, initiating a vicious circle of exacerbating the high rates of unemployment that the breaking of SGP rules sought to address.

As previously discussed in Chapters 2 and 3, macroeconomics is distinguished by theories based upon different schools of thought that possess alternative views on how the economy works at the aggregate level – hence, providing different arguments of the role of short-run economic stabilisation policies. However, these models have failed to explain and provide successful solutions to the fluctuations of the macro-economy, one after another, over different time periods. Consequently, since the 1990s a new model has been established that sought to combine the strengths of different approaches, to create a better model that can be used as a more appropriate tool to study macroeconomics (Fontana, 2009). As discussed in Chapter 3, the New Consensus Model (NCM), combines the elements of new classical, monetarism and the New Keynesians. For example, it shares the idea of the vertical Philips Curve in the long-term, but regards it as downward sloping in the short-term, whilst prices are sticky in the short-run and yet economic agents have rational expectations (Goodfriend and King, 1997; Fontana, 2009). Within this contemporary framework central banks operate monetary policy through interest-rate adjustment, not money-supply growth targets, given the endogeneity issue, such that the aim is to keep the economy close to its inflation target at the equilibrium level of output. Hence, the central bank's role is important due to the disturbances/shocks that shift inflation away from its target or output away from the equilibrium level, or both; thus the contemporary role for central banks is to minimise these sub-optimal fluctuations. To achieve this, the central bank will choose the interest rate to influence the output gap, as it seeks to achieve stabilisation of the economy; however, it cannot bring about instantaneous change in output; rather, it takes time for interest rate changes to affect firms/households and output.

To represent this policymaking, the NCM derives a monetary rule (MR) equation from the central bank's output–inflation trade-off, which shows the combination of output and inflation that the central bank will choose given the Phillips Curve it faces. In particular, the MP equation looks at how the monetary authority sets the level of interest rate in relation to its policy goal (i.e., price stability/inflation targeting). In NCM, the interest rate is the policy instrument the central bank can use explicitly to control the inflation and output; moreover, it also indicates the replacement of LM by MR curve since the money supply is endogenously determined (Romer, 2000). The most famous and widely accepted monetary rule (interest policy rule) is the Taylor Rule, which proposes the monetary authority should respond to changes in both price and aggregate demand in order to maintain the price stability or to achieve the target inflation (Taylor, 1999). In other words, the central bank needs to change the interest rate if inflation deviates from its target or positive output appears in the economy (see Figure 8.2). In particular, this emphasises that a decision taken today by the central bank to react to a shock will only affect the inflation rate two periods later (π_2), such that the central bank must forecast a further period ahead in the double-lag model to locate the appropriate Phillips Curve and optimal interest rate choice today.

There may, however, be problems for the central bank when seeking to use an interest rate rule to stabilise the economy. Investment or other components of aggregate demand fail to respond (or to respond sufficiently)

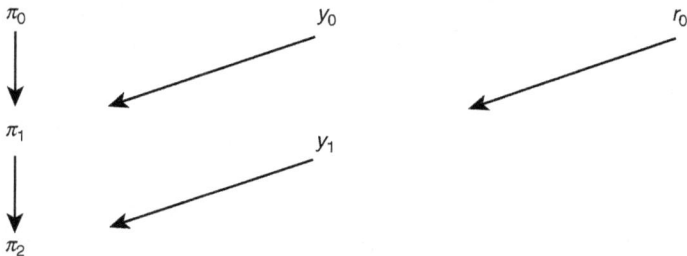

Figure 8.2 Lag structure in the IS-PC-MR model required to deliver a Taylor Rule
Source: Carlin and Soskice (2009).

to the change in the interest rate; if the central bank cuts the short-term interest rate to stimulate the economy because it fears a recession, but financial markets believe the underlying cause of the recessionary threat is likely to produce higher inflation in the long run, then a higher long-run real interest rate will be required, which will dampen interest-sensitive expenditure at the time the central bank is attempting to stimulate the economy. Finally, if the real interest rate required to stimulate the economy was negative then, if combined with low inflation, nominal interest rates cannot become negative; in other words the economy encounters a liquidity trap.

Consequently, the central bank reacts to the observed inflation and output gaps to set nominal interest rates to force the economy moving, or keep it around its target inflation level (Carlstrom and Fuerst, 2003). From this analysis several general points emerge: First, the central bank behaves in an active, but rule-based fashion; second, frequent adjustments of the interest rate are required by the monetary policy rule; third, due to inertia, inflation can only be eliminated by pushing output below (and unemployment above) the equilibrium. Hence, the central bank focuses on real interest rates when setting nominal interest rates such that it takes account of the higher expected inflation on the real interest rate, thereby pushing up the nominal rate to take this into account. However, it is commonly agreed that monetary policy may not have immediate effects on inflation, but with some lags (Friedman, 1961, Batini and Nelson, 2001, Carling and Soskice, 2005). Indeed, an empirical study conducted by the Bank of England (1999) adopted the two-lags model of NCM monetary policy to explain the process of inflation adjustments.

The eurozone as a flawed currency area?

As indicated above, fiscal policy should be used as a counter-cyclical tool; however, if this is the case, fiscal policy may become challenging within a monetary union through the occurrence of spill-over or free-rider effects (von Hagen and Wyplosz, 2008). The former may occur if members run large budget deficits over a prolonged period of time, leading to their fiscal stance being unsustainable which, given its financing through the financial markets, results in ever-higher interest rates on sovereign debt. Additionally, with such growing recourse to financial markets, the availability of liquidity may decrease and therefore further drive-up interest rates. Thus, one member's debt issue spills over to others as financing sovereign debt becomes more expensive for all countries (Arezki et al., 2011). The potential hazard of free-rider effects materialises when a country cannot meet the repayment of its outstanding debt; with default on the horizon, it can either undertake surprise devaluation or inflation to reduce its debt's real value. However, for eurozone members without sovereign monetary policy these methods are no longer available, thereby increasing the possibility of outright default

(McKinnon, 1996). Moreover, with the integration of financial markets, one country's bonds may be widely held by other members. Thus, outright debt default harms not only domestic bondholders, but also other government and private investors. Thus, as has been witnessed, eurozone governments become uniquely vulnerable to self-fulfilling panic over default.

Even with these inherent problems, such difficulties could have been tempered if the eurozone incorporated a coherent adjustment mechanism to meet inevitably changing economic circumstances. However, deflation with all its economic, political and social costs has become the eurozone's sole adjustment mechanism to the detriment of its citizens. Indeed, to date, the eurozone's response has been piecemeal; ad hoc loans have been provided, whilst minor revisions to the Lisbon Treaty have been agreed to enable the creation of a bail-out fund; however, such 'solutions', deal with the symptoms rather than the fundamental causes of the euro's structural weaknesses. The initial response was moral suasion through castigating debtor countries for their profligacy, but such a shaming process may exert a limited effect and is likely to be of only short duration, given its illogicality. Thus, Germany is urging budget cuts on the Mediterranean nations without acknowledging how its own surpluses were built partly upon their willingness to buy German commodities with borrowed money, as earlier illustrated by the BoP analysis. Indeed, the analysis of Chick and Pettifor (2001) indicates that implementation of austerity policies across the EU has been asymmetric, whereby government spending has risen in the 'core economies' so that budget deficits have remained steady whilst GDP has increased. In contrast, reductions in government spending in the 'periphery' (e.g., Greece, Ireland and Spain) have led to a range of budgetary outcomes and a decline in GDP.

Although such efforts may lead to economic remedies, a potentially more significant outcome from the eurozone crisis is to the body politic of the EU with greater long-term damage emerging through the imposition of 1930s-style austerity policies. In terms of the flawed economics of austerity, Blyth (2013) provides an account of how this has reared its head at moments of crisis only to persistently exacerbate the situation in the overwhelming majority of cases. In the contemporary context of the eurozone crisis, a number of studies (Alesina and Tabellini, 1987; Persson and Svensson, 1989; Giavazzi and Pagano, 1990; Alesina and Ardagna, 2010) were the touchstone of the shift towards so-called expansionary fiscal consolidation; subsequently, their findings have been rebutted by a further series of studies (Jayadev and Konczal, 2010; Leigh et al., 2010; Gravelle and Hungerford. 2011; Perotti, 2011; Guajardo et al., 2011; Battini et al., 2012; Jordà and Taylor, 2013). Overall, research on the effects of austerity on macroeconomic indicators remains problematic and complicated by the difficulty of identifying multipliers; however, the consensus has now shifted in favour of the latter studies refuting the applicability of fiscal consolidation. Moreover, they indicate that fiscal contraction prolongs the pain when an economy is weak compared to when the economy is strong; in other words, precisely not the policy to pursue in times of crisis.

In addition to a return to austerity-orientated economics and political discourse, a further aspect of the EU's response to the eurozone crisis has arguably been a weakening of the bonds of social cohesion through increasing internal and external discrimination, together with the rising spectre of racism in Europe. The twin concepts of internal and external discrimination are centred on the notion that, in contrast to EU integrationalist developments, for third country nationals there is a danger of Europe increasingly becoming a 'fortress', whilst internal discrimination occurs through the differences in the way individual member states treat their minority populations – treatment that is partially explicable in terms of their differing histories and patterns of migration. In terms of the extreme right in contemporary Europe, the conventional view has been that its rise in popularity is largely explained by the individual fortunes of political parties, as opposed to a particular phenomenon occurring. However, evidence suggests that the diminution of social cohesion along with the rise of racism as exemplified by support for the extreme right is a pan-EU phenomenon exacerbated by neoliberal deflationary policies as espoused by the eurozone and, now, austerity (Baimbridge et al., 1994).

Furthermore, a linked yet unintended consequence of the Global Financial Crisis and the subsequent eurozone sovereign debt crisis has been a distinct shift in the political landscape of several countries, with the advent of unelected technocrat governments (i.e., Greece and Italy), together with growing dissatisfaction of mainstream political parties with support for either the far-right (e.g., Golden Dawn), protest parties (e.g., Five Star Movement), anti-euro parties (e.g., Alternative for Germany Party), anti-EU parties (e.g., UKIP, True Finns), or member states losing confidence in the direction of 'ever-closer union' (e.g., the renegotiation and referendum pledge by the United Kingdom's ruling Conservative Party). The key issue is whether these are the first signs of a longer-term trend or merely a temporary phenomenon for which analysis is required to differentiate between the impulse and propagation mechanisms when explaining these new political fluctuations from the more familiar consensus. The former refers to the initial shock that is arguably the new economic reality of low growth, high unemployment and pressure upon the European social model (Whyman et al., 2012), whilst the latter encompasses forces that magnify the initial effect of the shock forward over time, causing deviation from the original steady-state position, in this case the series of policies adopted to resolve the eurozone crisis. Only the passage of time will reveal whether these developments will endure to signal a tectonic shift in Europe's political landscape.

Thus, there is the necessity to formulate a more efficient policy response that will significantly reduce damaging externalities. Experience has demonstrated that, in contrast to the advent of the euro when incentives to maintain the announced fiscal consolidation path were evident, the situation once member states were in the eurozone has proved to be politically inefficient (Buti and Giudice, 2002). Although resolving such political bias is likely to be problematic, potential solutions range from the introduction of 'rainy-day' funds, permitting countries to set aside revenue in good times (Buti et al., 2003), to the harmonisation of electoral cycles to reduce politically induced distortions (Sapir and Sekkat, 1999). However, the outcome in the guise of the European Fiscal Compact has been an increase of budgetary surveillance focussing on structural balances and using peer pressure and 'early warnings' to curb fiscal misbehaviour. In contrast, one potential stability-generating mechanism is that of fiscal federalism: MacDougall (1992, 2003) demonstrated that a redistributive federal fiscal structure requires an EU budget of 5–7% of EU GDP, compared to the minimum 20–25% of GDP that federal systems usually necessitate (Baimbridge and Whyman, 2004). However, the current EU budget remains too small to exert a significant stabilising effect upon the eurozone regions in the advent of an asymmetric external shock (Eichengreen, 1994; Bayoumi and Masson, 1995; EU Commission, 1996). Consequently, the alternative is a compromise of a more targeted version of fiscal federalism, aimed at stabilising growing divergence in unemployment rates and/or economic growth paths without additional (spill-over) redistribution of resources. This has been estimated to cost between 0.2–1.9% of eurozone GDP, depending upon the degree of stabilisation from an initial shock that the scheme is intended to deliver (Italianer and Vanheukelen, 1993; Whyman, 2010).

A more radical option to resolving eurozone imbalances would be the creation of a clearing union as originally suggested by Keynes (1942) on an international basis, a step that has more recently been advocated by Davidson (2002, 2009) from a Post-Keynesian perspective. A European Clearing Union (ECU) could not only remove the sovereign debt problems of particular countries but, more significantly, in the long term restore international confidence in the single currency. Under such a proposal the central bank of individual countries would buy and sell their currencies against debits and credits to their accounts at the ECU, whereby each central bank would have the right to an amount of bank money, essentially an overdraft facility. Keynes (1942) also emphasised the importance of transparency that provides 'an automatic register of the size and whereabouts of aggregate debtor and credit positions respectively. The danger signal is shown to all concerned'. At first sight, the eurozone appears to meet the essential aspects of this idea within its geographical area of application, but it lacks the underlying equilibrating mechanism to eliminate both deficits and surpluses. However, the proposal possesses the major advantage of redistributing resources within the eurozone without the political encumbrance of an apparatus of fiscal union, whilst addressing the problem of private, as well as public, debt.

Alternatively, so long as this state of affairs persists, consideration must eventually be given to a fifth response – the collapse of the euro, at least in its current form and with its current membership. The placement of all adjustment costs upon specific members has never worked in the long term, for which the periodic crises and the ultimate collapse of the Silver and Gold Standards are evident proof (Eichengreen, 1996). Although whilst unilateral ending of eurozone membership for outlier states would solve the worst problems in the short run, the fundamental design flaws would remain. However, the demise of the currently constituted eurozone would impose fewer costs than would the status quo or alternative scenarios. Moreover, these costs could be minimised if it were accomplished through an orderly process involving internal euro devaluation in each of the debtor economies, accompanied by capital and exchange controls on all external transactions until new non-euro currencies had been established. The main problem facing such a policy, however, arises from the substantial cross-border lending that has occurred within the EU over the last decade, which will leave many banks carrying large losses. Therefore, the key requirement becomes stopping banks from defaulting on their deposits, which would involve their widespread public ownership and support, including extending public ownership where necessary whilst the ECB concentrates its borrowing power on securing bank liabilities.

Conclusion

This chapter has sought to outline the shape of eurozone economic policy-making where the SGP reinforces the budgetary aspects of the TEU convergence criteria, leading to an unprecedented loss of national fiscal policy autonomy, together with the ECB's monetary-policy stance of a 'one-size-fits-all' interest-rate policy. However, this combination has proved particularly toxic following the Great Recession (induced by the Global Financial Crisis) when these contemporary crises are seen as the product of deficient policymaking in the suffering countries, where budgetary policy has been too expansive and economies are too competitively inflexible. Conventional wisdom declares that once fiscal consolidation has occurred and labour market flexibility has been introduced, the countries concerned can return to non-inflationary growth. Unfortunately, such conventional wisdom has been misplaced, subjecting the eurozone to inefficient and ultimately unsustainable tensions that cannot be resolved by fiscal austerity alone, but only by a large rise in the external demand for output. However, in a eurozone without monetary or exchange-rate offsets, any reduction in public expenditure generates at least an equivalent reduction in output (Holland, 1995). Such a diminution in purchasing power creates a spiral of debt deflation in which the cost of meeting unpaid debts leads to low growth, falling prices, loss of jobs and declining living standards (Minsky, 2008). This 'perfect storm' increases the risk of default and therefore is likely to cause long-term interest rates to rise, the very thing that the adjustment policy was designed to avoid. Such a scenario carries dire consequences for future productive potential, political dislocation and social distress (Baimbridge, et al., 2012).

Consequently, the sustainability of the eurozone in the medium- and long-term will partly depend upon the implementation of a fiscal-policy initiative, one located at the federal rather than national level and which is sufficiently well-resourced and targeted to stabilise member-state economies in the face of asymmetric external shocks. In the absence of exchange-rate or monetary autonomy, and with insufficient labour mobility and wage flexibility, individual regions may become characterised by persistent unemployment, low per-capita income and ensuing social tension. The EU leadership's priority is to prevent the single currency collapsing, but such a stance creates immense danger since the EU possesses only a limited volume of borrowing and political will. For example, the European Financial Stability Facility (EFSF) and European Stability Mechanism (ESM) were established with a capital base of €80bn to provide a lending ceiling of €500bn, but should a country such as Italy require a bailout, then even the combined might of the ESM and IMF would be severely tested. If these become exhausted, insufficient financial firepower may remain to prevent bank defaults when a number of countries decide to leave the single currency and devalue. This risk has been intensified by EU encouragement of cross-border loans within its jurisdiction, thus leaving European banks more exposed than they would otherwise have been. Moreover, as this chapter has discussed, the potential negative externalities resulting from the eurozone crisis encompass the body politic, which could possess longer-term implications for the EU as an 'ever-closer union'.

This section of the book firstly presented the background to the issue of monetary union where it is merely a step along a theoretical road of macroeconomic thought and international monetary systems. However, the adoption of an exchange-rate regime is not a decision for any country to take lightly, given that its practical consequences in terms of both economic and political national sovereignty are substantial and therefore require deep analysis. The lessons to be learnt from historical experience are: that an 'ideal' international monetary system is an elusive aspiration for policy-makers; that the key to understanding exchange-rate regimes is to realise their inherently temporary nature relative to the level of economic development experienced by the country in question and its main trading partners, together with the overall global trend in international monetary systems; hence, the need for countries to maintain a degree of 'philosophical' flexibility, given that an alternative regime might prove optimal as economic circumstances change. This calculation is required by eurozone member states; however, there are complications in that the various costs and benefits need to be assessed within the context of both the potential partner country and in relation to the already-established monetary union or the other prospective members. Each economy is unique in its blend of sectoral strengths and weaknesses and comparative advantage, therefore national interests will be distinctively different for potential participants. Further, there is no set rule by which to weigh the relative merits of the arguments associated with membership of a monetary union. Although economic theory suggests that a monetary union will prove generally beneficial if the participants are sufficiently converged, it is necessary to establish an unambiguous, comprehensive and theoretically sound set of convergence criteria: it is questionable, however, whether the eurozone's current convergence criteria fulfil this role.

Consequently, the view advocated in this book is that future potential eurozone members should adopt the more comprehensive guide offered by optimum currency area theory rather than the endogeneity assumption that a shared currency will generate economic convergence and political unity. As recent events have indicated this policy has resulted in the opposite as increasing divergence amongst members undermines eurozone performance and threatens the economic stability of the rest of the world. With that in mind, this book now turns to exploring a number of potential solutions to the eurozone crisis, together with alternative potential directions in relation to neoliberalism.

Part III
Solutions to the Eurozone Crisis

9
Moral Suasion, Financial Relief and Debt Default

Introduction

As previously discussed, the eurozone came under unprecedented strain, in particular as the credit crunch induced recession-triggered problems within the eurozone regarding sovereign debt, leading to a series of potential remedies instigated by the EU itself. This chapter consists of a critical evaluation of the solutions that have been instigated in relation to moral persuasion, financial relief measures and debt default. In contrast, the subsequent chapters of this section of the book address a series of alternative and perhaps more radical propositions concerning fiscal federalism and a European Clearing Union, and envisions a scenario in which the euro might even collapse.

The initial response to the eurozone crisis was that of moral suasion, namely, castigating debtor countries for their profligacy. Such a shaming process may have a limited effect, but is likely to be of only short duration, given its illogicality. For example, Germany is urging budget cuts on the Mediterranean nations, without acknowledging how its own surpluses were built partly upon their willingness to buy German commodities with borrowed money. Indeed, the analysis of Chick and Pettifor (2011) indicates that implementation of austerity policies across the EU has been asymmetric, whereby government spending has risen in the 'core economies', so that budget deficits have remained steady whilst GDP has increased. In contrast, reductions in government spending in the 'periphery' (e.g., Greece, Ireland and Spain) have led to a range of budgetary outcomes and a decline in GDP. Hence, if the euro is to prove permanent, it requires a firmly based equilibrating mechanism. Thus, the search continues for more secure foundations than the Treaty on European Union provides.

The offer of ad hoc financial relief measures, usually subject to guarantees of changed economic policy backed by market and political pressures, was the reaction to the eurozone crises during 2010 and the early months of 2011. As bailouts encompassed Greece, Ireland and Portugal, and with market sentiment indicating the possibility of future loans to Belgium,

139

Italy and Spain, a permanent source of funding was seen to be required. Consequently, eurozone members agreed to establish the EFSF to be replaced by the ESM after 2013, so that by 2017 the ESM will possess a fully paid-up capital base of €80 billion, which provides it with a lending ceiling of €500 billion, which is more than adequate to cover the cost of existing bailouts.

The causes of the debt crisis are the result of certain eurozone countries borrowing more than they could repay on time, with the result that they have had to (and in many cases will continue to) suffer years of austerity as they try to meet their obligations – while their creditors suffer the uncertainty of not knowing when or whether they will be repaid. A common reaction to such crises is 'neither a borrower nor a lender be' and such views tend to gain particular currency after periodic financial crises, as both borrowers and lenders recover their equilibrium. In general, however, such isolationism is not a sensible response, for borrowing has an important role in economic development, as a glance at economic history amply illustrates. However, the eurozone debt crisis raises many questions: how the crisis came about; how international banks lent so much money to these countries; why indebted countries did not go into outright default; how the debt crisis has been managed since the emergence of the problem, and what various solutions have been proposed to resolve the crisis.

Moral suasion

Moral suasion can be defined as the attempt to coerce economic activity via exhortation in directions not already defined or dictated by existing statute law, such that it carries at a minimum the implied threat of future legislation. The necessary conditions for a moral suasion policy to be successful in achieving any desired goal constitute a special, not a general, case in the economy; and the presence of these necessary conditions may well be promoted by existing trends in the economy so that over time we may expect to see a continued increase in both the incidence and effectiveness of policies implemented through moral suasion (Romans, 1966). In relation to the eurozone crisis, moral suasion appeared to be a policy tool undergoing a contemporary resurrection, whereby there has been a marked increase in intra-governmental pressure, led by Germany, and to a somewhat lesser extent by elements of the EU, such as the Commission and ECB (El-Erian and Roubini, 2012; van Riet, 2013). Indeed, from late 2011 to early 2012 many commercial banks reportedly became subject to moral suasion by their national governments to take advantage of the ECB's offer of cheap liquidity for three years and to park these funds in sovereign debt (Buiter and Rahbari, 2012). The European Parliament also argued that a government under financial stress could take all necessary measures to encourage private investors to maintain their overall exposure on a voluntary basis. In addition, it proposed to allow the countries concerned to initiate measures aimed at stabilising markets and preserving the good functioning of their financial sector. As these proposals were adopted, the new EU regulation could in principle legitimise national regulatory actions and moral suasion in support of government debt financing.

However, although there is little evidence that moral suasion is being used wholly as a substitute for other instruments of economic policy, it is nevertheless interesting to see its occurrence, given the plethora of more conventional economic policies (i.e., fiscal, monetary and supply-side) that governments are familiar with. Indeed, it is perhaps this re-emergence of moral suasion as a major policy instrument that has raised so many objections in that it is inequitable because it: rewards noncompliance; constitutes extra-legal coercion without judicial review; is in violation of the 'rule of law'; entails the danger of an overly familiar relationship between regulator and regulatee, where promises, implicit or explicit, are involved; has an ad-hoc character that adds an additional and unnecessary element of uncertainty to business decisions; and may frequently be used in lieu of (i.e., as an excuse for not implementing) more effective legislation (Romans, 1966). However, this does not prove that moral suasion is inferior, per se, to other types of policy instruments, since all policies have opportunity costs, both in terms of their administrative and enforcement costs as well as their allocative effects on the economy. Whether moral suasion is inferior to other instruments, or whether a partially effective moral suasion policy is even superior to a policy of doing nothing at all depends upon the relative costs and effectiveness of alternative policies and the value system within which the relative costs and benefits are weighed (Romans, 1966). Indeed, in terms of the actions of central banks, this was a familiar policy before being replaced in the Great Depression by more actively interventionist policies (Smits, 1997).

Proponents of moral suasion argue that it is to the long-run benefit of the erring national governments to comply with the persuasion, implying that they are presently acting irrationally and not maximising their welfare in the long run. On the other hand, opponents of moral suasion argue that such a position is misguided, for compliance would not increase national welfare – for example, it is not in the national interest to remain within the eurozone. However, crucially, under such circumstances neither side addresses itself to the only real dilemma, namely the situation in which both parties are acting rationally in light of their own objective functions. Moreover, there are two necessary conditions for the success of a moral suasion policy: first, a long-run condition whereby the public must support the EU/ECB/IMF position, such that strong involvement with the public interest increases both the scope for altruism as well as the probability that threats will be carried out. A glare of publicity can increase the power of persuasion ex ante (by increasing the expected cost of noncompliance) and the degree of censure on non-compliers ex post. However, this is only a necessary condition for an effective moral suasion policy in the long-run, for fear of public displeasure is only one of the possible threats or promises with which EU/ECB/IMF might back a moral suasion policy. In the short-run it may be possible to establish sufficient expectations of other costs for non-compliers; however, in the long-run, given that economic policies are (at least notionally) made in a democratic framework, the public must support these policies politically. This is particularly true when moral suasion is used recurrently against the same group. Second, there is both a short- and long-run condition in that moral suasion appears to be completely ineffective when exerted upon a large population. Fewness makes non-compliers readily identifiable and places responsibility for the success of the policy specifically and directly upon a small number of individual units, so that credit for success, or blame for failure, can be levied. However, simultaneously the fewness condition imposes a severe limitation on the applicability of moral suasion as an instrument of policy, and it cannot be artificially satisfied by arbitrarily delineating a small population to be persuaded. Generally, the population to be persuaded must be as large as the population policymakers desire to affect. Additionally, fewness also implies the existence of sufficient market power to affect the public interest. Given that some level of restraint on economic activity is required, substitute restraints must come from either increased EU/ECB/IMF controls or from moral suasion. This offers a possible reason why we have observed, and may continue to observe, the use of moral suasion as an economic policy.

Fiscal compact and financial relief measures

The first option available for the EU to seek to address the issues raised by the financial crisis, and subsequent tensions laid bare within the eurozone, involves a reaffirmation of the essential features of the original design for the eurozone, but strengthened by additional monitoring of nation states and sanctions against fiscal imprudence.

This may be termed an orthodox solution in that it borrows from neo-classical and monetarist economic theories. It rejects the necessity for fiscal flexibility to seek to maintain a sufficient level of aggregate demand in each national economy, which is the Keynesian position, doing so partly because of variable lags in implementation that may cause fiscal intervention to be destabilising. Reliance upon annual budgets would certainly increase the time lag inherent in implementation, although, during the Keynesian era, this was surmounted by multiple budgets during the year where necessary. It has been noted that tax cuts are quicker to enact and transmission lags are shorter than public-works schemes, although delays in identification of areas in which to invest can be significantly shortened if implementing advance investment planning, whereby public agencies maintain a list of preferred investments in advance of recessionary periods during which these works can be started on relatively short notice.

A second rationale concerns a belief in the significance of crowding out, whereby an increase in public expenditure will cause the interest rate to rise (as demand for money rises relative to supply according to neo-classical perceptions of financial markets), which displaces an equivalent amount of private-sector investment. A stronger variant of this approach is to assume that private-sector activity is, de facto, more efficient than public-sector activity, and therefore crowding out would result in a net aggregate fall in productive capacity. One final theoretical justification for the orthodox approach rests upon the assumption of Ricardian equivalence, as rational economic agents respond to an increase in budget deficits by anticipating future tax rises to pay for the additional spending. Hence, they respond by reducing immediate consumption to raise their levels of savings against this future expense. As a result, fiscal policy is ineffective (Barro, 1974, 1989).

These conclusions, however, depend upon a number of fundamental assumptions. For example, crowding out is not likely to be much of a problem unless the economy is at, or close to, its full employment level. New classical economists, who believe in instant market clearing, adopt the assumption that this is always the case, barring the intervention of market imperfections, whereas neo-classical and monetarist economists accept that there might be some deviation from full-employment equilibrium in the short run, but that this will not last very long. Recent events may question these optimistic assumptions and may provide further evidence, if it is really needed, that the Keynesian identification of demand-deficient unemployment can persist for a considerable time – the importance of which is that crowding out is less likely to have negative effects when there are under-used resources in the economy that would benefit from public spending bringing them back into use.

There is, however, a more fundamental problem with the crowding-out theory, and that is the assumption of a neo-classical money market, determining the demand and supply of money, and hence the price or interest rate. However, this is not how money is allocated in a modern economy, as it is the banking sector that creates credit used in public and private investment, and it does so more in line with expectations of risk, the level of activity in the economy and future prospects of growth. Money is endogenous not exogenous.

The 'fiscal compact' – more properly entitled the intergovernmental Treaty on Stability, Coordination and Governance in the Economic and Monetary Union – was devised by the EU in 2011, signed in 2012 by all but two member states, the United Kingdom and the Czech Republic, and enacted the following year. It introduced six new measures – five regulations and one directive – which became nicknamed the 'six pack'. This set of measures sought to tighten the SGP and governance surrounding the eurozone more generally, through:

1. implementation of a common set of accounting systems and statistics;
2. regular surveillance of public finances to evaluate risks of imbalances; and
3. a system of graduated sanctions enforcing budget prudence – imposition of an interest-bearing deposit, amounting to 0.2% of GDP, for those member states that the EU Council of Ministers believes have not taken sufficient corrective action following an adverse judgement by the EU Commission on budget balance – the deposit is converted into a fine if recommended corrective actions are not implemented (Degryse, 2012: 30)

These rules only bind eurozone members, although other member state signatories would be automatically bound should they join the single currency.

To compliment this set of measures, a set of national reform programmes was agreed to promote prudent public finances in each of the member states. This encompasses areas of social and employment policy, including public-sector employment, welfare-expenditure, pensions, infrastructure expenditure and actions pertaining to tackling social exclusion (Degryse, 2012: 41). The intention is for this element of increased coordination of social and economic policies to reinforce the SGP, promote competitiveness by controlling labour costs and facilitate employment through increased use of 'flexicurity' (Degryse, 2012: 46).

The fiscal framework was further tightened in January 2012, with the adoption of the European Fiscal Compact treaty, requesting that all states introduce a 'golden-rule' balanced budget principle in their national constitutions. This involved:

- commitment to achieving a balanced or surplus budget, with the structural deficit limited to 0.5% GDP, except in exceptional circumstances;
- public debt to be kept below 60% GDP;
- failure to meet these targets would trigger a requirement to submit a structural reform package to the EU Commission and the Council, for approval and implementation;
- failure to incorporate these rules into national law would be subject to the EU Court of Justice and to potential imposition of a fine.

In essence, debt brakes were, therefore, to be introduced in each member state using the euro.

These reforms have led to an 'unprecedented extension of the surveillance powers of the EU over the member states' (Degryse, 2012: 67), alongside a similar strengthening of the accompanying enforcement measures available to the EU to ensure compliance.

Alongside this combination of fiscal discipline, enshrined in national law, reinforced by external oversight and by sanctions imposed against breaches of this new system of fiscal rules, a system of macro-prudential regulations has been introduced. Accordingly, a range of indicators is to be closely monitored, with the intention that these will highlight external imbalances sufficiently rapidly for national governments to devise adequate policy responses. Indicators include house prices, credit expansion and external balance. Whilst, undoubtedly, a positive development, doubt remains over whether national governments have the capacity to adequately design and implement a range of policy instruments of sufficient force to successfully mitigate against the full range of risk factors – particularly given the fiscal constraints imposed by the other aspects of the fiscal compact regime (Lane, 2012: 63).

The European Financial Stability Mechanism

In addition to the adoption of the new fiscal compact rules, the response to the 2008 financial crisis and to the subsequent sovereign debt crisis for certain members of the eurozone – as government attempts to rescue and recapitalise their banking sectors have caused a rapid increase in public deficits and indebtedness – the EU has introduced the European Financial Stability Mechanism (EFSM). At first glance, this might appear similar to the EFTS schemes advocated by Italianer and Vanheukelen (1993) and Whyman (1997), however, they are quite different in both intent and design. Whereas the EFTS was proposed to provide a continual element of fiscal stabilisation to protect the eurozone from the worst of the asymmetric shocks it will inevitably and periodically experience, the EFSF has been established with the more limited, and more immediate, objective of seeking to prevent insolvency amongst high-risk eurozone member states from undermining the single-currency project.

The European Commission created three new instruments to facilitate borrowing on the international money markets in order to make loans to member states that are threatened with debt default. The European Financial Stability Mechanism was established with a borrowing limit of €60bn, whilst the European Financial Stability Facility was established as a temporary instrument, but with a larger borrowing capacity: €440bn. In 2012, the European Stability Mechanism was established with capital injection of €80bn from EU member states, and this fund can borrow against this up to a total of €500bn. The intention is that these instruments will intervene on secondary financial markets to purchase the bonds of struggling debtor-participant nations from the private-sector investors who currently hold the assets. The intention is to prevent fears over the insolvency of the debtor nations from causing a withdrawal of credit and substantially raising interest rates, thereby exacerbating their existing financial problems. Essentially, the EFSF would be nationalising (or perhaps, more accurately, Europeanising) potentially bad debts, in the same way as many governments responded in their own markets during the recent 'credit crunch' financial crisis. Private investors would take a 'haircut' (receiving less than the full paper value of the assets) to prevent creating undue moral hazard, which would occur if the investors did not suffer any consequences for poor lending decisions. Whilst money loaned to a distressed member state would normally be charged a lower rate of interest than prevailing market rates available to that nation (although lower than rates available to other member states without such debt problems, it would still have to repay the loan and interest payments).

The interventions, to date, have been substantial, albeit four EU member states have been the primary recipients:

- Greece – €347bn, 179% GDP
- Spain – €100bn, 9.5% GDP
- Ireland – €85bn, 47.5% GDP
- Portugal – €78bn, 42.7% GDP
- Cyprus – €17bn, 97% GDP
- Hungary, Lithuania, Romania – €50bn

The ESM is, as yet, untested, and doubts remain about whether it is of sufficient size to resist the threatened default of a member state the size of Spain or Italy. Moreover, criticism is targeted at the fact that, despite the appearance of an economic and monetary union, individual member states still borrow money individually, and therefore are subject to significantly differing rates of interest, resulting from different perceptions of the risk of inflation and/or default.

The creation of the EFSF is an interesting watershed moment for the eurozone. At one level, it demonstrates the practical and political problems inherent in the creation of fiscal federalism – for example, that even at a time of considerable crisis, it has proven difficult to craft an innovation that all parties find acceptable. Indeed, the detail remains imprecise about how this new fiscal policy instrument would operate and evolve in the future. Yet, the fact remains that this first, tentative step in the creation of some form of federal fiscal intervention has been taken, and the pressure of events will necessitate further developments during the following months and years, as the destabilisation caused by the 'credit crunch' plays out. This is comforting for those advocates of fiscal federalism being a necessary, but not sufficient, feature of a sustainable eurozone.

A second aspect of the EFSF is less advantageous, however, since the financial support packages are intended to be reinforced by a stricter interpretation of the SGP. This is perhaps not a surprising condition to be placed upon debtor nations, as contributors to the schemes wish to limit their payments (under pressure from discontented taxpayers at home), and so they require a rapid fiscal consolidation on behalf of debtor nations, bringing deficits within the SGP limits during a very-short, two-year time period. Moreover, the 15-point proposal additionally includes proposals to strengthen the scrutiny of individual nations' fiscal plans and legal restraints being placed upon national budgets. Thus, the combination of the financial rescue schemes appears to be to provide sufficient short-term credit to debtor nations to enable them to deflate their economies in order to return to close to financial balance, without the ability to devalue (due to participation in the single currency) and, at a time when most of the rest of the world is experiencing constrained economic growth prospects. This would appear to be too close to the United Kingdom preoccupation – the best part of a century ago – with the maintenance of the gold standard at an uncompetitive rate, combined with the disastrous response to budget deficits arising amidst the Great Depression, both squeezing growth prospects in order to try and balance the economy and, instead, pushing the economy onto a downward spiral of negative growth and a deteriorating budgetary position.

In summary, the financial crisis has highlighted weaknesses in the economic infrastructure established to sustain the eurozone. However, there is not unanimity in diagnosis of the inherent causes, nor in terms of policy prescriptions. More orthodox economic opinion holds that the sovereign-debt crisis in Europe was caused by fiscal profligacy, whereas Keynesian opinion holds that the eurozone has not been established correctly to deal with asymmetric shocks that are likely to persist. Accordingly, there are two broadly different policy responses to this problem (or three, if the option of abandoning the eurozone is included), namely: (a) to tighten the rules relating to national budgetary management to enshrine debt brakes in legislation and broaden the range of social and economic policies coming under the auspices of the EU Commission as it monitors individual member state actions; and, (b) to introduce greater budgetary flexibility in order to prioritise macroeconomic demand-management at national level, perhaps supplemented by a supra-national fiscal policy instrument, whether through significant extension of federal budgetary competences or through a more targeted EFTS, with the specific intention to minimise the asymmetric nature of external shocks and thereby stabilise the eurozone.

There is nothing preventing a combination of the two approaches and, indeed, it has been suggested that the U.S. experience might indicate that option (a) might not be sustainable in the long term in its proposed form, due to a lack of local 'ownership' of the initiative, and resulting adverse reaction to the perception of externally imposed negative economic consequences (i.e., the protests in Greece). Moreover, and perhaps more significantly, option (b), since debt brakes or balanced budget rules do not allow for counter-cyclical fiscal policy, their adoption in the majority of U.S. states has occurred only because the federal government has a large budget and can take the strain of macroeconomic management (Henning and Kessler, 2012). As previously stated, the present EU central budget is currently insufficient to perform this task.

Nevertheless, the policy selections made by the eurozone members in the aftermath of the financial crisis would appear to be more heavily slanted towards the former option, with a short-term series of (repayable) loans distributed subject to the implementation of domestic austerity, imposed by an external EU 'troika', and with tighter rules established in the attempt to constrain national fiscal policy in the future. The fact that member states in distress were all located in the eurozone periphery and had large public deficits, suggested to many that the problem had been fiscal profligacy and, therefore, austerity and an enhanced stringency in curtailing national budget deficits were perceived to be significant elements of the solution (Zezza, 2012: 41). Indeed, the obfuscation of the Greek failure to comply with the pre-crisis fiscal rules helped to form an influential political narrative, blaming the crisis on fiscal irresponsibility of individual nations rather than on more fundamental macroeconomic imbalances and weaknesses in the design of the eurozone itself (Lane, 2012: 56).

This analysis is incorrect. It is not the case that all struggling member states had pre-existing budget deficits. Indeed, Ireland and Spain had budget surpluses, in the year before the financial crisis, whereas only Greece exhibited the type of budgetary ill-discipline that corresponds to this neo-liberal critique (Bird and Mandilaras, 2013). Moreover, a more-detailed examination of the evidence would indicate that the financial crisis resulted from excess levels of private-sector debt, allowed or encouraged to occur due to the deregulation of the financial sector and misapplication of estimation of risk. Bird and Mandilaras (2013) have, for example, estimated that fiscal deficits have not been a significant, never mind primary, cause of the European economic crisis. This was not a crisis caused by fiscal profligacy. Consequently, responses to the crisis focus on a symptom of the crisis and not on the fundamental causes (Calcagno, 2012: 24).

It has been suggested that the future of the ESM, within the framework of the EU austerity measures, is considered to be 'bleak' (Degryse, 2012: 73), as member states pursue a 'competitiveness state' agenda, increasingly utilising social policy as a means of promoting national competitiveness. Indeed, Degryse (2012: 72) claims this austerity approach 'is a road to nowhere', whilst Zezza (2012: 52) argues that the further implementation of fiscal austerity may lead to either the stagnation of the periphery of the eurozone or else the collapse of the euro.

What can be predicted, with a reasonable degree of certainty, is that the current eurozone fiscal framework is unlikely to remain in its present form in the medium term. Pressures arising from the weaknesses in competitive austerity approaches, and the insistence that member states already experiencing weak economic performance bear the disproportionate brunt of any adjustment costs, would seem to be ultimately defeating in the absence of broader supportive fiscal measures. These could take the form of Eurobonds, or an EFTS scheme, or even the centralising of federal budgetary competences as originally advocated by the MacDougal Report four decades ago. However, evaluating these issues in the aftermath of a substantial shock to the EU economy – a shock which, although it impacted negatively upon all member states, the effects were experienced asymmetrically in terms of the scale of the resultant consequences arising from the initial event – it would seem that the case for fiscal federalism to stabilise and sustain the eurozone is more persuasive, whereas the neo-liberal critique of the approach has been fundamentally weakened by recent events.

The economics of the sovereign debt crisis

A key issue to examine in relation to the crisis is the economics of borrowing, in order to analyse how the debt problem arose: Why were certain eurozone countries eager to borrow and commercial banks so willing to supply the funds in the first place? From the perspective of these countries, the combinations of relatively low incomes and poorly developed capital markets meant that there were frequently insufficient domestic savings to provide the finance for domestic investment. However, their relatively low capital stock suggests that there are plenty of opportunities for profitable investment. Thus, by borrowing funds from abroad and in particular from other eurozone members, they could raise domestic investment above domestic savings, leading to a higher rate of economic growth and the rapid expansion of productive resources. At the later date, when the borrowing economies had to repay the principal and interest on the loans, the expectation is that the additional resources created by the loan-financed investment will be at least sufficient to meet the repayments.

In contrast, for the lending countries, their relatively high incomes and sophisticated financial markets lead to high savings ratios. Simultaneously, high levels of capital stock means that a large proportion of savers will look to place their funds abroad to achieve higher returns than are available domestically. Hence, the potential exists for profitable exchange between the two types of eurozone countries, whereby the borrowing nations can utilise the excess savings of the lending countries for investment while the lending countries have higher prospective returns from such investments rather than domestic investments.

However, with the largely unanticipated drying-up of international capital markets, this relationship proved not to be so mutually beneficial, and history contains numerous previous similar episodes. For example, Argentina borrowed to finance large fiscal deficits incurred because of political instability in the 1970s, inefficient state enterprises and heavy military expenditure in the 1980s; none of which constituted productive investment with which to repay the loans. Mexico, on the other hand, used its loans to finance heavy investment in the oil industry, which was based upon overtly optimistic future price expectations and which, with the benefit of

hindsight, proved unable to provide the flow of additional resources anticipated to repay the initial loans. In contrast, the supposedly more-sophisti-
cated Western governments and banking sectors within the eurozone were
regarded as immune to such financial sleight-of-hand.

Such a situation, then, frequently becomes exacerbated via the dynamics of
international debt: when investment begins to exceed domestic savings once
borrowing occurs, then the country is running a current account deficit, the
counterpart of which is the capital inflow on the capital account. In other
words, the increase in a country's net foreign indebtedness is equal to the
current account deficit that has to be financed by borrowing from abroad.
Using the national income accounting identities, the proximate causes of a
current account deficit are: $(X - M) - R_F = (S - I) + (T - G)$ where the current
account (the trade account $X - M$) together with net interest paid abroad
(R_F) is equal to the sum of net private- and public-sector saving. It follows
that if net foreign indebtedness is not increased, the trade surplus must be
large enough to finance interest payments abroad. Thus, if $(X - M) < R_F$ then
debt increases, if $(X - M) > R_F$ then debt decreases, and if $(X - M) = R_F$ then a
stable state exists, with debt neither growing nor falling. For a trade surplus
to occur, net domestic saving (i.e., public plus private) must be positive. Thus,
anything that causes I to rise relative to S, G relative to T, M relative to X, or
R_F to increase, can cause net foreign indebtedness to increase.

A further way to review the economics of sovereign debt is in relation to
the national budget in the following formula:

$$\frac{B_t}{Y_t} - \frac{B_{t-1}}{Y_{t-1}} = (r - g)\frac{B_{t-1}}{Y_{t-1}} + \frac{G_t - T_t}{Y_t}$$

Where:

Bt = government debt at the end of year t
Gt = government spending during year t
Tt = taxes minus transfers during year t
Yt = national income during year t
r = the real interest rate
g = real growth rate

The equation implies increases in debt-to-GDP ratio will be larger under
the following set of mutually exclusive circumstances: the higher the real
interest rate, the lower the growth rate of output and the higher the primary
deficit and debt ratio. Unfortunately, for several of the eurozone economies
these were likely to happen as ECB lowered its interest rate, because uncertainty led to slower growth that was already occurring in many eurozone
countries. Consequently, to prevent debt accelerating, primary surplus as

a percent of GDP required to maintain the debt ratio constant varied from around 2% for Spain to over 40% for Greece; in contrast, Germany could afford to run a primary deficit of nearly 3%.

As a broad generalisation, the onset of the Great Recession resulted in an unfavourable movement in several of these factors for the indebted euro-zone countries as a group. Therefore both internal and external factors were ultimately responsible for the debt crisis. Whilst it would be unfair to blame solely the banks for the debt crisis, one may ask whether they acted entirely prudently. Although there was little to indicate any problem with sovereign lending, they could have considered whether borrowers' policies were such that they could have serviced their debt from own resources rather than new borrowing. Moreover, several features distinguished those eurozone countries that suffered most from the debt crisis, among them inappropriate fiscal policies, with traditions of large budget deficits, whereby foreign borrowing provided a simple solution by financing the deficits in a relatively non-inflationary manner. Also, the related problem of capital flight by which, fearing increased taxes, the wealthy sections of the private sector sent their assets abroad while the government borrowed them back from foreign banks to finance the resulting decline in reserves. The prevailing trade regime also affected countries' exposure to borrowing crises, where outward-oriented regimes such as Germany provided robust and diversified export revenues on which to borrow, whilst more inward-looking regimes tended to be rigid and inefficient.

The difficulties imposed upon several eurozone countries by the debt crisis leads to the discussion of regarding the potential costs and benefits of default, given the severity of the situation and the long-term damage wrought on their economies and even on social cohesion. Indeed, since many of the loans taken out were undertaken (or guaranteed) by government, any default in repayments would represent 'sovereign default'. As a consequence, there would not be a legal remedy for creditors to retrieve their money; nevertheless, debtors are typically reluctant to default because their savings on repayments are perceived as being typically lower than the costs of defaulting. Although the costs of default are uncertain and difficult to quantify, as witnessed in the eurozone crisis, the reluctance of debtor governments to default means that the costs must potentially be more important than the benefits accrued by saving repayments. In such cases the most common costs tend to concern exclusion from future borrowing, such that foreign creditors would be unlikely to lend to defaulting countries as such loans would appear unduly risky and, even if the loans would occur, they would attract very high rates of interest and probably the requirement for some form of loan-guarantee collateral. Thus, the country would be constrained to finance future investment from its already relatively low domestic savings, which would impede economic growth. In addition, borrowing would be unavailable to smooth out adverse external shocks, exposing the nation to sudden changes in economic conditions and, in turn, associating long-term investment with higher risk. Second, there is the issue of reduced gains from international trade, whereby the defaulting country would risk an increased possibility of protectionist trade measures being imposed against it, with the additional risk that debtors might seize its goods as they crossed international borders. Consequently, trade credits may also be more difficult to secure, potentially resulting in a reduction in the volume of trade and thereby causing significant welfare losses for the citizens of the defaulting nation. Third, there is the potential danger of the seizure of overseas assets. Whilst legal recourse for creditors does not exist, they may be able to persuade their governments or legal systems to freeze (or confiscate) defaulting countries' assets held in their jurisdiction, as in the case of the Icelandic banks. Alternatively, one method of reducing the possibility of penalties would be for debtor countries to form defaulting cartels. Defaulting *en masse* would make it more difficult for creditor governments to maximise pressure on all participants simultaneously. Thus, it is in the interest of creditor governments to avoid the formation of organised default by maximising the potential costs of such default, whilst minimising the potential benefits.

In contrast, the potential benefits of defaulting gained by the nation concerned is that it saves the repayment of the principal that is due as well as the interest due on the outstanding debt. Thus, we can derive the following equation: $DS = P + rD$ where DS represents debt-service repayments, P the principal and interest due, r the rate of interest and D the stock of debt remaining. This equation represents the gross repayments a government would save through default, but it does not represent the net resource transfer (NRT) which also takes account of new loans received. Obviously, if the debtor country continued to receive new loans, this would reduce its immediate burden in terms of the repayment of its initial loans, and therefore reduce the immediate incentive to default. The NRT can be illustrated in the equation: $NRT = P + rD - L = DS - L$ where L represents new loans received by the debtor nation. Consequently, we can deduce that a debtor government will not default if the immediate benefit of doing so is less than the perceived costs of default. In other words, if the net resource transfer (NRT) is less than the perceived costs (C). Thus, if $NRT = P + rD - L < C$ then a country should not default, whilst if $NRT = P + rD - L > C$ then a country should default. These equations are important to understand the various strategies adopted by the banks and creditor governments to avoid default by either raising the costs of default or lowering its benefits.

The previous section of this chapter discussed how the eurozone debt crisis has been managed largely on a 'case-by-case' approach in relation to each debtor nation – on an individual basis rather than collectively, largely grounded on the rationale that this was the only realistic option because the problem confronting each debtor has its own particular characteristics, requiring its own solutions. However, from a historical experience, numerous plans have been developed for resolving debt crises such that it is useful to examine the common principles in the treatment extended to debtors. The first of these is debt relief such that even if countries were willing to undertake domestic adjustment, debtors still have the problem of borrowing new money. Experience suggests that debtors usually need a period of a significantly reduced debt-service burden in which to stabilise their economies and start adjustment. Such periods may be engendered by interest holidays, negotiated debt reductions, increased lending, or unilateral suspension of debt-service payments. However, debt relief raises the potentially serious problem of moral hazard with both sovereign lending and debtor governments. Additionally, in the knowledge that they will be bailed out again, banks may pursue a high-risk strategy of lending with insufficient monitoring. Furthermore, if a country owes more than it could ever pay off, then stabilisation programmes only increase the proportion of debt it can pay off; however, if no benefits accrue from this policy, why should a rational government pursue such austerity policies?

In contrast, the option of debt rescheduling is when pressure is put upon countries to maintain interest repayments if debt relief (i.e., reduction) has been ruled out and yet there is no money to meet the payments. Although under such circumstances rescheduling would be the only option, there is the implicit aspect within this structure that no creditor receive more favourable treatment than any other. Nevertheless, the difficulty of making rescheduling agreements raises the question of why debtors do not default on their loans. A common answer is that it would close them off from new money; however, this argument is frequently exaggerated – rather, it is the involvement of debtor governments in foreign borrowing that is important where official default is an explicit and political act. Indeed, it was the level of political capital invested in the eurozone project that meant it could not be allowed to fail. The flipside to default is debt forgiveness, whereby advocates of this policy view the plight of the debtor nations as so serious that the best means of helping them is to partially write off their debts. Proponents of this option argue that banks realise that they are unlikely to recover a large proportion of the loans made and, consequently, partial repayment is preferable to none at all. It is claimed that initial debt forgiveness will, in the long run, reduce the amount of write off, particularly if debt forgiveness is linked to economic reform, since this provides debtors with the incentive to continue to struggle to meet their loan obligations. However, potential problems associated with this approach include the question of who bears the cost of debt forgiveness in the creditor countries (i.e., commercial banks or government). Indeed, this was the dilemma surrounding the so-called 'haircut' experienced by banks in relation to Greek debt. Furthermore, it is claimed that debt forgiveness suffers from moral hazard since it gives encouragement to profligate economic policies and penalises those countries, like Greece, that suffered considerable domestic hardship in attempting to repay its debts. Finally, it is suggested that debt forgiveness is not based upon as clearly a 'moral' case as its proponents imply, which instead might be to argue for an increase in development assistance to the indebted countries; for example, through some form of enhanced fiscal federalism, as we discuss in the next chapter.

However, if either default or forgiveness remains unfeasible and the reality of the debt burden remains, a nation might wish to alter the nature and structure of its debt. Frequently, it this is type of proposal that banks more generally support, since they are loath to simply write off debt, with potential strategies, including: the lengthening of the time horizon for repayment, making its servicing more manageable; converting floating debt into fixed-interest bonds, so debtors are more certain of future debt-service commitments; 'debt-equity' swaps through selling debt at a discount of its face value to a third party who then has the right to exchange the debt for local currency, which in turn can be exchanged for equity in debtor-country enterprises; and 'debt for trade' swaps between developing countries as a means of settling debt obligations and debt reduction as part of a package to privatise state-owned companies. Similarly, to fundamentally decrease the pervasiveness of debt the only long-term solution is that of economic reform; indeed, banks and institutions such the IMF historically have been keen to promote economic reform in debtor countries on the basis that reform will improve their ability to service debt. Whilst typical measures can be summarised as devaluation, deflation and deregulation, the applicability of these for eurozone countries is clearly problematic, with the first ruled-out and the second (in the guise of austerity) having proved damaging. This leaves the third option, deregulation, but whilst the EU has sought to address such issues through initiatives such as the Lisbon Agenda and its successor Europe 2020, these have largely failed to deliver. Moreover, in the short term, such reforms may lead to increased unemployment, thereby making them politically destabilising for debtor nations to implement. Hence, the absence of any long-term solution to the sovereign debt problem continues to pose a threat to international financial stability. Current management is not dealing with the source of the crisis, nor does this management help to contain the random shocks that were responsible for precipitating the crisis.

Conclusion

While the loan market may not voluntarily increase its exposure to the indebted eurozone economies, the magnitude and nature of the current agreements mean that commercial bank lenders will continue to play an important part in the determination of debtor nations. There are, however, some worrying trends in the present situation: first that rescheduling packages usually roll the debt over in the medium term, yet the rationale for eurozone borrowing is based on the idea that foreign debt should be used for long-term supply-side-driven growth. Hence, there is clearly some degree of incompatibility within the time frame of this arrangement. The indebted eurozone economies have witnessed both capital flight and a decline in savings and investment as a share of GDP. While the pace of capital flight has diminished, it remains a source of concern. However, the decline in savings will reduce gross domestic investment, thereby discouraging growth, which in turn will discourage future investment and encourage further capital flight. This vicious circle of events, should it occur, would clearly be extremely serious for economic growth. Finally, there is the issue of what degree of the burden of the problem falls on lender countries in terms who should absorb it: shareholders of lender banks, their depositors, or the central bank and, hence, the taxpayer? Most observers believe it should be the shareholders; however, whilst capital and reserves remain insufficient to absorb the full burden, the potential for commercial bank failure will persist. Consequently, the absence of any long-term solution to the sovereign debt problem continues to pose a threat to the eurozone and, potentially, to international financial stability.

10
Fiscal Federalism

Introduction

The 2008 international financial crisis, which was triggered by problems related to sub-prime housing loans and securitisation via collateralised loan obligations and credit-default swaps, led to a deep economic recession across most of the industrialised world. It highlighted not only the fragility of the European banking system, but additionally the flaws in design of the particular form of Economic and Monetary Union (the eurozone) established amongst a number of European Union (EU) member states. The tensions caused by the financial crisis have not caused these problems, however, but rather magnified pre-existing weaknesses that have long been recognised by a number of academic commentators who have written on this topic over the past two decades or more (Eichengreen, 1992; de Grauwe and Vanhaverbeke, 1993; Burkett et al., 1996; Feldstein, 1997; Arestis and Sawyer, 2000; Lane, 2006). Moreover, it is not only the design of the eurozone, and the rules established to limit participation to suitable candidate nations, which have been found to be at fault, but also the economic architecture introduced in an attempt to sustain this new arrangement (Degryse, 2012: 6).

The response to these problems has been threefold. Firstly, the EU member states have sought to provide emergency loans in order to assist the eurozone members in immediate and pressing difficulties and thereby prevent nations being forced to leave the single currency or, indeed, keep the eurozone from disintegrating. This approach has been called 'kicking the can down the road', as it is a temporary 'sticking plaster' and does not solve fundamental problems, although it might create time for this to occur. Financial assistance has evolved into the more substantive European Stability Mechanism (ESM) but, where financial loans are provided, they are subject to the implementation of austerity measures and reforms in national labour and/or social policy, intended to reduce public expenditure. This 'fiscal compact' is the second element of the response. The third element is the ongoing negotiation of a tighter set of budgetary rules, tightening the former Stability and

Growth Pact (SGP) by having more restrictive limits on budget deficits and stricter enforcement of any breaches of these new rules. In essence, this is similar in effect to the mandatory establishment of balanced-budget rules for all participating member states. Once this regime has been enacted, the suggestion is that one or more elements of fiscal federalism may be introduced to help stabilise the eurozone over the long term.

This chapter seeks to examine the potential for fiscal federalism to play a significant role in sustaining the eurozone, and also to contrast variants of fiscal innovations for fulfilling this role.

Why might the eurozone benefit from fiscal federalism?

Participation in the eurozone involves national governments relinquishing exchange-rate and monetary policy instruments to federal economic authorities. The significance of this reduction in policy tools available to manage individual economies depends upon the extent to which devaluation retains a real effect in the medium to long term, and whether the financial markets within Europe are so closely integrated that independent monetary policy has been rendered impotent. However, should both of these conditions be satisfied, the eurozone would remain susceptible to destabilisation to the extent that external shocks exert an asymmetric impact upon individual economies. Asymmetric shocks are minimised if monetary union occurs between countries with comparable industrial structures that are, simultaneously, highly diversified. The expectation is that diversification will cause industry-specific shocks to offset one another whilst broad similarities between economies implies that a given external shock will possess a similar impact and require a matching policy response, which could be satisfactorily accomplished by the ECB or another federal financial authority.

In relation to external shocks, the literature has indicated the persistence of significant differences between specific EU member states that the pressures of the single currency magnify in importance. Thus, oil and gas production in the Netherlands and the United Kingdom, the manufacturing sector in Germany and the financial and media sectors in the United Kingdom, and the agricultural sector within many of the new member states, are each more developed than throughout the majority of EU nations. Similarly, the propensity for home ownership is different in Ireland and the United Kingdom than in continental Europe – a propensity which, when combined with a higher proportion of variable-rate mortgages, causes changes in monetary policy to have a faster and larger impact upon Irish and British domestic consumption than in the rest of the EU. Moreover, differences in financial systems can have a significant impact upon the economic consequences of movements in a common the eurozone-wide interest rate for nations (such as the United Kingdom) with a much greater proportion of corporate and household debt paid at variable rates of interest (Burkitt et al., 1997: 10–12).

The empirical analysis ascertaining whether the eurozone will predominantly experience symmetric or asymmetric shocks is therefore of fundamental importance to the design of the policy framework established to reinforce the union. Two such studies were undertaken, by Weber (1991) and by Bayoumi and Eichengreen (1993). The former found that shocks to nominal variables, such as inflation rates, and supply-side shocks were largely and increasingly symmetric, whereas labour market and demand shocks were primarily asymmetric. Furthermore, Bayoumi and Eichengreen discovered that EU member states suffered from more inflationary shocks and a higher proportion of supply shocks than did comparable U.S. states. Moreover, EU countries experienced particularly pronounced asymmetric external shocks, with the average correlation of supply shocks measuring 0.33 amongst EU member states compared to 0.46 amongst U.S. regions, whilst average demand shocks measured a particularly asymmetric 0.18 compared to 0.37 in the United States. Thus, whereas 46% of supply shocks and 37% of demand shocks were found to be symmetric in the United States, the corresponding figures for the EU were only 33% and 18% respectively.

This problematic conclusion would be eased if the eurozone were to be limited to a 'core' group comprising Germany, France, Belgium, Denmark and the Netherlands, potentially extended to Austria and one or two new member states in due course, since external shocks had a profoundly more symmetric effect upon this group of countries than on the rest of the EU member states. For this core group, correlation coefficients of 0.58 and 0.31, for supply and demand shocks, respectively, compares favourably with the values calculated for U.S. regions. The correlation coefficients of 0.14 and 0.10 for the remaining EU member states demonstrates that their participation in the eurozone would severely strain the ability of the ECB to formulate a monetary and exchange-rate policy that would be equally appropriate for all countries. Thus, current discussions about whether Greece should withdraw from the euro, potentially being followed by one or more struggling economies (i.e., Ireland, Spain, Portugal), would, on this evidence, appear to be beneficial both for these nations and the eurozone zone as a whole. Whilst a two-speed Europe has never proven to be a politically appealing scenario for EU leaders, it does appear to conform more closely to the available economic evidence (Bayoumi and Eichengreen, 1993).

The high degree of external shock asymmetry amongst EU member states highlights the potential cost of the eurozone in the absence of countervailing forces or government policies. In the absence of devaluation, a nation experiencing a loss of competitiveness due, for example, to slow productivity growth or a cost-push raw material price shock would experience rising unemployment unless price flexibility or factor mobility were sufficient to maintain full employment. However, the available evidence from academic studies suggests that neither of these mechanisms can provide more than marginal assistance. The consensus reached by most of the literature on nominal and real wage rigidity in Europe is that between 25% and 75% of price rises are passed on to wages, depending upon the country in question, thereby weakening real wage flexibility as an equilibrating mechanism to restore full employment in the aftermath of an asymmetric shock (Bruno and Sachs, 1985; Sala-i-Martin and Sachs, 1992; Goodhart, 1995).

Labour mobility within European countries has been estimated to be three times lower than in the United States, despite the existence of greater regional inequality and unemployment in Europe, implying that EU labour mobility is less responsive to employment and income incentives than is the U.S. labour market (OECD, 1986; Eichengreen, 1992). This is despite evidence that the dispersion of external shocks to labour markets was of a broadly similar frequency and magnitude for Britain, Italy and the United States (Eichengreen, 1993b: 155). Moreover, these estimates relate to labour mobility *within* individual countries, whereas mobility *between* countries is likely to be much lower due to language barriers, differences in culture and residual non-recognition of qualifications (Goodhart and Smith, 1993: 422). Thus, it may require substantially higher unemployment and regional inequality to generate labour mobility on the scale required to resolve regional imbalances in the absence of devaluation and wage/price flexibility. This would be equally destabilising for eurozone cohesion due to the political implications of large-scale emigration, together with the tensions created by unemployment and relative poverty within a Europe made more transparent through the introduction of a single currency. Indeed, it is possible that, as in Germany after reunification, labour market rigidity will increase as pay-differential transparency generates demands for pay equalisation between employees performing equivalent work in different countries, irrespective of productivity equalisation, with potentially damaging effects to competitiveness, output and employment (Doyle, 1989; Horn and Zwiener, 1992; Goodhart, 1995).

Capital mobility can, in principal, substitute for labour mobility in the long run, as the relocation of productive processes to depressed, inexpensive areas may occur. Indeed, Foreign Direct Investment (FDI) from established to new member states, may over the long term play a significant role in reducing the disparities in GDP per capita between member states. However, given the time lags involved in the movement of physical as opposed to financial capital, such movements are likely to reduce long-term regional disparities rather than offset short-term external shocks. The weakness of capital mobility to reduce long-term structural inequalities within existing nation states, together with the insights provided by studies in cumulative causation and endogenous growth theory, caution against over-optimistic assumptions of a rapid elimination of unemployment caused by shocks (Myrdal, 1957; Romer, 1994). Moreover, due to the transactions costs involved, factor movements are an inefficient means of reacting to transitory regional shocks (von Hagen, 1993: 278).

One argument frequently presented in the literature is that the further economic integration of Europe may reduce the probability of asymmetric shocks, so that existing policy instruments would be sufficient to moderate these disturbances (Emerson et al., 1992). However, the prevalence of regional asymmetric shocks within existing EU nation states may equally indicate that the industrial concentration accompanying economic integration may magnify the frequency and importance of asymmetric shocks (de Grauwe and Vanhaverbeke, 1993: 112–125). Enlargement of the EU has magnified the diversity of the single economy, whilst the current financial crisis amidst the Southern European members of the eurozone would appear to point to additional tensions between the longer-established EU member states. In view of the divergence of academic opinion on this point, it would be unwise for the architects of the eurozone to rely upon economic integration to provide a sufficient, permanent reduction in asymmetric shocks in the absence of the introduction of economic instruments designed to ensure the stability of the monetary union.

The persistence of asymmetric shocks within an the eurozone – where monetary and exchange-rate policy is determined at the federal level, and where price flexibility and labour mobility are insufficient to sustain full employment equilibrium – leaves fiscal policy as the primary stabilising instrument (Kenen, 1969, 1995: 81; Masson, 1996: 1002). Critics of the stabilising potential of fiscal policy argue that automatic stabilisers are counter-productive since they reduce the strength of price flexibility and labour mobility (Goodhart and Smith, 1993: 441; van der Ploeg, 1993: 144). A non-accommodative monetary and fiscal stance is claimed to reduce the time lag involved in adjusting to a new equilibrium position as individual economic actors internalise more of the costs of their actions, whilst the operation of the eurozone may reduce persistent rigidities (Majocchi and Rey, 1993). Furthermore, it is suggested that international policy coordination may undermine central bank credibility and cause an unanticipated increase in inflation by weakening the disciplining effects of excessive monetary growth upon the exchange rate (van der Ploeg, 1993: 156). Finally, von Hagen (1993: 265) rejects what he terms the 'parallel unification proposition', namely that currency unification requires fiscal policy unification, although without examining the merits of a policy framework being developed between the extremes of either full fiscal autonomy or complete centralisation at the federal level. However, despite these criticisms, unless the discipline effect of the eurozone is powerful and immediate, the persistence of price and factor rigidities would appear to necessitate the use of fiscal policy as a stabilising instrument to reduce the incentive for any country to leave the eurozone and, as a substitute (albeit an imperfect one) for exchange-rate flexibility.

The conclusion that fiscal policy may become the principal instrument with which to counteract asymmetric external shocks, and therein prevent the destabilisation of the eurozone, raises the issue of whether it should be deployed at the national or federal level. The adoption of the decentralisation theorem, or 'layer-cake' concept, whereby functions are performed by the lowest efficient layer of government, accords with the EU's professed belief in subsidiarity and would indicate an initial preference for national fiscal autonomy within the eurozone (Oates, 1972: 35; Bayoumi and Masson, 1995: 268). However, the operation of the SGP, in restricting the pursuit of counter-cyclical fiscal policy, has significantly constrained the operation of national fiscal policy (Burkitt et al., 1996, 1997: 3–6).

Autonomous fiscal policy is further undermined by the operation of the Single Market and the loss of tax revenue for certain member states caused by the eurozone. The requirement for the abolition of exchange controls, contained within the single market legislation, not only contributed to the currency instability during 1992–1993, but was intended to enhance financial market integration within the EU. However, such integration reduces the ability of member states to borrow cheaply to enable debt-financed fiscal expansion (Courchene, 1993: 152).

The potential reduction in fiscal flexibility would be compounded for those member states that currently depend upon seigniorage for a significant proportion of their total tax revenue. This relates to the circumstances wherein the purchasing power of government securities is eroded by inflation, thus providing an inexpensive method to finance public expenditure by, in effect, borrowing at very low real rates of interest. A stable eurozone would require a convergence in national inflation rates and, assuming that the European Central Bank achieved the low inflation target established in its founding chapter, seigniorage would be limited to an estimated 0.4% of GDP for all participants. This would particularly affect Portugal, as seigniorage revenues totalled 3.6% of its GDP in 1990, whilst Greece (2.3%), Spain (1.9%) and Italy (1.3%) would also lose a significant proportion of budget revenue (Dornbusch, 1988: 26; Eichengreen, 1993: 1335–1336; Spahn, 1993: 577). Thus, the fiscal drain experienced by certain member states would cause fiscal retrenchment independent of the additional requirements imposed by the Maastricht convergence criteria (Masson, 1996).

The restrictions placed upon national fiscal policy, both during the transition to (for new entrants) and the subsequent operation of the eurozone may, therefore, necessitate the enlargement of federal fiscal expenditure to ensure the stability of the European economy. This conclusion is reinforced by three further considerations. Firstly, governments may not undertake an optimal level of counter-cyclical stabilisation due to the existence of regional spill-overs or externalities, whereby non-residents derive some benefit from the policy whilst residents must bear the full cost through higher debt or taxation. Factor mobility could also constrain governments from incurring high levels of debt, since the risk of higher future taxes may encourage factor relocation to other regions, thus reducing the tax base and providing short-term stability at the price of long-term instability. To the extent that this 'prisoner's dilemma' constrains government fiscal flexibility, the solution requires a coordinated stabilisation strategy solution typical of non-cooperative game settings, necessitating either horizontal cooperation amongst member states or centralisation under a federal authority (Rompuy et al., 1993: 112–113).

Secondly, assuming that adverse shocks occur randomly, an inter-regional public insurance scheme can redistribute income from 'favourably shocked' to 'adversely shocked' regions to prevent an 'unlucky' area bearing a disproportionate financial burden. Moral hazard is minimised by ensuring that no incentives exist that encourage potential beneficiaries to manipulate the scheme to their advantage and in so doing to discourage participation from other regions (Wyplotz, 1993: 181; Courchene, 1993: 134–135).

Finally, the need to strengthen the cohesion of the eurozone through redistribution of resources to weaker regions, which reinforces political and social solidarity throughout all participating member states, may entail a significantly enhanced role for federal financial authority. It does appear to be the case that all mature monetary unions exhibit a significant degree of redistribution between wealthy and poorer regions (Bayoumi and Masson, 1995).

Finally, the experience of existing federations confirms the necessity for a federal system of fiscal transfers between regions to promote stabilisation and redistribution across the eurozone zone. The path-breaking study conducted by Sala-i-Martin and Sachs (1992) claimed that U.S. federal fiscal policy offset approximately 40% of an initial $1 decline in average Gross Regional Product (GRP). However, this was challenged due to its failure to differentiate between the cyclical and structural effects of fiscal policy. Von Hagen (1992) argued that the stabilisation effect of U.S. federal fiscal policy was a mere 10%, whilst Goodhart and Smith (1993) found 14% of an initial reduction in GRP offset by a combination of fiscal transfers and federal taxes. These later studies were criticised, in turn, for underestimating the degree of stabilisation by narrowly focusing upon federal income taxes, thereby neglecting other federal taxes. The importance of this omission is clear from the simulation undertaken by Pisani-Ferry et al. (1993), where non-income federal taxation generated a greater stabilising influence than income taxation, leading to a 17.1% stabilisation effect for the United States, whilst Bayoumi and Masson (1995) found 30.2% fiscal stabilisation using a similar methodology. The conflicting results produced by these studies impair the formation of a consensus concerning the scale of fiscal federalism necessary to stabilise the eurozone. However, the weight of evidence suggests that U.S. fiscal policy produces a stabilising effect between 17% and 30% of an initial external shock.

The generality of the conclusions reached by the literature require a comparison of the U.S. results with those from additional federations. Accordingly, both Goodhart and Smith (1993) and Bayoumi and Masson (1995) reproduced their analyses using Canadian data and found a significantly larger stabilising effect, calculated at 24% and 17.4% respectively. Furthermore,

Pisani-Ferry et al. (1993) calculated that Germany achieved 42% stabilisation through the interaction of taxation policy and fiscal transfers. These estimates are largely consistent with the range of results from the United States, although the apparently more-pronounced counter-cyclical effectiveness of European fiscal policy cannot be relied upon on the basis of only one study.

Fiscal federalism appears to perform a necessary stabilising function through the counter-cyclical impact of taxation and fiscal transfers, moderating between 17% and 30% of an initial shock for North American federations. The degree to which evidence gleaned from North America can legitimately be applied to the eurozone does, perhaps, necessitate further research; however it would seem to be a reasonable hypothesis to assume that a European eurozone federation might prefer a degree of stabilisation at the higher end of this range, as a result of a historically more-vigorous pursuit of social solidarity demonstrated through their higher welfare expenditure.

The current EU budget, equivalent to only 1.24% of EU GDP, is too small to exert a significant stabilising effect upon the eurozone regions in the advent of an asymmetric external shock, with structural funds accounting for a minority of this expenditure. Indeed, the present budget size limits the EU's ability to enhance member-state stabilisation to an estimated paltry 3%, which is clearly inadequate in relation to the stabilisation achieved by mature federations (Eichengreen, 1994: 186; Bayoumi and Masson, 1995: 266). Therefore, a plausible case exists for the enlargement of federal fiscal capability. This conclusion is amplified by the introduction of a more proscriptive SGP limiting the former stabilisation secured through national fiscal policy measures. To the extent that national fiscal operations are constrained by the new federal rules, there is a stronger argument for federal fiscal policy expansion. The question concerns whether this occurs as part of the existing EU budget, thereby facilitating discretionary fiscal policy, or whether a system of automatic stabilisers should be established.

Discretionary of automatic stabilisers

Discretionary fiscal federalism was most notably advanced by the EU Commission's MacDougall Report. This report suggested that asymmetric shocks could be countered by counter-cyclical grants made to regional or local governments, triggered by regional unemployment or GDP trend indicators, supplemented with an EU unemployment fund that would provide a direct fiscal injection into areas experiencing above-average unemployment (MacDougall, 1977). The unemployment fund could be partly financed through individual contributions, although this would require unanimity across all member states concerning the absolute or proportionate payments made by taxpayers and companies to the fund, as well as the level of benefits received by individuals. Germany's reunification experience suggests that such a scheme might increase demands for wage and benefit equalisation throughout the eurozone, as differentials become more visible, irrespective of productivity differences, with the resultant negative economic consequences. However, the transfer of certain social insurance programmes to the federal level receives wide support within the literature (Masson and Mélitz, 1990; MacDougall, 1992). The MacDougall Report further advocated the expansion of redistributional transfers to reduce inter-regional differences in capital endowment and productivity. Thus, MacDougall's combination of policy measures required the gradual extension of the EU budget from 2–2.5% of GDP, in the transition period to the eurozone formation, to 5–7% of EU GDP in the early years of the eurozone, and ultimately expanding to 20–25% of EU GDP in a mature economic and monetary union (MacDougall, 1992: 65; Majocchi and Rey, 1993: 473).

Discretionary fiscal policy is criticised, however, on two principal grounds. First, the New Classical approach perceives no justification for discretionary fiscal policy, and certainly not for its use as a counter-cyclical Keynesian mechanism, preferring instead to encourage economic authorities to develop a reputation for economic orthodoxy, which would facilitate rule-based fiscal policy (Kydland and Prescott, 1977). This critique should have disappeared in the aftermath of the 2008 financial crisis, as a failure of neo-liberal economics became apparent and the effectiveness of counter-cyclical macroeconomic management was demonstrated. However, it has not disappeared. Instead, the neo-liberal critique has reappeared in the guise of claiming that sovereign debt crises prove that nations cannot afford active policy measures, even if these are successful.

A second criticism, however, concerns the imperfect availability of information that causes recognition and implementation time lags, thereby delaying the impact of discretionary policies by a sufficiently large margin that their effects may become *de-stabilising* (Friedman, 1953; Baumol, 1961; Fisher and Cooper, 1973). Automatic stabilisers eliminate the implementation lag experienced in democratic countries, where major fiscal decisions are typically presented in an annual budget. Therefore, they reduce the probability of any destabilising impact. Goodhart and Smith (1993: 432) further claim that the transparency of automatic stabilisers enables economic actors to internalise their effects when forming expectations.

A European Federal Transfer Scheme (EFTS) could ensure an equitable distribution of the gains and losses resulting from the impact of asymmetric shocks within the eurozone, whilst conforming to the subsidiarity principal because transfers are determined at the federal level but implemented locally (van der Ploeg, 1993: 144). Moreover, if borrowing is permitted to promote counter-cyclical stabilisation whilst ensuring that the budget is balanced over the economic cycle, the EFTS would avoid intertemporal debt redistribution (van der Ploeg, 1993: 144). Careful design can generate an EFTS that is a more efficient stabiliser than existing tax and transfer systems, which are developed to fulfil alternative objectives.

One proposal made by Italianer and Vanheukelen (1993) aims to achieve a degree of stabilisation similar to the fiscal federalism of the United States, for an average annual cost of €11.2 billion, which is the equivalent of only 0.23% of EU GDP (Italianer and Vanheukelen, 1993: 500). A more recent EFTS proposal places the average annual cost at between 0.17% and 0.86% of EU GDP for securing an 18% stabilisation of an initial shock within the eurozone, consisting of all current member states, whereas a more substantial 40% stabilisation target would cost between 0.38 and 1.9% of EU GDP per annum, depending upon precise estimates of the elasticity of output loss associated with higher unemployment (Whyman, 1997; Baimbridge and Whyman, 2008). Thus, these studies conclude that a similar degree of stabilisation may be achieved at a fraction of the central budget increases advocated by MacDougall, due to the greater efficiency of a stabilisation system designed solely to perform that function. Moreover, it is possible that smaller, better-targeted fiscal interventions can have a greater proportionate impact upon redistribution and income inequality than do larger fiscal programmes (Costello, 1993: 274–277).

Evaluation of discretionary and automatic federal fiscal policy measures depends upon their ability to stabilise the eurozone, combined with their distributional impact upon the individual member states. Put simply, fiscal federalism works through the transfer of funds from economies outperforming the eurozone average to those underperforming, with the amounts determined by the size of the schemes involved and the scale of stabilisation intended to be achieved. Even assuming a particularly targeted initiative, the net transfers for individual member states can be quite substantial. Admittedly, the responses should be available out of the net gains the 'winners' receive as a direct result of participating in the eurozone; perhaps, as in the case of Germany, by enjoying a currency undervalued relative to what would have been the case had the deutschmark still been in existence. One estimate suggests that the fiscal burden for the largest contributors to a fiscal federal scheme would have to be significant – comprising upwards of 3% of GDP and figures exceeding 6% of national budgetary expenditure – for any scheme to make an appreciable macroeconomic difference (Whyman, 1997b; Baimbridge and Whyman, 2008: 138–145). Amounts of this magnitude would require significant tax rises and/or expenditure reductions or, alternatively, the transfer of substantial elements of current national spending to a federal level.

Eurobonds

Eurobonds or 'Stability Bonds' are often presented as an alternative method of resolving many of these same issues. These would provide a form of common insurance, through the common issuance of sovereign bonds. Since the eurozone necessarily requires some form of risk sharing, the suggestion is that this can be channelled into a form of common debt. Moreover, it has been suggested that Eurobonds can enhance the effectiveness of monetary-transmission mechanisms, enhance fiscal surveillance upon member states (and, hence, improve fiscal discipline), reduce default probability through pooling risk and facilitate financial integration (Claessens et al., 2012: 6). This was first advocated for the EU two decades ago by the Giovanni Group (2000) and has been advocated subsequently by academic commentators and market professional associations (AFME, 2011; De Grauwe and Mosen, 2009; Gros and Micossi, 2009). Nevertheless, over a decade later, euro-area government bond markets remained highly fragmented. One reason is that the issuance of common debt raises questions of moral hazard, as individual member states have the ability to free ride upon the rest of the eurozone. Hence, proposals have tended to focus upon ways in which to enforce fiscal discipline. The resultant proposals for policy surveillance and coordination has, in turn, implications for national sovereignty, which has required protracted discussions in eurozone member states (EU, 2011: 4, 7–8, 21–24). A second complication would involve designing a system of common insurance and the pooling of risk which, nevertheless, did not breach Article 125 of the treaty on the functioning of the European Union, which prohibits one member state from assuming the liabilities of another (EU, 2011: 11).

Originating with a proposal made by Delpha and Weizsächer (2011), and subsequently adopted by the EU Commission, entitled 'Stability Bonds', one approach would be for member states to pool and assume joint liability for up to 60% of their national debt, with 'Blue Bonds' issued for this amount. The expectation would be that, due to the greater liquidity in the pooled market and lower risk premiums, it could be financed at lower interest rates than any debts individual nations had above this 60% figure. Any remaining debt above this 60% of GDP threshold would remain a nation state's individual responsibility, with borrowing occurring through nationally issued 'Red Bonds', and with interest rates set by the market in accordance with that state's relative creditworthiness. A three-to-four-year transition would be required to gradually mutualise the qualifying proportion of national into European common debt (EU, 2011: 14–15).

A second variant of the Eurobond proposal was advanced by the German Council of Economic Experts, which proposed a Redemption Pact that would transfer any national debt exceeding 60% of a member state's GDP into a European Debt Redemption Fund, for which eurozone participants would be jointly liable. Nations holding debt in this new fund would be obligated to repay it within a 25-year period, and with obligations taking precedence over other debt formats (Claessens et al., 2012: 9–10).

The 'euro-nomics' group advocated a third Eurobond alternative, namely the establishment of a European Safe Bond (ESBies) from a pooled and balanced portfolio of eurozone sovereign debt. As investors are exposed to combined eurozone risk, and not national sovereign risk, the suggestion is that any investor flight would be to, and not from, this new safe bond type, thereby creating greater stability within the single currency zone. Moreover, since it would not require sovereign guarantees, it would sit more easily within the treaty obligations prohibiting bailouts (Claessens et al., 2012: 9). This scheme would appear to hold advantages when individual member states get into fiscal difficulties, but the majority of the eurozone remains a good investment prospect, altrhough it would have difficulty dealing with circumstances wherein a majority of member states were considered to be a bad risk, or where the future of the single currency came into question.

Two final conceptions of Eurobonds have been proposed to resolve the issue of potential over-borrowing through only issuing bonds of short-term maturity. In this way, any member states exhibiting fiscal ill-discipline could have their access restricted relatively quickly (Claessens et al., 2012: 10; Lane, 2012). Alternatively, access to Eurobond borrowing could be limited to only those nations meeting criteria for sound fiscal and macroeconomic management (Muellbauer, 2011).

The strength of the Eurobond proposal would appear to be its ability to combine the pooling of risk associated with sovereign debt with restrictions placed upon the ability of member states to free ride upon the scheme through taking on excessive and unsustainable debt. Solutions have embraced short-term lending, to strengthen market discipline, or restrictions placed upon the proportion of lending that can be accommodated through the common insurance scheme. Furthermore, extra surveillance and restrictions upon national fiscal policy is considered to be essential to the success of this scheme, in addition to the enhanced powers provided to supra-national bodies through the fiscal compact initiatives. However, this highlights the disconnect between the fiscal federalism proposals, outlined in the rest of this chapter, and the various Eurobond schemes. Whereas the former is intended to generate additional fiscal flexibility, intended to stabilise the eurozone against the destabilisation of asymmetric shocks, given the loss of exchange rate and monetary policy instruments for individual member states, the Eurobond scheme focuses upon seeking to reassure financial markets concerning sovereign risk and, therefore, expecting to secure lower long-term interest rates. It is, in short, a difference between Keynesian assumptions of demand deficiency and the desire to utilise active fiscal policy to stabilise the eurozone and hence promote growth and employment, counterpoised against neo-classical/monetarist assumptions that the economy will automatically tend towards full employment and therefore the role of fiscal policy is to prevent profligacy, with resultant benefits of lower interest rates to facilitate growth. The two proposals, as currently presented, provide two quite different solutions to two quite different problems, based upon theoretical propositions from two quite different economic traditions. There is nothing to prevent Eurobonds providing a useful supplement to moves towards fiscal federalism in the eurozone; however, as currently constituted, they are not a viable substitute.

How would this fit with the current fiscal policy architecture of the eurozone?

The form of economic and monetary union (the eurozone) adopted by the EU developed a number of core features, namely: (a) the pooling of monetary policy under the auspices of the ECB, and (b) the adoption of fiscal rules intended to prevent free-rider problems arising from the ability of individual member states from borrowing in a common currency, and potential moral hazard if political pressure necessitates the bailout of any nation borrowing excessively (Lane, 2012: 49). The fiscal rules, therefore, sought to prevent member states from running large budget deficits and public sector debts, which have been determined as incompatible with the long-term stability of the system (EC Commission, 1992). The fiscal rules formed two parts, both focused upon emphasising the self-discipline of participating member states (Degryse, 2012: 12).

The first, pre-participation, involved the TEU convergence criteria, which set out five financial tests that potential members were supposed to meet prior to acceptance as full members of the eurozone. These rules were criticised as being too narrowly focused on financial rather than real-economy effects; nevertheless, whether or not the convergence criteria were insufficiently developed, the failure to adequately police their implementation has cast its shadow over the contemporary problems with public debt in Greece, Cyprus, Italy and Spain. Post-participation, the Stability and Growth Pact (SGP), derived from the 1997 Amsterdam Treaty, sought to make permanent and transparent the public-finance obligations contained in the TEU convergence criteria. Articles 121 and 126 of the Treaty on the Functioning of the European Union (TFEU) provide the legal basis of the SGP and established the proscribed limits of 3% of GDP for budget deficits and 60% of GDP for public debt. It has been suggested that fiscal 'discipline' is 'fundamental' for macroeconomic stability and, hence, for laying the foundations for future economic growth (ECB, 2005: 7). Thus, the fiscal architecture of the eurozone is essentially laying a constraint upon the autonomy and flexibility of national fiscal policy amongst the eurozone participants.

This is based upon the assumption that the economy fluctuates around the economic concept of the Non-Accelerating Inflation Rate of Unemployment (NAIRU), whereby supply-side factors determine real economic variables such as unemployment and output (Layard and Nickell, 1985; Carlin and Soskice, 1990). Hence, the resulting policy stance is to maintain a neutral fiscal policy and rely primarily upon monetary policy, through the medium of the interest-rate policy instrument, in order to smooth demand shocks and thereby enable supply-side factors to determine development in the real economy. There is, therefore, no need for democratic control over fiscal or monetary policy, as these policies are supportive of the primary drivers of economic growth, and therefore these instruments can be subcontracted to technocratic specialists in the ECB and/or be constrained by the operation of the SGP.

The design and operation of the SGP has, however, been criticised in two rather different ways. The first argues that the design of the SGP is viewed as flawed in a number of respects, including: its rigidity, with the one-size-fits all nature of its operations (based upon no review of the evidence to suggest that fiscal policy should be run in the same way in different nations); its tightening of the TEU convergence criteria obligations (in terms of smaller budget deficits and public-debt positions); lack of credibility, as sanctions are rather onerous and imposed post-event; the fact that the SGP demands a pro-cyclical macroeconomic stance amidst economic downturns; and, by focusing upon deficits and not surpluses, the pact is asymmetric in reinforcing national budgetary behaviour to the benefit of the monetary union as a whole (Monperrus-Veroni and Saraceno, 2006: 33–34). Moreover, the theoretical foundations of NAIRU are certainly not without quite substantive criticism (Setterfield et al., 1992; Galbraith, 1997; Whyman, 2006: 65–68).

A variant of such criticism goes further, claiming that the SGP is an impediment to successful national macroeconomic management. Viewed through the prism of Keynesian economic theory, detractors point to the rigidity of budget-deficit limits, together with the ability of the EU to compel member states to adhere to this approach as frustrating the flexibility required to operate counter-cyclical demand-management policies. According to this viewpoint, governments should be aiming to promote economic stability and economic growth through the maintenance of a sufficient level of effective demand in the economy, together with interventions aimed at enhancing the performance of labour markets and industrial competitiveness. This may require a greater flexibility in public finances than allowed under the SGP, and therefore the latter may prevent corrective measures necessary to prevent recessionary conditions, with the resultant loss of economic potential and with also a human cost.

The second critique of the SGP claims that, rather than it being a flawed concept, it is incomplete and thereby not sufficiently robust to secure the financial integrity required of all participants in a monetary union. This claim is reinforced by the ability of large member states, including France and Germany, to periodically ignore the proscriptive nature of the SGP when they find the rules inconvenient, and when they are faced with determined domestic opposition by organised labour (Bieler, 2006: 210; Mathers, 2007: 3). Consequently, reforms have been advocated to strengthen existing rules intended to prevent the emergence of large fiscal deficits and public debt within individual member states, and thereby prevent the eurozone being undermined by individual nations either requiring bailouts by other members, or defaulting and placing the future of the single currency at risk.

Instead of the SGP being replaced by a more flexible set of budgetary rules intended to ensure that a sufficient level of aggregate demand exists in each member state to facilitate full employment, the EU's response to the 2008 financial crisis was to further tighten fiscal scrutiny and place narrower limits upon fiscal manoeuvrability. As noted in Chapter 9, the fiscal compact has caused eurozone member states to enshrine balanced-budget targets into national law, with external surveillance and mandatory penalties for breaches of the new fiscal rules.

Conclusion

The studies outlined in this chapter indicate that the sustainability of the eurozone, in the medium and long term, may partly depend upon the implementation of a fiscal policy initiative at the federal rather than national level, one which is sufficiently well resourced and targeted to stabilise member state economies in the face of asymmetric external shocks. Failure to do so leaves the monetary union fatally exposed to asymmetric external shocks and divergent economic forces. Whilst the 2008 international financial crisis has proven to be a particularly destructive shock to the eurozone economy, and has resulted in a range of policy responses, this should not diminish the fact that the probability of asymmetric shocks of different types and magnitudes was always going to prove problematic for the eurozone in the absence of some form of compensatory policy mechanism.

Potential solutions may include greater flexibility in national fiscal policy, the introduction of fiscal federalism at supra-national level (whether through an enlarged EU budget or targeted EFTS), or the introduction of a form of Eurobonds. Yet, whilst these options have been discussed across the eurozone, the hesitancy in taking action leaves the fiscal compact, and restrictions upon national macroeconomic action, as the primary responses to the financial crisis. This is not a sufficient response. Indeed, in the absence of exchange-rate or monetary autonomy, and with insufficient labour mobility and wage flexibility, individual regions may become characterised by persistent unemployment, low per-capita income and ensuing social tension: troubled regions coexisting in the eurozone zone with neighbours enjoying full employment, high growth and greater prosperity. The cost in terms of lost output and avoidable human misery is compounded by the probability of countries withdrawing from the eurozone should such inequalities continue over a prolonged period. The reluctance of many economists and policymakers to address this problem has long been of concern.

11
European Clearing Union

Introduction

In previous chapters, the limitations inherent within the current eurozone economic framework have been highlighted. These include: design flaws in the methods to assess initial convergence; the lack of fiscal federalism to moderate inevitable asymmetric shocks to the currency union; and, more recently, a slow recognition of the problems caused by the international financial crisis and its fiscal after-effects, together with a presently inadequate policy response.

This examination has, however, raised a more fundamental issue, one that has undermined previous attempts at fixed exchange-rate systems (including the gold standard and Bretton Woods), namely persisting weaknesses, not only within the eurozone, but within the current international monetary and financial system as a whole. Specifically, four aspects of the international payments architecture have been advanced as problematic (Stiglitz and Greenwald, 2010: 12):

1. The association with large, unsustainable, payments imbalances;
2. Persistent high levels of volatility, both in terms of exchange rates, interest rates, and/or access to capital;
3. Policy responses to the volatility tend to result in increased demand for international reserves, which has the unfortunate consequence of reducing global aggregate demand;
4. The inequitable nature of the system, as differentials in risk premia result in less affluent nations providing net loans to richer countries at low interest rates, whilst borrowing back funds at higher interest rates.

All of these factors are interrelated, and therefore a solution to payments imbalances should ameliorate the other problems. Whilst a fixed-currency system – or, as in the case of the eurozone, a single currency adopted by a group of participating nation states – should reduce or eliminate exchange-rate volatility, the other issues remain. Indeed, solutions arguably become more pressing as exchange-rate variation can no longer play the role of an escape valve for other aspects of international payments disequilibria.

Excessive reserves and macroeconomic consequences

There are multiple motivations for holding international reserves, motivations that do not necessarily remain constant over time. Volatility and resultant perceptions of increased risk associated with economic activity tend to increase precautionary savings, in the form of reserves. Another reason may include high levels of price volatility for natural resources (especially oil). A third may arise from policy responses to the fragility of the international economic system.

One example of the latter may refer to the fact that substantial reserves do allow policymakers more flexibility in responding to periods of economic turbulence. China and Russia were both better able to sustain the strengths of their economies and, particularly in China's case, due to the previous build-up of reserves, to launch a sizeable Keynesian stimulus package in response to the recent financial crisis (Stiglitz and Greenwald, 2010: 8). This might be considered as a case of macro-precautionary motives, albeit that sometimes the trade policies of both of these nations appear to be more inspired by mercantilism. A second example may derive from the export-led growth model, which has proven successful in, amongst others, East Asia, Japan, China and Germany (Stiglitz and Greenwald, 2010: 10). However, the problem created by structural surpluses is that other nations must endure persistent deficits, given that the global trade surplus (deficit) must be zero. If surplus nations persist in their attempts to maintain their current account positions, this makes it more difficult for deficit countries to return to balance, as devaluations or deflation may be offset by actions taken by credit-balance nations. Moreover, to the extent that deficits can be reduced, if surplus nations do not accept a compensatory reduction in their positive balances, then this will lead to a deficit appearing elsewhere in the system. This tendency may be reinforced by the combination of neoclassical orthodox hegemony and successive WTO rounds, which have made industrial policy more difficult and hence less attractive. This, in turn, places more emphasis upon exchange-rate policy or else attempts to reduce wages or the social wage in order to improve international competitiveness. By facilitating increased net exports, these policies promote trade surpluses (Stiglitz and Greenwald, 2010: 8, 11).

To place the issue into context, the reserves held by monetary authorities across the globe more than quadrupled over the decade before the recent international financial crisis, rising from less than $2 trillion in 1999 to more than $8 trillion in 2009, with developing economies accounting for more than two thirds of that increase. This figure is equivalent to in excess of 12% of world output at market exchange rates (Costabile, 2010: 7; Stiglitz and Greenwald, 2010: 8). The cost of these reserves is, therefore, an opportunity cost, whereby these funds could have been invested in productive activity and, thereby, the world economy is poorer and has a slower potential growth trajectory as a result (Stiglitz and Greenwald, 2010: 8). This large proportion of potential demand being withdrawn from the global economy leads Stiglitz and Greenwald (2010: 12) to conclude that the current arrangements produce a 'chronically unstable global macroeconomic situation with a strong deflationary bias' (Stiglitz and Greenwald, 2010: 12).

To the extent that this is an accurate depiction of some of the problems facing the international economy, it has resonance for nations sharing a single currency, where exchange-rate policy is no longer available, and where the current approach is to utilise a combination of deflation and social wage reductions to restore competitiveness in deficit nations. Surplus nations, primarily Germany, which currently has amongst the largest trade surpluses in the world, appear determined to persist with the export-led growth model, thereby insuring that other eurozone members will find it more difficult to improve their own trade balances without more drastic action than might otherwise be needed. Moreover, as highlighted in the previous chapter, although German reserves, built up through this trade policy, are being utilised to provide temporary loans to those EU member states suffering fiscal distress, this provides only temporary relief, whilst loans are accompanied by demands for quite severe fiscal tightening. The persistence of trade surpluses and the lack of pressure upon governments to take corrective action create further problems for nations posting trade deficits.

There have been a number of different proposals advanced as potential solutions to the problems inherent within the global financial architecture, with some of the most notable examples summarised in Riese (2008). However, perhaps the most important contribution was made by Keynes, in the context of the discussion surrounding the shape of the post-Second World War international monetary system.

The Keynes Plan

The Keynes Plan for an International Clearing Union (ICU) originated during the period of the Second World War, as economists from the Allies considered the suitability of international economic foundations capable of promoting reconstruction and economic prosperity. The proposals were developed through a number of drafts, which are outlined in Keynes (1980), and cumulated in a U.K. government white paper, in 1942. The proposals were not ultimately adopted, although elements were included in the establishment of the IMF and the Bretton Woods international system of monetary arrangements (Skidelsky, 2000; Steil, 2013).

As befits his broader focus upon inadequate effective demand and under-employment of resources, Keynes proposed a form of international monetary system that combined the benefits of fixed exchange rates (less uncertainty leading to increased investment, trade and economic growth) with an attempt to ensure the maintenance of a sufficient level of effective demand to sustain global full employment. In the same way that a withdrawal from the circular flow of income, in a particular country, reduces aggregate demand and thereby potentially results in under-employment equilibria, he registered concern over the inability for an international payments system to prevent excess reserves from withdrawing money from the global economy. If surpluses were to remain unused, as would be the case in mercantilist strategy, the result would be a suboptimal level of aggregate demand, and insufficient to maintain full employment.

Attempts made by deficit nations to restore balance would exacerbate this problem, through deflation and other adjustment programmes (Piffaretti, 2009b: 47). Domestic deflation and devaluation, both of which seek to reduce the international price of exports relative to imports, with the elasticities of demand for imported and exported goods and services determining whether a modest or very large correction would be required to restore balance. Deflation will reduce the demand for imports, as a result of declining wages (or the social wage, via reductions in welfare expenditure) and/or increasing unemployment, whilst devaluation makes exports cheaper overseas and encourages import-substitution at home.

Kalecki (1946: 323–327) concurred with this position, arguing that no country would experience persistent problems with its balance-of-payments position if all nations maintained their expenditure levels sufficient to secure full employment. Net foreign expenditure would be financed through international long-term lending, the latter to be facilitated through the establishment of an international clearing union similar to Keynes's proposals, combined with an international investment office. Hence, in Keynes's own words, 'the plan aims at the substitution of an expansionist, in place of a contractionist, pressure on world trade' (Keynes, 1942).

The ICU proposal sought to establish an international system of payments that facilitated global full employment. The proposal had six main elements, namely:

- Establishment of a currency union, based on international bank money;
- Creation of a closed payments system, enabling central banks to regulate the flow of international payments;
- The need for symmetric, not asymmetric, rebalancing;
- Ensuring that international reserves are limited and re-circulated;
- Restrictions upon speculative and other short-term flows of capital;
- Ability to readjust fixed exchange-rate values to reflect changes in efficiency wages

The proposal was to create a currency union, provisionally named the International Clearing Union, utilising the creation of international bank money, which Keynes named 'bancor', and it was to be fixed, at least nominally in terms of gold – with national currencies within the ICU thereby fixed in relation to one another. Bancor would not, however, be convertible into gold (Keynes, 1980: 95). The closest current equivalent would be Special Drawing Rights (SDRs), operated by the International Monetary Fund (IMF), although, in the absence of a complete system like ICU within which to operate, SDRs have had little influence upon the international monetary system. Nevertheless, Stiglitz and Greenwald (2006) have advocated a similar scheme to the Keynes Plan, utilising SDRs as their bank money of choice.

The purpose of the new currency (bancor or SDRs) would be its use in settling international balances between participating member states, through accounts maintained by national central banks. Those nations with a surplus on their balance-of-payments account, with respect to other ICU participants, would accrue a credit account, whereas those with a balance-of-payments deficit would generate a debit account. The supply of bancor was to be perfectly elastic up to the maximum set for each country (Meltzer, 1983: 17). Moreover, there would be one-way convertibility only, from gold or national currencies to bancor (Keynes, 1942). Thus, bancor reserves can never leave the system, thereby negating the possibility of a run on the currency (Arestis, 1999: 7).

The ICU would be established such that the provision of foreign exchange would be located solely within the central bank of each participating nation. Where requested by individuals or businesses, other domestic banks would be required to apply to the central banks for release of these funds. Central banks would, therefore, have unqualified control over the outward transactions of national citizens (Keynes, 1980: 33–34). Bancor would not necessarily be utilised for all transactions between individual businesses or banks, but rather would be the sole means of settling the final outstanding balances between the central banks of each participating nation. It would operate in a manner similar to physical shipments of gold, under the gold standard, to settle balance-of-payments deficits (Keynes, 1942).

This plan largely reflected the position pertaining in the United Kingdom at the time Keynes was drafting the ICU proposals, although it would require a significant reversal of contemporary reality, where international financial markets operate without this restraint. However, D'Arista (2003: 737) notes that an ICU would eliminate what she regards as the 'wasteful' foreign exchange activities of multinational banks, thereby curbing speculation and reducing the volatility in currencies that hamper economic activity in the real economy.

The purpose of the ICU would be to extend the banking principle that exists within any closed system, namely that the sum of credits and debits (assets and liabilities) must balance (Keynes, 1980: 44). If credits are not permitted to exit the system, then the ICU has the freedom of action to advance loans to any member, knowing that the proceeds will be transferred to the clearing account of another member. Loans made to Greece may end up in the clearing account of Germany, if the former has a trade deficit with the latter, but, because the resources cannot leave the ICU system, they remain available for use rather than to sit as idle reserves. Given that reserves represent potential purchasing power, were they to remain unused, this would withdraw money from circulation and deflate the global economy. However, within the ICU, balances would not remain idle, but would be utilised to finance business in another participating member state, thereby maintaining the existing circular flow of income within the system (Keynes, 1942).

Given that the sum of the worldwide balance of payments must be zero, such that the sum of all surpluses must equal the sum of all deficits within a set period of time, surpluses cannot exist without an equivalent deficit occurring elsewhere in the world. Therefore, if the latter are a problem, the former must be a significant contributor to this problem occurring and persisting. This should imply that both surplus and deficit countries be treated equally in seeking to eliminate trade imbalances, but this is not typically the case. Deficit countries endure compulsion to reduce trade imbalances, whilst surplus countries do not. The ICU therefore sought to prevent *systematic* disequilibria by creating a system of incentives and penalties to be imposed on both deficit and surplus countries in order to discourage disequilibria (Costabile, 2010: 18–19). In this endeavour, the ICU would mimic the actions of national central banks in pursuing international 'symmetric rebalancing', and thereby achieving simultaneous debtor and creditor adjustment (Piffaretti, 2009b: 46).

Each national central bank would be allocated an index quota equal to the sum of its imports and exports, averaged over the previous five years, and would be entitled to overdraw its clearing account by up to the value of its index account. If a deficit remained above one quarter of the index value for more than a year, the 'deficiency bank' would be allowed to borrow from the clearing account of a bank running a surplus, whilst the deficit nation would be entitled to devalue its exchange rate by up to 5% per year. If the deficit exceeded half the index quota, this devaluation would be *required*, whilst outward movements of capital would be prohibited without the express permission of the governors of the central bank itself.

Meanwhile, surplus banks would be encouraged or required (if the surplus balance exceeded 50% of the index quota) to introduce corrective measures involving currency appreciation, to the maximum of 5% per annum, or easing the restrictions upon the outward flow of capital. At year's end, surplus balances still exceeding the value of the index quota would be transferred to the reserve fund of the central bank. In addition, surplus nations would be caused to transfer into the central bank's reserve fund 5% of the annual excess above one quarter of its index quota and 10% above half the quota figure (Keynes, 1980: 35–37). In essence, this imposed the equivalent of a rate of interest upon credit balances, in the attempt to provide a deterrent against the development of a persistent surplus position. In later drafts, this element was reluctantly dropped, albeit (as will be considered later in this chapter) this element of the proposal may have particular relevance to the circumstances facing the eurozone (Keynes, 1980: 96).

Problems with debtor countries can only occur, according to Keynes, if creditor countries are not making full use of the purchasing power derived from their trade surplus (Keynes, 1980). Viewed in this way, surplus countries tend to export deflationary consequences to other nations, and therefore any sustainable global financial system should have the means of disciplining surplus nations (Stiglitz and Greenwald, 2006: 11; 2010: 6–7). In the absence of an ICU-type arrangement, the health of the global economy depends upon the willingness of surplus countries to expand aggregate demand in order to maintain a necessary level of international effective demand, and thereby full employment (Richardson, 1985: 24).

One of the main design features of the bancor system was the attempt to avoid the accumulation of inactive balances held in individual national reserves. Bancor was, therefore, meant to be a means of payment but not a store of value (Meltzer, 1983: 17). Countries that did not wish to use their surplus balances immediately could store them in the ICU without this leading to deflationary consequences, as deficit nations could utilise this source of funds and thereby a level of effective demand adequate to maintain global full employment (Riese, 2008: 39). Kalecki and Schumacher (1943) believed that the combination of an ICU and institutional investment office should be sufficient to provide sufficient short- and long-term lending to prevent unsustainable foreign exchange problems.

Keynes (1980: 30–31) noted that the 19th-century system of international finance worked initially because the flow of capital funds was directed from surplus to debtor nations, at least in part to develop national infrastructure, and thereby maintained approximate balance of international payments. When this pattern shifted towards capital flowing from debtor to creditor nations, the international payments system became unstable. Consequently, he concluded that the object of any new system should be to encourage (or require) a similar initiative from creditor nations, whilst imploring sufficient discipline upon debtor nations so that they did not exploit the situation to live perpetually beyond their means.

Keynes (1980: 52, 86) stated quite clearly that he viewed the 'central control of capital movements, both inward and outward' to be a 'permanent feature of the post-war system', requiring 'exchange control for *all* transactions'. The Keynes Plan recognised the potential damage that 'fugitive' or 'floating' funds could inflict upon an economy, and therefore no country should henceforth accept international capital movements that sought to evade taxation or were made for reasons other than international trade or fixed investment (Keynes, 1980: 185). Indeed, he claimed that 'nothing is more certain than that the movement of capital funds must be regulated' (Keynes, 1980: 31).

Control over capital movements was intended to perform two primary functions: (a) to enable Britain to regulate interest rates without regard to foreign balances, and (b) to prevent periods of economic expansion being brought to a premature end through a rise in net foreign lending, resulting in a rise in interest rates as domestic banks sold bonds to raise capital with which to make domestic loans (Meltzer, 1983: 14–15).

It was intended that capital flows financing fixed investment would be treated differently, and more favourably, than speculative capital flows (Riese, 2008: 39). Thus, international trade in goods and services, and payments arising from these transactions, would be automatically permitted and capital movements would be more tightly regulated. Licences would regulate trade, whilst remittance of interest or other transfer payments would be limited, and speculation in purely financial instruments would be prohibited (Keynes, 1980: 52–53, 212–213). In the ICU system, this would be more effective as the regulation would apply at 'both ends' of any potential transfer. The intent would be to distinguish between, on the one hand, flows to finance trade, finance foreign direct investment (FDI) and/or maintain balance-of-payments equilibrium between surplus and deficit nations; and on the other hand, destabilising flows of capital, often for speculative purposes or flight out of deficit nations (Keynes, 1980: 53, 87).

Mélitz (1983: 23) argued that Keynes became convinced that no international monetary system was capable of achieving internal and external stability, high employment and economic freedom, and therefore he chose to sacrifice freedom through the introduction of a permanent system of exchange controls. The combination of fixed but adjustable exchange rates, capital controls and multilateral clearing was intended to smooth the trade cycle and facilitate the expansion of trade, thereby setting the foundations for the maintenance of a higher level of effective demand without inflationary consequences (Keynes, 1980: 155 – cited in Meltzer, 1983: 20).

Whilst the ICU was conceived as supporting a fixed exchange-rate system, it is important to note that Keynes did not view this fix as unalterable (Keynes, 1942). Indeed, devaluation would be permitted if efficiency wages increased relative to wages abroad (Meltzer, 1983: 19). This element of period readjustment to exchange-rate values was a feature of the Bretton Woods system, although, as successive speculative attacks upon the ECU (in the 1980s) and the ERM (in the early 1990s) amply demonstrated, this is made more difficult in the absence of capital controls. The creation of very large foreign exchange reserves might provide some protection in this respect but, due to their 'dead money' nature, this would draw demand away from the global economy.

Issues arising from the Keynes Plan

Many of the initial reactions to the Keynes Plan are summarised in the *Collected Writings* (Keynes, 1980), which caused subsequent drafting changes to the original conception of the proposal. The development of the Keynes concept is, moreover, documented elsewhere (de Vegh, 1943; Horsefield, 1969; Riese, 2008). There were, however, a number of issues arising out of the plan, which were raised as potentially problematic for the adoption and operation of the scheme.

The first relates to relations between ICU participants and non-members. Given that the ICU was devised as a means of resolving problems for the global economy, it would operate more smoothly if all nation states participated. However, this was always going to be unlikely and, indeed, Keynes (1942) appeared to accept this as well, at least in the early years of the ICU, when he discussed the advisability of the central banks of non-member states establishing *credit* clearing accounts with the ICU in order to facilitate trade with participants. This would suggest that non-members would have no right to borrow from the system, but if they had a trade surplus with ICU participants they could receive bancor credits as payment. However, it is unclear why they would wish to do so, as they would have to be subject to the same rules as members in terms of the non-convertibility of bancor reserves, or else this would represent a withdrawal from the union, circumventing the closed system and withdrawing purchasing power from the system. Given that, as non-members, they would have no influence over the development of the rules or management of the system, this would seem to provide little incentive for non-members to participate.

A second related point concerns the withdrawal of members from the scheme. Keynes (1942) allowed for this, subject to one year's notice, as long as any debits were discharged in advance of withdrawal, but also that existing credit balances would remain within the system. Non-convertibility of bancor would prevent exiting nations from withdrawing any credit balances. These balances would, therefore, remain within the ICU unless or until the withdrawing nation ran a deficit in relation to ICU participants and was able to utilise its previous credit balance to settle this account. Given that nations generating trade surpluses would be subject to greater constraint within the ICU than outside, this may provide an incentive for these nations to avoid participation in the system. Indeed, Riddle (1943: 15) argues that it is difficult to conceive of any prospective creditor nation agreeing to abide by this type of provision. Furthermore, their ability, once outside the ICU, to free ride upon the scheme, would weaken its positive effects. Thus, any sustained higher level of global demand, arising from the operation of the scheme, would enable these nations to build up even larger trade surpluses, whilst their expanding reserves would not be available to fund loans to deficit nations, thereby gradually undermining the purpose the ICU was intended to fulfil.

A third issue is related to the first, in that nations are reluctant to surrender sovereignty in economic matters. Keynes (1942) dismissed this issue as necessitating no greater loss than might occur under a standard commercial treaty. However, this is not the case, as commercial contracts do not restrict what one party can do with the proceeds of the activity in the way that the ICU would impose upon creditor nations. Indeed, the discipline inherent within the Keynes system would imply the creation of a new instrument of economic leadership and economic governance (de Vegh, 1943: 544, 547).

The ICU would also eliminate currency asymmetry, since no nation would be able to reap seigniorage (Riese, 2008: 41). Whilst this would be beneficial to most nations, it would remove a source of finance for those nations whose currencies would otherwise act as international reserve currencies. As a result, Stiglitz and Greenwald (2010: 19) suggest that it might be difficult to create a global financial system using the ICU model. However, they noted that spillovers across countries within a specific region of the world economy, and a potentially higher feeling of solidarity arising from spatial location, may make the introduction of regional clearing unions more feasible.

A fifth issue arising from the ICU proposal, and one that Keynes identified as perhaps the most difficult issue to resolve, relates to the demarcation of rules and discretion in the design of the system. In Point 15 of the final version of the Keynes Plan, the author wrestled with the necessity to use rules to prevent 'indiscipline' and 'unwarrantable liberties'. By contrast, in his wider work, Keynes argued for government policy to have the discretion to adapt to circumstances and take whatever measures necessary at the time. He noted the theoretical preference for rules, but that discretion is probably necessary to make the system work more effectively in practice. Yet, in paragraph 52 of the plan, Keynes seems to have resolved his conflict of thought in favour of rules, by stating:

> Surely it is an advantage, rather than a disadvantage, of the scheme that it invites the member States and groups to abandon that licence to promote indiscipline, disorder and bad-neighbourliness which, to the general disadvantage, they have been free to exercise hitherto.

In terms of the choice of a supranational body that has the strength and authority to be able to manage an international monetary system, Davidson (1992: 8) proposed that a central bank similar to the current European Central Bank (ECB), albeit with rather different objectives, could be a viable solution. Arestis (1999: 9) agrees with Davidson that the enshrining of full employment policy at the heart of the ICU system, and thereby as the leading objective for a supranational central bank or other management body, would be an essential prerequisite of the scheme. As a result, he argues that an ECB-type organisation would require radical reform in structure, strategic objectives and its willingness to use a broader use of differential policy tools, before it would be an acceptable conduit.

Interestingly, Davidson (2009: 136–142) has more recently developed what he terms a 'more modest' variant of the original Keynes Plan, by avoiding the need for a supranational central bank to manage the clearing union.

Instead, he proposed the introduction of a closed, double-entry bookkeeping clearing institution able to account for net international payment positions between participating trading nations, and to monitor the compliance with the mutually agreed rules intended to solve problems of persistent trade and payments imbalances.

A final issue concerns potential inflationary effects arising from the operation of the ICU. For example, Meltzer (1983: 19) claims that Keynes was aware of the possible inflationary bias of his scheme, due to an excess supply of money, but that this flaw was not addressed – perhaps, he suggests, because the scheme was unlikely to be accepted by the American negotiators at the Bretton Woods summit. The argument is advanced that the ICU provides surplus nations with an incentive to expand their economy, rather than allow build-up of surpluses triggering an exchange-rate appreciation. If the economy was already operating at full employment, this would be inflationary. Similarly, persistent deficit nations would be expected to devalue, which would improve the competitiveness of their exports but also provide an expansionary effect. In combination, these two measures would provide a stimulus to economic activity across the ICU. If economies were already operating at full employment levels, then this would be inflationary.

This critique ignores the basic starting point that led to the development of the Keynes Plan in the first place, namely that the operation of the current international payments system – through asymmetric treatment of deficit and surplus nations, alongside the amassing of idle reserves – has a profound deflationary effect upon the global economy. The ICU was *supposed* to reverse this effect, thereby providing better global balance. If this analysis is correct, then it would be unlikely that all economies (deficit or surplus) would be simultaneously operating at full employment, given the withdrawal from the system arising from idle reserves and the necessity for debtor nations to deflate to reduce trade deficits. Certainly, the global economy would 'run hotter', with less wasted resources, and the varied evidence arising from the Phillips Curve, NAIRU and other policy trade-off analysis, would indicate that inflationary pressures may arise at slightly less than full-employment equilibrium. Nevertheless, even if this analysis is correct, this is more of a problem for the correct use of macroeconomic policy tools rather than a justification to reject the ICU system.

Relevance to the eurozone

Having outlined the fundamental elements of the Keynes Plan, the relevance to the difficulties faced by the eurozone in 2013 should be obvious. Were an ICU reform to be introduced, the asymmetric nature of the current eurozone rescue plans, which dampen demand in already struggling member states and provide only temporary relief, could be exchanged for a system which would automatically ensure a *symmetric* rebalancing of the eurozone.

Creditor nations would be encouraged to spend their reserves, either by increasing the economic activity in their own economies or, if already at or near full employment, these reserves would be automatically available, within the clearing union mechanism, to be lent to debtor nations. This might be via a European investment foundation, as suggested by Arestis (1999: 9–10). The result should be the union experiencing a higher level of aggregate demand, as resources are not withdrawn as the result of a build-up of reserves or deflation imposed upon deficit nations, and thereby growth should rise and unemployment fall across participating member states.

The adoption of an ICU would not, however, be without quite significant difficulties. The first of these relates to the current state of the international finance system. Compared to the more managed economies characterising the period in which Keynes developed his ideas, contemporary central banks are far less in control of the creation of credit and the establishment of interest rates (Arestis, 1999: 9). Liberalisation of the sector, particularly during the 1980s, together with the subsequent internationalisation of financial markets, have combined to weaken the control of central banks.

The relevance of the necessity to regulate financial capital were amply demonstrated by the 2008 financial crisis. Writing well in advance of this event, Cartapanis and Herland (2002: 273–274) had already noted that 'rarely in the course of history has the international markets experienced such violent adjustments' as had been experienced in the previous decade. Indeed, the IMF has itself recognised that the period since the demise of the Bretton Woods system has been characterised by 124 systemic banking crises (Laeven and Valencia, 2008: 5). One significant factor underpinning this increase in financial volatility has been the liberalisation of capital movements (Cartapanis and Herland, 2002: 274). Consequently, some re-regulation would appear overdue. This, however, is problematic due to the hegemonic dominance of neo-classical orthodoxy, which does not seem to have been as fatally wounded by the crisis as might have been anticipated.

Capital restrictions would additionally appear, at least superficially, to conflict with the 'four freedoms' enshrined in the Treaty of Rome, one of which being the freedom of movement of capital. The clearing union would, at its heart, have restrictions upon the convertibility of currencies into bancor and the regulation of the supranational clearing agency authority of all capital movements not related directly to trade or long-term productive investment. This would necessarily constrain the freedom of movement of capital. However, the EU has never been absolutist in its adherence to these principles when they conflict with other objectives. For example, current discussions regarding the advisability of introducing a form of Tobin tax (1978), to prevent short-term speculative financial transactions from undermining economic stability, would imply that the principle of freedom of movement of capital is not sacrosanct. Moreover, the ICU proposal would encourage the expansion of international trade in goods and services alongside long-term productive investment, so only short-term capital movements would be severely curtailed. This would not hamper the completion of the European single internal market and, indeed, may facilitate its progress.

One advantage the EU has over supporters of the original 1940s Keynes Plan is that part of the infrastructure necessary for the operation of the scheme is already in place. The ECB already exists as an accepted supranational economic authority, and as such, this could form the basis for the clearing agency proposed by Keynes to manage the clearing union. This would, of course, require a fundamental change of theoretical underpinning for the ECB, in addition to a radical revision of its objectives. Thus, the narrow focus upon low inflation would need to be superseded by the task of managing the clearing union and, as a consequence, to prioritise the facilitation of full employment across the union. This is incompatible with a theoretical adherence to economic orthodoxy with a neo-liberal flavour, and hence the ECB and its officers would need to accept the tenets of Keynesian theory. This would prove problematic, given the dominance of orthodox economic perspectives in the finance sector and, albeit to a lesser extent, to academia – the two areas from which potential ECB officials might be drawn. Nevertheless, given the importance of the new institution for the success of the new policy orientation, sufficient candidates could be found amongst the minority heterodox economist communities.

There is, however, one final and potentially even more difficult problem for the EU in adopting an ICU proposal, and that arises from the pre-existing single currency, onto which a clearing union would need to be grafted. This could allow an 'ICU-light' version of the scheme, but for a comprehensive implementation of the scheme, more fundamental changes would be required. In terms of the 'ICU-light' variant, the euro could either become the international banking currency, or else a separate currency (let us call it the Eurobancor) could be established. In either case, this could operate much as in the Keynes Plan, with each nation having a clearing account to settle net balances between eurozone participants, with one-way convertibility of their domestic currencies (in this case, the euro for each nation) and the clearing account. For those creditor economies, limitations would be placed upon the size of the credit balances in the clearing account, and similarly for deficit nations, and once these were reached, corrective action would be required. This, however, is where the original Keynes Plan would need to be amended, as his original plan to seek to correct fundamental trade imbalances through changes in exchange rates is not available for a clearing union formed between nations sharing a single currency.

To take one example, if Germany has a large surplus with other members of the clearing union and Greece a deficit, it is not possible to attempt to rectify differentials in international competitiveness through the means of appreciating the German currency relative to Greece, since they both share the euro. Seeking to achieve the same end through internal devaluation would be possible if the EU Commission were willing to go beyond its existing monitoring of national economic policies and enforcing recommendations of policy changes to comply with existing agreements related to the eurozone. They could insist, for example, that Germany increase domestic activity and Greece deflate. This would not be straightforward, however, as the German memory of the hyperinflationary episode in the 1920s would cause resistance to this recommendation, and without the means to enforce this policy change, the result would be somewhat similar to current circumstances – that is, Germany would prefer to amass large reserves and Greece would be forced to deflate its economy, thereby reducing total clearing-union demand below the full employment equilibrium position.

Conclusion

Even with this deviation from the Keynes Plan, the 'ICU-light' option could still make a useful contribution to the present eurozone crisis. It would still require much tighter financial regulation, with central bank control over financial flows limiting the destabilising effect arising from short-term speculative flows. Moreover, since surpluses would be built up within the clearing-union payments system and could not be withdrawn from the system, these funds would be made available to finance productive investment in deficit nations. Additional incentives could be introduced to encourage creditor nations to expand their domestic demand rather than continue to build up surpluses, including the requirement to transfer excess account balances into a special holding account in the supranational clearing union institution, an account that could either pay no interest (hence imposing a real terms cost); or else consider the imposition of a negative interest rate, payable by the creditor nation, upon these excess balances. If this approach achieved its aim, and surplus nations inflated their economies, this would achieve a form of internal devaluation capable of gradually shifting relative competitive positions, although this would be slower and potentially more disruptive than the exchange-rate alternative not available to members of a single currency.

The 'ICU-light' version of the Keynes Plan would, therefore, achieve some of the stated goals, but the full variant would be a superior solution. For this to be achieved, however, there would need to be some form of reintroduction of national currencies for the rebalancing to work more effectively. In this scenario, each member of the eurozone would possess its individual currency and use the euro as the international bank currency to resolve balance of payments. As credit or debit balances grew, the option of encouraged or enforced currency revaluation and devaluation would be possible, thereby securing a quicker and more-effective symmetric rebalancing of the clearing union than could be accomplished through the alternative plethora of incentives outlined in the previous paragraph.

This would, of necessity, require the EU Commission and current participants in the eurozone to acknowledge that the form of monetary union they chose to implement is fatally flawed – and neither politicians nor economists appear to welcome having to admit previous mistakes. However, once this step has been taken, the future for this alternative vision of a currency union would have far greater potential for long-term sustainability. It would be possible, for example, for shifts in international competitiveness to be swiftly dealt with, in the absence of painful adjustment that stretched internal solidarity. It would also encourage the eurozone economy to operate closer to full employment, with faster rates of economic growth, which would mark a significant improvement over what has been achieved since the advent of the single currency. Moreover, the creation of a more flexible system, in which the objectives of employment and economic prosperity appeared to dominate over financial motives, and where participation does not seem to be such a permanent solution if circumstances for individual nations were to change, might encourage more nations to participate in the system. The United Kingdom, for example, would find it much easier to consider membership in a clearing union of this type, rather than in the current version of the eurozone.

None of this is to suggest that the ICA would prove to be a panacea for all economic problems facing the European economy (Arestis, 1999: 1). But it has the potential to provide a superior alternative to the present solutions. Perhaps it might be time for EU economists and policymakers to dust off their copies of the Keynes Plan and familiarise themselves with the contents – it might prove instructive.

12
The Collapse of the Eurozone: Disaster or Liberation?

Introduction

The current crisis and potential ultimate demise of the European single currency in its exiting format was predictable because it stems from deep-seated flaws within its structure. If policy-makers understood fully the impact of their action, they would never have launched the euro, unless, of course, ideology simply overrode common sense. Only fear of the conse-quences of a break-up is now keeping it together, and doing so at great cost, both in terms of bailout resources and, more importantly, degrading the life chances of a great number of eurozone citizens, clearly never the intention of the European integration project. The present chapter seeks to remove this fear through an analysis of the probable consequences.

A crucial idea introduced by Keynes (1936) into the corpus of economic thought is that the level of output and employment under market capitalism depends upon interaction between total spending and the economy's capacity to produce. Decisions to produce are made primarily by private profit-making firms; production, the source of employment, takes place only if companies anticipate a market in which goods and services can be sold at a profit. If demand is insufficient, productive capacity will stand idle and people will be without jobs. There is no automatic mechanism that guarantees output and spending decisions always coincide. Imbalances between aggregate demand and aggregate supply require active policy by government to change either its own or private expenditure through budgetary or monetary instruments. The neo-classical assumption of an automatic tendency towards market clearing is replaced by the necessity for active government intervention to secure simul-taneous internal and external balance in the economy.

Such a Keynesian framework is explicitly diminished by the monetarist ideology of the TEU, which laid the basis for the eurozone. A clear example of its approach is the reliance upon monetary tests of convergence rather than the examination of real variables of output growth and rates of unemploy-ment. Its convergence criteria include restrictions upon discretionary fiscal policy through the implementation of maximum permitted budget deficits backed by the possibility of levying fines on non-compliant economies. The transfer of monetary and exchange-rate policy to an independent ECB, whose sole legally defined objective is to secure stable prices through the use of a single economic policy instrument, a common Euroland interest rate, is at complete variance with a Keynesian approach. The political imperative to comply with this mandarin platform led to the EU suffering a prolonged period of slow growth and high levels of unemployment.

This chapter highlights the incompatibility between the monetarist model upon which the eurozone is constructed, and the possibility of creating an alternative economic strategy grounded in the Post-Keynesian tradition. Despite the inability of theorists to develop a universal Post-Keynesian theoretical model, due in large part to the complexity and dynamic nature of modern economies, it is nevertheless possible to identify a number of important themes that denote the essence of Post-Keynesian thought. We also outline the framework within which such an independent Post-Keynesian policy could operate.

Fundamental flaws of the eurozone

As previously discussed in Chapter 4, the countries forming the eurozone did not meet the requirements laid down by economists for an Optimum Currency Area (OCA) (Eichengreen, 1992). Consequently, eurozone proponents were reduced to the weaker proposition that adoption of a single currency and uniform monetary policy across participant nations would generate greater convergence amongst them in terms of the endogeneity OCA hypothesis. In fact, as a decade of experience has demonstrated, establishing the apparatus of a currency union created ever-wider divergence between the members. Thus, youth unemployment in Spain has hovered around 50% whilst fighting against an estimated 30% overvaluation of Spanish output against Germany. Far from binding member nations together, a one-size-fits-all monetary policy is driving them apart.

Second, the eurozone lacks any equilibrating mechanism to narrow different performances across member states, other than the production-losing option of deflation. Therefore, a clamour for fiscal union has arisen, either overtly or via Eurobonds, to redistribute resources from the strongly performing to weaker national economies. However, such proposals possess inherent weaknesses. For example, in practice they merely *contain* spatial disparities rather than *eliminate* them. Thus, after two decades of reunification, no part of the former East Germany is as rich as the poorest region of the former West Germany, whilst a century of subsidies has failed to eradicate the inequality between Northern and Southern Italy. If transfers within a single nation exert only a limited impact, their effect will be less when applied to countries with different languages and ways of life. Moreover, to be effective, regional resource redistribution requires political acceptability, based upon a shared citizenship amongst the peoples involved. Such feelings are hard to generate within the boundaries of one state, but are almost impossible to secure across a eurozone of countries with varying histories and cultures.

Third, the basic economic philosophy and governing institutions of the eurozone rest upon a pre-Keynesian mindset that seeks to achieve stability through balanced budgets and the prioritisation of anti-inflation targets to the neglect, and at times the detriment, of economic growth and job creation. The loss of credibility created by the crisis goes beyond the single currency to the ideology that shaped its creation: one of deregulation, privatisation and the privileging of corporate power despite modest employment rights introduced to limit social dumping. There was always a disconnect between this neo-liberal economic framework for the single currency and the European Social Model advocated by social democratic and other progressive political forces. Moreover, no mainstream European politicians are addressing the failure of that model nor recognising that a eurozone based on one-sided deflationary adjustment must ultimately fail. If they insist on maintaining that policy, they will have to accept the results and prepare for the consequences.

Fourth, the institutional structure of the eurozone is anti-democratic since none of its key decision-making bodies (e.g., the Council of Ministers, the European Central Bank and the European Commission) are transparent in procedure or accountable to the electorate. Such a situation is unacceptable to those who believe that decisions that profoundly affect peoples' lives should only be made by bodies whose authority derives from, and is renewable by, voters. National parliaments face such a sanction, whereas none of the eurozone's governing institutions do so. Consequently, in times of crisis they enjoy no reservoir of public support to fall back on. Their elite decision-makers are concentrated in the Frankfurt Group, an unelected cabal of eight people: IMF managing director Christine Lagarde; chancellor of Germany, Angela Merkel; French president, Nicolas Sarkozy; ECB President Mario Draghi; European Commission President Jose Barroso; President of the Euro Group Jean-Claude Juncker; President of the European Council Herman Van Rompuy; European Commissioner for Economic and Monetary Affairs Olli Rehn. This group took the key decisions for the eurozone based on financial-market sentiment, not on the electorate's opinions. Governments change, but policies remain unaltered, creating a democratic deficit of alarming proportions. Such a fundamental problem cannot be resolved by radical, let alone piecemeal, reforms; it requires a total structural dismantling followed by an equally profound recreation process.

A break-up of the eurozone?

Despite these inherent and largely insurmountable difficulties, the single currency precariously survives because of the nearly universally accepted belief that its break-up would be catastrophic. Consequently, the development of a plan B to cover such a probability is deterred. However, the time is overdue to consider how to manage a break-up with minimum collateral economic cost, because yesterday's unthinkable is becoming tomorrow's reality – particularly given that EU leaders in October 2011 broke their own taboo by admitting publically that Greece (and by implication other countries) could default and leave the eurozone. Any cost–benefit analysis of a break-up is inevitably problematic because it depends upon the unpredictable behaviour of the manifold actors whc would be involved and each of whose decisions potentially affect the outcome. However, certain critical issues can be identified.

The first is the time scale over which the impact is assessed as the short-term withdrawal effects become dwarfed, over a longer period, by the impact of lost production, employment and the subsequent social dislocation imposed by the eurozone's sole equilibrating mechanism: deflation. Dissolution of the eurozone would create uncertainty in an already unpredictable environment, but its outcome is unlikely to be more costly than years of diminished output, joblessness and the associated social ills, such as increased crime and greater sickness, already being witnessed across Southern Europe. Each temporary bailout postpones eventual break-up, as witnessed by a short-lived market rally frequently regarded as 'good news', but over the long-run these rallies are the opposite, as they prolong the burdens of deflation. The uncertainty facing weaker economies, and the risk premium paid on borrowing, suggest that there would be little additional net cost involved in a reconstitution of currency arrangements, as long as it appears to be credible and constitutes a long-term solution. The second issue concerns the manner in which the eurozone is dissolved; an enforced, disorderly breakdown under the pressure of events would entail greater costs than would a planned dissolution. An orderly break-up would not be easy to organise, but a chaotic implosion would be far worse. Therefore, it is in the interests of both members and non-members that its leaders retract their mantra that a collapse of the single currency is 'unthinkable' and, instead, devise detailed mechanisms to minimise the costs of its occurrence. The United Kingdom should also be prepared for such as eventuality; if it is, short-term losses would be small compared to long-term gains from greater flexibility and, hence, economic efficiency, together with enhanced accountability in decision-making. On 5 November 2011 George Osborne finally admitted that the Treasury was undertaking planning for the event of a eurozone collapse, whilst on 24 November 2011 the Financial Services Authority told British banks to prepare a contingency strategy for a single-currency break-up.

The eurozone's debt crisis is not about state profligacy, but is the result of a recession-induced slump in tax revenues triggered by the 2008 crash's repercussions upon the financial institutions that caused it. The surface debt crisis is actually one of economic growth and employment, whereby private investment has fallen and, until governments support the real economy with public infrastructure expenditure to stimulate growth and redistribution of income to boost consumption, 'rescue' packages will continue to fail. If every country simultaneously belt-tightens, aggregate demand will decline and there will be a reduced market for goods and services. Policy-makers who appear to deny this link, seem to have learnt none of the lessons posed by the 20th century's Great Depression – lessons such as that a series of national deflation strategies, intended to eliminate budget deficits, are self-defeating if they create an international deflationary spiral. However, recognition of such lessons requires a major policy shift among core eurozone states, which shows no sign of materialising. Therefore, the demise of the single currency in its existing structure will be hastened. However, so much political capital has been poured into the euro project that it is inevitable that policy-makers would try to buy time until they piece together a politically acceptable form of fiscal union to bolster monetary union. However, these attempts encounter severe difficulties, such as they take time to organise, time the eurozone does not possess; they involve less-competitive nations being dictated to by the more-competitive, even more directly than they are currently; they require, not years, but decades of self-defeating, production-losing deflation; they ignore the obvious conclusion that the single currency is based upon deficient economics.

The alternative to integration is disintegration which, despite short-run problems, constitutes a more efficient long-run strategy. Restoring national currencies would not be easy, since countries would have to nationalise their banks (although this may prove desirable for other reasons, such as financial stability) and re-impose capital controls to prevent destabilising currency movements. Moreover, they would need to be aware that the inflationary potential of a devalued currency could eliminate some of its gains in competitiveness; however, it would restore to governments a degree of control over their national destinies and provide an alternative to deflation (which creates mass unemployment and has associated costs, such as crime, ill-health and social exclusion, as well as wealth-creating opportunities being lost forever). Due to the difficulties involved, detailed studies of the costs of a eurozone break-up are highly problematic: a study made by economists at UBS (Deo et al., 2011) makes depressing reading, whereby if Germany were to leave the eurozone, it would incur costs worth 20–25% of GDP in the first year and roughly half that in each subsequent year. In contrast, if Greece were to quit, the first-year costs would be 40–50% of GDP, whilst succeeding annual costs would amount to some 15%. However, under close analysis these figures are problematic, since the report is based on the extreme assumption that countries exiting the eurozone would be compelled to leave the EU itself. Although there is a legal argument for this position, real-politics mean that this would be unlikely, as it would benefit no one to have embittered neighbours in the eastern Mediterranean (or elsewhere), nor to cut Germany adrift. Policy-makers would be determined to preserve the single market rather than immolate it in a bonfire of euros.

Therefore the costs of break-up would be significantly smaller than envisaged by the UBS estimations; however, more importantly, they failed to consider the potential benefits following the dissolution of the eurozone – benefits to which we now turn.

Potential eurozone break-up scenarios

Fortunately a workable alternative exists to the dilemma of long-run depression in the eurozone (under the present system) or to uncontrolled currency depreciation (if debtor countries are forced out of the single currency by market or political pressures). First, Germany could leave the single currency, taking with it Austria, Finland and the Netherlands (if they so desire) to form a German-mark area. Exiting from a position of strength would generate less panic, reducing the threat of bank runs and contagion. Many legal and technical challenges would remain, but the reputation of the Bundesbank and the relevant economies' competitive performance would permit time to erect the required institutions and controls. Such a move would initially be painful for German exporters, who have thrived on the basis of an undervalued euro and the credit-fuelled boom in peripheral nations. However, they also thrived previously with a strong deutschmark and will appreciate the absence of long-term costs in the form of permanent transfers to less-competitive eurozone members. Moreover, by Germany no longer having to impose, inappropriately, its own disciplines upon others, and withdrawing voluntarily, all would benefit. That would improve the existing situation, in which Germany is paralysed between two constituencies of a policy elite remaining wedded to concepts of European 'ever-close union' and most of its population, who do not wish to subsidise permanently other eurozone countries.

Second, the current state of the French economy, with large private and public-sector debt, substantial bank exposure to indebted euro regions and a lack of competitiveness, makes it ill-suited to share a currency with Germany, as demonstrated by the record gap between their bond yields in 2011. However, a period of devaluation and orderly debt restructuring could see France ready to join a new German-mark zone within a decade. Alternatively, a two-tier structure could emerge, with Germany leading a Hanseatic-style northern league and France a Mediterranean zone. Such a transformation of the 60-year-old Franco-German axis may seem remote, but events could lead to its development.

Third, Greece and, less spectacularly, other creditor states (e.g., Spain, Portugal and Italy) remain stuck in the type of vicious cycle of insolvency, low competiveness and ever-deepening depression, as documented by Minsky (2008). To escape, they must begin an orderly default and voluntarily exit the eurozone, since all other options that might restore competitiveness are problematic and require currency depreciation as a necessary, albeit not sufficient, condition. The first option, a sharp weakening of the single currency is unlikely, whilst the United States is economically weak and Germany ultra-competitive. The second option, a rapid reduction in unit labour costs through increased productivity growth in excess of wages, is equally improbable. Germany took a decade to reduce its competitiveness; even if Greece and other countries could emulate its example, they cannot wait so long. The third option is price and wage deflation of some 20%; however, this would cause many years of intensified depression, while making public debts unsustainable. Hence, as none of these options is feasible in practice, the only effective strategy for Greece and other similarly affected countries is to leave the eurozone and return to a depreciated national currency that would restore growth and competitiveness. This is a tired and tested route, for example: Argentina after 2002, and other emerging markets that abandoned their currency pegs. Argentina subsequently grew by 9% in 2003 and carried on around that rate until checked by the 2008 financial crisis and 2009 global recession; it is currently growing at close to 10%, providing a decade-long resurgence of national prosperity.

Therefore, countries that exit the eurozone should do so in a manner that is in the interests of the real economy rather than the financial economy, whereby finance is intended to facilitate productive activity in the real economy and not dictate the framework/environment within which the real economy must operate. Contrary to conventional wisdom, these countries will not collapse. Instead it should be recognised that monetary unions always possess a limited life, and the eurozone is an especially badly structured one. Exit is the most efficient way for certain nations to recreate long-term competitiveness and commence short-term recovery. A decisive government would take several immediate steps; switch rapidly to a new currency, nationalise the banks and reintroduce capital controls. Administrative measures to ensure supplies of food, medicine and oil will be required along with income and wealth redistribution to promote the consumption necessary for job creation. New contracts executed under domestic law, plus taxation and government expenditure, would be denominated in the new currency, whilst existing contracts remain in euros. Banks will possess both legacy single currency accounts and new currency accounts such that recovery should commence in a few months, spurred by devaluation that would allow industry to increase exports and recapture the domestic market. Hence, the immediate crisis is an opportunity to restructure the economy, changing the balance of power in favour of the majority. If such a remedy sounds drastic to the orthodox, they should compare it to the cost of eurozone-imposed deflation on suffering countries. Only a complete break from EU neoliberal ideology and policy can initiate productive and democratic regeneration.

Of course, problems would occur. The most substantial will be capital losses for core eurozone institutions. However, such difficulties can be navigated; Argentina did so in 2001, when it converted its dollar debts into pesos; and the United States performed a similar feat in 1933, when it depreciated the dollar and repealed the gold clause. Major eurozone banks would require adequate recapitalisation, whilst effective capital controls can prevent a post-exit implosion of peripheral banking systems. Collateral damage is limited by an orderly exit process and by international support to finance the fiscal transition. Via depreciation, the exit will restore growth quickly, avoiding at least a decade of depression. The recent experience of Ireland, which defied the dictates of global financiers, together with many emerging countries in the last 20 years, demonstrates that the orderly restructuring of foreign debts can restore debt sustainability, competitiveness and job creation. As in a broken marriage that requires dissolution, it is fairer and more efficient to establish rules that make separation less costly to all parties.

A Post-Keynesian alternative

The monetarist bias institutionalised at the core of the eurozone project, which will prove difficult to reverse given its centrality to the TEU, is in sharp contrast to the theoretical predictions and policy prescriptions that emerge from the broad Keynesian tradition (see Table 12.1 for a summary).

In relation to the twin concepts of disequilibrium and cumulative causation, the 1990s decade of deflation amongst EU economies was not a simple 'one-off' loss of potential income, but was a long-term process of relative decline fuelled by cumulative causation. The latter term was first used by Myrdal (1957) to convey the reinforcing processes whereby patterns of uneven development may be perpetuated and even accentuated. It constitutes a challenge to orthodox equilibrium theory, which holds that, if divergences in economic phenomenon exist, forces come into play that narrow these differences and ultimately eliminate them. However, in Myrdal's model of cumulative causation, markets reinforce inequality, so that focus on positions of static equilibrium is inappropriate and misleading. The deflationary impact of pursuing the Maastricht convergence criteria lowers current sales and profits, which in turn leads to falling investment, thereby reducing demand in the future. By contrast, a Post-Keynesian strategy of achieving full employment with growth (prohibited under the monetarism of Maastricht) would fuel an upward spiral of rising income, demand, investment and profitability (Whyman et al., 2005). Moreover, within capitalism many factors operate that work towards disequilibrium rather than equilibrium once initial differences in economic and social phenomena arise. It is the process of change that should occupy the centre of analytical attention; this process is not a moving series of equilibria, but a chain reaction of mutual feedback. The existence of destabilising feedback mechanisms implies that temporary disturbances may involve substantial social and economic consequences, which often gather speed at an accelerating rate. Under cumulative causation, social forces interact with technical, economic and psychological factors, whilst the evolution of the

Table 12.1　Comparison between features of Post-Keynesianism and the eurozone

	Post-Keynesianism	Neo-liberal eurozone
Macroeconomic assumptions		
Economy tends towards full employment	No, capitalism is inherently unstable	Yes
Demand side		
Aggregate demand level	Vital, but unstable	Important
Aggregate demand management	Essential prerequisite for fully employed economy	Not important, no federal instrument to manage demand
Fiscal policy	Main instrument to manage AD	Unimportant, prerogative of nation state
Monetary policy	Supportive to fiscal policy; cheap money to stimulate investment and growth	Uniform interest rate – set to produce price stability
Counter-cyclical	Yes	Limited by TEU convergence criteria and SGP on budget deficits
Status of central bank	Democratically controlled – given multiple objectives	Independent – sole target is price stability
Supply side		
What causes unemployment?	Demand deficiency and supply-side problems	Structural/supply side factors
Model of unemployment	Hysteresis; tendency towards disequilibrium	Natural rate/NAIRU
Policies to reduce unemployment	Demand management, labour-market policies, incomes policy (or wage bargaining coordination) industrial policy (including socialisation investment)	Level and duration of benefits
External balance		
Exchange-rate regime	Short-term stability, long-term flexibility	Single currency
How to defeat destabilising speculation?	Capital controls, financial regulation	Large single economy less prone to destabilisation
Globalisation?	National autonomy remains possible	Integrated financial markets, no room for independent monetary policy

Source: Baimbridge et al. (2007).

economy depends upon, and is reflected by, the institutional organisation of economic phenomena (Baimbridge et al., 2007).

Furthermore, in relation to increasing returns to scale and economic growth, Hardin (1982) related cumulative causation to the existence of increasing returns. The latter jeopardises the existence of standard neoclassical equilibria but, more significantly, it creates dynamic tendencies of uneven development, whereby both comparative success and comparative failure exert self-reinforcing effects, whilst the combination of profit-driven production and investment decisions, free trade and capital mobility produces inherent tendencies towards asymmetrical growth. Hence, growth is perceived to be an endogenous, cumulative process based on increasing returns activities rather than being the outcome of exogenously given expansion-of-factor endowments (Baimbridge et al., 2007). Additionally, cumulative causation also depends upon technology gaps, which represent the differences in technical advancement between rival nations, between industries in different countries or between firms in a given industry in one economy. Such gaps imply that technology is not uniform and that technical progress is not instantaneously diffused. If these gaps are not simply a function of market failure, technology is more than an endowment, and scarcity does not determine the resource-allocation process. It is the learned ability to innovate and to imitate existing commodities and ways of producing that is the driving force behind higher productivity and competitiveness. The rejection of scarcity and of a crucial role for endowments changes the character of economic policy. In a scarcity-driven world, the state's function is to overcome market failure; in a world of technology gaps, economic policy promotes the innovation process support of research and development, subsidies, demand management and workplace democracy. Moreover, it essential to note that technical change is cumulative and path-dependent, such that it is neither random nor predictable. Agents do not usually share identical knowledge or competence; indeed, the diffusion of technology requires time; the discontinuity of this diffusion process implies that, even with a steady rate of innovation (itself highly unlikely), technology gaps reinforce the conclusion of cumulative causation theory that convergence is by no means a guaranteed, nor even a frequent, occurrence. Therefore, active government economic policy, restricted by the TEU, is essential to achieving an upward spiral of cumulative causation (Whyman et al., 2005).

The inherent instability of capitalist economies requires government intervention to maintain a sufficiently high level of aggregate demand to ensure the full employment of all resources. However, Post-Keynesianism emphasises that the level of aggregate demand simultaneously influences the level of capacity utilisation and employment in both the short and long run. The simulation of investment in the short run will facilitate full employment but also produces additional capacity for an expansion of production in future time periods (Sawyer, 1995). In the absence of sufficient future capacity, an economy could be 'too small' to employ all resources and expand at its optimum rate. Consequently, any strategy to reduce the natural instability of capitalist economies would focus upon one of the main causes of fluctuations in output, namely entrepreneurial expectations and their resultant impact upon private-sector investment. The maintenance of a sufficiently high level of aggregate demand can contribute towards enhancing expectations of future profitability, whilst simultaneously facilitating a current budget surplus capable of financing a considerable proportion of future investment. However, this strategy leaves the investment function in private hands and, therefore, dependent upon unstable expectations. Keynes (1936 and 1943–1944) predicted recurrent problems of market coordination and under-utilisation of resources due to a fundamental conflict between industry and finance, where, in a world of uncertainty, the short-run behaviour of rentiers tends to prevail in the market for financial securities. The ability of rentiers to impose a constraint on the liquid funds available for the long-term finance of enterprises and their desire for liquidity results in rates of investment that lie below the level necessary to achieve full employment.

Keynes's solution to both these problems was the socialisation of investment. Only the state could remain impervious to speculative financial gain and, therefore, approve sufficient projects 'so as to preserve stability of aggregate investment ... at the right and appropriate level'. When pressed by fellow economists in 1943 as to how far he would socialise investment, Keynes replied, 'Two-thirds or three-quarters would be indirectly influenced by public and semi-public bodies'. Thus, full employment could be secured through the establishment of the National Investment Bank (NIB), charged with the strategic regulation of the aggregate flow of investment. This would ensure 'an adequate demand for them, partly by making them available at a rate that would attract a sufficient demand, and partly be stimulating for the undertaking of particular investment projects'. More recent proposals of this type have advocated the democratic control of capital formation through pension-fund or employee-investment-fund socialism (Burkitt and Whyman 1995). They are only feasible outside the constraints imposed by eurozone membership.

Finally, the relationship between aggregate demand and aggregate supply is one of significant insights to emerge from Post-Keynesian thought (Sawyer, 1995). Whilst a high level of aggregate demand is a necessary precondition for the full employment of resources, it is insufficient if the economy suffers from supply-side deficiencies. For example, active labour-market policy is advocated where skill shortages and labour-market bottlenecks threaten to destabilise the economy. Training and educational programmes can match skills to the demand for labour, whilst employment services enhance the efficiency of the search process (Layard et al., 1991; Trehorning, 1993). Similarly, incomes policy and/or the coordination of wage bargaining can deliver a superior trade-off between inflation and unemployment than decentralised, deregulated bargaining in those economies in which trade unions are present. Though internalisation of the costs of imprecise wage levels into the decision-making parameters of all parties to the negotiations, there is an increased likelihood of reaching a compromise between labour and capital over their respective shares of national income without damaging international competitiveness, growth and employment. Moreover, the degree to which wage bargaining is coordinated is associated with real-wage flexibility, because centralised structures provide a more flexible adaptation to market conditions.

Economic policy outside the eurozone

The policy imperatives imposed upon the state by cumulative causation and technology gaps are unlikely to be achieved over all of the EU's member states, with their different trade cycles, economic structures, histories, languages and cultures. Advanced capitalist economies are inherently unstable; left to themselves, they cannot maintain full-employment resources whilst being marred by inequalities in the distribution of market power, income and wealth. Unfettered market forces tend, via cumulative causation, to exacerbate these instabilities and disparities. Considerable scope exists for government involvement in initiating, pursuing and implementing economic policies; or the demand side, insufficient aggregate demand and the instability of investment are the key problems to resolve, whilst on the supply side, planning of prices and incomes, training plus active industrial measures to direct investment to resolve any balance-of-payments problems are central. The prospect of an EU-wide strategy to achieve these objectives is remote, although supra-national directives may prevent the implementation of effective national policies.

However, in order to implement Post-Keynesian economic policies, EU member states need to avoid the uniform monetary policy and the constraints upon budgetary measures imposed by the eurozone; therefore, the crucial issue becomes: What framework is needed for the formation or macroeconomic policy? The initial stage is a national information campaign to acquaint the public and industry with the opportunities created by, and the dangers averted through, the break-up of the eurozone. In particular, a decision to reject participation in the single currency restores to national government those economic instruments essential to the management of its economy. Therefore, democratic accountability is re-established, because citizens can once again enjoy the opportunity to choose the economic strategy pursued by the government of the day, rather than a policy being dictated by unelected central bankers. Moreover, governments will be able to develop a balanced economic programme, pursuing the multiple objectives of full employment, rapid economic growth and a sustainable balance-of-payments. as well as low inflation. The opportunities are substantial.

In particular, a Post-Keynesian economic strategy seeks to achieve both internal and external balance. Internal balance refers to more than the Maastricht target of price stability. Accordingly, aggregate demand management could reduce unemployment, whilst a mixture of budgetary and monetary measures, a prices and incomes policy, the re-introduction of credit controls and coordinated national wage bargaining could restrain inflation. Although direct controls are unpopular with orthodox economists, who prefer the supposed allocative efficiency of free markets, the reality of sticky prices within oligopolistic markets creates the potential for governments to increase employment and growth. Moreover, a majority of the world's nations still retain capital controls as part of their economic management, whilst Ireland's recent remarkable growth was facilitated by social contracts with the trade unions. Furthermore, the Post-Keynesian approach stresses a positive role for government action to enhance the competitiveness of industry. Hence, outside the single currency, the governments could strengthen their economy's competitiveness by enhancing the production potential of already-strong sectors through targeted reductions in corporation tax, research and development, and greater spending upon education.

However, an argument frequently advanced by advocates of the eurozone is that the degree of economic autonomy for the nation state advocated in the present book is largely illusory due to globalisation and the international integration of financial markets. To the extent that national economies fail to insulate themselves from international financial markets through exchange controls or 'Tobin taxes', economies became prisoners of the neoclassical assumptions held by the majority of economists. For example, an expansionary fiscal policy is seen by orthodoxy as a prelude to an increase in inflation and a decline in international competitiveness, rather than as a precursor to a higher level of aggregate demand, increased investment in future capacity and therefore the creation of a potentially higher future rate of economic growth. Thus non-orthodox economic policy is penalised by the withdrawal of inward investment, perhaps triggering a currency crisis of a sufficient magnitude to undermine the entire strategy. An extension of this thesis argues that, due to financial integration, nation states can no longer operate a distinct monetary policy. Interest rates will be set internationally, with a premium equivalent to the degree of the perceived risk of currency devaluation, problems caused by political instability or threats to foreign investment. The argument implies that eurozone membership will be costless since monetary autonomy no longer exists. Indeed, the greater anti-inflation credibility formerly associated with the Bundesbank, assumed to pass to its successor the ECB, should ensure a lower long-term real interest rate than would be possible for an independent nation state.

Additionally, the effectiveness of devaluation as a means of establishing an international competitive advantage is also dismissed, because the preponderance of subsidiaries of foreign transnational corporations (TNCs) rises as a proportion of the manufacturing sector. Subsidiaries of a parent company will not respond to devaluation by allowing their prices to fall, which would imply competing with their own parent company in foreign markets at a lower price. Thus, they are more likely to maintain real prices and take higher sterling profits, thereby nullifying the effectiveness of the policy. Hence, in essence the economic case for participation in the eurozone rests upon the assertion that the economic effectiveness of the nation state is over, so that only as part of regional economic blocs can governments reassert the use of traditional economic tools, such as monetary and exchange-rate policy. Indeed certain socialist theorists argue that European economic integration can make possible a form of Euro-Keynesianism, which can no longer work at the national level (Holland, 1985). However, the contested ratification of the TEU suggests that there will be little appetite for renegotiation, whilst the EU Commission's attacks upon 'expansionary' budgetary policy under the auspices of the SGP indicates that a bias towards deflation remains at the heart of EU economic policy decision-making within the eurozone.

Our arguments do not dismiss the reality of a shift towards increasingly globalised trade and financial structures, although it would be more accurate to describe the process as 'triadisation', as the world economy becomes increasingly dominated by three main trading groups – NAFTA, the EU and an Asian block built around Japan. Many parts of the world (for example almost the entire African continent) play little or no part in these supposedly 'global' markets. Nevertheless, it is true that an explosion in international movements of financial capital, particularly associated with speculation rather than with trade in goods and services, has altered the environment within which national economic strategy is determined. Nevertheless, the majority of countries in the world continue to operate controls on the international movement of capital, whilst the financial destabilisation inflicted upon Mexico, Russia, the ERM and the 'Asian tiger' economies has served to warn world governments of the perils of unregulated capital movements. The policy prescriptions should not come as a surprise, as Keynes outlined it decades ago, whilst the post-war economy was based upon the tight regulation of capital to prevent international economic instability. Therefore the choice is between eurozone membership and becoming increasingly immersed in a neo-liberal, triadised system, or pursuing a strategy protected by a re-regulation of financial capital.

In summary, it is essential to note that EU member states enjoy an effective long-run option concerning their future economic strategy; they can embrace an essentially monetarist eurozone identity or, if they decide to abandon the euro, they can pursue an alternative policy direction. The widely held view that Britain possesses 'no alternative' but to participate in further monetary integration is at odds with the facts, such that by decoupling them from the eurozone's integrationist momentum the outcome will be enhanced economic prosperity and restored democratic choice to their electorates. Indeed, if Post-Keynesian insights into the working of the economy in the real world are ever to influence government policy, they are more likely to be effective outside the eurozone than if countries remain a prisoner of its neo-classically designed institutions.

Conclusion

The recurrent eurozone crises since 2010, when national problems were magnified onto a regional and indirectly global scale, illustrate that a break-up cannot be postponed indefinitely. A 50-year fiction is over; as frequently before in history, a new Europe must be built on the ruins of the old. This poses the existential question: What sort of countries do EU member states wish to be? That choice is not ultimately technical, or even economic, but political.

A single currency may conceivably improve the performance of converged economies, such as Germany with certain of its northern neighbours, but a single currency cannot become an efficient, permanent tool of Brussels's control over 17 diverse nations, as is currently advocated by proponents of eurozone policy centralisation. To develop a recently repeated remark by Angela Merkel, whatever the question, 'more Europe' cannot conceivably be an effective answer. The states of the eurozone must resort to floating exchange rates to adapt to different lifestyles and working practices, a truth Britain discovered painfully after Winston Churchill re-adopted the Gold Standard in 1925. No amount of 'pro-Europe' rhetoric can find jobs for millions of unemployed workers – the ones who are the single currency's chief victims. Differences between states must ultimately be reflected in their terms of exchange.

The EU was always a creation of elitist diplomacy, supported by voters only so long as they either believed it would bring prosperity or were frightened by the supposed dangers of independence. The EU sought to craft a political entity from cultures whose variations defied Hapsburgs, Bourbons, Napoleon and Hitler. Hence, what prospects of defeating such odds have Angela Merkel, François Hollande and the unelected EU bureaucrats? A new, more flexible European constitution is urgently required; one that restores and reasserts the sovereignty of countries. It should abandon the dogma that free trade is everywhere and always an absolute objective. Governments should recognise that democracy is a greater good, with its untidy edges and its acknowledgement of national self-interest driven by public discourse. Democracy is, and for the foreseeable future will remain, located in nation states. Recognition of democracy's supremacy removes the need for the demands of European peoples – with proud and different histories, cultures and political, economic and social structures – to be reconciled in an artificial compromise that satisfies no one and potentially creates sources of conflict (for instance, between suppliers and recipients of transfers in a sub-optimal currency union).

Thus, the EU is a confederation that requires a working constitution detoxified of 'ever-closer union' specifying clear boundaries of sovereign discretion. Nation states need legislative space, even when the outcome is many distorted playing fields. Rather than perceiving a euro break-up as failure, proponents of democracy see break-up to be the harbinger of a new settlement in which the wider interest is expressed by allowing citizens and parliaments self-determination, sometimes merging institutions and sometimes maintaining their separation as enlightened democracy permits. A Europe based on friendship and cooperation, not on an institutional restriction of diversity, is the path to a self-governing and prosperous future.

13
From the Eurozone to National Economic Self-Governance

Introduction

Participation in further EU integration will place a continued straight-jacket upon EU member states' macroeconomic policy and thus increase the difficulty of their pursuing their national interest. For example, the model for the eurozone seeks to impose a particular institutional framework that restricts the flexibility of action of individual countries in order to enable economic policy to be determined, or at least co-ordinated, from the centre. Many economists (Jamieson, 1998; Michie, 2000; Minford, 2000; Ormerod, 1999) argue that greater autonomy for individual nation states, under the principle of subsidiarity, might provide a more stable economic environment in which to pursue further co-operation between countries. However, largely due to the political desire to tie members more closely together, the EU is seeking to progressively replace economic autonomy for a nation state by the requirement to coordinate its economic strategy with the EU norm or else be subject to sanctions levied by the EU Commission (Pennant-Rea et al., 1997). A decision to reject such developments would restore to national government those economic instruments essential to the management of its economy. Governments would be able to devise different economic programmes and, once endorsed by the electorate, would possess the means by which to pursue their chosen objectives. Democracy would, therefore, be restored, so that citizens can once again enjoy the opportunity to choose the economic strategy pursued by the government of the day. Moreover, governments will be able to engage in a more balanced economic programme, pursuing the multiple objectives of full employment, high economic growth and a sustainable balance of payments as well as low inflation. The opportunities are substantial.

To illustrate the broad range of different policies that could be enacted, this chapter outlines a number of broad, alternative economic strategies that could be pursued once a nation is freed from the restrictive grip of the ECB and the requirements of the TEU, let alone any future developments.

Additionally, it discusses the development of complementary industrial strategy and exchange-rate policy. The former can only prove effective if supplemented by fiscal and monetary policies that target growth and reject deflation. Inflation and unemployment is not the European disease but the symptom of economies that cannot produce enough to satisfy domestic demand: the basic economic problem is insufficient production. The solution is to boost demand but channel it to EU industry, improving profits, stimulating production and, hence, productivity, and providing the incentive to invest, thereby cutting unit costs and inflation through a considered policy of economic expansion. This solution can be achieved, free from eurozone constraints, through control of the exchange rate and the accompanying interest-rate changes. Such a policy makes it profitable to produce in the EU member states by utilising the price mechanism to boost exports, encourage import substitution and lure EU industry back into sectors it has abandoned, whilst a tax on imports would provide crucial support. An effective exchange-rate policy is critical to the successful implementation of the outlined options for macroeconomic policy. The intention is to demonstrate that national economic management is not only still feasible, but also that it is preferable to transferring the main levers of macroeconomic policy into the hands of the EU, which is incapable of using them consistently and in the best interests of all EU member states simultaneously.

Developing a macroeconomic policy strategy

The first potential economic strategy seeks to follow the framework whereby national monetary authorities, whether in the hands of an independent or democratically controlled central bank, seek a higher long-term growth rate by providing a favourable climate for industrial expansion through low inflation and, hence, reduced long-term interest rates. Fiscal policy is used to support the more dominant monetary policy by restraining inflationary pressures, thereby reinforcing the low-interest-rate objective. The globalisation of financial markets prevents governments from 'persuading' financial institutions to finance public-sector borrowing at less than the market rate. Consequently, the higher the level of public-sector borrowing on the international money markets, the higher the price for that borrowing in terms of long-term interest rates. This approach assumes crowding-out in the financial markets due to limited resources for lending to prospective borrowers because, were banks to create money simply to meet the additional demand for funds so that the supply of loanable funds was relatively elastic, interest rates would be unaffected. However, the strategy seeks to reduce government expenditure in order to reduce borrowing and, hence, interest rates. In 'hard' versions of this strategy, the government endeavours to maintain a high value for the currency in order to squeeze inflation further. The objective is comparatively easy to accomplish if the country enjoys a trade surplus, because the pressure on its exchange rate is upwards due to the country's competitive position, assuming the absence of speculative motives to counter this fundamental relationship. However, for those eurozone member states that typically suffer from a current-account trade deficit, a rise in short-term interest rates is needed to attract sufficient short-term capital investment into securities to counterbalance trade-related downward pressures on the currency; although, these developments will impact upon long-term interest rates and thus conflict with the fundamental goal of the strategy. Nevertheless, unemployment remains the greatest economic problem for Europe to solve; thus it is probable that, sooner rather than later, the ECB will come under pressure to permanently loosen monetary policy now that it has established its anti-inflation credibility and to demonstrate that it can ensure the long-term stability of the eurozone.

A second distinctive economic strategy involves the more active use of fiscal as well as monetary policy in order to pursue both internal and external balance for the economy. Internal balance refers to more than just low inflation, but also to low unemployment and to high rates of economic growth. Accordingly, a mixture of demand-side reflation and supply-side labour market policies, particularly measures encouraging retraining and labour mobility, could reduce unemployment. Thus, the net stimulative effect is targeted upon specific sectors of the economy that most require assistance, rather than raising aggregate demand per se and creating inflationary bottlenecks. Economic growth could be facilitated by the maintenance of a competitive exchange rate through managed floating, perhaps based upon a trade-weighted basket of currencies, together with tax incentives for firms that increase productive investment. A mixture of fiscal and monetary policy could restrain inflation; if this proved difficult to achieve, rather than abandon the other internal objectives, governments could enact additional measures to restrain inflationary pressures. These might include the temporary re-introduction of credit controls, an incomes policy (tax-based or otherwise) or co-ordinated national bargaining. Although currently unpopular amongst economists who prefer the allocative efficiency of free markets, the reality of sticky wages and prices, due to oligopolistic markets as much as to the existence of trade unions, gives rise to the possibility of market failure resulting in persistently high unemployment and slower-than-trend output growth. In this case, government intervention is justified to achieve a superior outcome. It is a fact that the majority of the world's nations still retain exchange controls to assist them to manage their economies, whilst Ireland's remarkable recent growth rates have been facilitated by 'social contracts' with trade unions to prevent wage pressures undermining its competitive position. Finally, external balance can be achieved through the provision of a competitive exchange rate, although structural problems in export sectors may require supplementary supply-side measures to improve product quality and reliability and to encourage a shift of resources to provide goods and services in growing, rather than stagnant, markets.

This 'Keynesian' strategy is notably different from the first approach due to its positive role for government action in wider areas of economic activity. Accordingly, an approach of this nature would be facilitated by an industrial policy designed to enhance the long-run competitiveness of EU industry. An analysis of trade flows indicates that the EU enjoys a comparative advantage in financial and media services, and in those areas of manufacturing that rely upon a high degree of scientific innovation, such as telecommunications, pharmaceuticals, aerospace, energy exploration and generation, biochemicals and computer-related activity, together with lower value-added manufactures, most notably in engineering and metalworking sectors. Consequently, the EU could strive to strengthen its competitive position by enhancing the productive potential of already-strong sectors through *targeted* reductions in corporation tax, research and development tax credits, and greater spending upon education. If higher growth is to be forthcoming, innovative research undertaken by universities and publicly funded research centres requires prioritisation in terms of the allocation of government resources. Labour-market programmes designed to re-equip workers for the requirements of industries with a competitive advantage ensure that their maximum growth potential is not undermined by the lack of a skilled workforce, whilst facilitating the shift of resources to more productive uses.

Developing a supply-side strategy

An active industrial strategy must be based upon understanding of what promotes industrial competitiveness. Porter's (1990) exhaustive research demonstrated that economic success is achieved through the development of 'clusters' of mutually reinforcing internationally competitive industries. EU member states once enjoyed the benefits of clustering, as one sophisticated industry spawned and reinforced others; where goods pulled services into overseas markets and vice versa, its multinationals served as loyal customers abroad, and the cluster of financial services and trade-related industries was highly self-reinforced. However, a gradual unwinding of industrial clusters occurred, with limited areas of competitive advantage remaining. As some EU industries became uncompetitive, they were increasingly poor buyers for other domestic products. The spiral continues downward, cushioned only by long tradition and the remnants of technological innovation. Thus, many EU manufacturing companies lag behind those of other industrial countries, such as Japan, in process technology and in their willingness and ability to invest in new plants, undermining competitive advantage in industries producing manufacturing equipment. The sectors in which EU firms sustain competitive advantage partly owe it to a cluster of related, supporting industries. In consumer goods and services, a vibrant retail industry creates pressures to innovate, whilst the City of London, and to a lesser extent Frankfurt, provide another sector where strength relies upon the advantages of clustering.

However, the EU's industry overall lacks dynamism and the ability to upgrade its competitive position unaided; this is due to cumulative disadvantages that reinforce each other negatively in the spiral of relative decline. Problems in one industry hurt other industries. Falling competitiveness reduces relative living standards, making consumer demand less sophisticated. Downward pressure on government revenue leads to cutbacks in resource-creation and social services, weakening still more industries. Consequently, it is questionable whether remaining levels of competitive advantage are insufficient to generate enough well-paid jobs for all its citizens; therefore, the danger is that the EU economy is caught in the downward spiral of clustering, and its relative living standards suffer accordingly. Loss of competitiveness creates its own momentum and, once established, it is hard to reverse without a major policy initiative. Indeed, lingering market positions and customer loyalties allay any sense of urgency about the need for change. A significant proportion of growth in skilled and value-added EU employment has occurred from investment by foreign firms. Much of this, however, is attracted by relatively low production costs. Foreign investments are largely in assembly facilities, taking advantage of poorly paid, mostly unskilled labour, or in service industries such as hotels, golf courses and retail outlets. While overseas capital benefits EU industry, an economy whose growth depends on the assembly outposts of foreign companies will be constrained in terms of productivity increases. Certainly, such investment alone cannot break the vicious circle between a weak balance of payments, slow growth and declining manufacturing, which has developed across much of the eurozone economy. Hence, it demonstrates the problems facing an economy needing to restart the upgrading process whereby a number of fundamental problems must be tackled by a co-ordinated industrial strategy if recovery is to occur.

The EU cannot regain innovation-driven competitiveness without a world-class educational and training system encompassing all socioeconomic and ability levels. The rate of investment in human skills must rise substantially, standards must be improved and technical expertise must be stressed. This is perhaps the most pressing issue over the next decade, for the need to improve the quality and quantity of the EU's labour force is great. Research conducted in France and Germany by the National Institute for Economic and Social Research (Prais and Wagner, 1988; Steedman, 1988; Jarvis and Prais, 1989) has demonstrated that a high level of technical qualifications of craft workers is crucial. Further, EU companies, as well as member state governments, face a busy skills agenda. They need to realise that without a broader pool of trained human resources, their competitive advantage will be limited, such that unless companies accept greater responsibility for internal training of all workers, they will make little progress relative to their competitors. The multi-skilling of the industrial workforce provides the route to productive flexibility, quality and innovation, while enhancing individuals' occupational status. The inability of individuals to contribute to their full potential is reflected in the stunted economic performance of many sectors, where narrow vocational training is a contradiction in an economy that seeks to place workers at the forefront of innovation. Consequently the emphasis must be on quality training to reflect new economic requirements.

Additionally, EU investment levels need to increase to match the improved labour force, primarily in manufacturing but also in the infrastructure of essential services. Machinery and plant in many sectors are currently antiquated, so that the development of advanced technologies as a basis for expanding into modern high value-added production is held back. The future competitive advantage of EU firms can only be based on innovation in new products and new processes of production. Government aid to industry enabling the maintenance of high investment can play a crucial role in this process. Moreover, many of the EU member states lag behind other industrial nations in the share of GDP allocated to research and development (R&D) spending in firms. A reallocation of both government and company resources towards commercial R&D is necessary for successfully reversing the spiral of relative decline, by stimulating both the generation and the diffusion of innovation. Supporting reform of the accounting treatment of R&D expenditure would also prove beneficial.

In addition to pure supply-side issues, it is crucial to remember that without sophisticated buyers, innovation and dynamism will be stunted. The EU already enjoys demand-side advantages in luxury and leisure-related commodities, but the challenge is to upgrade industrial demand to broaden the sphere over which EU companies benefit from well-informed buyers. Furthermore, economic prosperity will never be complete without a faster rate of new business formation to make headway in reducing unemployment, because revitalisation of established industries sometimes reduces the size of the workforce. However, new business formation depends on skills and ideas, on appropriate motivation and goals, on active competition and access to capital. One of the urgent reasons for upgrading British education, especially in universities, is to seed new ventures.

These measures should reduce the level of joblessness, leading to the long-term restoration of full employment. By reducing, and eventually eliminating, the long-run growth of imports and by stimulating an expansion in exports, the strategy aims to reconcile full employment with the simultaneous achievement of payments equilibrium. However, the question becomes whether such an industrial strategy can be reconciled with current EU regulations, let alone any future federal aspirations, thus EU member states' essential interests potentially conflict directly with EU moves towards greater integration. However, with determination and imagination, there is no reason why the EU cannot acquire again the significant comparative advantages in the production of goods that once made it the workshop of the world. Services are a crucial complement to this process but do not, alone, provide the growth momentum of manufacturing industry, nor can they be relied upon to substitute for the deficits in overseas visible trade. In our view the construction of such a competitive economy involves the unravelling and reconstruction of central aspects of the EU, such that the policies required to revitalise EU industry run counter to current EU rules and would be frustrated by movement towards economic and political union. Major historical trends cannot be reversed quickly; a permanent increase in the EU rate of productivity growth, for instance, requires sustained economic expansion, a difficult endeavour given the deflationary tendencies of the eurozone.

Hence, EU membership tends to frustrate the achievement of these objectives through three fundamental mechanisms. Firstly, to recover a relatively weak competitive trade position prevents market forces from generating, unaided, the profits required for industrial regeneration whereby experience demonstrates that market operations tend to accentuate strengths and deficiencies rather than eliminate them. Secondly, the Treaty of Rome severely limits aid to industry, whilst the public expenditure needed to complement the price mechanism in promoting industrial regeneration is circumscribed by the TEU convergence criteria and the SGP. Thirdly, the current functioning of the eurozone limits the scope for discretionary national economic policies. Therefore, both markets and governments are prevented from addressing the EU's basic problems by the very essence of EU operations and developments. The scale of de-industrialisation is significant across the EU, thereby requiring the implementation of a solution geared specifically to this rather than the more blunt, less-sensitive EU-wide programmes such as the Lisbon Agenda and Europe 2020 that have been devised. However, any strategy designed to confront the EU's deep-seated trading crisis will take many years to come to fruition. Therefore, a danger arises that, in the face of short-term pressures, such a strategy could be jettisoned before it has had sufficient time to be effective. This consideration suggests that government funds for industrial restructuring should be exempt from any immediate requirement for reducing public expenditure. Consequently, a programme to stimulate industrial investment, boost jobs creation and improve the quality of education and training must be rigorously maintained in the face of potential short-run problems. The benefits from such a programme would be reaped over a five- to ten-year period if the constraints imposed by EU integration are prevented from undermining its potential. Survival in the interim requires the creation of a breathing space for the EU economy until the programme becomes effective. The preservation of this essential space depends upon the EU possessing an active exchange rate and trade policy with discretionary control over movements in the external value of the euro, together with freedom to pursue independent fiscal and monetary policies. However, the latter are inimical to eurozone membership, whilst the former requires the development of a pro-growth exchange-rate policy.

Developing an exchange-rate policy

Export-led growth occurs because the firms that are competitive in world markets commence with the advantage of costs at least as low as their competitors, given that an economy is usually required to sell its output to the rest of the world at a competitive price. If it does so, it will embark on export-led growth; otherwise import-led stagnation is likely to follow. Moreover, once export-led growth is established a number of forces operate to keep fast-growing economies moving ahead. Particularly significant is the impact of successive waves of investment, which tend to reduce the cost of goods in the internationally traded goods sector, thereby rendering export prices increasingly competitive. However, a key determinant of competitiveness is establishing and maintaining a competitive exchange rate, that is, one that achieves balance of payments equilibrium at full employment. If a policy of expanding the eurozone economy through the export-led growth engendered by a competitive exchange rate is adopted, it is unlikely, on the available evidence, to cause substantial inflation during its early stages. Indeed, it could lead to inflation falling. However, a further potential generator of price increases may be an overexpansion of domestic demand, so that the economy becomes overheated. Once demand exceeds the capacity to supply, prices begin to rise. Such a scenario must be avoided. However, these problems are not insurmountable; they can be contained through a variety of channels. First, the more resources that are deployed into sectors facing falling cost curves and engaged in foreign trade, the easier it is for self-sustaining growth to be achieved. Large returns on investment that can be obtained in these sectors can provide sufficient new profitability to finance additional new capital requirements. Second, for at least some shortages there is considerable scope for importing what cannot be obtained from domestic production. For many commodities there exists an elastic supply of foreign output to meet domestic shortages. Third, any attempt to reflate the eurozone economy in order to achieve full employment must include a commitment to training, retraining and education, particularly with regard to engineering and technical work. However, a competitive exchange rate cannot in itself be a panacea for all the eurozone's economic problems. It will take some years to recreate full employment. When the euro's external value ensures competitive exports, it will still require price changes to produce substantial increases in output.

Hence, over a period of time the desired objectives of exchange-rate policy are short-term stability and long-term flexibility. The dangers to avoid are long-term fixity and short-term volatility. The only way of achieving these goals is a system that permits long-run change whilst avoiding violent short run fluctuations. Various policies are available to secure this end, but membership of the euro prevents them being implemented by establishing a permanent fixity that imposes deflation upon less-competitive national economies. However, this does not reduce relative prices automatically; it does so by creating unemployment and stifling the future prospects for economic growth. That is what is meant by those who advocate eurozone membership as a 'discipline' upon its member countries. Fundamentally, it is essential to remember that the exchange rate is a price like any other, whereby its movement enables economies to achieve trade and payments balance. If one country's exchange rate is over-valued its exports become more expensive in the foreign currency, while imports become cheaper in its own currency. Therefore, export volumes tend to decline and import volumes to increase, so that eventually the trade balance moves into deficit and unemployment rises. Conversely, when a country lowers its exchange rate, exports became cheaper and expand, while imports are constricted. The trade balance usually improves, but at some contemporary sacrifice of real income due to higher internal prices. The correct level for the exchange rate at any one time is that which enables an economy to combine full employment of productive resources simultaneously with approximate balance-of-payments equilibrium. A higher exchange rate generates overseas deficits and unemployment; a lower exchange rate leads to the build-up of excessive foreign currency reserves and domestic inflation. However, it has been emphasised that this 'correct' exchange rate varies in value over time (Jay, 1990). The variety of influences affecting economic performance (trade balances, productivity, price movements, discoveries of natural resources, etc.) combines to ensure that the 'correct' value of the exchange rate alters with the years. Therefore, a country needs to retain its ability to adjust the external value of its currency. To fix it irrevocably forever is as difficult as attempting to maintain in perpetuity the rate of income tax or the price of oil. The endeavour to do so generates economic inefficiency, usually in the form of accelerating inflation or a rise in unemployment.

Consequently, an economy's optimal strategy is to retain the national policy instruments required to increase its competitiveness in a socially acceptable manner; hence, it is essential that a country retain control over its interest rate, uses central bank intervention to smooth speculative fluctuations, encourages world-wide co-operation between central banks (through the G8) and aims for the maximum long-term exchange rate flexibility combined with the maximum practical short-term stability. Under such a regime, the exchange rate fulfils its role as facilitator of greater growth, higher living standards and full employment, without becoming an end in itself, as is the eurozone. Indeed, there is always a rate of exchange that enables each country to employ fully its productive resources. In an ever-changing environment, the rate frequently alters to secure simultaneous full employment and trade balance. Therefore, when formulating economic policy any suggestion that the euro should 'shadow' a particular currency must be rebutted. Such targeting makes domestic objectives harder to achieve. However, as the Chinese government has illustrated, it is possible for a nation to choose where it wants the exchange rate to be and, over the long term, to hold it there within narrow margins. Of course, there will be short-term fluctuations, but these are not important. It is the medium-term trend that counts. The issue then becomes one of which policies can governments pursue to change the exchange rate and then maintain it near the preferred level. A range of options is available, which can be co-ordinated to generate a viable, nation-wide strategy. Firstly, is the monetary and interest rate stance that the government adopts, where strong evidence exists to indicate that tight monetary policies and the high interest rates that accompany them pull the exchange rate up, while more accommodating monetary policies and lower interest rates bring it down. Secondly, the actions of both the government and the central bank, when dealing with the foreign-exchange market, exert a powerful influence in an area in which expectations are crucial. If the government expresses a clear view that the exchange rate is too high or too low, the market will respond. Thirdly, the government possesses a defined strategy to eliminate the foreign-trade imbalance. Such a strategy requires a commitment to achieving a long-term competitive exchange rate that achieves balance-of-payments equilibrium at full employment. This rate will, of course, alter over time. Fourthly, tariff protection may be crucial in order to restrict the flows of imports to a level consistent with the targeted short-term exchange rate. Fifth, on the capital side of the balance of payments the government can control international financial flows to maintain a competitive exchange rate. Potential policies range from taxes to quantitative restrictions on speculative movements.

However, if the value of the currency falls, there is an initial tendency for imports to stay at their previous volume, while the domestic revenue from exports falls because the exchange rate has gone down: the 'J curve' effect. A slow decline in the exchange rate generates a succession of such effects flowing from each successive decrease, giving the impression that no improvement is in sight. Nonetheless, the empirical evidence of exchange-rate movements and of the availability of a battery of policy instruments to sustain a targeted external currency value, demonstrates that in the medium-term governments can determine exchange rates. As we have discussed in Chapter 5, the exchange-rate policy of industrialised nations has lurched from the ultra-fixed systems such as the gold standard, through Bretton Woods and the ERM, to the free-floating days when monetarism and the rule of markets swept through governments across the industrialised world. Rarely has the decision to enter, or exit, one particular system been taken for any proven economic reason. Instead, the main driving force is whatever the current vogue politicians and their advisers happen to follow. This is clearly an inefficient method of managing an economy and of determining peoples' employment potential and standard of living. Rather, within the context of this discussion concerning the development of an active exchange-rate policy to facilitate national economic renewal, we argue that its overriding function is to convert domestic prices of all factors of production – including, labour, energy and raw materials – into international prices at such a level as to encourage economic growth through the full use of resources and, simultaneously, to achieve trade balance. If the exchange rate cannot fulfil these functions over a sufficient period of time (to counter fluctuations), this offers conclusive evidence that the exchange rate is misaligned, so that the existing system must come under scrutiny.

An exchange-rate system to suit all economies for all seasons is an impossible reality given the complexity of determining the exact exchange-rate regime for a country in light of the arguments concerning flexible and fixed exchange rates (Baimbridge and Whyman, 2008). Two systems, however, offer the greatest potential for combining an exchange rate that secures balance-of-payments equilibrium with full employment. Firstly, managed floating does not involve parities that the government is obliged to preserve. Instead, the currency is free to float, but the authorities intervene to avoid what they regard to be undesirable consequences of excessive appreciation or depreciation. A weak currency may lead to excessive depreciation that the government may wish to avoid because of its repercussions on the domestic price of imports and the internal cost structure. Alternatively, countries with a strong currency may seek to avoid appreciation if they want to accumulate reserves and are indifferent to the effect on the money supply. Moreover, a country may even attempt to engineer the depreciation of its currency, which would otherwise appreciate if the foreign-exchange market were left to operate freely. Secondly, multiple exchange rates offer a system whereby different exchange rates are enforced for different transactions, either on the current or capital account. The IMF's official definition of a multiple exchange rate is 'an effective buying or selling rate which, as a result of official action, differs from parity by more than 1 per cent'. Multiple exchange rates can be viewed both as a form of exchange control (particularly over capital transactions) and as a rational response to the fact that different classes of goods have different price elasticities in world trade. Many countries, including Britain in the past with the 'dollar premium', charge a higher domestic price for foreign currency than the prevailing market rate for investment abroad in capital assets such as shares and property. Such a device acts, in essence, as a form of exchange control.

Conclusion

The design of a macroeconomic framework for a complex advanced economy depends upon a multiplicity of diverse factors, including recognition of its unique industrial structure, monetary and fiscal policy transmission mechanisms, the practice of wage formation, propensity for owner-occupation, national savings rates and technological progress. A combination of differences in consumer tastes, political choices, natural resources and centres of competitive excellence, together with the actions of institutions established to implement economic and social policy, necessitates differences in economic policy between nations. Moreover, exchange-rate regimes tend to have a greater impact upon smaller, export-orientated nations than upon their larger neighbours, where only a relatively small proportion of GDP is traded. Consequently, it is extremely difficult for one international economic authority to replace national macroeconomic management by one common interest or exchange rate. As discussed in Chapter 4, too many economies of EU member states are too divergent from their neighbours, cyclically and structurally, for any claim of prior convergence to be convincing and, without such evidence, a common economic strategy is unlikely to be simultaneously in their individual interests. In view of such fundamental weakness at the heart of the EU project, the decision to reject participation retains, for national government, the economic instruments vital to successful macroeconomic management. Exchange rates can fulfil their function of equalising the demand and supply for a currency by the variation of its price, thereby preventing a basic uncompetitive imbalance from causing mass unemployment and falling standards of living. Fiscal policy, freed from the twin restrictions of the TEU convergence criteria and the SGP, can smooth cyclical fluctuations, avoiding periodic unemployment that wastes productive resources and generates associated human misery. The purpose of monetary policy is, then, to prevent unstable boom-and-slump conditions in housing and financial markets whilst seeking to ensure a low interest rate for investors in productive capital. Supply-side policies, including selective labour-market programmes and investment in the economy's physical and IT superstructure, do not require a rejection of the single currency to be applied, although the benefit of a macroeconomic structure tailored to the needs of the economy would provide a more fertile environment for their implementation. Thus, rather than being weakened by the refusal to be dominated by an EU agenda that will often conflict with the interests of its economy, the national government would be both stronger and possess a superior ability to adapt to changing international market conditions.

In view of the overwhelming evidence supporting the maintenance of national self-determination of economic policy, two factors remain to provide the momentum towards further integrationalist economic participation. The first relates to the determination of a small political elite, together with the representatives of multinational corporations, to complete the European integration project; the former perhaps seek the increased influence that a 'United States of Europe' would play in world events, whereas the latter desire to evade national regulatory regimes and thereby enhance profits. However, as demonstrated by the outcome of the 2014 European parliamentary elections, these small elites are increasingly neither representative of the wider electorate, nor even of the majority of businesses. The second factor undermining the vigorous assertion of national independence is the fear of failure, whereby the notion of the EU as a declining economic entity, through bouts of 'eurosclerosis', has long sapped its resolve and caused many member states to prefer safety in 'Fortress Europe'.

Yet, as illustrated in this chapter, there is no reason for such defeatism. Fear is the enemy of innovation and, as a group of the largest economies in the world, the EU possesses a significant number of advantages. The question remains whether these advantages can better be realised within an EU model of deeper economic and political integration, or through a looser relationship – through a more independent arrangement. This is a question for considered evaluation of all the evidence and should not be closed off due to political prejudice or an ill-considered agenda that conflicts with contemporary debate. This is an important question, since it goes to the very heart of what the EU will make of itself and whether it places artificial limitations upon its ability to deliver the priorities espoused by its citizens.

Bibliography

Abbas, S.A., Belhocine, N., El Ganainy, A. and Horton, M. (2010) A Historical Public Debt Database. IMF Working Paper WP/10/245. Available at: http://www.imf.org/external/pubs/ft/wp/2010/wp10245.pdf.

Abbott, D. (2000) The Case against the Maastricht Model of Central Bank Independence; in Baimbridge, M., Burkitt, B. and Whyman, P. (eds) *The Impact of the Euro: Debating Britain's Future*, Macmillan, London.

Abbott, K. (1997) The European Trade Union Confederation: Its Organisation and Objectives in Transition, *Journal of Common Market Studies*, 35(3) 465–481.

Ackrill, R. (2005) The Common Agricultural Policy; in van der Hoek, M.P. (ed.) *Handbook of Public Administration and Policy in the European Union*, CRC Press, New York.

Addison, J.T. and Sieber, W.S. (1991) The Social Charter of the European Community: Evolution and Controversies, *Industrial and Labour Relations Review*, 44(4) 597–625.

AFME (2011) Proposals for Common Eurozone Sovereign Issuance, Discussion Paper, Association for Financial Markets in Europe, London.

Agell, J. (1996) Why Sweden's Welfare State Needed Reform, *Economic Journal*, 106(439) 1760–1771.

Aglietta, M. and Uctum, M. (1996a) Europe and the Maastricht Challenge, Research Paper 9615, Federal Reserve Bank of New York.

Aglietta, M. and Uctum, M. (1996b) Europe and the Maastricht challenge, Research Paper 9616, Federal Reserve Bank of New York.

Agresti, A.-M. and Mojon, B. (2001) Some Stylised Facts on the Euro Area Business Cycle, EC3 Working Paper, No. 95.

Ahearne, A. Schmitz, B. and von Hagen, J. (2007) Current Account Imbalances in the Euro Area. Available at: http://www.hkimr.org/uploads/seminars/213/sem_paper_0_245_current_account_imbalances.pdf.

Aisen, A. and Jos Veiga, F. (2005) The Political Economy of Seigniorage. IMF Working Paper, 1(1) 3.

Albert, M. (1993) *Capitalism against Capitalism*, Whurr, London.

Alesina, A. (1987) Macroeconomic Policy in a Two-Party System as a Repeated Game, *Quarterly Journal of Economics*, August.

Alesina, A. (1988) *Macroeconomics and Politics*, NBER Macroeconomic Annual 1988, NBER, Cambridge, MA.

Alesina, A. (1989) Politics and Business Cycles in Industrial Democracies, *Economic Policy*, 8 58–98.

Alesina, A. and Ardagna, S. (2010) Large Changes in Fiscal Policy: Taxes versus Spending; in Brown, J.R., *Tax Policy and the Economy*, vol. 24, University of Chicago Press, Chicago, 35–68.

Alesina, A. and Bayoumi, T. (1996) The Costs and Benefits of Fiscal Rules: Evidence from the US States. NBER Working Paper No. 5614. Available at: http://www.nber.org/papers/w5614.pdf.

Alesina, A. and Drazen, A. (1991) Why Are Stabilizations Delayed? *The American Economic Review*, 81(5) 1170–1188.

Alesina, A. and Grilli, V. (1991) *The European Central Bank: Reshaping Monetary Policies in Europe*, Discussion paper 563, CEPR, London.

Alesina, A. and Perotti, R. (1995a) The Political Economy of Budget Deficits. *IMF Staff Papers*, 42(1) 1–31.

Alesina, A. and Perotti, R. (1995b) Fiscal Expansions and Adjustments in OECD countries. *Economic Policy,* 10(21) 205–248.

Alesina, A. and Perotti, R. (1998) Economic Risk and Political Risk in Fiscal Unions, *Economic Journal*, 108(449) 989–1008.

Alesina, A. and Summers, L.H. (1993) Central Bank Independence and Macroeconomic Performance: Some Comparative Evidence, *Journal of Money, Credit and Banking*, 25(2) 151–162.

Alesina, A. and Tabbellini (1987) A Positive Theory of Fiscal Deficits and Government Debt in a Democracy, NBER working paper 2308, Cambridge, MA.

Alesina, A. and Tabellini, G. (2005) Why Is Fiscal Policy Often Procyclical? NBER Working Papers, No. 11600. Available at: http://www.nber.org/papers/w11600.

Alesina, A., Blanchard, O., Galì, J., Giavazzi, F. and Ulhig, H. (2001) Defining a Macroeconomic Framework for the Euro Area, Monitoring the European Central Bank 3, CEPR, London.

Alesina, A., Cohen, G. and Roubini, N. (1992) Macroeconomic Policy and Elections in OECD Democracies. *Economics and Politics,* 4(1) 1–30.

Alesina, A., Perotti, R., Tavares, J., Obstfeld, M. and Eichengreen, B. (1998) The Political Economy of Fiscal Adjustments, Brookings Papers on Economic Activity, 1, 197–266.

Alesina, A., Roubini N. and Cohen G. (1997) *Political Cycles and the Macroeconomy.* Cambridge, MA: MIT Press.

Allsopp, C. and Artis, M.J. (2003) The Assessment: EMU Four Years on, *Oxford Review of Economic Policy*, 19(1) 1–29.

Allsopp, C. and Vines, D. (2000) The Assessment: Macroeconomic Policy, *Oxford Review of Economic Policy*, 16(4) 1–32.

Almunia, M., Bénétrix, A., Eichengreen, B., O'Rourke, K.H. and Rua, G. (2010) From Great Depression to Great Credit Crisis: Similarities, Differences and Lessons, *Economic Policy*, 25(62) 219–265.

Alogoskoufis, G. and Portes, R. (1991) The International Costs and Benefits from EMU; in The economics of EMU, *European Economy*, Special edition 1, Office for the Official Publications of the European Communities, Luxembourg.

Alogoskoufis, G. and Portes, R. (1992) European Monetary Union and International Currencies in a Tripolar World; in Canzoneri, M., Grilli, V. and Masson, P.R. (eds) *Establishing a Central Bank: Issue in Europe and Lessons from the US*, Cambridge: Cambridge University Press.

Alt, J. and Lowry, R. (1994) Divided Government, Fiscal Institutions, and Budget Deficits: Evidence from the States. *American Political Science Review*, 88(4) 811–828.

Altavilla, C. (2004) Do EMU Members Share the Same Business Cycle? *Journal of Common Market Studies*, vol. 42 Issue 5, 869–896.

Amoroso, B. and Jespersen, J. (1992) *Macroeconomic Theories and Policies for the 1990s: A Scandinavian Perspective*, St Martins Press, New York.

Anderson, K. and Tyers, R. (1993) Implications of EC expansion for European Agricultural Policies, Trade and Welfare, *Centre for Economic Policy Research*, Discussion Paper 829.

Andrikopoulos, A., Loizdes, I. and Prodromidis, K. (2004) Fiscal Policy and Political Business Cycles in the EU. *European Journal of Political Economy.* 20(1) 125–152.

Angeloni, I., Gaspar, V. and Tristani, O. (1999) The Monetary Policy Strategy of the ECB; in: Cobham, D. and Zis, G. (eds) *From EMS to EMU*, Macmillan, London.

Arestis, P. (1999) The Independent European Central Bank: Keynesian Alternatives, *Jerome Levy Economics Institute Working Paper No. 274*, Bard College, Annandale-on-Hudson, NY.

Arestis, P. (2009) New Consensus Macroeconomics: A Critical Appraisal, Levy Economics Institute, Working Paper 564.

Arestis, P. and Chick, V. (eds) (1992), *Recent Developments in Post-Keynesian Economics*, Edward Elgar, Cheltenham.

Arestis, P. and Sawyer, M. (1996) Making the euro palatable, *New Economy*, 3(2) 89–92.

Arestis, P. and Sawyer, M. (2000) Deflationary Consequences of the Single Currency'; in Baimbridge, M., Burkitt, B. and Whyman, P.B., (eds) *The Impact of the Euro: Debating Britain's Future*, Macmillan, London.

Arestis, P. and Sawyer, M. (2004) *Re-examining Monetary and Fiscal Policy for the 21st Century*, Edward Elgar, Cheltenham.

Arestis, P. and Sawyer, M. (2006) What Type of European Monetary Union?; in Whyman, P., Bamibridge, M. and Burkitt, B. (eds) *Implications of the Euro: A Critical Perspective from the Left*, Routledge, London, 52–59.

Arestis, P. and Sawyer, M. (2008) A Critical Reconsideration of the Foundations of Monetary Policy in the New Consensus Macroeconomics Framework, *Cambridge Journal of Economics*, 32(5) 761–779.

Arestis, P. and Sawyer, M. (2012) Can the Euro Survive after the European Crisis? in: Arestis, P. and Sawyer, M (eds) *The Euro Crisis*, Palgrave Macmillan, Basingstoke.

Arestis, P., McCauley, K. and Sawyer, M. (2001) An Alternative Stability and Growth Pact for the European Union, *Cambridge Journal of Economics*, 25(1) 113–130.

Arezki, R., Candelon, B. and Sy, A.N.R. (2011) Sovereign Rating News and Financial Markets Spillovers: Evidence from the European Debt Crisis, IMF Working Paper 11/68, International Monetary Fund, Washington, DC.

Armingeon, K., Weissstanner, D., Engler, S., Potolidis, P. and Gerber, M. (2012) *Comparative Political Data Set 1960–2009*. Institute of Political Science, University of Berne. Available at: http://www.ipw.unibe.ch/content/team/klaus_armingeon/comparative_political_data_sets/index_ger.html.

Artis M. and Zhang W. (1995) International Business Cycles and the ERM: Is There a European Business Cycle?, CEPR Discussion Paper No. 1191.

Artis, M.J. and Zhang, W. (1999) Further Evidence on The International Business Cycle and The ERM: Is There a European Business cycle?, *Oxford Economic Papers*, vol. 51, 120–132.

Artis, M.J. and Buti, M. (2001) Setting Medium-Term Fiscal Targets in EMU; in Brunila, A., Buti, M. and Franco, D. (eds) *The Stability and Growth Pact: The architecture of fiscal policy in EMU*, Palgrave Macmillan, London.

Artis, M.J., Krolzig, H.-M., Toro, J. (2004) The European Business Cycle, *Oxford Economic Papers* 56, 1–44.

Aspinwall, M. (2003) Britain and Europe: Some Alternative Economic Tests, *Political Quarterly*, 74(2) 146–157.

Atkinson, A.B. (1999) *The Economic Consequences of Rolling Back the Welfare State* MIT Press, London.

Auerbach, A.J. and Feenberg, D. (2000) The Significance of Federal Taxes as Automatic Stabilizers, NBER Working Paper No.7662.

Ayuso-i-Casals, J., Hernandez, D. G., Moulin, L. and Turrini A. (2006) *Beyond the SGP–Features and Effects of EU National-Level Fiscal Rules*. Available at: https://www.bancaditalia.it/studiricerche/convegni/atti/fiscal_policy/session%203/ayuso_gonzalez_moulin_turrini.pdf.

Backus, D.K. and Driffill, J. (1985) Inflation and Reputations, *American Economic Review*, June.

Bade, R. and Parkin, M. (1988) Central Bank Laws and Monetary Policy, Working Paper, University of Western Ontario.

Baimbridge, M. (1997) Is EMU Ready for Take-Off?, *The Review of Policy Issues*, 3(4) 25–33.

Baimbridge, M. (2005a) EUphoria to Apathy: EP Turnout in the New Member States; in Lodge, J. (ed.) *The 2004 Elections to the European Parliament*, Palgrave Macmillan, London.

Baimbridge, M. (2005b) The Euro; in van der Hoek, M.P. (ed.) *Handbook of Public Administration and Policy in the European Union*, CRC Press, New York.

Baimbridge, M. (2006) The ECB in Theory and Practice; in Whyman, P., Baimbridge, M. and Burkitt, B. (eds) *Implications of the Euro: A Critical Perspective from the Left*, Routledge, London.

Baimbridge, M. and Burkitt, B. (1995a) Equitable Voting in the EU?: Options for Change, *Politics*, 15(2) 79–87.

Baimbridge, M. and Burkitt, B. (1995b) Council of Ministers Voting Rights, *Politics Review*, 4(3) 31–33.

Baimbridge, M. and Philippidis, G. (eds) (2006) *EU Enlargement: Challenges and Prospects*, Copenhagen Business School Press, Copenhagen.

Baimbridge, M. and Whyman, P. (1997) Institutional Macroeconomic Forecasting Performance of the UK Economy, *Applied Economics Letters*, 4(6) 373–376.

Baimbridge, M. and Whyman, P. (2004) Fiscal Federalism and EMU: An Appraisal; in Baimbridge, M. and Whyman, P. (eds) *Fiscal Federalism and European Economic Integration*, Routledge, London.

Baimbridge, M. and Whyman, P.B. (2008) *Britain, the Euro and Beyond*. Ashgate, Aldershot.

Baimbridge, M. and Whyman, P.B. (2004) *Fiscal Federalism and European Economic Integration*, Routledge, London.

Baimbridge, M., Burkitt, B. and Macey, M. (1994) The Maastricht Treaty: exacerbating racism in Europe?, *Ethnic and Racial Studies*, 17(3) 420–441.

Baimbridge, M., Burkitt, B. and Whyman, P. (1997) A Critical British Perspective, *New Political Economy*, 2(3) 488–492.

Baimbridge, M., Burkitt, B. and Whyman, P. (1998a) Evaluation of Convergence Criteria, in *Preparations for Stage Three of Economic and Monetary Union*, Treasury Committee, House of Commons, HMSO, London.

Baimbridge, M., Burkitt, B. and Whyman, P. (1998b) Is Europe Ready for EMU? Theory, evidence and consequences, Occasional Paper 31, The Bruges Group, London.

Baimbridge, M., Burkitt, B. and Whyman, P. (1999a) Convergence Criteria and EMU Membership: Theory and Evidence, *Journal of European Integration*, 21(4) 281–305.

Baimbridge, M., Burkitt, B. and Whyman, P. (1999b) *The Bank that Rules Europe? The ECB and Central Bank Independence*, Bruges Group, London.

Baimbridge, M., Burkitt, B. and Whyman, P. (2000) An Overview of European Monetary Integration; in Baimbridge, M., Burkitt, B. and Whyman, P. (eds) *The Impact of the Euro: Debating Britain's Future*, Macmillan, London.

Baimbridge, M., Burkitt, B. and Whyman, P. (2002) The Bank That Rules Europe: The ECB and Central Bank Independence; in Holmes, M. (ed.) *The Eurosceptical Reader II*, Palgrave, London.

Baimbridge, M., Burkitt, B. and Whyman, P. (2005) *Britain and the European Union: Alternative Futures*, CIB, London.

Baimbridge, M., Burkitt, B. and Whyman, P. (2012) The Eurozone as a Flawed Currency Area, *The Political Quarterly*, 83(1) 96–107.

Baimbridge, M., Burkitt, B. and Whyman, P.B. (1999) Economic Convergence and EMU Membership: Theory and Evidence, *Journal of European Integration* 21(4) 281–305.

Baimbridge. M., Burkitt, B. and Whyman, P.B. (2006) Alternative Relationships between Britain and the EU: New Ways Forward?, *The Political Quarterly*, 77(3) 402–412.

Baimbridge, M., Harrop, J. and Philippidis, G. (2004) *Current Economic Issues in EU Integration*, Palgrave Macmillan, London.

Baimbridge. M., Whyman, P. and Mullen, A. (2007) The 1975 Referendum on Europe: current analysis and lessons for the future, Imprint Academic, Exeter and Charlottesville, VA.

Baimbridge M., Whyman, P.B. and Burkitt, B. (2007) Beyond EU Neoliberalisation: A Progressive Strategy for the British Left, *Capital and Class*, Special Issue: The left and Europe, 93 (Autumn) 67–91.

Baker, D., Gamble, A., Ludlam, S. and Seawright, D., with Bull, K. (1999) MPS and Europe: Enthusiasm, Circumspection or Outright Scepticism; in Fisher, J., Cowley, P., Denver, D. and Russel, A. (eds) *British Elections and Parties Review* – vol. 9, Frank Cass, London, 171–185.

Baker, D., Gamble, A. and Seawright, D. (2002) Sovereign Nations and Global Markets: Modern British Conservatism and Hyperglobalism, *British Journal of Politics and International Relations*, vol. 4. No. 3, 399–428.

Baker, D., Gamble, A., Ludlum, S. and Seawright, D. (1996) Labour and Europe: A Survey of MPs and MEPs, *Political Quarterly*, 67(4) 353–371.

Bakhoven, A.F. (1989) *The Completion of the Single Market in 1992: Macroeconomic Consequences for the European Community*, Central Planning Bureau, No. 56, The Netherlands.

Balanyá, B., Doherty, A., Hoedeman, O., Maanit, A. and Wesselius, E. (2000) *Europe Inc: Regional and Global Restructuring and the Rise of Corporate Power*, Pluto Books, London.

Balassone, F. and Franco, D. (2001) Public Investment, the Stability Pact and the Golden Rule; in Brunila, A., Buti, M. and Franco, D. (eds) *The Stability and Growth Pact: The architecture of fiscal policy in EMU*, Palgrave Macmillan, London.

Ball, L. Mankiw, N.G. and Romer, D. (1988) The New-Keynesian Economics and the Output-Inflation Trade-Off, Brookings Papers on Economic Activity.

Bank for International Settlements (1994) *Financial Structure and the Monetary Transmission Mechanism*, Basle, Switzerland.

Bank for International Settlements (1996) *Central Bank Survey of Foreign Exchange and Derivatives Market Activity*, Basel, Switzerland.

Bank of England (1992) The Foreign Exchange Market in London, *Bank of England Quarterly Bulletin*, 32.

Bank of England (2002) *Practical Issues Arising from the Euro*, May, Bank of England, London.

Barber, T. (2010) *Greece Condemned for Falsifying Data*. Available at: http://www.ft.com/cms/s/0/33b0a48c-ff7e-11de-8f53–00144feabdc0.html#axzz2MFAUD4Xr.

Barclay, C. (1995) The Common Agricultural Policy and Eastern Europe, House of Commons Library Research Paper, No. 13, House of Commons, London.

Barnard, C. and Deakin, S. (1997) European Community Social Law and Policy: Evolution or Regression?, *Industrial Relations Journal* (European Annual Review) 131–153.

Barr, D., Breedon, F. and Miles, D. (2003) Life on the Outside: Economic Conditions and Prospects Outside Euroland, *Economic Policy*, 37, 573–613.

Barr, N. (1992) Economic Theory and the Welfare State: A Survey and Interpretation, *Journal of Economic Literature*, 30, 741–803.

Barrel, R. and te Velde, D.W. (2003) German Monetary Union and the Lessons for EMU; in Baimbridge, M. and Whyman, P. (eds) *Economic and Monetary Union in Europe: Theory, Evidence and Practice*, Edward Elgar, Cheltenham.

Barro, R. (1979) On the Determination of Public Debt. *The Journal of Political Economy*, 87(5) 940–971.

Barro, R. and Gordon, R. (1983) Rules, Discretion and Reputation in a Model of Monetary Policy, *Journal of Monetary Economics*, 12(1) 101–121.

Barro, R.J. (1974) Are Government Bonds Net Wealth?, *Journal of Political Economy*, 81, 1095–1117.

Barro, R.J. (1989) The Ricardian Approach to Budget Deficits, NBER Working Paper No. 2685.

Barro, R.J. (1997) Determinants of Economic Growth: A Cross-Country Empirical Study, MIT Press, London.

Battini, N., Callegari, G. and Melina, G. (2012) Successful Austerity in the United States, Europe and Japan, IMF Working Paper 12/190.

Baumol, W.J. (1961) Pitfalls in Counter-Cyclical Policies: Some Tools and Results, *Review of Economics and Statistics*, 43(1).

Baxter M. and Koupartitas M. (2005) Determinants of Business Cycles Movement: A Robust Analysis, *Journal of Monetary Economics*, vol. 52, 113–157.

Baxter M. and Stockman A.C. (1989) Business Cycles and the Exchange Rate Regime: Some International Evidence, *Journal of Monetary Economics*, 23, 3, 377–400.

Bayar, A. and Smeets, B. (2009) Economic, Political and Institutional Determinants of Budget Deficits in the European Union. CESifo Working Paper No. 2611. Available at: http://www.cesifo-group.de/portal/pls/portal/docs/1/1186372.PDF.

Bayoumi, T. and Eichengreen, B. (1992) *Shocking Aspects of Monetary Unification*, NBER Working Paper, No.3949.

Bayoumi, T. and Eichengreen, B. (1993) Shocking Aspects of European Monetary Integration, in Torres, B. and Giavazzi, F. (eds) *Adjustment and Growth in the European Monetary Union*, Cambridge University Press, Cambridge.

Bayoumi T. and Eichengreen B. (1996) Operationalizing the Theory of Optimum Currency Areas, CEPR Discussion Paper Series, No. 1484.

Bayoumi, T. and Masson, P.R. (1995) Fiscal Flows in the United States and Canada: Lessons for Monetary Union in Europe, *European Economic Review*, 39, 253–274.

Bean, C.R. (1998) Discussion, *Economic Policy*, 26, 104–107.

Begg, D., Canova, F., De Grauwe, P., Fatás, A. and Lane, P. (2002) *Surviving the Slowdown*, Monitoring Europe, 3rd Report of the CEPS Macroeconomic Policy Group, London.

Begg, I. (2000) Reshaping the EU Budget: Yet Another Missed Opportunity, *European Urban and Regional Studies*, 7, 51–62.

Behnisch, A.J. (2002) For Britain, Joining Europe was Associated with National Decline and Loss of Great Power Status, *New Statesman*, 16 December.

Beine, M., Candelon, B. and Sekkat, K. (2003) EMU Membership and Business Cycle Phases in Europe: Markov-Switching VAR Analysis, *Journal of Economic Integration*, vol. 18, 214–242.

Belo, F. (2001) Some Facts about the Cyclical Convergence in the Euro Zone, Banco de Portugal Working Paper, No. 7–2001.

Benn, T. (2006) The establishment of a Commonwealth of Europe; in Whyman, P., Baimbridge, M. and Burkitt, B. (eds) *Implications of the Euro: A Critical Perspective from the Left*, Routledge, London.

Bergman U,M. (2004) How Similar are European Business Cycles?, University of Copenhagen, EPRU Working Paper Series, No. 04–13.

Berry, R., Kitson, M. and Michie, J. (1995) *Towards Full Employment: The First Million Jobs*, Full Employment Forum, London.

Berthold, N. and Fehn, R. (1998) Does EMU Promote Labour-Market Reforms?, *Kyklos*, 51(4) 509–536.

Bieler, A. (2006) *The Struggle for a Social Europe: Trade Unions and EMU in Times of Global Restructuring*, Manchester University Press, Manchester.

Bini-Smaghi, L. and Vori, S. (1992) Rating the EC as an Optimum Currency Area: Is It Worse Than the US?; in O'Brien, R. (ed.) *Finance and the International Economy*, Oxford University Press, Oxford.

Bird, G. and Mandilaras, A. (2013) Fiscal Imbalances and Output Crises in Europe: Will the Fiscal Compact Help or Hinder?, *Journal of Economic Policy Reform*, 16(1) 1–16.

Black, C.M. (2000) *The European Union, Britain and the United States: Which Way to Go?*, Nixon Center Perspectives, 4(2).

Blair, A. (2000) Managing Change: A National and International Agenda of Reform?, speech given at the World Economic Forum, Davos, Switzerland, 28 January.

Blair, T. (1998a) Speech to the New York Stock Exchange, 28 September.

Blair, T. (1998b) Speech at The Hague, 20 January.

Blanchard, O. and Katz, L. (1992) Regional Evolutions, Brookings Papers on Economic Activity, 1, 1–61.

Blanchard, O.J. and SaKong II (2011) *Reconstructing the World Economy*. International Monetary Fund Publication Services, Washington, DC, 126.

Blankart, C.B. and Kirchner, C. (2004) The Deadlock of the EU Budget: An Economic Analysis of Ways in and Ways Out; in Blankart, C.B. and Mueller, D.C. (eds) *A Constitution for the European Union*, MIT Press, Cambridge, MA.

Blokker, N.M. and Muller, A.S. (1994). *Towards More Effective Supervision by International Organizations, Volume 1*. The Netherlands: Kluwer Academic Publishers.

Blyth, M. (2013) *Austerity: The History of a Dangerous Idea*, Oxford University Press, Oxford.

Bodart, V. (1990) *Central Bank Independence and the Effectiveness of Monetary Policy: A Comparative Analysis*, International Monetary Fund, Central Banking Department, IMF, Washington, DC.

Bohn, H. and Inman, R. P. (1996) Balanced Budget Rules and Public Deficits: Evidence from the US States. *Carnegie-Rochester Conference Series on Public Policy*, 45(1) 13–76.

Booker, C. and Jamieson, B. (1994) How Europe cost us £235bn, *Sunday Telegraph*, 9 October.

Bordo M.D. and Helbling T. (2003) Have National Business Become More Synchronised?, NBER Working Paper, No. 10130.

Bordo, M. and Jonung, L. (2000) *Lessons for EMU from the History of Monetary Unions*, IEA Readings 50, Institute of Economic Affairs, London.

Bordo, M.D. (1993) The Gold Standard, Bretton Woods and Other Monetary Regimes: A Historical Appraisal. *Federal Reserve Bank of St. Louis Review*. [online]. Available at: http://research.stlouisfed.org/publications/review/93/03/Gold_Mar_Apr1993.pdf.

Bordo, M.D. and Eichengreen, B. (1993) A Retrospective on the Bretton Woods System: Lessons for International Monetary Reform. USA: National Bureau of Economic Research, xi.

Brauninger, T. (2005) A Partisan Model of Government Expenditure. *Public Choice*, 125(3–4) 409–429.

Brender, A. and Drazen, A. (2005) Political Budget Cycles in New Versus Established Democracies, *Journal of Monetary Economics*, 52(7) 1271–1295.

Breton, A. (1974) *The Economic Theory of Representative Government*, Macmillan, London.

Brown, A.J. (1985) *World Inflation Since 1950*, Cambridge University Press, Cambridge.

Brunila, A., Buti, M. and Franco, D. (eds) *The Stability and Growth Pact: The Architecture of Fiscal Policy in EMU*, Palgrave Macmillan, London.

Bruno, M. and Sachs, J.D. (1985) *Economics of Worldwide Stagflation*, Blackwell, Oxford.

Buechtemann, C.F. and Schupp, J. (1992) Repercussions of Reunification: Patterns and Trends in the Socio-Economic Transformation of East Germany, *Industrial Relations Journal*, 23(2) 90–106.

Buiter, W. (2001) Notes on 'A Code for Fiscal Stability', *Oxford Economic Papers*, 53, 1–19.

Buiter, W.H. (2006) The sense and Nonsense of Maastricht Revisited: What Have We Learnt about Stabilization in EMU? *Journal of Common Market Studies*, 44(4) 687–710.

Buiter, W., Corsetti, G. and Roubini, N. (1993) Excessive Deficits: Sense and Nonsense in the Treaty of Maastricht, *Economic Policy*, 16, 57–100.

Buiter, W.H. (1999) *Alice in Euroland*, CEPR Policy Paper No. 1, Centre for Economic Policy Research, London.

Buiter, W.H. (2003) Ten commandments for a Fiscal Rule in the E(M)U, *Oxford Review of Economic Policy*, 19(1) 84–99.

Buiter, W.H. and Rahbari, E. (2012) The European Central Bank as Lender of Last Resort for Sovereigns in the Eurozone, *Journal of Common Market Studies*, 50 (s2) 6–35.

Bulmer, S. (2000) European Policy: Fresh Start or False Dawn?, in Coates, D. and Lawler, P. (eds) *New Labour in Power*, Manchester University Press, Manchester, 240–254.

Bulmer, S. and Burch, M. (1998) Organising for Europe: Whitehall, the British State and the European Union, *Public Administration*, 76, 601–628.

Burdekin, R.C.K, and Willett, T.D. (1990) Central Bank Reform: The Federal Reserve in International Perspective, Paper prepared for the special issue of *Public Budgeting and Financial Management*.

Burkitt, B. (2006) The European social model; in Whyman, P., Baimbridge, M. and Burkitt, B. (eds) *Implications of the Euro: A Critical Perspective from the Left*, Routledge, London.

Burkitt, B. and Baimbridge, M. (1990a) Britain, the European Economic Community and the Single Market of 1992: A Reappraisal, *Journal of Public Money and Management*, 10(4) 57–61.

Burkitt, B. and Baimbridge, M. (1990b) The Performance of British Agriculture and the Impact of the Common Agricultural Policy: a Historical Review, *Rural History*, 1(2) 265–280.

Burkitt, B. and Baimbridge, M. (1991) The Cecchini Report and the Impact of 1992, *European Research*, 2(5) 16–19.

Burkitt, B., Baimbridge, M. and Mills, J. (1993) *What Price the Pound? The Exchange Rate and Full Employment*, Full Employment Forum, Watford.

Burkitt, B., Baimbridge, M. and Reed, S. (1992) *From Rome to Maastricht: A Reappraisal of Britain's Membership of the European Community*, Anglia Press, Sudbury.

Burkitt, B., Baimbridge, M. and Whyman, P. (1996) *There is an Alternative: Britain and Its Relationship with the EU*, Nelson and Pollard, Oxford.

Burkitt, B., Baimbridge, M. and Whyman, P. (1997) *A Price Not Worth Paying: The Economic Cost of EMU*, Nelson and Pollard, Oxford.

Busch, K. and Knelangen, W. (2004) German Euroscepticism; in Harmsen, R. and Spiering, M. (eds) *Euroscepticism: Party Politics, National Identity and European Integration*, Rodopi, Amsterdam.

Busemeyer, M.R. (2004) *Chasing Maastricht: The Impact of the EMU on the Fiscal Performances of Member States*. Available at: http://eiop.or.at/eiop/texte/2004–008a.htm.

Buti, M. and Giudice, G. (2002) Maastricht Fiscal Rules at Ten: An Assessment, *Journal of Common Market Studies*, 40(5) 823–847.

Buti, M. and Martinot, B. (2000) Open Issues in the Implementation of the Stability and Growth Pact, *National Institute Economic Review*, 174, 92–104.

Buti, M. and Nava, M. (2003) *Towards a European Budgetary System*, Group of Policy Advisors, European Commission, Brussels.

Buti, M. and Sapir, A. (1998) *Economic Policy in EMU: A study by the European Commission Services*, Oxford University Press, Oxford.

Buti, M. and van den Noord, P. (2003) Discretionary Fiscal Policy and Elections: The Experience of the Early Years of EMU. OECD Economics Department Working Paper No. 351. Available at: http://dx.doi.org/10.1787/378575422756.

Buti, M., Eijffinger, S. and Franco, D. (2003) Revisiting EMU's Stability Pact: A Pragmatic Way Forward, *Oxford Review of Economic Policy*, 19(1) 100–111.

Buti, M., Franco, D. and Ongena, H. (1998) Fiscal Discipline and Flexibility in EMU: The Implementation of the Stability and Growth Pact, *Oxford Review of Economic Policy*, 14. 81–97.

Butler, D. and Kitzinger, U. (1996) *The 1975 Referendum*, Macmillan, London.

Cabral, A.J. (2001) Main Aspects of the Working of the Stability and Growth Pact; in Brunila, A., Buti, M. and Franco, D. (eds) *The Stability and Growth Pact: The Architecture of Fiscal Policy in EMU*, Palgrave Macmillan, London.

Calcagno, A. (2912) Can Austerity Work?, *Review of Keynesian Economics*, 1(1) 24–36.

Callaghan, J. (2000) *The Retreat of Social Democracy*, Manchester University Press, Manchester.

Calmfors, L. and Driffill, J. (1988) Bargaining Structure, Corporatism and Macroeconomic Performance, *Economic Policy*, 6, 13–62.

Calmfors, L. and Nyomen, R. (1990) Real Wage Adjustment and Employment Policies in the Nordic Countries, *Economic Policy*, 5(2) 397–448.

Camachoa M., Perez-Quirosb G. and Saizc L. (2008) Do European Business Cycles Look Like One?, *Journal of Economic Dynamics & Control*, vol. 32, 2165–2190.

Cambridge Econometrics (1990) *Regional Economic Prospects*, Cambridge Econometrics, Cambridge.

Cameron, D.R. (1984) Social Democracy, Corporatism, Labour Quiescence and the Representation of Economic Interest in advanced Capitalist Society; in Goldthorpe, J.H. (ed.) *Order and Conflict in Contemporary Capitalism*, Clarendon Press, Oxford.

Cameron, S. (2005) *Econometrics*, Maidenhead, McGraw-Hill Education.

Canzoneri, M.B. and Diba, B.T. (2000) *The Stability and Growth Pact revisited: A Delicate Balance or an Albatross?* Mimeo.

Carlin, W. and Soskice, D. (2006) *Macroeconomics: Imperfections, Institutions and Policies*. Oxford University Press, Oxford.

Carling, W. and Soskice, D. (2005) *The 3-Equation New Keynesian Model – A Graphical Exposition*, University College London, UCL Discussion Papers in Economics, No. 05–03.

Carling, W. and Soskice, D. (2009) Teaching Intermediate Macroeconomics Using the 3-Equation Model; in Fontana, G. and Setterfield, M. (eds) *Macroeconomic Theory and Macroeconomic Pedagogy*, Palgrave, London.

Carlstrom, C.T and Fuerst, T.S. (2003) *Comments on backward-looking interest-rate rules, interest-rate smoothing, and macroeconomic instability*, Working Paper 0319, Federal Reserve Bank of Cleveland.

Cartapanis, A. and Herland, M. (2002) The Reconstruction of the International Financial Architecture: Keynes' Revenge?, *Review of International Political Economy*, 9(2) 271–297.

Casella, A. (2001) Achieving Fiscal Discipline through Tradable Deficit Permits; in Brunila, A., Buti, M. and Franco, D. (eds) *The Stability and Growth Pact: The Architecture of Fiscal Policy in EMU*, Palgrave Macmillan, London.

Cash, W. (2001) *The Associated European Area: A Constructive Alternative to a Single European State*, European Foundation, London.

Castelnuovo, E., Altimari, S.N. and Rodriguez-Palenzuela, D. (2003) *Definition of Price Stability, Range and Point Inflation Targets: The Anchoring of Long-Term Inflation Expectations.* Background Study for ECB Governing Council, ECB, Frankfurt.

Castro, V. (2007) The Causes of Excessive Deficits in the European Union. The University of Warwick Research Papers No. 805. Available at: http://www2.warwick.ac.uk/fac/soc/economics/research/workingpapers/2008/twerp_805.pdf.

Cecchetti, S. (2000) Making Monetary Policy: Objectives and Rules, *Oxford Review of Economic Policy*, 16(4) 43–59.

Cecchetti, S., McConnell, M.M. and Perez-Quiros G. (1999) Policy Makers Revealed Preferences and the Output-Inflation Variability Trade-Off. Implications for the European System of Central Banks. Mimeo.

Cecchetti, S.G. and O'Sullivan, R. (2003) The European Central Bank and the Federal Reserve, *Oxford Review of Economic Policy*, 19(1) 30–43.

Cecchetti, S.G. and Wynne, M.A. (2003) Inflation Measurement and the ECBs Pursuit of Price Stability: A First Assessment, *Economic Policy*, 37, 395–434.

Cecchini, P. (1988) *The European Challenge – the Benefits of a Single Market*, Wildwood House, Aldershot.

Cerny, P.G. (1990) *The Changing Architecture of Politics*, Sage, London.

Chen, R., Milesi-Ferretti, G.M. and Tressel, T. (2012) External Imbalances in the Euro Area, IMF Working Paper 12/236.

Chick, V. (1983) *Macroeconomics after Keynes: A Reconsideration of the General Theory*, MIT Press, Cambridge MA.

Chick, V. and Pettifor, A. (2011) *The Economic Consequences of Mr. Osborne*, Policy Research in Macroeconomics, London.

Chorev, N. and Babb, S. (2009) The Crisis of Neoliberalism and the Future of International Institutions: A Comparison of the IMF and World Trade Organization. Springer Science and Business Media B.V.

Church, C. (1993) Switzerland and Europe: Problem or Pattern?, *European Policy Forum*.

Church, C. (2004) Swiss Euroscepticism: Local Variations on Wider Themes; in Harmsen, R. and Spiering, M. (eds) *Euroscepticism: Party Politics, National Identity and European Integration*, Rodopi, Amsterdam.

Claessens, S., Mody, A. and Vallee, S. (2012) Paths to Eurobonds, IMF Working Paper No. WP/12/172.

Clarida, R., Gali, J. and Gertler, M. (1999) The Science of Monetary Policy: A New Keynesian Perspective, *Journal of Economic Literature*, vol. 37, Issue 4, 1661–1707.

Clift, B. (2001) New Labour's Third Way and European Social Democracy, in Ludlam, S. and Smith, M.J. (eds) *New Labour in Government*, Macmillan, London, 55–73.

Clift, B. (2004) New Labour's Second Term and European Social Democracy, in Ludlam, S. and Smith, M.J. (eds) *Governing as New Labour: Policy and Politics under Blair*, Palgrave, London, 34–52.

Coates, D. (1999) Models of Capitalism in the New World Order, *Political Studies*, 47, 643–660.

Coenen G. (2003a) Downward Nominal Wage Rigidity and the Long-run Phillips Curve: Simulation-Based Evidence for the Euro Area; Background study for ECB Governing Council, ECB, Frankfurt.

Coenen G. (2003b) Zero Lower Bound: Is It a Problem in the Euro Area?, background study for ECB Governing Council, ECB, Frankfurt.

Colander, D.C. (1988) The Evolution of Keynesian Economics: From Keynesian to New Classical to New Keynesian; in: Hamouda, F.O and Smithin, N.J. (eds) *Keynes and Public Policy after Fifty Years*, vol. 1: *Economics and Policy*, Edward Elgar, Aldershot and Brookfield, VT.

Committee for the Study of Economic and Monetary Union (1989) *Report on Economic and Monetary Union in the European Community* (Delors Report), Office for Official Publications of the European Communities, Luxembourg.

Corden, M. (2003) Monetary Integration: The Intellectual Pre-history; in Baimbridge, M. and Whyman, P. (eds) *Economic and Monetary Union in Europe: Theory, Evidence and Practice*, Edward Elgar, Cheltenham.

Costabile, L. (2010) The International Circuit of Key Currencies and the Global Crisis: Is there Scope for Reform?, PERI Working Paper 220, Political Economy Research Institute, University of Massachusetts, Amherst.

Costello, D. (1993) The Redistributive Effects of Inter-regional Transfers: A Comparison of the European Community and Germany, *European Economy*, Reports and Studies, 5, 271–273.

Courchene, T.J. (1993) Reflections on Canadian federalism: Are there implications for European Economic and Monetary Union?, *European Economy*. Reports and Studies, 5. 127–166.

Court of Auditors (1995) Annual Report Concerning the Financial Year 1994 Together with the Institutions' Replies, *Official Journal of the European Communities*, 38(C303) 14 November, 1–328.

Crockett, A. (1982) *International Money: Issues and Analysis*, Thomas Nelson and Sons, Surrey.

Crouch, C. (1985) Corporation in Industrial Relations: A Formal Model; in Grant, W. (ed.) *The Political Economy of Corporatism*, Macmillan, London.

Croux, C., Forni, M. and Reichlin, L. (2001) A Measure for Comovement of Economic Variables: Theory and Empirics, *Review of Economics and Statistics*, vol. 83, 232–241.

CSO (1995) *Family Spending – A Report on the 1994–95 Family Expenditure Survey*, HMSO, London.

Cukierman, A. (1992) *Central Bank Strategy, Credibility and Independence*, MIT Press, Cambridge MA.

D'Arista, J. (2003) Reforming the Privatised International Monetary and Financial Architecture, in Mullineux, A.W. and Murinde, V. (eds) *Handbook of International Banking*, Cheltenham, Edward Elgar, 721–750.

Dalsgaard, T. and de Serres, A. (2001) Estimating Prudent Budgetary Margins for EU Countries: A Simulated SVAR Model Approach; in Brunila, A., Buti, M. and Franco, D. (eds) *The Stability and Growth Pact: The architecture of fiscal policy in EMU*, Palgrave Macmillan, London.

Daniels, P. (2003) From Hostility to Constructive Engagement: The Europeanisation of the Labour Party, in Chadwick, A. and Heffernan, R. (eds) *The New Labour Reader*, Polity Press, Cambridge, 223–230.

Darvas Z. and Szapary G. (2004) Business Cycle Synchronization in the Enlarged EU: Comovements in the New and Old Members, Central Bank of Hungary Working Paper, No. 2004/1.

Davidson, P. (1988) A Technical Definition of Uncertainty and the Long Run Nonneutrality of Money, *Cambridge Journal of Economics*, vol. 12, 329–337.

Davidson, P. (1991) *Controversies in Post-Keynesian Economics*, Edward Elgar, Cheltenham.

Davidson, P. (1992) Reforming the World's Money, *Journal of Post Keynesian Economics*, 15(2) 153–179.

Davidson, P. (1994) *Post-Keynesian Macroeconomic Theory*, Edward Elgar, Cheltenham.

Davidson, P. (1998) Post Keynesian employment analysis and the macroeconomics of OECD unemployment, *The Economic Journal*, 108(448) 817–831.

Davidson, P. (2002) *Financial Markets, Money and the Real World*, Elgar, Cheltenham.

Davidson, P. (2009) *The Keynes Solution: The Path to Global Economic Prosperity*, Palgrave Macmillan, London.

De Grauwe, P. and Mongelli, F. (2005) Endogeneities of Optimal Currency Area: What Brings Countries Sharing A Single Currency Closer Together? ECB Working Paper, No. 468.

De Grauwe, P. (1994) *The Economics of Monetary Integration*, Oxford University Press, Oxford.

De Grauwe, P. (2002) *The Economics of Monetary Integration*, Oxford University Press, Oxford.

De Grauwe, P. (2003) *Economics of a Monetary Union*, Oxford University Press, Oxford.

De Grauwe, P. and Mosen, W. (2009) Gains for All: A Proposal for a Common Eurobond, CEPS Commentaries, 3 April; http://aei.pitt.edu/11091/1/1823[1].pdf.

De Grauwe, P. and Vanhaverbeke, W. (1993) Is Europe an Optimum Currency Area?; in Masson, P.R. and Taylor, M.P. (eds) *Policy Issues in the Operation of Currency Unions*, Cambridge University Press, Cambridge, 111–129.

De Haan, J. and Sturm, J. (1997) Political and Economic Determinants of OECD Budget Deficits and Government Expenditures: A Reinvestigation. *European Journal of Political Economy*, 13(4) 739–750.

De Vegh, I. (1943) The International Clearing Union, *American Economic Review*, 33(3) 534–556.

Dearlove, J. and Saunders, P. (2000) *Introduction to British Politics*, Polity, Cambridge.

Debrun, X., Moulin, L., Turrini, A., Ayuso-i-Casals, K. and Kumar, M.S. (2008) Tied to the Mast? National Fiscal Rules in the European Union, *Economic Policy*, 23(54) 297–362.

Degryse, C. (2012) The New Economic Governance, *ETUI Working Paper* No. 14, Brussels.

Delpla, J. and von Weizsäcker, J. (2010) The Blue Bond Proposal, *Bruegel Policy Brief* No. 2010/03.

Deo, S., Donovan, P. and Hatheway, L. (2011) Euro break-up – the consequences, UBS Investment Research, Global Economic Perspectives, London.

Deva, N. (2002) *Who Really Governs Britain?*, The June Press, Totnes.

Developed Democracies, 1956–1990; in Strauch, R. and Von Hagen, J. (eds) *Institutions, Politics and Fiscal Policy*, Kluwer Academic Publishers, Dordrecht. Available at: http://www-personal.umich.edu/~franzese/E&PBCinDebt.pdf.

Di Mascio, F. and Natalini, A. (2012) Fiscal Retrenchment in the 'PIGS' of Southern Europe: Changing Patterns of Public Management in Greece, Italy, Portugal and Spain. Available at: http://www.sisp.it/files/papers/2012/fabrizio-di-mascio-e-ales-sandro-natalini-1421.pdf.

Dixon, H. (1997) The Role of Imperfect of Competition in Keynesian Economics, in Snowdon, B. and Vane, R.H. (eds) *Reflections on the Development of Modern Macroeconomics*, Edward Elgar, Cheltenham and Lyme, NH.

Dixon, H. and Rankin, N. (1994) Imperfect Competition and Macroeconomics: A Survey, *American Political Sciences Review*, March.

Dobson, W. (1991) Economic policy coordination: requiem or prologue?, *Policy Analysis in International Economics*, 30, Institute for International Economics, Washington, DC.

Dominguez, K.M. (1993) The Role of International Organizations in the Bretton Woods System; in Bordo, M.D. and Eichengreen, B. (eds) *A Retrospective on the Bretton Woods System: Lessons for International Monetary Reform*. University of Chicago Press. [online]. Available at: http://www.nber.org/chapters/c6874.

Dornbusch, R. (1988) The European Monetary System, the Dollar and the Yen; in Giovazzi, F., Micossi, S. and Miller, M. (eds) *The European Monetary System*, Cambridge University Press, Cambridge.

Dougherty, C. (2007) *An Introduction to Econometrics*, Oxford University Press, Oxford.

Dowd, K. (1989) The case against a European Central Bank, *The World Economy* 12(3) 361–372.

Dowd, K. (1994) The political economy of central banking, *Critical Review*, 8(1) 49–60.

Dowrick, S. (1996) Sweden's economic performance and Swedish economic debate: a view from outside, *Economic Journal*, 106(439) 1772–1779.

Doyle, M.F. (1989) Regional policy and European economic integration, in Committee for the Study of Economic and Monetary Union, *Report on Economic and Monetary Union in the European Community* – collection of papers, Office for Official Publications of the European Communities, Luxembourg.

Drazen, A. (2000a) *Political Economy in Macroeconomics*, Princeton: Princeton University Press.

Drazen, A. (2000b) The Political Business Cycle after 25 Years. *NBER/Macroeconomic Annual* (MIT Press), 15(1) 75–117.

Dréze, J. and Bean, C.R. (1990) European unemployment: lessons from a multi-country econometric study, *Scandinavian Journal of Economics*, 92(2) 135–165.

Duggan, M.C. (2013) Taking Back Globalization: A China–United States Counterfactual Using Keynes' 1941 International Clearing Union; in *Review of Radical Political Economics*, 45 (4), 508–516.

Duwicquet, V., Mazier, J. and Saadoui, J. (2012) *Exchange Rate Misalignments, Fiscal Federalism and Redistribution: How to Adjust in a Monetary Union*. Available at: http://www.euroframe.org/fileadmin/user_upload/euroframe/docs/2012/EUROF12_Duwicquet_Etal.pdf.

Eatwell, J. (2000) Unemployment: National Policies in a Global Economy, *International Journal of Manpower*, vol. 21, No. 5, 343–373.

EC Commission (1990) One money, one market, *European Economy*, 44, Office for the Official Publications of the European Communities, Luxembourg.

EC Commission (1992) *Treaty on European Union*, Office for the Official Publications of the European Communities, Luxembourg.

EC Commission (1996) The Community Budget – 1996 edition, Office for the Official Publications of the European Communities, Luxembourg.

ECB (2005) The reform of the Stability and Growth Pact, *Monthly Bulletin*, August.

ECB (2012) Competitiveness and External Imbalances within the Euro Area. Occasional paper 139.

Edin, P.A. and Ohlsson, H. (1991) Political determinants of budget deficits: Coalition effects versus minority effects, *European Economic Review*, 35(8) 1597–1603.

Edmonds, J. (2000) The single currency and the European Social Model; in Baimbridge, M., Burkitt, B. and Whyman, P. (eds) *The Impact of the Euro: Debating Britain's Future*, Macmillan, London.

Ehrmann, M., Gambacorta, L., Martinez-Pages, J., Sevestre, P. and Worms, A. (2003) The effects of monetary policy in the euro area, *Oxford Review of Economic Policy*, 19(1) 58–72.

Eichener, V. (1996) Die Ruckwirkungen der europaischen Integration auf nationale Politikmuster, in Jachtenfuchs, M. and Kohler-Koch, N. (eds) *Europasiche Integration*, Leske & Budrich, Opladen.

Eichengreen, B. (1990) One money for Europe? Lessons from the U.S. currency union, *Economic Policy*, 10, 118–187.

Eichengreen, B. (1992a) Is Europe an optimum currency area?; in Borner, S. and Grubel, H. (eds) *The European Community after 1992: Perspectives from the Outside*, Macmillan, London, 138–161.

Eichengreen, B. (1992b) Should the Maastricht Treaty be saved?, *Princeton Studies in International Finance*, 74, International Finance Section, Princeton University, Princeton.

Eichengreen, B. (1993a) European monetary unification, *Journal of Economic Literature*, 31(3) 1321–1357.

Eichengreen, B. (1993b) Labour markets and European Monetary Unification; in Masson, P.R. and Taylor, M.P. (eds) *Policy Issues in the Operation of Currency Unions*, Cambridge University Press, Cambridge.

Eichengreen, B. (1994) Fiscal policy and EMU; in Eichengreen, B. and Frieden, J., (eds) *The Political Economy of European Monetary Integration*, Westview Press, Oxford.

Eichengreen, B. (1996) *Golden Fetters: The Gold Standard and the Great Depression, 1919–1939*, Oxford University Press, Oxford.

Eichengreen, B. (2000) Saving Europe's automatic stabilisers; in Baimbridge, M., Burkitt, B. and Whyman, P. (eds) *The Impact of the Euro: Debating Britain's Future*, Macmillan, London.

Eichengreen, B. and Wyplosz, C. (1995) *What Do Currency Crises Tell Us About the Future of the International Monetary System?*, Center for International and Development Economics Research (CIDER) Working Papers, University of California at Berkeley C95-057, University of California at Berkeley.

Eijffinger, S.C.W. and De Haan, J. (2000) *European Monetary and Fiscal Policy*, Oxford University Press, Oxford.

EIU Viewswire (2012) *Greece: Finance Outlook*. Available at: http://search.proquest.com. ezproxy.brad.ac.uk/docview/1035340590/139B662F1E32316BE8/4?accountid=17193.

El-Erian, M. and Roubini, N. (2012) A euro breakup: cardiac arrest for Europe, *New Perspectives Quarterly*, 29: 47–50.

Eltis, W. (1996) If EMU happens should Britain join?, *International Currency Review*, 23(3) 61–66.

Eltis, W. (2000) EMU membership would destabilise the British economy; in Baimbridge, M., Burkitt, B. and Whyman, P. (eds) *The Impact of the Euro: Debating Britain's Future*, Macmillan, London.

Emerson, M. (1990) One market, one money, *European Economy*, No. 44, Commission of the European Economies, Luxembourg.

Emerson, M., Gros, D., Italianer, A., Pisani-Ferry, J. and Reichenbach, H. (1992) *One Market, One Money: An Evaluation of the Potential Benefits and Costs of Forming an Economic and Monetary Union*, Oxford University Press, Oxford.

Ermisch, J. (1991) European Integration and external constraints on social policy: Is a social charter necessary?, *National Institute Economic Review*, No. 136, May, 93–108.

Ersboll, N. and Ludlow, P. (1995) *Preparing for 1996 and a larger European Union*, Centre for European Policy Studies, Brussels.

Esping-Andersen, G. (1990) *The Three Worlds of Welfare Capitalism*, Polity Press, Cambridge.

EU (2000) *European Economy*. Economic Trends (Supplement A) No. 1/2, Office for the Official Publications of the European Communities, Luxembourg.

EU (2011) *Green Paper on the Feasibility of Introducing Stability Bonds*, COM 818, European Commission, Brussels.

EU (2012) New Crisis Management Measures to Avoid Future Bank Bailouts, Press Release, June, European Commission, Brussels.

EU Commission (1996) *The Community Budget – 1996 edition*, Office for the Official Publications of the European Communities, Luxembourg.

EU Commission (1997) The Stability and Growth Pact, *InfEuro*, Office for the Official Publications of the European Communities, Luxembourg.

EU Commission (1998) *Financing the European Union: Commission Report on the Operation of the Own Resources System*, Office for the Official Publications of the European Communities, Luxembourg.

EU Commission (2000) *Public Finances in EMU – 2000*, Report of the Directorate General for Economic and Financial Affairs, Brussels.

EU Commission (2002) *Public Finances in EMU – 2002*, Report of the Directorate General for Economic and Financial Affairs, Brussels.

EU Commission (2004a) *General budget of the European Union for the Financial Year 2004*, Office for the Official Publications of the European Communities, Luxembourg.

EU Commission (2004b) *Allocation of 2003 EU Operating Expenditure by Member State*, Office for the Official Publications of the European Communities, Luxembourg.

EU Commission (1996) *The Community Budget – 1996 edition*, Office for the Official Publications of the European Communities, Luxembourg.

EU (2011) *Green Paper on the Feasibility of Introducing Stability Bonds*, COM 818, European Commission, Brussels.

EU (2012) New Crisis Management Measures to Avoid Future Bank Bailouts, Press Release, June, European Commission, Brussels.

Europa (2006) *Introducing the Euro: Convergence criteria*. Available at: http://europa.eu/legislation_summaries/other/l25014_En.htm.

European Central Bank (1998) *A Stability Oriented Monetary Policy Strategy for the ESCB*, ECB, Frankfurt.

European Central Bank (1999) *Monthly Bulletin*, Frankfurt: ECB.

European Central Bank (2001) *Monthly Bulletin*, ECB, Frankfurt.

European Central Bank (2002) *Evaluation of the 2002 Cash Changeover*, ECB, Frankfurt.

European Central Bank (2003) *Overview of the Background Studies for the Reflections on the ECB's Monetary Policy Strategy*, ECB, Frankfurt.

European Central Bank (2008) *Data on EU Membership*. Available at: http://www.ecb.int/stats/payments/paym/html/data.en.html.

European Central Bank (2012) *History: Economic and Monetary Union*. Available at: http://www.ecb.int/ecb/history/emu/html/index.en.html#stage3.

European Commission (1992) Treaty on European Union. Office for the Official Publications of the European Communities. Luxembourg.

European Commission (1998) *A Review of Possible Own Resources for the European Union*, European Commission, Brussels.

European Commission (2003) *Second Progress Report on Economic and Social Cohesion*, European Union, Brussels.

European Commission (2012a) *Economics and Financial Affairs: AMECO*. Available at: http://ec.europa.eu/economy_finance/ameco/user/serie/SelectSerie.cfm.

European Commission (2012b) *The Euro*. Available at: http://ec.europa.eu/ economy_finance/euro/index_En.htm.

European Communities (1991) *Amendments to the EEC Treaty – Economic and Monetary Union*, Conference of the Representatives of the Governments of the Member States – Economic and Monetary Union, CONF-UEM 1621/91.

European Monetary Institute (1997) *The Single Monetary Policy in Stage Three*, EMI, Frankfurt.

Eurostat Yearbook (1998–1999) *A Statistical Eye on Europe Data 1987–1997*.

Evans, G.W. and Honkapohja, S. (1999) Learning Dynamics; in J.B. Taylor and M. Woodford (eds) *Handbook of Macroeconomics*, North-Holland, Amsterdam.

Fatás A. (1997) EMU: Countries or Regions? Lessons from The EMS Experience, *European Economic Review*, vol. 41, 743–751.

Favero, C. and Giavazzi, F. (2007) Debt and the effects of fiscal policy. NBER Working Paper No. 12822. Available at: http://www.nber.org/papers/w12822. pdf?new_window=1.

Favretto, I. (2003) *The Long Search for a Third Way: The British Labour Party and the Italian Left Since 1945*, Palgrave, MacMillan.

Featherstone, K. (2011) The Greek Sovereign Debt Crisis and EMU: A Failing State in a Skewed Regime, *Journal of Common Market Studies*, 49(2) 193–217.

Feld, L.P. and Kirchgassner, G. (1999) Public Debt and Budgetary Procedures: Top Down or Bottom Up? Some Evidence from Swiss Municipalities; in Poterba, J.M. and Von Hagen, J. (eds) *Fiscal Institutions and Fiscal Performance*, Chicago University Press, Chicago. Available at: http://www.nber.org/chapters/c8027.pdf?new_window=1.

Feld, L.P. (2005) European public finances: much ado about nothing; in van der Hoek, M.P. (ed.) *Handbook of Public Administration and Policy in the European Union*, CRC Press, New York.

Feld, L.P. and Kirchgassner, G. (2004) The role of direct democracy in the European Union; in Blankart, C.B. and Mueller, D.C. (eds) *A Constitution for the European Union*, MIT Press, Cambridge, MA.

Feldstein, M. (1997) The Political Economy of an European Economic and Monetary Union: Political Sources of an Economic Liability, *Journal of Economic Perspectives*, 11(4) 23–42.

Feldstein, M.S. (1974) Social security, induced retirement and aggregate capital accumulation, *Journal of Political Economy*, 82, 905–926.

Feldstein, M.S. (1976) Temporary layoffs in the theory of unemployment, *Journal of Political Economy*, 84, 937–957.

Fidrmuc, J. (2004) *The Endogeneity of the Optimum Currency Area Criteria, Intra-Industry Trade, and EMU Enlargement*, Contemporary Economic Policy, 22 (1), 1–12.

Fischer, J. and Giudice, G. (2001) Fiscal surveillance under the pact: the stability and convergence programmes; in Brunila, A., Buti, M. and Franco, D. (eds) *The Stability and Growth Pact: The architecture of fiscal policy in EMU*, Palgrave Macmillan, London.

Fisher, S. and Cooper, J.P. (1973) Stabilisation policy and lags, *Journal of Political Economy*, 81(4).

Fitoussi, J.-P. and Creel, J. (2002) *How to Reform the European Central Bank*, Centre for European Reform, London.

Fleming, J.M. (1971) On exchange rate unification, *Economic Journal*, 81, 467–488.

Flockton, C. (1998) Germany's long-running fiscal strains: unification costs or unsustainability of welfare state arrangements?, *Debatte*, 6(1) 79–93.

Flood, C. (2002) The challenge of Euroscepticism; in Gower, J. (ed.) *The European Union Handbook*, Fitzroy Dearborn, London.

Fontana, G. (2003) Post Keynesian Approach to Endogenous Money: A Time Framework Explanation, *Review of Political Economy*, vol. 15, No. 3, 291–314.

Fontana, G. (2009) Whither New Consensus Macroeconomics? The Role of Government and Fiscal Policy in Modern Macroeconomics, Levy Economics Institute, Working Paper 563.

Foreman-Peck, J. (1995) *A History of the World Economy: International Relations Since 1850*, Harvester Wheatsheaf, London.

Forster, A. (2002) *Euroscepticism in Contemporary British Politics: Opposition to Europe in the British Conservative and Labour Parties Since 1945*, Routledge, London.

Fouskas, V. (2001) The Complexity of New Labour, in Ludlam, S. and Smith, M.J. (eds) *New Labour in Government*, Macmillan, Basingstoke, 256–267.

Frankel, J. (1999) No Single Currency Regime Is Right For All Countries or at All times, NBER Working Paper, No. 7338.

Frankel, J. and Rose, A. (1997) Is EMU more justifiable ex-post than ex-ante?, *European Economic Review*, 41, 753–760.

Frankel, J.A. and Wei, S.J. (1993) Trade blocs and currency blocs, CEPR Conference on The Monetary Future of Europe, La Coruna, Spain.

Franzese, R.J. (2000) *Electoral and Partisan Manipulation of Public Debt in Developed Democracies*, 1956–90.

Franzese, R.J. (2001) *The Positive Political Economy of Public Debt: An Empirical Examination of the OECD Post-war Experience*. Available at: http://www-personal.umich.edu/~franzese/rjf.debt.paper.pdf.

Franzese, R J. (2002) Electoral and Partisan Cycles in Economic Policies and Outcomes. *Annual Review of Political Science*, 5(1) 369–421.

Frey, B.S. and Schneider, F. (1978a) An Empirical Study of Politico-Economic Interaction in the United States, *The Review of Economics and Statistics*, 60(2) 174–183.

Frey, B.S. and Schneider, F. (1978b) A Politico-Economic Model of the United Kingdom. *The Economic Journal*, 88(350) 243–253.

Frey, B.S. (1978) *Modern Political Economy*, Martin Robertson, Oxford.

Friedman, M. (1953a) The case for floating rates; in Friedman, M. (ed.) *Essays in Positive Economics*, University of Chicago Press, Chicago.

Friedman, M. (1953b) The lags of a full employment policy on economic stability: a formal analysis, in Friedman, M. (ed.) *Essays in Positive Economics*, University of Chicago Press, Chicago.

Friedman, M. and Schwartz, A.J. (1991) Alternative approaches to analysing economic data, *American Economic Review*, 81(1) 39–49.

Froyen, R.T. (2009) *Macroeconomics: Theories and Policies*, Pearson Prentice Hall, London.

Frydman, R. and Phelps, E.S. (eds) (1983) *Individual Forecasting and Aggregate Outcome: Rational Expectations Examined*, Cambridge University Press, Cambridge.

Fukuda, H. (1995) Speech at Chatham House conference, London, 29 March.

Funabashi, Y. (1989) *Managing the Dollar from the Plaza to the Louvre*, Institute for International Economics, Washington, DC.

Galbraith, J.K. (1997) Time to Ditch the NAIRU, *Journal of Economic Perspectives*, 11(1) 93–108.

Gali, J. (2001) Monetary policy in the early years of EMU. Paper presented at the European Commission Workshop on The Functioning of EMU: Challenges of the Early Years.

Gali, J. (2008) Monetary policy, inflation and the business cycle: an introduction to the New Keynesian framework, Princeton University Press, Princeton.

Gali, J. and Perotti, R. (2003) Fiscal policy and monetary integration in Europe, *Economic Policy*, 37, 533–572.

Garrett, G. (1995) Capital Mobility, Trade and the Domestic Politics of Economic Policy, *International Organisation*, vol. 49, 657–587.

Gaspar, V., Masuch, K. and Pill, H. (2001) The ECB's monetary policy strategy: responding to the challenges of the early years. Mimeo.

Gavin, F.J. (1996). Economic Myths Explained – The Legends of Bretton Woods, *Orbis*, 40 (2), 183–98.

Geddes, A. (2004) *The European Union and British Politics*, Palgrave, London.

George, S. (1998) *An Awkward Partner: Britain in the European Community*, Oxford University Press, Oxford.

George, S. (ed.) (1992) *Britain and the European Community: The Politics of Semi-detachment*, Clarendon Press, Oxford.

Ghosh, A.R., Gulde, A-M. and Wolf, H.C. (2002) *Exchange Rate Regimes: Choices and Consequences*, The MIT Press, Cambridge, MA.

Giannone D., Lenza M. and Reichlin L. (2010) Business Cycles in The Euro Area; in Alesina, A. and Giavazzi, F. (eds) *Europe and the Euro*, NBER c11669, University of Chicago Press, Chicago, 141–167.

Giavazzi, F. and Pagano, M. (1990) Can severe fiscal contractions be expansionary? Tales of two small European countries, NBER working paper 3372, Cambridge, MA.

Giddens, A. (2001) Introduction; in Giddens, A. (ed.) *The Global Third Way Debate*, Polity Press, Cambridge, 1–23.

Gill, S. (1998) European governance and the new constitutionalism *New Political Economy*, vol. 3 No. 1, 4–25.

Giovannini Group (2000) *Co-ordinated Public Debt Issuance in the Euro Area:* Report of the Giovanni Group, http://ec.europa.eu/economy_finance/publications/publication6372_En.pdf.

Glasman, M. (1997) The siege of the German social market, *New Left Review*, 225, 134–139.

Glick, R and Rose, A.K. (2002) Does a Currency Union Affect Trade? The Time-Series Evidence, *European Economic Review*, 46, 1125–1151.

Global Britain (1999) *UK Trade in 1998*, Global Britain, London.

Goodfriend, M. and King R.G. (1997) The New Neoclassical Synthesis and the Role of Monetary Policy, *NBER Macroeconomics Annual 1997*, vol. 12, 231–296.

Goodhart, C.A.E. (1992) National fiscal policy within EMU: the fiscal implications of Maastricht; in Goodhart, C.A.E. (ed.) *EMU and ESCB after Maastricht*, London School of Economics/Financial Markets Group, London.

Goodhart, C.A.E. (1995) The political economy of monetary union; in Kenen, P.B. (ed.) *Understanding independence: The Macroeconomics of the Open Economy*, Princeton University Press, Princeton.

Goodhart, C.A.E. and Hansen, E. (1990) Fiscal Policy and EMU, in Dornbusch, R., Goodhart, C.A.E. and Layard, R. (eds) *Britain and EMU*, Centre for Economic Performance, London School of Economics, December.

Goodhart, C.A.E. and Smith, S. (1993) Stabilisation, *European Economy*, Reports and Studies, 5, 419–455.

Gordon, R.J. (1990) What is New-Keynesian Economics? *Journal of Economic Literature*, September.

Gordon, R.J. (1993) Macroeconomics, 6th edn., HarperCollins, New York.

Gould, B. (2006) Preface; in Whyman, P., Baimbridge, M. and Burkitt, B. (eds) *Implications of the Euro: A Critical Perspective from the Left*, Routledge, London.

Gramlich, E.M and Wood, P.R (2004) Fiscal and monetary policies; in Baimbridge, M. and Whyman, P. (eds) *Fiscal Federalism and European Economic Integration*, Routledge, London.

Gravelle, J.G. and Hungerford, T.L. (2011) Can contractionary fiscal policy be expansionary?, Congressional Research Service 7–5700 R41849.

Gray, J. (1998) *False Dawn: the Delusions of Global Capitalism*, Granta, London.

Green, J. and Swagel, P.L. (1998) The euro area and the world economy, *Finance and Development*, 35(4) 8–11.

Grilli, V., Masciandoro, D. and Tabellini, G. (1991) Political and monetary institutions and public financial policies in the industrial countries, *Economic Policy*, 13, 341–392.

Gros, D. and Micossi, S. (2009) A Bond-Issuing EU Stability Fund Could Rescue Europe, Europe's World Discussion Paper No. 12; http://europesworld.org/2009/02/01/a-bond-issuing-eu-stability-fund-could-rescue-europe/

Gros, D., Jimeno, J., Monticelli, C., Tabellini, G. and Thygesen, N. (2001) Testing the speed limit for the European Central Bank, 4, CEPR, London.

Gross, D. and Thygesen, N. (1992) *European Monetary Integration*, Longman, London.

Grubel, H.G. (1977) *The International Monetary System*, 3rd edn. Penguin, Harmondsworth.

Guajardo, J., Leigh, D. and Pescatori, A. (2011) Expansionary austerity: new international evidence, IMF Working Paper 11/158.

Guichard, S., Kennedy, M., Wurzel, E. and André, C. (2007) What Promotes Fiscal Consolidation: OECD Country Experiences. OECD Economics Departments Working Paper No. 553. Available at: http://search.oecd.org/officialdocuments/di splaydocumentpdf/?doclanguage=en&cote=eco/wkp(2007)13.

Haberler, G. (1970) The international monetary system: some recent developments and discussions; in Halm, G.N. (ed.) *Approaches to Greater Flexibility of Exchange Rates*, Princeton University Press, Princeton.

Hainsworth, P., O'Brien, C. and Mitchell, P. (2004) Defending the nation: the politics of Euroscepticism on the French right; in Harmsen, R. and Spiering, M. (eds) *Euroscepticism: Party Politics, National Identity and European Integration*, Rodopi, Amsterdam.

Hall, S.G., Hondroyiannis, G., Swamy, P. and Tavlas, G.S. (2011). *Bretton Woods Systems, Old and New, and the Rotation of Exchange-Rate Regimes*, The Manchester School, 79 (2), 293–317.

Hallett, A.H. and Vines, D. (1993) On the possible costs of European Monetary Union, *The Manchester School*, 61(1) 35–64.

Hansson, A. (1987) Politics, institutions and cross-country inflation differentials, unpublished.

Hardin, R. (1982) *Collective Action*, Johns Hopkins Press, Baltimore.

Harding, D. and Pagan, A.R. (2002) Dissecting the Cycle: A Methodclogical Investigation, *Journal of Monetary Economics*, vol. 49, Issue 2, 365–381.

Harmsen, R. (2004) Euroscepticism in the Netherlands: stirrings of dissent; in Harmsen, R. and Spiering, M. (eds) *Euroscepticism: Party Politics, National Identity and European Integration*, Rodopi, Amsterdam.

Harrison, B. (1996) *The Transformation of British Politics 1860–1995*, Oxford University Press, Oxford.

Harrop, J. (2005) The internal market; in van der Hoek, M.P. (ed.) *Handbook of Public Administration and Policy in the European Union*, CRC Press, New York.

Hassel, A. (1999) The erosion of the German system of industrial relations, *British Journal of Industrial Relations*, 37(3) 483–505.

Hay, C. (1998) Globalisation, Welfare Retrenchment and the 'Logic of No Alternative': Why Second-Best Won't Do, *Journal of Social Policy*, vol. 27, No. 4, 525–532.

Hay, C. (1999) *The Political Economy of New Labour: Labouring Under False Pretences?*, Manchester University Press, Manchester.

Hay, C. and Rosamond, B. (2002) Globalization, European integration and the discursive construction of economic imperatives, *Journal of European Public Policy*, vol. 9, No. 2, 147–167.

Healey, N. (2000) The case for European Monetary Union; in Baimbridge, M., Burkitt, B. and Whyman, P. (eds) *The Impact of the Euro: Debating Britain's Future*, Macmillan, London.

Henderick, M. (1998) *The Euro and Co-operative Enterprises*, Co-operative Press, Manchester.

Henley, A. and Tsakalotos, E. (1995) Unemployment experience and the institutional preconditions; in Arestis, P. and Marshall, M. (eds) *The Political Economy of Full Employment*, Edward Elgar, Cheltenham.

Henning, C.R. and Kessler, M. (2012) Fiscal Federalism: US History for Architects of Europe's Fiscal Union, *Peterson Institute for International Economics Working Paper Series*, WP 12–1.

Henrekson, M. (1996) Sweden's relative economic performance: lagging behind or staying on top?, *Economic Journal*, 106(439)1747–1759.

Hettne, B. (1994) The Regional Factor in the Formation of a New World Order, in Sakamoto, Y. (ed.) *Global Transformation: Challenges to the State System*, United Nations University, Tokyo, 134–166.

Hibbs, D.A. (1977a) Political Parties and Macroeconomic Policy. *The American Political Science Review*, 71(4) 1467–1487.

Hibbs, D.A. (1977b) Political Parties and Macroeconomic Policy American Political Science Review, December.

Hill, R. (2001) *The Labour Party and Economic Strategy 1979–1997: The Long Road Back*, Palgrave, Basingstoke.

Hindley, B. and Howe, M. (1996) *Better-off Out? The Benefits or Costs of EU Membership*, IEA Occasional paper 99, Institute of Economic Affairs, London.

Hirst, P. and Thompson, G. (1996) *Globalisation in Question: The International Economy and the Possibilities of Governance*, Polity Press, Cambridge.

HM Treasury (1997) *UK Membership of the Single Currency: An Assessment of Five Economic Tests*, HMSO, London.

Hofstede, G. (1980) *Culture's Consequences*, Sage, London.

Holinski, N., Kool, C. and Muysken, J. (2012) Persistent Macroeconomic Imbalances in the Euro Area: Causes and Consequences. *Federal Reserve Bank of St. Louis Review*, 94(1) 1–20.

Holland, S. (1995) Squaring the Circle? The Maastricht convergence criteria, cohesion and employment, in Coates, K. and Holland, S. (eds.) *Full Employment for Europe*, Spokesman, Nottingham.

Honohan, P. and Lane, P.R. (2003) Divergent inflation rates in EMU, *Economic Policy*, 37, 357–394.

Hopkins, S. (1995) The Council of Ministers, *Politics Review*, 4(3) 32.

Horn, G.A. and Zwiener, R. (1992) Wage regimes in a United Europe; in Barrell, R. and Whitley, J. (eds) *Macroeconomic Policy Co-ordination in Europe*, Sage, London.

Horsefield, J.K. (1969) *The International Monetary Fund 1945–1965* – vol. 3: *Documents*, International Monetary Fund, Washington, DC.

Hughes-Hallett, A. and Lewis, J. (2008) European Fiscal Discipline Before and After EMU: Crash Diet or Permanent Weight Loss? *Macroeconomic Dynamics*, 12(3) 404–424.

Hutton, W. (1994) *The State We're In*, Cape, London.

Imbeau, L., Petry, F. and Lamari, M. (2001) Left–right party ideology and government policy: A meta-analysis, *European Journal of Political Research*, 40(1) 1–29.

IMF (2009) *World Economic Outlook Data:* October edition. Available at: http://www. imf.org/external/pubs/ft/weo/2009/02/weodata/index.aspx.

IMF (2012) *World Economic Outlook Data: October 2012 edition.* Available at: http://www.imf.org/external/pubs/ft/weo/2012/02/weodata/index.aspx.

Incomes Data Services (1990) *European Report*, April, 340.

Ingram, J. (1962) *Regional Payments Mechanisms: The case of Puerto Rico*, University of North Carolina Press, Chapel Hill, NC.

Ingram, J. (1969) Comment: the currency area problem; in Mundell, R.A. and Swoboda, A.K. (eds) *Monetary Problems of the International Economy*, University of Chicago Press, Chicago.

Inklaar, R. and de Haan, J. (2001) Is There Really a European Business Cycle? A Comment, *Oxford Economic Papers*, 53(2), 215–20.

Inklaar, R., Jong-A-Ping, R. and de Haan, J. (2008) Trade and Business Cycle Synchronisation in OECD Countries: A Re-Examination, *European Economic Review*, vol. 52, Issue 4, 646–666.

International Monetary Fund (2001) *World Economic Outlook Database*, IMF, Washington, DC.

International Monetary Fund (2002) Concluding statement of the IMF mission on the economic policies of the euro area – in the context of the 2002 Article IV consultation discussions with the euro area countries, IMF, Washington, DC.

Issing, O., Gaspar, V., Angeloni, I. and Tristani, O. (2001) *Monetary Policy in the Euro Area: Strategy and decision making at the European Central Bank*, Cambridge University Press, Cambridge.

Italianer, A. and Vanheukelen, M. (1993) Proposals for Community stabilisation mechanisms: some historical applications, *European Economy*, Reports and Studies, 5, 495–510.

Jackman, R., Pissarides, C. and Savouri, S. (1990) Labour market policies and unemployment in the OECD, *Economic Policy*, 5(2) 449–490.

Jamieson, B. (1995) Worlds apart?, Occasional Paper No.19, The Bruges Group, London.

Jamieson, B. (1998) *Britain: Free to Choose*, Global Britain, London.

Jarvis, V. and Prais, S.J. (1989) Two nations of shopkeepers, *National Institute Economic Review*, 128, May, 58–74.

Jaumotte, F. and Sodsriwiboon, P. (2010) Current Account Imbalances in the Southern Euro Area, IMF Working Paper 10/139.

Jay, D. (1990) *The European Monetary System: The ERM Illusion*, Labour Common Market Safeguards Committee, London.

Jayadev, A. and Konczal, M. (2010) The boom not the slump: the right time for austerity The Roosevelt Institute.

Jespersen, J. (2004) The Stability Pact: A Macroeconomic Straightjacket! In: Ljungberg, J. (ed.) *The Price of the Euro*. Palgrave Macmillan, Basingstoke.

Jirankova, M. and Hnat, P. (2012) Balance of Payments Adjustment Mechanisms in the Euro Area. *Eastern Journal of European Studies*, 3(1) 67–86.

Johnson, G. (1991) *World Agriculture in Disarray*, Macmillan, London.

Johnson, K.H. (1994) International dimension of European monetary union: implications for the dollar, International Finance Discussion Paper, 496, Washington, DC, Board of Governors of the Federal Reserve System.

Jordà, Ò and A.M. Taylor (2013) The Time for Austerity: Estimating the Average Treatment Effect of Fiscal Policy; paper presented at the NBER Summer Institute.

Kaergard, N. and Henriksen, I. (2003) Historical experience with monetary unions: the case of Scandinavia 1875–1914; in Baimbridge, M. and Whyman, P. (eds) *Economic and Monetary Union in Europe: Theory, Evidence and Practice*, Edward Elgar, Cheltenham.

Kalecki, M. (1943) Political aspects of full employment, *Political Quarterly*, October–December, 322–331.

Kalecki, M. (1946) Multilateralism and Full Employment, *Canadian Journal of Economics and Political Science*, 12, 322–327.

Kalecki, M. and Schumacher, E.F. (1943) International Clearing and Long-Term Lending, *Bulletin of the Oxford Institute of Statistics*, 5(August, Supplement) 29–33.

Karanassou, M. and Snower, D. (1998) How labour market flexibility affects unemployment: long-term implications of the chain reaction theory, *The Economic Journal*, 108(448) 832–849.

Kavanagh, D. (2000) *British Politics: Continuities and Change*, Oxford University Press, Oxford.

Keller, B. and Sorries, B. (1997) The new social dialogue: procedural structuring, first results and perspectives, *Industrial Relations Journal* (European Annual Review) 77–98.

Kenen, P.B. (1969) The theory of optimum currency areas: an eclectic view; in Mundell, R.A. and Swoboda, A.K. (eds) *Monetary Problems of the International Economy*, University of Chicago Press, Chicago.

Kenen, P.B. (1989) *Exchange Rates and Policy Coordination*, University of Michigan Press, Ann Arbor.

Kenen, P.B. (1995) *Economic and Monetary Union in Europe: Moving beyond Maastricht*, Cambridge University Press, Cambridge.

Kenen, P.B. (1995) What have we learned from the EMS crises?, *Journal of Policy Modelling*, 17(5) 449–461.

Keynes, J.M. (1942) Proposals for an International Currency (or Clearing) Union, fourth draft of the Keynes Plan; reproduced in Horsefield, J.K. (1969) *The International Monetary Fund 1945–1965 – vol. 3: Documents*, International Monetary Fund, Washington, DC, 3–36.

Keynes, J.M. (1942) *Collected Works*, 25, 108–139, Macmillan, London.

Keynes, J.M. (1980) Activities 1940–1944: Shaping the Post-War World – The Clearing Union; in Moggridge, D. (ed.) *The Collected Writings of John Maynard Keynes*, Macmillan, London.

King, M. (1997) Changes in UK monetary policy: rules versus discretion in practice, *Journal of Monetary Economics*, 39, 81–97.

Klaeffling, M. and Lopez-Perez, V. (2003) Inflation targets and the liquidity trap. Background Study for ECB Governing Council, ECB, Frankfurt.

Knutsen, P. (1997) Corporatist tendencies in the Euro-polity: the EU Directive of 22 September 1994 on European Works Councils, *Economic and Industrial Democracy*, 18(2) 289–323.

Konstanty, R. and Zwingmann, B. (1996) Arbeitsschutzeform – bleibt Deutschland Schlu-lict in Europa?, *WSI-Meittelungen*, 49(2) 56–70.

Kontopolous, Y. and Perotti, R. (1999) Government Fragmentation and Fiscal Policy Outcomes: Evidence from OECD Countries; in Poterba, J.M. and Von Hagen, J. (eds.) *Fiscal Institutions and Fiscal Performance*, University of Chicago Press, London. Available at: http://www.nber.org/chapters/c8024.pdf.

Koop, G. (2008) *Introduction to Econometrics*, Wiley, Hoboken, NJ.

Koopman, S.J. and Azevedo, J.V. (2003) Measuring Synchronization and Convergence of Business Cycles, Tinbergen Institute Discussion Paper, No. 2003–052/4.

Kopecky, P. (2004) An awkward newcomer? EU enlargement and Euroscepticism in the Czech Republic; in Harmsen, R. and Spiering, M. (eds) *Euroscepticism: Party Politics, National Identity and European Integration*, Rodopi, Amsterdam.

Korkman, S. (2001) Should fiscal policy co-ordination go beyond the SGP?; in Brunila, A., Buti, M. and Franco, D. (eds) *The Stability and Growth Pact: The Architecture of Fiscal Policy in EMU*, Palgrave Macmillan, London.

Korpi, W. (1985) Economic growth and the welfare system: leaky bucket or irrigation system?, *European Sociological Review*, 1, 97–118.

Korpi, W. (1996) Eurosclerosis and the sclerosis of objectivity: on the role of values among economic policy experts, *Economic Journal*, 106(439) 1727–1746.

Kose, M.A, Otrok, C. and Whitman, C.H. (2003) International Business Cycles: World, Region, and Country-Specific Factors, *American Economic Review*, vol. 93, 1216–1239.

KPMG (2000) *Europe's Response to EMU*, KPMG Consultants, London.

Krugman P. (1993) What do we need to know about the international monetary system?; in Kenen, P. (ed.) Understanding Interdependence, Princeton University Press, Princeton, 509–530.

Krugman, P. (1980) Vehicle currencies and the structure of international exchange, *Journal of Money, Credit and Banking*, 12.

Krugman, P. (1984) The international role of the dollar: theory and prospect; in Bilson, J.F.O. and Marston, R.C. (eds) *Exchange Rate Theory and Practice*, University of Chicago Press, Chicago.

Kydland, F.E. and Prescott, E.C. (1977) Rules rather than discretion: the time inconsistency of optimal plans, *Journal of Political Economy*, 85, 473–499.

Laeven, L. and Valencia, F. (2008) Systematic Banking Crises: A New Database, *International Monetary Fund Working Paper 08/224*, IMF, Washington, DC.

Lamfalussy, A. (1989) Macro-coordination of fiscal policies in an Economic and Monetary Union in Europe; in Committee for the Study of Economic and Monetary Union [Delors Report] (ed.) *Report of Economic and Monetary Union in the European Community*, Office for the Official Publications of the European Communities, Luxembourg.

Lane, P.R. (2012) The European Sovereign Debt Crisis, *Journal of Economic Perspectives*, 26(3) 49–68.

Lane, P.R. (2006) The Real Effects of European Monetary Union, *Journal of Economic Perspectives*, 20(4) 47–66.

Lash, S. and Urry, J. (1987) *The End of Organised Capitalism*, Polity Press, Oxford.

Lavoie, M. (2004) The New Consensus on Monetary Policy Seen From a Post-Keynesian Perspective; in Lavoie, M. and Seccareccia, M. (eds.) *Central Banking in Modern World: Alternative Perspective*, Cheltenham, Edward Elgar.

Lavoie, M. (2006) A Post-Keynesian Amendment to the New Consensus on Monetary Policy, *Metroeconomica*, vol. 57, Issue 2, 165–192.

Lawrence, R. and Schultz, C. (1987) (eds) *Barriers to European Growth: A Transatlantic View*, Brookings Institution, Washington, DC.

Layard, R. and Nickell, S. (1985) The Causes of British Unemployment, *National Economic Institute Review*, 111, 62–85.

Layard, R., Nickell, S. and Jackman, R. (1991) *Unemployment: Macroeconomic Performance and the Labour Market*, Oxford University Press, Oxford.

Lea, R. (2010) Time for a Global Vision for Britain; in Baimbridge, M., Whyman, P.B. and Burkitt, B. (eds) *Britain in a Global World: Options for a New Beginning.*, Imprint Academic, Exeter.

Leach, R. (2000) EU membership: What's the bottom line? IoD Policy Paper, Institute of Directors, London.

Lee, J. (2012) Business Cycle Synchronisation in Europe: Evidence from a Dynamic Factor Model, *International Economic Journal*, vol. 27, Issue 3, 347–364.

Lehwald, S. (2012) Has the Euro Changed Business Cycle Synchronisation? Evidence from the Core and the Periphery, IFO Working Paper, No. 122.

Leibfried, S. (1994) The social dimension of the European Union: En route to positively joint sovereignty?, *Journal of European Social Policy*, 4(4) 239–262.

Leibfried, S. and Pierson, P. (1995) The dynamics of social policy integration; in Leibfried, S. and Pierson, P. (eds) *Fragmented Social policy: The European Community's Social Dimension in Comparative Perspective*, Brookings Institution, Washington, DC.

Leigh, D., Devries, P., Freedman, C., Guajardo, J., Laxton, D. and Pescatori, A. (2010) Will it hurt? Macroeconomic effects of fiscal consolidation, IMF World Economic Outlook.

Lindbeck, A. (1992) Macroeconomics Theory and the Labour Market, *European Economic Review*, April.

Lindbeck, A. (1998) New Keynesian and Aggregate Economic Activity, *Economic Journal*, January.

Lindbeck, A., Molander, P., Persson, T., Petersson, O., Sandmo, A., Swedenborg, B. and Thygesen, N. (1994) *Turning Sweden Around*, MIT Press, London.

Lockwood, C. (1994) Play the EU game: you can waste millions, *Daily Telegraph*, 16 November.

Lovell, M.C. (1986) Tests of the Rational Expectations Hypothesis, *American Economic Review*, March.

Lowery, D. (1985) The Keynesian and political determinants of unbalanced budgets: U.S. fiscal policy from Eisenhower to Reagan, *American Journal of Political Science*, 29(3) 429–460.

Lucas, R. (1976), Econometric policy evaluation: a critique, in Brunner, K. and Meltzer, A. (eds) *The Phillips Curve and Labour Markets, Carnegie-Rochester Conference Series on Public Policy*, 1, New York: American Elsevier, pp. 19–46.

Lucas, R.E. and Stokey, N.L. (1983) Optimal fiscal and monetary policy in an economy without capital. *Journal of Monetary Economics*, 12(1) 55–93.

Lucas, R.E. (1972) Expectations and the Neutrality of Money, *Journal of Economic Theory*, April.

Lucas, R.E. (1973) Some International Evidence on Output-Inflation Tradeoffs, *American Economic Review*, June.

Lucas, R.E. (1978) Unemployment Policy, *American Economic Review*, May.

Lucas, R.E. and Rapping, L.A. (1969) Real Wages, Employment and Inflation, *Journal of Political Economy*, September/October.

Lumley, R. (1996) Labour markets and employment relations in transition: the case of German unification, *Employee Relations*, 17(1) 24–37.

Lumsdaine, R.L. and Prasad, E.S. (2003) Identifying the Common Component of International Economic Fluctuations: A New Approach, *Economic Journal*, vol. 113, 101–127.

MacDougall, D. (1977) *The Role of public finance in the European Communities*, Office for the Official Publications of the European Communities, Brussels.

MacDougall, D. (1992) Economic and Monetary Union and the European Community Budget, *National Institute Economic Review*, May, 64–68.

MacDougall, D. (2003) Economic and monetary union and the European Community budget, in Baimbridge, M. and Whyman, P. (eds) *Economic and Monetary Union in Europe: Theory, Evidence and Practice*, Edward Elgar, Cheltenham.

MacRae, C.D. (1977) A political model of the business cycle, *Journal of Political Economy*, 85, 239–263.

Madsen, J.B. (1998) General equilibrium macroeconomic models of unemployment: Can they explain the unemployment path in the OECD?, *The Economic Journal*, 108(448) 850–867.

Magnifico, G. (1973) *European Monetary Unification*, Wiley, New York.

Majocchi, A. and Rey, M. (1993) A special financial support scheme in Economic and Monetary Union: need and nature. In The Economics of Community Public Finance, *European Economy*, Reports and Studies, 5, 459–480.

Mangano, G. (1998) Measuring central bank independence: a tale of subjectivity and of its consequences, *Oxford Economic Papers*, 50(3) 468–492.

Mankiw, N G. (1991) Comment on Rotemberg, J.J. and Woodford, M., Markups and the Business Cycle, *NBER Macroeconomics Annual*.

Mankiw, N.G. and Romer, D. (eds) (1991) *New Keynesian Economics*, MIT Press, Cambridge MA.

Marginson, P. and Sisson, K. (1996) Multinational companies and the future of collective bargaining: a review of the research issues, *European Journal of Industrial Relations*, 2(2) 173–197.

Marneffe, W., Van Aarle, B., Van Der Wielen, W. and Vereeck, L. (2010) The Impact of Fiscal Rules on Public Finances: Theory and Empirical Evidence for the Euro Area. CESifo Working Paper No. 3303. Available at: http://www.cesifo-group.de/portal/pls/portal/docs/1/1201052.PDF.

Marquand, D. (1999) Premature Obsequies: Social Democracy Comes in From the Cold; in Gamble, A. and Wright, T. (eds) *The New Social Democracy*, Blackwell, Oxford.

Marsden, D. (1992) Incomes policy for Europe? Or will pay bargaining destroy the single European market?, *British Journal of Industrial Relations*, 30(4) 587–604.

Marsh, D. (1992) *The Bundesbank – the Bank That Rules Europe*, Heinemann, London.

Marshall, M.G. (1995) Lessons from the experience of the Swedish model; in Arestis, P. and Marshall, M. (eds) *The Political Economy of Full Employment*, Edward Elgar, Cheltenham.

Massmann, M. and Mitchell, J. (2004) Reconsidering the Evidence: Are Eurozone Business Cycles Converging?, *Journal of Business Cycle Measurement and Analysis*, vol.1, Issue 1, 275–308.

Masson, P.R. (1996) Fiscal Dimensions of EMU, *Economic Journal*, 106(437) 996–1004.

Masson, P.R. and Mélitz, J. (1990) Fiscal policy independence in a European Monetary Union, *Open Economies Review*, 2.

Masson, P.R. and Taylor, M.P. (1993) Common currency areas and currency unions: an analysis of the issues, Parts I and II, *Journal of International and Comparative Economics*, 1(3–4) 231–294.

Masson, P.R. and Taylor, M.P. (1993) Currency Unions: A Survey of the Issues, in: Masson, P.R. and Taylor, M.P. (eds) *Policy Issues in the Operation of Currency Unions*, Cambridge University Press, Cambridge.

Masson, P.R. (1996) Fiscal dimensions of EMU, *Economic Journal*, 106(437) 996–1004.

Mathers, A. (2007) *Struggling for a Social Europe: Neo-Liberal Globalisation and the Birth of a European Social Movement*, Ashgate, Aldershot.

Mayes, D.G. (2003) The euro and the stabilisation of the Eastern European economy; in Baimbridge, M. and Whyman, P. (eds) *Economic and Monetary Union in Europe: Theory, Evidence and Practice*, Edward Elgar, Cheltenham.

McCallum, J. (1983) Inflation and social consensus in the seventies, *Economic Journal*, 93(372) 784–805.

McCombie, J.S.L. and Thirlwall, A.P. (1994) *Economic Growth and the Balance-of-Payments Constraint*, Macmillan, Basingstoke.

McGiffen, S.P. (2001) *The European Union: A Critical Guide*, Pluto, London.

McKay, D. (1999) *Federalism and the European Union: A Political Economy Perspective*, Oxford University Press, Oxford.

McKay, D. (2001) *Designing Europe: Comparative Lessons from the Federal Experience*, Oxford University Press, Oxford.

McKinnon, R. (1963) Optimum currency areas, *American Economic Review*, 53, 717–725.

McKinnon, R. (1996) *Default Risk in Monetary Union*; background report for the Swedish government commission on EMU, Stockholm.

McKinnon, R. (2003) Monetary regimes, collective fiscal retrenchment and the political economy of EMU; in Baimbridge, M. and Whyman, P. (eds) *Economic and Monetary Union in Europe: Theory, Evidence and Practice*, Edward Elgar, Cheltenham.

Mélitz, J. (1997) The Evidence about the costs and benefits of EMU, *Swedish Economic Policy Review*, 4, 359–410.

Mélitz, J. (2001), *Geography, Trade and Currency Union*, CEPR Discussion Paper No. 2987.

Meltzer, A.H. (1983) Keynes on Monetary Reform and International Economic Order; the Fifth Henry Thornton Lecture, 3 October, City University Business School, London. Available via: http://repository.cmu.edu/tepper/796/

Micco, A., Stein, E. and Ordonez, G. (2003) The currency union effect on trade: early evidence from EMU, *Economic Policy*, 37, 315–356.

Michie, J. (2000) The economic consequences of EMU for Britain; in Baimbridge, M., Burkitt, B. and Whyman, P. (eds) *The Impact of the Euro: Debating Britain's future*, Macmillan, London.

Michie, J. (2006) Economic consequences of EMU for Britain; in Whyman, P., Baimbridge, M. and Burkitt, B. (eds) *Implications of the Euro: A Critical Perspective from the Left*, Routledge, London.

Midelfart-Knarvik, K.H. and Overman, H.G. (2002) Delocation and European integration. Is structural spending justified?, *Economic Policy*, 323–359.

Miller, V. and Dyson, J. (1994) The European Communities (Finance Bill) House of Commons Library Research Paper, No. 94/117, London.

Mills, J. (2010) Questions and answers on the prospects for the euro, *Labour Euro-Safeguards Campaign Bulletin*, January.

Mills, J. (2011) Questions and answers on the future of the euro, *Labour Euro-Safeguards Campaign Bulletin*, January.

Milne, I. (1998) *The Facts about Direct Investment*, The June Press, London.

Milne, I. (2004) *A Cost Too Far? An Analysis of the Net Economic Costs and Benefits for the UK of EU Membership*, The Institute for the Study of Civil Society, London.

Milner, S. (2004) For an alternative Europe: Euroscepticism and the French left since the Maastricht Treaty; in Harmsen, R. and Spiering, M. (eds) *Euroscepticism: Party Politics, National Identity and European Integration*, Rodopi, Amsterdam.

Minford, P. (1996) *Britain and Europe: The balance sheet*, Macroeconomic Research, Liverpool.

Minford, P. (1996) Corporatism, the natural rate and productivity; in *Trade Unions and the Economy: Into the 1990s*, Employment Institute, London.

Minford, P. (2000) The single currency – will it work and should we join?; in Baimbridge, M., Burkitt, B. and Whyman, P. (eds) *The Impact of the Euro: Debating Britain's Future*, Macmillan, London.

Minford, P. (2002) *Should Britain Join the Euro?*, Institute of Economic Affairs, London.

Minford, P., Mahambare, V. and Novell, E. (2005) *Should Britain Leave the EU? An Economic Analysis of a Troubled Relationship*, Edward Elgar, Cheltenham.

Mink, M. and De Haan, J. (2006) Are there Political Budget Cycles in the Euro Area? *European Union Politics*, 7(2) 191–211.

Minsky, H. (2008) *John Maynard Keynes*, McGraw-Hill, London.

Missale, A. (2001) How should the debt be managed? Supporting the Stability Pact; in Brunila, A., Buti, M. and Franco, D. (eds) *The Stability and Growth Pact: The Architecture of Fiscal Policy in EMU*, Palgrave Macmillan, London.

Mitchell, A. (1993) Democracy and monetary policy; memorandum submitted to the Treasury and Civil Service Committee.

Mitchell, A. (2006) Euro versus the people; in Whyman, P., Baimbridge, M. and Burkitt, E. (eds) *Implications of the Euro: A Critical Perspective from the Left*, Routledge, London.

Molle, W. (2003) Are EU policies good or bad for convergence? Paper presented at the Experts Workshop, Cohesion in the European Union, College of Europe, Bruges.

Monfort, A., Renne, J.P., Rüffer, R. and Vitale, G. (2003) Is Economic Activity in the G7 Synchronized? Common Shocks versus Spillover Effects, CEPR Discussion Paper, No. 4119.

Monks, J. (2000) A single currency for Europe – considerations for workers; in Baimbridge, M., Burkitt, B. and Whyman, P. (eds) *The Impact of the Euro: Debating Britain's future*, Macmillan, London.

Monperrus-Veroni, P. and Saraceno, F. (2006) Whither Stability Pact? An Assessment of Reform Proposals, in Mitchell, W., Muysken, J., and Van Veen, T. (eds) *Growth and Cohesion in the European Union: The Impact of Macroeconomic Policy*, Edward Elgar, Cheltenham, 32–56.

Monvoisin, V. and Rochon L.-P. (2006) The Post-Keynesian Consensus, the New Consensus and Endogenous Money; in Gnos C. and Rochon L.-P. (eds) *Post Keynesian Principles of Economic Policy*, Edward Elgar, Cheltenham.

Moore, B.J. (1988) Horizontalists and Verticalists: the Macroeconomics of Credit Money, Cambridge University Press, Cambridge.

Muellbauer, J. (2011) Resolving the Eurozone Crisis: Time for Conditional Eurobonds *CEPR Policy Insight* No. 59.

Mueller, D.C. (2003) *Public Choice III*, Cambridge University Press, Cambridge.

Mulas-Granados, C. (2003) The Political and Economic Determinants of Budgetary Consolidation in Europe. *European Political Economy Review*, 1(1) 15–39.

Mulas-Granados, C. (2004) *Economics or Politics? A Theoretical Review of the Determinants of Fiscal Policy*. Available at: http://www.ucm.es/info/ecap2/mulas_carlos/articulos%20en%20revistas%20nacionales/Economis%20or%20Politics.pdf.

Mullen, A. (2007) From Imperial Third Force to the 1975 Referendum; in Baimbridge, M. (ed.) *The 1975 Referendum on Europe*, vol. 1: *Reflections of the Participants*, Imprint Academic, Exeter.

Mundell, R.A. (1961) A theory of optimum currency areas, *American Economic Review*, 51, 657–665.

Mundell, R.A. (1968) *International Economics*. Macmillan, London.

Muscatelli, V.A. (1998) Political consensus, uncertain preferences, and central bank independence, *Oxford Economic Papers*, 50(3) 412–430.

Musgrave, R.A. and Musgrave, P.B. (1973) *Public Finance in Theory and Practice*, McGraw-Hill, London.

Muth, J.F. (1961) Rational Expectations and the Theory of Price Movements, *Econometrica*, July.

Myrdal, G. (1957) *Economic Theory and Underdeveloped Regions*, London, Duckworth.

Nag, A. (2012) Sterling hits 1-month low versus dollar on economic worries. Available at: http://uk.reuters.com/article/2012/10/08/uk-markets-sterling-update-idUKBRE88K0EF20121008.

Nairn, T. (1972) *The Left against Europe?*, Penguin, London.

Nasad, N. (2012) *A History of Europe's Debt Crisis and Current Issues*. Available at: http://www.ibtimes.com/history-europe%E2%80%99s-debt-crisis-and-current-issues-413248.

National Consumer Council (1995) *Agricultural Policy in the European Union*, National Consumer Council, London.

Neck, R. and Sturm, J. (2008) *Sustainability of Public Debt*. MIT Press, Cambridge, MA.

Nevin, E. (1990) *The Economics of Europe*, Macmillan, London.

Nickell, S. (1998) Unemployment: questions and some answers, *The Economic Journal*, 108(448) 802–816.

Nordhaus, W.D. (1975) The Political Business Cycle, *Review of Economic Studies*, 42(2) 169–190.

Notermans, T. (2000) Europeanisation and the crisis of Scandinavian social democracy; in Geyer, R., Ingebritsen, C. and Moses, J.W. (eds) *Globalisation, Europeanisation and the End of Social Democracy?*, Macmillan, London.

O'Connor, M. (2009) The euro meltdown, *European Journal*, 3, December.

Oates, W.E. (1972) *Fiscal Federalism*, Harcourt-Brace and Jovanovich, New York.

Oates, W.E. (2004) An essay on fiscal federalism; in Baimbridge, M. and Whyman, P. (eds) *Fiscal Federalism and European Economic Integration*, Routledge, London.

OECD (1986) *Flexibility in the Labour Market*, OECD, Paris.

OECD (2001) *Economic Outlook*, OECD, Paris.

OECD (2007) *Fiscal Consolidation: Lessons from Past Experience*. Available at: http://www.oecd.org/economy/economicoutlookanalysisandforecasts/38628499.pdf.

Ohmae, K. (1990) The Borderless World: Power and Strategy in the Interlinked Economy, Collins, London.

Ohmae, K. (1995) *The End of the Nation-State: The Rise of Regional Economies*, Harper Collins, London.

Ormerod, P. (1999a) The Euro-attack on jobs; in Bush, J. (ed.) *Everything You Always Wanted to Know about the Euro*, New Europe, London.

Ormerod, P. (1999b) A currency for jobs?, *European Journal*, July, 7–8.

Ormerod, P. (2006) The euro: an outsider's perspective; in Whyman, P., Baimbridge, M. and Burkitt, B. (eds) *Implications of the Euro: A Critical Perspective from the Left*, Routledge, London.

Owen, D. (2006) Foreword; in Whyman, P., Baimbridge, M. and Burkitt, B. (eds) *Implications of the Euro: A Critical Perspective from the Left*, Routledge, London.

Pain, N. and Young, G. (2004) The macroeconomic impact of UK withdrawal from the EU, *Economic Modelling*, 21(3) 387–408.

Palley, T.I. (2006) A Post-Keynesian Framework for Monetary Policy: Why Interest Rate Operating Procedures Are Not Enough; in Gnos C. and Rochon L.-P. (eds) *Post-Keynesian Principles of Economic Policy*, Edward Elgar, Cheltenham.

Pamp, O. (2008) Partisan Preferences and Political Institutions: Explaining Fiscal Retrenchment in the European Union, *European Political Economy Review*, 8, 4–39. Available at: http://eper.htw-berlin.de/no8/pamp.pdf.

Panic, M. (1992) *European Monetary Union: Lessons from the Classical Gold Standard*, Macmillan, London.

Peele, G. (2004) *Governing the UK: British Politics in the 21st Century*, Blackwell, Oxford.

Pennant-Rea, R., Bean, C.R., Begg, D., Hardie, J., Lankester, T., Miles, D.K., Portes, R., Robinson, A., Seabright, P. and Wolf, M. (1997) *The Ostrich and the EMU – Policy Choices Facing the UK*, Centre for Economic Policy Research, London.

Perotti, R. (2004) Estimating the Effects of Fiscal Policy in OECD Countries. IGIER working paper No. 276. Available at: ftp://ftp.igier.uni-bocconi.it/wp/2004/276.pdf.

Perotti, R. (2011) The austerity myth: pain without gain, Bank of International Settlements Working Paper 362.

Perraton, J., Goldblatt, D., Held, D. and McGrew, A. (2000) The Globalisation of Economic Activity; in Higgott, R. and Payne, A. (eds) *The New Political Economy of Globalisation*, vol. 1, Edward Elgar, Cheltenham.

Persson, T. (2001) Currency Unions and Trade: How Large is the Treatment Effect?, *Economic Policy*, 33, 435–448.

Persson, T. and Svensson, L. (1989) Why a stubborn conservative would run a deficit: Policy with Time Inconsistent results. *Quarterly Journal of Economics*, 104(2) 325–345.

Petchey, J. and Wells, G. (2004) Australia's federal experience; in Baimbridge, M. and Whyman, P. (eds) *Fiscal Federalism and European Economic Integration*, Routledge, London.

Peters, T. (1995) European Monetary Union and labour markets: what to expect, *International Labour Review*, 134(3) 315–332.

Phelps, E.S. and Zoega, G. (1998) Natural-rate theory and OECD unemployment, *The Economic Journal*, 108(448) 782–801.

Piffaretti, N.F. (2009a) Reshaping the International Monetary Architecture: Lessons from Keynes Plan, *World Bank Policy Research Working Paper* Nr. 5034.

Piffaretti, N.F. (2009b) Reshaping the International Monetary Architecture: Lessons from Keynes' Plan, *Banks and Bank Systems*, 4(1) 45–54.

Pilbeam, K. (2006) *International Finance*, Palgrave Macmillan, Basingstoke.

Pindyck, R.S. and Rubinfeld, D.L. (1998a) *Microeconomics*, 4th edn. Englewood Cliffs, NJ: Prentice-Hall.

Pindyck, R.S. and Rubinfeld, D.L. (1998b) *Econometric Models and Economic Forecasts*. McGraw-Hill, London.

Pinho, M.M. (2004) Political Models of Budget Deficits: A Literature Review. University of Porto Working Paper No. 138. Available at: http://fep.up.pt/investigacao/workingpapers/_.old_WP_Fev09/04.03.08_WP138_Maria%20Pinho.pdf.

Pisani-Ferry, J., Italianer, A. and Lescure, R. (1993) Stabilisation properties of budgetary systems: a simulation analysis, *European Economy*, Reports and Studies, 5, 513–538.

Pissarides, C. (1997) The need for labour market flexibility in European Economic and Monetary Union, *Swedish Economic Policy Review*, 4(2) 513–546.

Podmore, W. and Katz, P. (1998) Sovereignty for what? Why European monetary union is just the start, *Tribune*, London.

Porter, M.E. (1990) *The Competitive Advantage of Nations*, Macmillan, London.

Posen, A (1993) Why central bank independence does not cause low inflation: there is no institutional fix for politics; in O'Brien, R. (ed.) *Finance and the International Economy*, 7, Oxford University Press, Oxford.

Posen, A (1998) Central bank independence and disinflationary credibility: a missing link, *Oxford Economic Papers*, 50(3) 335–359.

Poterba, J.M. (1996) Do budget rules work? NBER Working Paper No. 5550. Available at: http://www.nber.org/papers/w5550.pdf.

Prais, S.J. and Wagner, K. (1988) Productivity and management: the training in foremen in Britain and Germany, *National Institute Economic Review*, 123, February, 34–47.

Prestowitz, C. (2004) *Rogue Nation: American Unilateralism and the Failure of Good Intentions*. Perseus Books Group, Cambridge.

Radice, H. (1984) The National Economy – a Keynesian Myth?, Capital and Class, No. 22, 111–140.

Rae, D. (1968) A Note on the Fractionalization of Some European Party Systems. *Comparative Political Studies*, 1(3) 413–418.

Rau, N. (1985) Simplifying the Theory of the Government Budget Restraint, *Oxford Economic Papers*, New Series, 37(2) 210–229.

Redman, D.A. (1992) *A Reader's Guide to Rational Expectations*, Edward Elgar, Aldershot and Brookfield, VT.

Redwood, J. (1997) *Our Currency, Our Country: The Dangers of European Monetary Union*, Penguin Books, London.

Redwood, J. (2000) Sterling democracy or European bureaucracy?; in Baimbridge, M., Burkitt, B. and Whyman, P. (eds) *The impact of the euro: Debating Britain's Future*, Macmillan, London.

Reich, R. (1992) *The Work of Nations*, Vintage, New York.

Rhodes, M. (1992) The future of the social dimension: labour market regulation in post-1992 Europe, *Journal of Common Market Studies*, 30(1) 23–51.

Richards, D. and Smith, M.J. (2002) *Governance and Public Policy in the United Kingdom*, Oxford University Press, Oxford.

Richardson, D.R. (1985) On Proposals for a Clearing Union, *Journal of Post Keynesian Economics*, 8(1) 14–27.

Riddle, J.H. (1943) *British and American Plans for International Currency Stabilisation*, National Bureau for Economic Research (NBER) Cambridge, MA. Out of print edition, available via: http://www.nber.org/chapters/c4632.pdf.

Riese, M. (2008) *Reforming the Global Financial Architecture: A Comparison of Different Proposals*. Available via: http://www.singleglobalcurrency.org/documents/DAReformingtheGlobalFinancialArchitecturehyper.pdf.

Rochon, L.-P. (1999) Credit, Money and Production: an Alternative Post-Keynesian Approach, Edward Elgar, Cheltenham.

Rochon, L.-P. and Setterfield, M. (2007) Post Keynesian Interest Rate Rules and Macroeconomic Performance: a Comparative Evaluation, Post-Keynesian Economic Policies conference, Université de Bourgogne, November 30–December 1, 2007.

Rochon, L.-P. (2004) Wicksell after the Taylor Rule: a Post-Keynesian critique of the New Consensus, paper presented at the Robinson seminar, University of Ottawa.

Rogoff, K. (1985a) The optimal degree of commitment to an intermediate monetary target, *Quarterly Journal of Economics*, 100, 1169–1190.

Rogoff, K. and Sibert, A. (1988) Elections and Macroeconomic Policy Cycles. *The Review of Economic Studies*, 55(1) 1–16.

Rolnick, A.J. and Weber, W.E. (1986) Gresham's Law or Gresham's Fallacy. *Journal of Political Economy*, 94(1) 185–199.

Romans, J.T. (1966) Moral Suasion as an Instrument of Economic Policy, *The American Economic Review*, 56(5) 1220–1226.

Romer, D. (2000) Keynesian Macroeconomics without LM Curve, *Journal of Economic Perspectives*, vol. 14, Issue 2, 149–169.

Romer, P.M. (1994) The origins of endogenous growth, *Journal of Economic Perspectives*, 8(1) 3–22.

Rompuy, P.V., Abraham, F. and Heremans, D. (1993) Economic federalism and the EMU; in The Economics of EMU – Background Studies, *European Economy*, 44, 109–135.

Rooney, B. (2012) *Europe Strengthens Fiscal Ties*. Available at: http://money.cnn.com/2012/03/02/markets/european_union_fiscal_pact/index.htm.

Rosamond, B. (1993) National Labour Organizations and European Integration: British Trade Unions and 1992, *Political Studies*, vol. 41, No. 3, 420–434.

Rosamond, B. (1999) Discourses of globalization and the social construction of European identities, *Journal of European Public Policy*, vol. 6, No. 4, 652–668.

Rose, A.K. (2000) One Money, One Market: Estimating the Effect of Common Currencies on Trade, *Economic Policy*, 20, 7–45.

Rostagno, M., Hiebert, P. and Pérez-Garcìa, J. (2001) Optimal debt under a deficit constraint; in Brunila, A., Buti, M. and Franco, D. (eds) *The Stability and Growth Pact: The architecture of fiscal policy in EMU*, Palgrave Macmillan, London.

Roubini, N. and Sachs, J. (1989) Government Spending and Budget Deficits in Industrial Economies. *Economic Policy*, 4(1) 99–132.

Rowthorn, B. and Glyn, A. (1990) The diversity of unemployment experience since 1973; in Marglin, S.A. and Schor, J.B. (eds) *The Golden Age of Capitalism: Reinterpreting the Post-War Experience*, Clarendon Press, Cambridge.

Royal Society of Edinburgh (2004) *Inquiry into the Future of the Scottish Fishing Industry*, RSE, Edinburgh.

Sachs, J.D. (1999) Twentieth-Century Political Economy: A Brief History of Global Capitalism, *Oxford Review of Economic Policy*, December.

Sala-i-Martin, X. and Sachs, J. (1992) Fiscal federalism and optimum currency areas: evidence for Europe from the United States, in: Canzoneri, M.B. et al., (eds) *Establishing a Central Bank: Issues in Europe and lessons from the US*, Cambridge University Press, Cambridge.

Sapir, A. and Sekkat, K. (1999) Optimum electoral areas: should Europe adopt a single election day?, *European Economic Review*, 43, 1595–1619.

Sapir, A., Sekkhat, K. and Weber, A. (1994) The impact of exchange rate fluctuations on European Union trade, CEPR Discussion Paper, 104.

Sargent, T.J. and Wallace, N. (1975) Rational Expectations, the Optimal Monetary Instrument and the Optimal Money Supply Rule, *Journal of Political Economy*, April.

Sargent, T.J. and Wallace, N. (1976) Rational Expectations and the Theory of Economic Policy. *Journal of Monetary Economics*, April.

Sarno, L. and Taylor, M.P. (2002) *The Economics of Exchange Rates*, Cambridge University Press, Cambridge.

Sassoon D. (1999) European Social Democracy and New Labour: Unity in Diversity?, in Gamble, A. and Wright, T. (eds) *The New Social Democracy*, Blackwell, Oxford, 19–37.

Sawyer, M. (1988) *Post-Keynesian Economics*, Edward Elgar.

Sawyer, M. (1995) Obstacles to full employment in capitalist economies; in Arestis, P. and Marshall, M. (eds) *The Political Economy of Full Employment*, Cheltenham, Edward Elgar.

Sawyer, M. (2012) Remedies for the eurozone crisis: quack and otherwise. Available at: http://ssrn.com/abstract=2078821.

Sawyer, M. and Arestis, P. (2006) What type of European monetary union?; in Whyman, P., Baimbridge, M. and Burkitt, B. (eds) *Implications of the Euro: A Critical Perspective from the Left*, Routledge, London.

Schaltegger, C.A. and Frey, R.L. (2004) Fiscal federalism in Switzerland: a public choice approach; in Baimbridge, M. and Whyman, P. (eds) *Fiscal Federalism and European Economic Integration*, Routledge, London.

Scholte, J.A. (2000) *Globalisation: A Critical Introduction*, Macmillan, Basingstoke.

Schoors, K. and Gobbin, N. (2005) Enlargement; in van der Hoek, M.P. (ed.) *Handbook of Public Administration and Policy in the European Union*, CRC Press, New York.

Schumpeter, J.A. (1942) *Capitalism, Socialism and Democracy*, George Allen and Unwin, London.

Seater, J.J. (1993) Ricardian Equivalence, *Journal of Economic Literature*, 31(1) 142–190.

Setterfield, M. (2004) Central Banking, Stability and Macroeconomic Outcomes; in Lavoie M. and Seccareccia, M. (eds) *Central Banking in the Modern World: Alternative Perspectives*, Cheltenham, Edward Elgar.

Setterfield, M., Gordon, D.V. and Osberg, L. (1992) Searching for a Will O' Wisp: An Empirical Study of the NAIRU in Canada, *European Economic Review*, 36(1) 119–136.

Shackle, G.L.S. (1967) *The Year of High Theory*, Cambridge University Press, Cambridge.

Shi, M. and J. Svensson (2006) Political Budget Cycles: Do They Differ Across Countries and Why? *Journal of Public Economics*, 90(8–9) 1367–1389.

Shore, P. (2006) Fighting against federalism; in Whyman, P., Baimbridge, M. and Burkitt, B. (eds) *Implications of the Euro: A Critical Perspective from the Left*, Routledge, London.

Sidschlag, I. and Tondl, G. (2011) Regional Output Growth Synchronisation with the Euro Area, *Empirica*, vol. 38, Issue 2, 203–221.

Simon, D. (2000) EMU and the opportunities for British business; in Baimbridge, M., Burkitt, B. and Whyman, P. (eds) *The Impact of the Euro: Debating Britain's Future*, Macmillan, London.

Sisson, K. and Marginson, P. (1995) Management: systems, structures and strategy; in Edwards, P. (ed.) *Industrial Relations: Theory and Practice in Britain*, Blackwell, Oxford.

Skidelsky, R. (2000) *John Maynard Keynes: Fighting for Britain, 1937–1946*, vol. 3, Macmillan, London.

Sleath, P. (1995) Fish Facts, *European Journal*, March, 20.

Smithin, J. (2004) Interest Rate Operating Procedures and Income Distribution; in Lavoie, M. and Seccareccia, M. (eds) *Central Banking in the Modern World: Alternative Perspectives*, Edward Elgar, Cheltenham.

Smithin, J. (2007) A Real Interest Rate Rule for Monetary Policy?, *Journal of Post Keynesian Economics*, vol. 31, Issue 1, 101–118.

Smits, R. (1997) *The European Central Bank: Institutional Aspects*, Kluwer, The Hague.

Snoddon, T.R. (2004) Fiscal institutions, regional adjustment and convergence in Canada's currency union: lessons for EMU; in Baimbridge, M. and Whyman, P. (eds) *Fiscal Federalism and European Economic Integration*, Routledge, London.

Snowdon, B. (1997) Politics and the Business Cycle, *Political Quarterly*, July.

Snowdon, B. and Vane, H.R. (2005) *Modern Macroeconomics: Its Origins, Development and Current State*, Edward Elgar, Cheltenham.

Södersten, B. and Reed, G. (1994) *International Economics*, Basingstoke, Macmillan.

Spahn, B. (1993) The consequences of Economic and Monetary Union for fiscal relations in the Community and the financing of the Community Budget, in The Economics of Community Public Finance, *European Economy*, Reports and Studies, 5, 543–584.

Spiegel, P. (2012) Greek bailout clears last Eurozone hurdle. Available at: http://www.ft.com/cms/s/0/c68890f6–6dce-11e1-b98d-00144feab49a.html#axzz2DhbZ35qY.

Spiering, M. (2004) British Euroscepticism; in Harmsen, R. and Spiering, M. (eds) *Euroscepticism: Party Politics, National Identity and European Integration*, Rodopi, Amsterdam.

Stanners, W. (1993) Is low inflation an important condition for high growth?, *Cambridge Journal of Economics*, 17(1) 79–107.

Stark, J. (2001) Genesis of a Pact; in Brunila, A., Buti, M. and Franco, D. (eds) *The Stability and Growth Pact: The Architecture of Fiscal Policy in EMU*, Palgrave Macmillan, London.

Steedman, H. (1988) Vocational training in France and Britain, *National Institute Economic Review*, 126, November, 57–70.

Steil, B. (2013) *The Battle of Bretton Woods: John Maynard Keynes, Harry Dexter White, and the Making of a New World Order*, Princeton University Press, Princeton.

Stiglitz, J.E. and Greenwald, B. (2003) *Towards a New Paradigm in Monetary Economics*, Cambridge University Press, Cambridge.

Stiglitz, J.E. and Greenwald, B. (2010) Towards a New Global Reserve System, *Journal of Globalisation and Development*, 1(2) 1–24.

Strange, G. (2002) *British Trade Unions and European Union Integration in the 1990s: Politics versus Political Economy*, *Political Studies*, vol.50, No. 2 332–353.

Strange, G. (1997) The British labour movement and Economic and Monetary Union in Europe, *Capital and Class*, 63, 13–24.

Strange, S. (1996) The Retreat of State: The Diffusion of Power in the World Economy, Cambridge University Press, Cambridge.

Strange, S. (2000) The Defective State, in Higgott, R. and Payne, A. (eds) (2000) *The New Political Economy of Globalisation*, vol. 1, Edward Elgar, Cheltenham.

Streeck, W. (1992) *Social Institutions and Economic Performance: Studies of Industrial Relations in Advanced Capitalist Economies*, Sage, London.

Streeck, W. and Schmitter, P.C. (1991) From national corporatism to transnational pluralism: organised interests in the single European market, *Politics and Society*, 19(2) 133–164.

Sunnus, M. (2004) Swedish Euroscepticism: democracy, sovereignty and welfare; in Harmsen, R. and Spiering, M. (eds) *Euroscepticism: Party politics, national identity and European integration*, Rodopi, Amsterdam.

Surico, P. (2003) Asymmetric reaction functions for the euro area, *Oxford Review of Economic Policy*, 19(1) 44–57.

Svaljek, S. (1997) Public debt boundaries: A review of the theories and methods of the assessment of public debt sustainability. *Economic Trends and Economic Policy*, 7(61) 34–64.

Svensson, L.E.O. (2002) A reform of the Eurosystems monetary policy strategy is increasingly urgent; Briefing Paper, Committee on Economic and Monetary Affairs, European Parliament.

Svensson, L.E.O. (2003) How should the Eurosystem reform its monetary strategy?; Briefing Paper, Committee on Economic and Monetary Affairs, European Parliament.

Swinburne, M. and Castello-Branco, M. (1991) Central bank independence: issues and experience, International Monetary Fund Working Paper No. 91/58, IMF, Washington, DC.

Szczerbiak, A. (2004) Polish Euroscepticism in the run-up to EU accession; in Harmsen, R. and Spiering, M. (eds) *Euroscepticism: Party politics, national identity and European integration*, Rodopi, Amsterdam.

Tamny, J. (2013) Keynes, White, and The Battle Of Bretton Woods. Available: http://www.forbes.com/sites/johntamny/2013/03/31/keynes-white-and-the-battle-of-bretton-woods/

Taylor, J.B. (1993) Discretion versus policy rules in practice; Carnegie-Rochester Conference Series on Public Policy, 39(1) 195–214.

Taylor, J.B. (2000a) Reassessing Discretionary Fiscal Policy, *Journal of Economic Perspective*, Summer.

Taylor, J.B. (2000b) Teaching Modern Macroeconomics at The Principle Level, *American Economic Review*, vol. 90, Issue 2, 90–94.

Taylor, M. (1995) A single currency – implications for the UK economy, Institute of Directors, London.

Teague, P. (1991) Introduction to the cross-national research, Seminar on *Workers Rights in Europe*, London School of Economics and Political Science, London, 13 April.

Teague, P. (1997) Lean production and the German model, *German Politics*, 6(2) 76–94.

Teague, P. (1998) Monetary Union and social Europe, *Journal of European Social Policy*, 8(2) 117–139.

The Economist (1991) Japanese spoken here, *The Economist*, 14 September.

The Economist (2005) A working model, *The Economist*, 13 August.

Thirlwall, A.P. and Gibson, H.D. (1992) *Balance of Payments Theory and the United Kingdom Experience*. Macmillan, Basingstoke.

Thirlwall, A.P. and Barton, C.A. (1971) Inflation and growth: the international evidence, *Banca Nazionale del Lavoro – Quarterly Review*, 98, 682–695. EDITED.

Tinbergen, J. (1952) *On the Theory of Economic Policy*, North-Holland, Amsterdam.

Tober, D. (1993) One World – One Vision for Business, in S. Bushrui et al. (eds) *Transition to a Global Society*, Oneworld, Oxford, 98–107.

Tobin, J. (1978) A Proposal for International Monetary Reform, *Eastern Economic Journal*, 4(3–4) 153–159.

Tobin, J. (1993) Price Flexibility and Output Stability: An Old Keynesian View, *Journal of Economics Perspectives*, Winter.

Tobin, J. (1994) Speculators tax, *New Economy*, 1, 104–109.

Tobin, J. (1996) *Full Employment and Growth: Further Essays on Policy*, Edward Elgar, Cheltenham and Brookfield, VT.

Tondl, G. (2002) Will the new EU regional policy meet the challenges of enlargement?; in Cuadrado-Roura, J. and Parellada, M. (eds) *Regional convergence in the European Union: Advances in Spatial Science*, Springer, Heidelberg.

Tondl, G. (2005) European Union regional policy; in van der Hoek, M.P. (ed.) *Handbook of Public Administration and Policy in the European Union*, CRC Press, New York.

Toniolo, G. (1988) *Central Banks Independence in Historical Perspective*, Walter de Gruyter, Berlin.

Tower, E. and Willett, T.D. (1970) The concept of optimum currency areas and the choice between fixed and flexible exchange rates; in Halm, G.N. (ed.) *Approaches to Greater Flexibility of Exchange Rates*, Princeton University Press, Princeton.

Trades Union Congress (1993) *European Common Currency*, TUC, London.

Treaty of Nice (2000) Intergovernmental Conference on Institutional Reform, 12 December 2000, Conference of the Representatives of the Governments of Member States, Nice.

TUC (1992) Europe 1992: Maximising the Benefits, Minimising the Costs, TUC, London.

Tufte, E. (1978) *Political Control of the Economy*, Princeton University Press, Chichester.

Tujula, M. and Wolswijk, G. (2004) What determines Fiscal Balances? An empirical investigation in determinants of changes in OECD Budget Balances. European Central Bank Working Paper No. 422. Available at: http://195.128.1.78/pub/pdf/scpwps/ecbwp422.pdf.

Turner, L. (1996) The Europeanisation of labour: structure before action, *European Journal of Industrial Relations*, 2(3) 325–344.

UNCTAD (1996) *Trade and Development Annual Report*, UNCTAD, New York.

United States International Trade Commission (2000) The impact on the US economy of including the United Kingdom in a free trade arrangement with the United States, Canada and Mexico, Investigation No. 332–409, Publication 3339, August.

Van Apeldoorn, B. (2002) *Transnational Capitalism and the Struggle over European Integration*, Routledge, London.

van der Hoek, M.P. (ed.) (2005) *Handbook of Public Administration and Policy in the European Union*, CRC Press, New York.

van der Ploeg, F. (1993) Macroeconomic policy co-ordination: issues during the various phases of Economic and Monetary Integration in Europe; in The Economics of EMU, *European Economy*, Special Edition, 1, 136–164.

van Riet, A. (2013) Financial repression to ease fiscal stress: turning back the clock in the eurozone?, Banco Central do Brasil VIII Annual Seminar on Risk, Financial Stability and Banking São Paulo, 8–9 August 2013.

Vaubel, R. (1976) Real exchange rate changes in the European Community: the empirical evidence and its implications for European currency unification, *Weltwirtschaftliches Archiv*, 112, 429–470.

Vaubel, R. (1978) *Strategies for Currency Unification*, J.B.C. Mohr, Tubingen.

Vaughan-Whitehead, D.C. (2003) EU Enlargement versus Social Europe? The Uncertain Future of the European Social Model, Edward Elgar, Cheltenham.

Verdun, A. (2005) A history of Economic and Monetary Union; in van der Hoek, M.P. (ed.) *Handbook of Public Administration and Policy in the European Union*, CRC Press, New York.

Veseth, M. (1998) *Selling Globalisation: The Myth of the Global Economy*, Lynne Rienner, London.

Viren, M. (2001) Fiscal policy, automatic stabilisers and policy co-ordination in EMU; in Brunila, A., Buti, M. and Franco, D. (eds) *The Stability and Growth Pact: The Architecture of Fiscal Policy in EMU*, Palgrave Macmillan, London.

Volkerink, B. and De Haan, J. (2001) Fragmented Government Effects on Fiscal Policy: New Evidence, *Public Choice*, 109(3/4) 221–242.

Von Hagen, J. (1991) A note on the empirical effectiveness of Formal Fiscal Restraints. *Journal of Public Economics*, 44(2) 199–211.

von Hagen, J. (1992) Fiscal Arrangements in a Monetary Union: Evidence from the US; in Fair, D.E. and de Boissieu, C., (eds) *Fiscal Policy, Taxes and the Financial System in an Increasingly Integrated Europe*, Kluwer, Deventer.

von Hagen, J. (1993) Monetary Union and Fiscal Union: A Perspective from Fiscal Federalism, in Masson, P.R. and Taylor, M.P. (eds) *Policy Issues in the Operation of Currency Unions*, Cambridge University Press, Cambridge.

von Hagen, J. (2003) EMU: Monetary Policy Issues and Challenges; in Baimbridge, M. and Whyman, P. (eds) *Economic and Monetary Union in Europe: Theory, Evidence and Practice*, Edward Elgar, Cheltenham.

von Hagen, J. and Brückner, M. (2002) Monetary policy in Unknown Territory: The European Central Bank in the Early Years, ZEI Working Paper, B18.

von Hagen, J. and Wyplosz, C. (2008) EMU's Decentralized System of Fiscal Policy, *European Economy – Economic Papers*, No. 306, 1–19.

Wagner, R.E. (1977) Economic Manipulation for Political Profit: Macroeconomic Consequences and Constitutional Implications, *Kyklos*, 30, 395–410.

Walsh, C.E. (2002) Teaching Inflation Targeting: An Analysis of Intermediate Macro, *Journal of Economic Education*, vol. 33, 333–346.

Walsh, J., Zappala, G. and Brown, W. (1995) European Integration and the Pay Policies of British multinationals, *Industrial Relations Journal*, 26(2) 84–96.

Warr, P. (1987) *Work, Unemployment and Mental Health*, Oxford University Press, Oxford.

Watson, M. (2002) Sand in the Wheels, Or Oiling the Wheels of International Finance? New Labour's Appeal to a New Bretton Woods', *British Journal of Politics and International Relations*, vol. 4, No. 2, 193–221.

Watson, M. (2006) The European Social Model: Between a Rock and a Hard Place?; in Whyman, P., Baimbridge, M. and Burkitt, B. (eds) *Implications of the Euro: A Critical Perspective from the Left*, Routledge, London.

Weber, A.A. (1991a) EMU and Asymmetries and Adjustment Problems in the EMS, in The Economics of EMU, *European Economy*, Special Edition 1.

Weber, A.A. (1991b) Reputation and Credibility in the European Monetary System, *The European Economy*, 12, 57–102.

Wehner, J. (2011) Electoral Budget Cycles in the EMU: A Challenge to Context Conditionality. Available at: http://www.wcfia.harvard.edu/sites/default/files/emu.pdf.

West, K. (1995) *Economic Opportunities for Britain and the Commonwealth*, Royal Institute for International Affairs, London.

Wheare, K.C. (1963) *Federal Government*, Oxford University Press, Oxford.

Whyman, P. (1997a) Fiscal Policy Consequences of Economic and Monetary Union in Europe, Working Paper No. 97:1, Department of Social and Economic Studies, University of Bradford, Bradford.

Whyman, P. (1997b) Fiscal Federalism and EMU: A Proposal for a European Federal Transfer Scheme, Working Paper No. 97.10.5, Department of Social and Economic Studies, University of Bradford.

Whyman, P. (2001a) Can Opposites Attract? Monetary Union and the Social Market, *Contemporary Politics*, 7(2) 113–128.

Whyman, P. (2001b) The Impact of Economic and Monetary Union upon British business, *European Business Journal*, 13(1) 28–36.

Whyman, P. (2002) British trade unions and EMU: natural supporters or conflicting interests?, *Industrial Relations*, 41(3) 467–476.

Whyman, P. (2006a) *Third Way Economics: Theory and Evaluation*, Palgrave, Basingstoke.

Whyman, P. (2006b) Trade unions and EMU; in Whyman, P., Baimbridge, M. and Burkitt, B. (eds) *Implications of the Euro: A Critical Perspective from the Left*, Routledge, London.

Whyman, P. (2010) Stabilising Economic and Monetary Union in Europe: The potential for a semi-automatic stabilisation mechanism, in Columbus, F. (ed.) *Progress in Economics Research*, vol. 18, Nova Science Publishers, Hauppauge, NY.

Whyman, P., Baimbridge, M. and Burkitt, B. (2006) *Implications of the Euro: A critical perspective from the left*, Routledge, London.

Whyman, P., Baimbridge, M. and Mullen, A. (2012) *The Political Economy of the European Social Model*, Routledge, London.

Whyman, P., Burkitt, B. and Baimbridge, M. (2000) Economic policy outside EMU: strategies for a global Britain, *Political Quarterly*, 71(4) 451–462.

Whyman, P., Burkitt, B. and Baimbridge, M. (2005) Post-Keynesianism and a neo-liberal EMU: the case for economic independence, *Contemporary Politics*, 11(4) 259–270.

Whyman, P., Burkitt, B. and Baimbridge, M. (2006) A post-Keynesian strategy for the UK economy; in Whyman, P., Baimbridge, M. and Burkitt, B. (eds) *Implications of the Euro: A Critical Perspective from the Left*, Routledge, London.

Wierts, P. (2008) Fiscal rules and fiscal outcomes in EMU: Theory and evidence. Available at: http://www1.fee.uva.nl/toe/content/people/content/Old/wierts/downloadablepapers/WiertsThesisFiscalRules.pdf.

Williamson, J. and Milner, C. (1991) *The World Economy*, Harvester Wheatsheaf, Hemel Hempstead.

Windolf, P. (1989) Productivity coalitions and the future of European corporatism, *Industrial Relations*, 28(1) 1–20.

Winters, L A. (2003) EMU and the rest of the world: thinking about the effects on the real economy; in Baimbridge, M. and Whyman, P. (eds) *Economic and Monetary Union in Europe: Theory, Evidence and Practice*, Edward Elgar, Cheltenham.

Woldendorp, J., Keman, H. and Budge, I. (2011) *Party Government in 40 Democracies 1948–2008*. Composition–Duration–Personnel. Available at: http://www.fsw.vu.nl/en/departments/political-science/staff/woldendorp/party-government-data-set/index.asp.

Woo, J. (2003) Economic, political, and institutional determinants of public deficits. *Journal of Public Economics*, 87(3–4) 387–426.

Woodford, M. (1999) *Revolution and Evolution in Twentieth-Century Macroeconomics*, Unpublished, Princeton University.

Woodford, M. (2001) The Taylor Rule and Optimal Monetary Policy, *American Economic Review*, vol. 91, No. 2, 232–237.

Woodford, M. (2002) *Interest and Prices: Foundations of a Theory of Monetary Policy*, Princeton University Press, Princeton.

World Bank (1993) *The East Asian Miracle: Economic Growth and Public Policy*, Oxford University Press, Oxford.

World Gold Council. (2014) Monetary History: July 22nd 1944. Available: http://www.gold.org/value/reserve_asset/history/monetary_history/vol3/1944jul22.html.

Wray, L.R. (2007) A Post Keynesian View of Central Bank Independence, Policy Target, and the Rules versus Discretion Debate, *Journal of Post Keynesian Economics*, 30(1) 119–141.

Wynne, M. and Rodriguez-Palenzuela, D. (2002) Measurement bias in the HICP: What do we know and what do we need to know?, ECB Working Paper, 131, ECB, Frankfurt.

Wyplosz, C. (1993) Monetary Union and fiscal policy discipline, in the Economics of EMU – Background Studies, *European Economy*, 44, 165–184.

Wyplosz, C. (2003) Policy challenges under EMU; in Baimbridge, M. and Whyman, P. (eds) *Economic and Monetary Union in Europe: Theory, Evidence and Practice*, Edward Elgar, Cheltenham.

Yates T. (1998) Downward nominal rigidity and monetary policy, Bank of England Working Paper, 82, Bank of England, London.

Yates, T. (2002) Monetary policy and the zero bound to interest rates: a review, ECB Working Paper, 190, ECB, Frankfurt.

Young, J. (1998) *This Blessed Plot: Britain and Europe from Churchill to Blair*, Macmillan, London.

Zezza, G. (2012) The Impact of Fiscal Austerity in the Eurozone, *Review of Keynesian Economics*, 1(1) 37–54.

Index

Lightning Source UK Ltd.
Milton Keynes UK
UKOW05n0910210916

283481UK00016B/299/P